Joseph R. Brown

ADVENTURER

On The Minnesota Frontier

1820 - 1849

BY

Nancy & Robert Goodman

Lone Oak Press, Ltd.

Joseph R. Brown

ADVENTURER

On The Minnesota Frontier

1820 - 1849

BY

Nancy & Robert Goodman

Published
BY
Lone Oak Press, Ltd.
304 11th Avenue Southeast
Rochester, Minnesota 55904-7221
507-280-6557

First Edition
ISBN Number 1-883477-12-3
Library of Congress Card Catalog Number 96-78129

Cover: *Travelers Meeting with Minataree Indians*,
colored engraving after Carl Bodmer, 1842.
Courtesy of Gilcrease Museum, Tulsa.
J. R. Brown from daguerrotype ca. 1853, Minnesota Historical Society.
Back cover photos by Dave Hanson

CONTENTS

TABLE OF FIGURES

MAPS

AUTHORS' NOTE

ON SEMANTICS & SPELLING

Understanding Joseph R. Brown necessitates learning something about the people with whom he came into contact and his relationships with those people. For at least his earliest years in Minnesota, most of his associates were of French Canadian, Indian or mixed descent. We are not ethnologists and this book does not pretend to reconstruct the social structures of these groups nor to comment on the "rightness" or "wrongness" of their various motives, belief systems and deeds. We are equally uneasy about making assumptions concerning the lifestyles and subcultures of the various white groups Brown encountered (which included British army officers, the unemployable masquerading as soldiers, American Board missionaries, Swiss and German immigrants, eastern businessmen, lumbermen, European travelers, etc.) because we do not really know how those people thought, what "truths" they knew and what motives inspired them. This book is a biography, and while we have attempted to show Brown's relationships with members of these groups and speculate on his seeming influence over so many disparate people, we have tried to base all discussion on discoverable facts, such as the written words and preserved opinions of his contemporaries.

That brings up a second point: many of the ideas and opinions quoted were politically correct in their day but are not now. History is about what people did and thought in former times, whether palatable or not. Whitewash does no service, as can be easily determined by reading a "politically correct" Victorian biography. Admittedly, the views of most of the Indians (except for the few who could write English) have been filtered through the medium of at least a transcriber, if not a translator. We made no attempt to have these versions of events interpreted or corrected by present-day Indians with recourse to oral traditions. We have tried to understand the people with whom Brown interacted as individuals, with their own agendas, not as representatives of particular cultural groups. One way to get a different grasp of that slippery thing, the historical event, is to look at it from the viewpoint of one of the actors and try to determine what influenced his actions. This book presents the world of the 1800s through the eyes of Joseph R. Brown and his contemporaries, however prejudiced by cultural differences. We hope the picture thus presented adds to, rather than detracts from, our historical knowledge of this period.

Terminology and orthography present some problems. American Indians have been called many names – Native Americans, Amerinds, red men. In this narrative they will be called "Indians" (quotes after this are to be understood). For lack of another term that encompasses them all, Europeans and Americans of European ancestry will be called "whites." Those of mixed descent were legally and inevitably referred to as "halfbreeds," and we retain the term. Names used historically for indigenous peoples with which this book is concerned were Sioux, Chippewa, Sac/Fox and Winnebago. Today preferred terms are Dakota for the Santee Sioux (Mdewakanton, Wahpekute, Wahpeton, Sisseton), Nakota for the Yankton and Yanktonai, Lakota for the Teton, Ojibwe or Anishinabe for the Chippewa, Mesquakie for the related Sac and Fox and Hochunk for the Winnebago. We have kept the historic names for these nations to avoid confusion between the quoted texts and the narrative, and have reserved the terms Dakota, Ojibwe and Mesquakie for the languages spoken by those groups. (The term Sioux, according to one writer, was originally a nickname used by the French to avoid giving offense to the Dakota bands who held names sacred and were uneasy when addressed directly by name.)[1]

Names and words in Winnebago, Menominee, Mesquakie and Ojibwe dialects have been spelled as consistently as possible, given the many variant orthographies used by different ethnic groups that encountered them. None were written languages in Brown's time. Dakota, however, was and we have followed the orthography developed by Rev. Samuel Pond in 1835 and used by Brown and his Indian correspondents. Many Dakota words have entered the English vocabulary with technically incorrect spellings, and we retain these spellings simply to avoid confusion. Joe Brown, who wrote good Dakota, often used an anglicized version of a Dakota word when writing in English, for example, Chanwakan for *canwakan*, Sintomonee for *sintomni*, Mendota for *mdote* or, for that matter, Dacotah for *Dakota*, and so do we. As an aid to pronunciation, for those interested: *c* always has a ch sound; *g* and *k* are always hard; *h* is always pronounced and always begins a syllable. Several letters represent sounds unique to Dakota: *x* represents sh (although many names in which it appears are commonly spelled with sh, as Wabasha); *j* is used for zh (although, again, we adhere to conventional spellings, as Kaposia); and *r* is used for a guttural resembling the German strong ch, as in *nacht*. (The word Wahpekute has this latter sound and was properly written Warpekute, pronounced wa-kpe-ku-te, however spelled.) We have chosen to write Indian names as one unhyphenated word, and have provided the English equivalent, if known. Any errors are ours alone.

---

1. This statement is given by William Joseph Snelling, a trader with the Sioux in the 1820s, in notes to *Tales of the Northwest: Sketches of Indian Life and Character by a Resident Beyond The Frontier* 237 (reprint Minneapolis 1936)

PREFACE

This is the story of one of Minnesota's most amazing characters. The first of a planned two-volume work, this volume takes the reader through the first two-thirds of Joseph R. Brown's life, from his birth to the beginnings of the Territory of Minnesota, which owed so much to his foresight and resourcefulness, not to say machinations. In a sense, it covers the man nobody knows, and suggests how the J.R. Brown of the history books – "Jo the Juggler," the politico, the insider in the Indian treaties that opened the state to settlement and the "chief counselor of the agents and the government" – came to be.[1] Everyone knew that Brown had come to the state with the first American soldiers and stayed to become a trader, pioneer, legislator and one of the most widely known public men of Minnesota and was, at his death, its oldest white settler.[2] No one knew much of what he had done before the opening up of the territory to settlement, except that his experiences had been mildly unsavory, at least to his Victorian memorialists. One epitaph contained this assessment of his life: "A drummer-boy, soldier, Indian trader, lumberman, pioneer, speculator, founder of cities, legislator, politician, editor, inventor, his career – though it hardly commenced till half his life had been wasted in the obscure solitudes of this far Northwestern wilderness – has been a very remarkable and characteristic one, not so much for what he has achieved, as for the extraordinary versatility and capacity which he has displayed in every new situation." The same somewhat sanctimonious writer called Brown's death "the sad culmination of a life which seems one chequered waste of unfulfilled dreams."[3]

Half a life wasted. Could that really have been true? No in-depth biography of Brown has hitherto been attempted because of the paucity of material available on these early "wasted" years. Brown himself was too busy to write his memoirs and, besides,

---

1. *St. Paul Press*, Nov. 12, 1870.
2. John Fletcher Williams "Memoir of Joseph R. Brown," *Minnesota Historical Collections* III: 212 (St. Paul 1880).
3. *St. Paul Press*, ibid.

could see no remunerative purpose for doing so. His own personal records were scattered and destroyed, and the public record is so filled with inconsistencies and discrepancies concerning his career, it has effectively prevented anyone else from producing a meaningful account of a life that even to his contemporaries seemed contradictory and filled with restless wanderings. Minnesota historian William Watts Folwell, fascinated by the man who had been called "the brainiest of them all, a sort of intellectual lion, who sported with the savage Sioux, or ruled a political caucus, with equal power,"4 couldn't figure Brown out either, finally capitulated by including the semilegendary man in his history of the state, relegating the mystery man and his misadventures to an appendix in which he lamented that "this man of energy and genius, of admirable personal qualities, for whom a great career might have been expected, left a scantier record behind him than many other public men by far his inferior in capacity," and wondered if this lack was due to character or environment. Folwell concluded that a "truthful biography of the real 'Joe' Brown might be not only a fascinating story but a highly valuable contribution to the early history of Minnesota."5

A fascinating story it is, and, it is to hoped, a contribution as well. For in digging out the vivid life of the unknown Joe Brown hidden in the correspondence of his contemporaries, the books and diaries and newspapers of the period and the public records everywhere – literally hundreds of city, county, territorial, state and national archives – we have also dug out many details of the scarcely better known pre-territorial history of the state we call Minnesota. Few Minnesotans have any clear idea of how people lived and traveled in the early days of the nineteenth century, of what the life of a fur trader was like, or that of a soldier or homesteader or timbercutter or Indian. The story of Joseph R. Brown knits together all these facets in the settlement and politics of the upper Mississippi country, spanning the period from Dakota dominance to the rise of an industrial society. This is not meant to be a history of the period arranged for convenience around one man; it is rather an account of the adventures and aspirations of an individual (as much as this can be ascertained) augmented by the historical detail necessary to understand him. This first volume attempts to separate a few kernels of historical truth from the chaff of obscurity to which Minnesota's pre-territorial period is now consigned by throwing light on some of the experiences that made Joseph R. Brown into one of the major players in early Minnesota

---

4. Charles D. Gilfillan "The Early Political History of Minnesota," *Minnesota Historical Collections* IX:179. (St. Paul 1901)
5. William Watts Folwell *A History of Minnesota* III: 350–351 (revised St. Paul 1969).

politics. We are less concerned with painting the broad historical picture than with illuminating details that show how Brown's character was shaped, and how that, in turn, shaped his achievements (and failures). Further discussion of some historical points can be found in the appendices following the text.

Other young men came west to the Minnesota country as fur traders, lived intimately with the Indians and yet remained to become staid and prominent public figures in a highly structured Victorian world. Joe Brown does not fit into this mold. It has been assumed that he relished the lawless life of the wild, living sometimes in the Indian culture, sometimes in the white world, but never wholly accepting the restrictions of civilization.[6] This assumption turns out to be not entirely true. A pragmatic businessman, Brown went where his speculative nature took him, but always lived life, as one writer so neatly phrased it, "to the hilt of his circumstances."[7] Brown's relationship to the Indians was pretty thoroughly misunderstood by people whose first contact with Brown or the Sioux was in the 1850s, after the Indians had been removed to reservations. He was called by some erratic and visionary in private matters, although generous to a fault.[8] Far from being a dilettante who flitted about from activity to activity, Brown was in truth one of the most doggedly persistent and least capricious of men. He always had sound reasons for what he did, but those reasons are not readily apparent today because of what Brown himself would call "a wrong turn of fortune's wheel."[9] He was a man who could laugh at himself and stare misfortune in the face. His chief ambitions have scarcely been guessed at. To many, then and now, he was an enigma; he did not subscribe to the proprieties and conventions of mid-nineteenth century society and cared little what anyone thought of him, disdaining even to correct the inaccuracies that were published about him before his death.

Even today there is a strange tendency for people to think of Minnesota's settlement history as beginning with the Stillwater convention, which is where this volume ends, and to ignore the first fifty years of the century that were so significant in determining its form. "No history of Minnesota can be written which shall omit from its pages the scenes and incidents wherein, for half a century, he moved conspicuously," wrote a fellow editor commemorating Brown's death.[10] But perhaps Brown's truest epitaph was penned fifty years after his death by another prolific Minnesotan, Sinclair

---

6. Folwell, ibid.
7. Evan Jones *The Minnesota: Forgotten River* 126. (New York 1962).
8. *St. Paul Dispatch* Nov. 12, 1870.
9. Joseph R. Brown Account Book, Brown papers, MHS.
10. Earle S. Goodrich in the *St. Paul Pioneer* Nov. 15, 1870.

Lewis, who recognized and appreciated the essential quality of Brown's character:

> "If he had lived ten years longer – he died suddenly in a hotel in New York in 1870 – he might have been more famous than Henry Ford and have hustled up history by forty years.... He had more of Lorenzo de' Medici in him than would be supposed by that seventy per cent of the present virtuous citizenry of Minnesota who know nothing about him, or by the ninety-eight point five per cent of the general American population who have never heard his name. When the definitive book about him is written, it will be translated into Czech, Urdu and Hollywood."[11]

Here's a try at it.

---

11. Sinclair Lewis *The God-Seeker, a novel*, 421-422 (New York 1949). Lewis' reference is to Brown's last hurrah, a self-propelled steam wagon he was building and promoting for use on the railroad-less prairies.

Joseph Renshaw Brown

Photo by J. Byerly, Frederick, MD. Minnesota Historical Society

Map 1 Area of Joseph R. Brown's origins: Brown was born near York, raised near Black Horse and Columbia, apprenticed at Downingtown, recruited at Philadelphia, and sent on his way west from Fort Mifflin

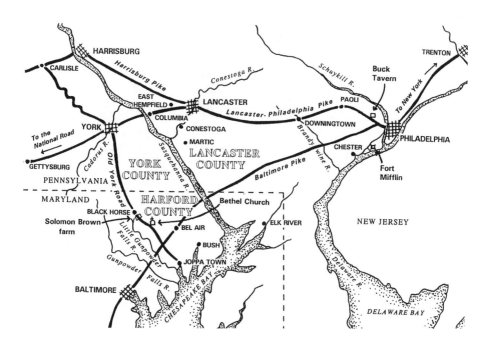

14

CHAPTER I

Joseph Renshaw Brown, not quite two years old, didn't remember leaving his father and his home. He was too young to retain any conscious memory of his mother's death in York County, Pennsylvania, where he had been born, or of his journey to Grandmother Brown's farm in Maryland. But Margaret Henderson never forgot. She had held the squirming two-year-old on her lap all the way, a distance of more than thirty-five miles, because he was yet too small to sit alone on the high wagon seat. A wagon journey was hard enough at anytime over the rutted tracks that passed for roads in this part of the country, and could be particularly grueling if the weather, as so often happens in late fall, became wet and blustery. And Margaret, very young and newly married, was pregnant with her first child.

Joseph, the only son of Emily Renshaw and Samuel Brown, had been born January 5, 1805, in York County. When Emily died, perhaps bearing a second child, Samuel Brown (according to one family story, distraught with grief) appealed to his sister Margaret and her new husband, Robert Henderson, to take the little boy into their home. The Hendersons lived with Joseph's grandmother, Althea Brown, on the farm where his father had been born and raised, at Black Horse, just across the state line in northern Maryland. Samuel had been married on the farm, too, but soon after took his bride to York. Joseph assumed he had been born in Harford County in the home in which he grew up, looked after by his three young aunts – two still unmarried – and his grandmother. He was the eldest child in the Henderson family, and when Margaret's first baby died within the year he became the only child, perhaps somewhat spoiled and coddled in consequence. However, he soon had cousins who must have seemed like siblings: Andrew was born in the spring of 1809, John in 1811, and seven others soon followed.[1]

---

1. Three accounts of Brown's childhood are given in David Henderson to Lydia Ann Carli, Jan. 13, 1871; Ellen Henderson to Ellen Brown Allanson, Feb. 6, 1871; Andrew Henderson to Samuel J. Brown, Feb. 19, 1871, all in Brown papers, MHS. All biographical sketches of Brown say he was born in Harford

Joseph's grandfather, Solomon Brown, had been born in Scotland in 1729 and probably immigrated to America in the 1750s. He settled first in New Jersey, as had many Scots had who were induced to come by eastern New Jersey's Scottish proprietors, but within a few years he moved to Harford County, Maryland, where he began to acquire land. He married at least twice. With his first wife, Huldah Smith, daughter of Harford landowner Ralph Smith, he raised five children to adulthood. The sons of this marriage were described by a nephew as men of mechanical talent as well as "men of mind," all having had "Fair Plan" educations. John Brown, born in 1761, was a millwright and carpenter; in the 1780s he moved to "the western country" (then western Pennsylvania), and soon his sister Mary, married to John Chambers, and brother James followed him west. John possessed considerable property at Bethany (now in West Virginia) which he gave to his daughter Margaret and her husband, Alexander Campbell, founder of the religious sect called Disciples of Christ or Campbellites. Two younger brothers, Thomas and Solomon, left the farm for Baltimore where they worked as cooper and carpenter. According to a family story, both were wounded in the War of 1812 and both subsequently died of their injuries, Solomon in 1813 and Thomas in 1816, leaving no families.2

Some time after his first wife's death, Solomon married Althea Foster, thought to have been Welsh. She bore him three more daughters – Holliday (or Huldah) who became the wife of Edward M. Guyton in 1810, Margaret who married Robert Henderson in 1806 and Martha who died unmarried in 1815 – and one son, Joseph's father, Samuel.3 There is a gap of some years between the two families of Solomon Brown; John was nearly thirty when Althea's youngest child was born. When Solomon died, aged seventy-four, in December of 1803 he left the farm in trust for his widow Althea to be divided among his children at her death. He may have expected one of more of his sons to stay on the land; however, the eldest had moved west and the youngest pursued careers as skilled craftsmen, Solomon and Thomas in Baltimore and Samuel in York, leaving the farm to their sister Margaret and her husband, Robert Henderson, who later bought it from the estate. Althea survived until November 1815, outliving her youngest stepson and daughters Martha and Holliday.

Shortly before the father's death his youngest son, Samuel, married Emily Renshaw, daughter of Joseph Renshaw Junior, a neighboring farmer. Emily's family had been substantial landholders in Bush River

Co., and he himself undoubtedly believed so for a time. He gave "Hartford (sic) County, Maryland" for place of birth on his reenlistment papers in 1825, but by 1850 he had discovered the error, giving "Pennsylvania" on the census, and "York County, Penn." as a Territorial Legislator in 1854. Henderson family records are in the Henderson papers, Maryland Historical Society, Baltimore. See Appendix A for further genealogical material.

2. Andrew Henderson to Brown, Feb. 19, 1871; Lydia Carli to S. J. Brown, May 20, 1902, in Brown papers; will of Solomon Brown Oct. 20, 1803, and final distribution of estate of Solomon Brown Sep. 30, 1817, Harford County records, Bel Air, MD; will of Solomon Brown (junior), Mar. 11, 1813, and probate May 19, 1813, of estate of Solomon Brown (junior), Baltimore Co. records, Baltimore, MD; Brown family records, collections of T. W. Phillips Memorial Library, Bethany College, Bethany, WV.

3. Harford Co. marriage records.

Lower Hundred since before 1710 and her grandfather had inherited that part of the family plantation having the dwelling and improvements and also the slaves, which at his death in 1810 totaled thirteen – ten women and girls, three lads and boys. As late as 1777 Joseph Renshaw Senior and all his sons took the oath of loyalty to the crown, although Emily's father later joined the colonists' militia. Their slaveholding or their British sympathies may furnish a reason why except for Emily the Browns "did not esteem" the Renshaws. Emily was not brought up on this plantation, which eventually went to her unmarried aunts, but on a 136-acre farm her father purchased in Bush River Upper Hundred, not far from Solomon Brown. It may not have been a happy family. Joseph Renshaw was estranged from Emily's sisters and perhaps from Emily also. When he died in 1830, he cut them off – and cut them down as well – willing nothing to Harriet, "who had so little affection for me that I think twenty-five cents is as much as she deserves," and the same to Fanny, "who disobliged me by marrying a drunken, dissipated Irish weaver by the name of Johnson," and leaving all to their brother, Otho.**4**

Samuel Brown left very little to know him by. No record has been found of his marriage, his son's birth or his wife's death; in the early nineteenth century such events often did not become part of the public record. However, it could not have been long after their marriage that the young couple moved north to York County. Samuel, who was well educated and a good carpenter, could easily have found work there. Indeed, there was little to hold him in Harford, for he knew that his mother would have the use of his father's property for her lifetime, and since she was some twenty years younger than her late husband that might be a long time. Family records give Joseph's birth date as January 5, 1805, and indicate his mother died when he was about two; late 1806 fits well with the family story that Margaret Henderson brought him to the Brown farm on her lap, as she was wed in April of that year and her first baby was born in March of 1807. A later date is ruled out because it is difficult to believe she would make the trip if she was far advanced in pregnancy or had a nursing baby, one, moreover, that may have been sickly for her first baby did not live long. Neither is the date of Samuel's second marriage known, but it could not have been more than three years after Emily's death that he moved across the Susquehanna River to Lancaster County and there met and married Mary Hart, as their first child was born in 1810. About this time Samuel, raised a Presbyterian but converted to Methodism, decided to become a preacher. Indeed, Methodism flourished in York and the chance to join a church there may have prompted his decision to move north. Whatever his circumstances, it appears to have

---

4. Census records 1776 to 1830; Joseph Renshaw (senior) estate appraisal, Aug. 15, 1810; will of Joseph Renshaw (junior) entered for probate May 10, 1830, Harford Co. records; Federal Tax List Bush River Upper and Eden, 1798, Maryland Hall of Records, Annapolis; Grace Parke Renshaw *Renshaw Reflections* (Baltimore 1983). Emily Renshaw's forebears were English, had lived near Perryman, Harford County for a century or more. Emily's father owned "Renshaw's Delight," a plantation not far from Brown's in Upper Bush Hundred.

been several years before Samuel Brown was in a position to send for his first-born son. As he struggled to make a living and start a new family in Pennsylvania, Joseph was being raised by his relatives in Maryland, where life had changed little since the first farmers had pushed inland from the seaboard better than 150 years earlier.[5]

Brown's farm lay on the Old York Road that followed the high ground between the Little Gunpowder Falls River and the headwaters of Deer Creek. No rural backwater, this was then the main route from York to Baltimore and Joppa Town (until 1768 the Baltimore County seat). Just to the north was the well-known Black Horse Tavern (later owned by Solomon's grandson Thomas Henderson), a popular stopping place for farmers on their way to market and Pennsylvanians on their way to Baltimore and even, in 1773, for George Washington on his way back to Mount Vernon. A few miles south was the humble log structure of Bethel Presbyterian Church; among its early subscribers was Solomon Brown, who is buried in its churchyard along with many of his family. By 1787 Solomon Brown owned a 94-acre farm called "Poteet's Pleasure," which, according to the property tax assessment list for Bush River Hundred, had a wood barn 20 by 27 feet, a dwelling house and outhouse.[6] The land was fertile but hilly and cut up into small odd-shaped fields that followed the contours of the tillable land, interspersed with plentiful woods. There were no large villages in this part of the county, but each crossroads seemed to have a cluster of farms with a smithy or mill or tavern. Most of the small farms were largely self-sufficient. Each farmer raised a few animals to provide meat and milk for his family, planted enough grain to feed his stock and raised flax or tobacco to furnish a cash crop. Solomon Brown had followed this pattern and his son-in-law, Robert Henderson, did the same. Their crops were wheat, rye and flax, and they kept a few cows, horses and pigs. Solomon also owned a pair of sheep shears and two spinning wheels, evidence that he raised sheep as well. It was a great place for a boy to grow up.

The documents which most suggest the way of life at Poteet's Pleasure are an inventory of Solomon Brown's estate made in 1804 and a second made at the estate sale in 1816. They reveal a comfortable existence without luxuries or elegance. The fact that the two inventories, made twelve years apart, are nearly identical speaks of the care that was taken of these manufactured goods and the value that was set on them. The family's prized possessions were the four large featherbeds, one of which weighed almost sixty pounds, with bolsters and pillows. There were five bedsteads and cords with three quilts, two pairs of blankets, an old coverlet and rug, eleven sheets and seven pillowcases to cover them and a warming pan to take off the chill on wintery nights. The table was set with

---

5. Ellen Henderson to Allanson Feb. 6, 1871; Andrew Henderson to Brown, Feb. 1871

6. Walter W. Preston *History of Harford County* 170–173 (Baltimore 1901); Harford County Land Records Vol. 104, Bel Air, MD; Federal tax list Bush River 1798. Poteet's Pleasure was described as being on the headwaters of the Little Gunpowder Falls River, east of Lord Baltimore's reserve (Maryland Land Office, patent #653 Harford Co., to Thomas Poteet, Annapolis).

six pewter plates, a pewter dish and other vessels of pewter that total twenty-one pounds; the other less valuable "cupboard furniture" is not named. There were at least one tablecloth and two napkins worth mentioning. The looking glass and knife box were obviously items of value, and some store may have been set by the "lott of books." Much of the furniture must have been home-built and therefore of little value, but the cradle, three chests, two tables and seven chairs – one an armchair – were good enough to evaluate. In the kitchen were a churn and two wash tubs, the wooling wheels, two flat irons and one bake iron, a pot rack, iron pot, dutch oven, ladle and meat fork.

Solomon's crop of rye in the ground, flax from the swingle, even the beehive and bacons were inventoried. He owned a grey mare and horse, a bay riding horse and a "rhoan colt," which he willed to his son Solomon. In the barn were four cows and two heifers, a bull and six hogs. There was a wagon, harness and collars for the horses, a riding saddle and saddlebags, plough and singletrees, harrow and flax hackles. They must have had apple trees, for there were a cider press and three cider barrels, plus various casks, hogsheads and kegs suitable for containing home-brewed beer or flour ground at nearby grist mills. All the various tools and appurtenances of a farm were listed, right down to the axes and knives and the grindstone to keep them sharp.[7]

There is little to indicate how old Joseph was when he returned to his father. His cousins had the impression that it was not long after his father's remarriage, yet he was old enough to have developed a distinct personality and to have gained a reputation in the Henderson family as a mischievous boy. Joe's cousin Ellen, who was too young to have known him at this period, thought that he was a "pet boy." Andrew, four years younger than Joseph, recalled that he was "an energetic, go-ahead boy," but did not remember him well at all. Joe told his family that he had had some schooling in Maryland, so we may guess he was at least seven when he was returned to his father.[8] By then Joseph surely thought of himself as a Henderson. If he had seen his father at all during the interim, he could not have known him well. It must have been a shattering experience for him to be taken from the only family he had ever known and deposited with virtual strangers in a far-away place! The farm had provided Joseph with security in a substantial, stable and well-ordered world. It would be otherwise in the household of his father.

About 1810 Samuel Brown had become a Methodist-Episcopalian local preacher – a calling that paid no stipend and required that its practitioners work at some other trade to keep body and soul together. Shortly after Emily's death he moved eastward to Lancaster County,

7. Will of Solomon Brown, Oct. 20, 1803; appraisal of estate of Solomon Brown by Crispin Tredway and Joshua Guyton, Apr. 20, 1804; final distribution of estate of Solomon Brown, Sep. 30, 1817, Harford Co. records. For more on the area's history, see Edward C. Papenfuss, Gregory A. Stiverson, Susan A. Collins, Lois Green Carr, editors, *Maryland: New Guide to the Old Line State* 35–38, 414–416 (Baltimore 1976) and Preston *Harford County*.

8. E. Henderson to Allanson, Feb. 6, 1871; A. Henderson to Brown, Feb. 19, 1871; Allanson to Brown, Jan 9, 1871.

probably stopping first in Conestoga Township, south of Lancaster City, where a Samuel Brown is listed in the 1810 census. Conestoga was then a hotbed of Methodism, although there had been no churches or ordained ministers in the county until 1809. Circuit preachers brought the sacraments to local assemblies only infrequently; the rest of the time the membership was served by lay exhorters such as Samuel Brown. Among the early Methodists in nearby Martic Township was a cordwainer (shoemaker) named Valentine Hart, a veteran of the revolution who had fought at Bunker Hill and owner of considerable property. Samuel Brown also worked as a shoemaker according to his family; he may have worked with Hart. In any case, he soon married Hart's daughter Mary. Their first son, Solomon, was born in 1810. Solomon was quickly followed (although not necessarily in this order) by Mary, Jeremiah, Wilson, John Wesley, Lydia Ann, Samuel Fletcher, Florence, Welsley (who did not live past his third year) and Nathaniel Reeder (the youngest, born in 1827). By 1816, when John Wesley was born, Samuel was renting a farm in East Hempfield, a location convenient to the burgeoning Methodist assembly in Columbia and near the grounds where huge open-air camp meetings were often held. He later moved to a farm nearer Lancaster, and may have moved around even more than is apparent, for he disappears from the public records after 1812, not to reappear until his insolvency proceedings in 1819.9

For Joseph, it is plain that life was very different in Pennsylvania. His father seemed never to be out of debt. In all his life Samuel Brown never owned enough personal or real property to pay taxes. Although he twice came into small cash inheritances, at the death of his mother in 1816 and at that of his wife's father in 1826, it didn't seem to go far in paying the creditors. However, according to his daughter Lydia, he was the kind of man who puts little stock in worldly things, being convinced of God's provenance. He considered himself a follower of Christ, she said, and tried to save men's souls, but he was not a minister: even though he was twice offered $1,000 per annum, a princely sum, to take a pulpit, he declined both offers. Presumably he felt he could do more good exhorting small gatherings of country folk than by guiding an established congregation. He was, said Lydia, an honest man and believed every man to be so, an attitude which goes far toward explaining his lack of financial success.10

9. Carli to Brown, May 20, 1902; John W. Brown to John R. Case, notes in John R. Case papers, MHS; John R. Case "Pioneer Days In And Around Hastings" in *The Hastings Gazette* Dec. 4, 1920 (for family information supplied by J. W. Brown); Federal tax lists, Conestoga, Columbia, Hempfield, Manor and Providence townships 1807–1822, Pennsylvania Historical Society, Harrisburg; Federal census records. Samuel Brown may very well have preached in York where there was a large Methodist assembly founded in 1781; the Lancaster circuit, which includes Columbia, was formed in the 1780s, but there was no permanent assembly there until Henry Boehm's chapel was founded in Willow Street in 1809. Early records are sketchy and we cannot tell if Samuel Brown was a member of either congregation. Columbia was handy for the large tent meetings held near there—Bishop Herbert Asbury preached to crowds of 2,000 and more on the site in 1807 and 1810. For more see Franklin Ellis *History of Lancaster County* (1888) and William G. Carter *History of York County* (1834).

10. Carli to Brown, May 20, 1902; final settlement of estate of Solomon Brown 1817; final settlement of estate of Valentine Hart Sep. 17, 1827, Lancaster County probate records, Lancaster, PA.

Samuel Brown was a man of high principles, good education and keen intellect. He was said to have been a compelling speaker, although Andrew Henderson, who had heard him preach, said only that he was "above mediocrity." In looks and bearing his son Joseph resembled him strongly, so we may safely picture him as tall and straight, firm-jawed, with piercing blue eyes, perhaps tending toward a solid squareness of figure. Joseph R. Brown never wrote or said a word that has been recorded about his parent, but it may be significant that Lydia Carli described their father as harsh and tyrannical. Samuel may have subscribed to the teaching of the zealous Methodist-Episcopal Bishops Coke and Asbury, that "children be indulged with nothing that the world calls play... for those who play when they are young will play when they are old." The importance of his father's character should not be overlooked. If Samuel was such an exacting parent, or perhaps so caught up in his religious life that he seemed indifferent, it is easy imagine the effect he might have had on a spirited boy, getting him, as it were, after the twig was bent. It would be strange, indeed, if young Joseph didn't offer some resistance to the changed circumstances and harbor some resentment against his parent, especially if he had been a pet in the Henderson family. What his relationship with his young stepmother might have been, we are offered no clue. But as might be expected, by his teens Joseph R. Brown was reputed to be headstrong, impudent and cheeky – qualities, however, that mask a developing self-reliance that would become one of Brown's greatest strengths.[11]

Joe Brown acquired very little formal education. Andrew Henderson implies that Cousin Joe's father wanted him at home to work on the farm, and it may be that once the boy was big enough, he was taken from school for that purpose. His daughter Ellen said that he had had only three terms of schooling, in Maryland and Pennsylvania, she thought.[12] It is probable that his father instructed him as well. Joe Brown was, luckily, a natural scholar, possessed of a quick mind for ciphering, excellent penmanship and a keen grasp of spelling and grammar. What knowledge of history, philosophy and literature he had was probably acquired through voracious reading. We can suppose that as a boy he had the same bold and imaginative mind, eagerly absorbing all he read, that characterized him as a man. Certainly a minimum of formal study was sufficient to educate Joe Brown.

While Samuel Brown was preaching and farming near Columbia, struggling to keep his increasing family together, his eldest son was undoubtedly gaining an education of another kind. There's no reason not to assume that Joseph R. Brown possessed, as a boy of ten or twelve, the same curiosity, unbounded energy and enthusiasm for life that distinguished him throughout his life. He would have found a wonderful

---

11. Carli to Brown, ibid; A. Henderson to Brown, Feb. 19, 1871; Lydia Carli to John Fletcher Williams, Sep. 20, 1871, notes of interview in J. F. Williams papers, MHS. Quotation from rules of Cokesbury College given in Papenfuss et al., *Maryland* 35.
12. Allanson to Brown, Jan. 9, 1871.

focus for his energies in Columbia, a small town of perhaps fifty houses just fifteen miles west of Lancaster and only a few miles from their farm. It was a lively and stimulating place. and probably the largest settlement that Joseph had ever seen. Columbia supported several schools, both private and public, one of which Joseph may have attended. It was also the scene of great commercial activity. Situated at the lowest place where the Susquehanna River could be safely navigated, it had become the point of crossing of the great road west. From the Appalachians came coal, wheat, lumber, whiskey, iron to be transferred at Columbia from pack animals or from the flat-bottomed "arc" in which it had descended the river to wagons for the trip to Philadelphia. Traveling in the other direction were settlers heading for western Pennsylvania. It's no coincidence that the Conestoga wagon, the pioneers' freighter, was built nearby. In Columbia an inquisitive boy could meet wagoners, mule skinners, boatmen, merchants and travelers of every description, and no doubt young Joseph made the most of his opportunities.[13] The lure of the western frontier being dangled before his eyes daily in Columbia may very well have first attracted his interest in moving west.

At about age twelve, Joseph was apprenticed to a printer. It may have been an economic necessity or a growing inability to influence his unruly offspring, or both, that caused Samuel Brown to seek a master for Joseph. However, in the early nineteenth century indenture was still common and was the usual way for boy to enter a skilled trade. Others of Samuel's children were probably apprenticed: Jeremiah went to the painter's trade; Samuel Fletcher to a tailor; Mary, the crippled daughter, became a milliner; Wilson, who according to Lydia "went to a Methodist minister who put him out of the way and we never heard of him since," may also have been indentured. Joseph Brown was certainly well-suited for the printing business as he later proved and it may well have been his choice of vocation, or, indeed, a convenient way to escape from a home in which he was not content. Usually a starting apprentice would be in his mid-teens – witness an advertisement in the *Lancaster Journal* in the summer of 1817 requesting a boy of fourteen for a printer's apprentice – but Joseph was probably younger. His age may have been misrepresented, because the printer for whom he was working in 1820 was under the impression that Brown (actually fifteen) was then a seventeen-year-old but small for his age. Since his apprenticeship had then three years to run, and the usual contract was for six, it is likely Joseph was apprenticed in 1817 when he was twelve.[14]

---

13. Ellis, *Lancaster County*.

14. Although the guild-like system of apprenticeship to the trades was beginning to break down, especially in printing, it was still very much in use in 1818. Some terms had been shortened from six to three years, but that does not seem to apply to Joseph. He may have been lucky to get taken on at all. In eastern cities there was a superabundance of learners, runaway apprentices and half-way journeymen who would "elope from their masters as soon as they acquire sufficient knowledge of the art to be enabled to earn their bread." See John R. Commons, *History of Labor in the United States* I: 110–116 (New York 1921).

By 1818 Samuel Brown was in very real financial trouble. Sometime that year he was cast into debtor's prison in Lancaster and was only able to free himself by declaring insolvency. He wasn't alone in his quagmire of debt; from 1816 on there had been general business stagnation in the aftermath of the war with the British. Many banks had folded, money was devalued and the papers were full of notices of insolvencies and bankruptcies. With all his debts (two of his largest creditors were doctors, which may point to sickness as a contributing factor), Samuel Brown might have been able to stave off ruin, but a neighbor to whom he owed $12 was taken up for debt and Brown was drawn up in the same net.[15] Binding out his son may have been an attempt to provide for both the boy and himself.

And so in early 1820 Joseph R. Brown found himself in the printing offices of Charles Mowry, editor of *The American Republican* in Downingtown, Pennsylvania, some fifty miles from home. Now there is a discrepancy here: all the family accounts and all subsequent sketches of Brown, agree that he was apprenticed to a printer in Lancaster City. Was this an assumption made by everyone, or was Joseph first bound to a Lancaster printer and later to Mowry in Downingtown? The latter is likely, because the story goes that he was with the particular printer for only a short time, maybe a year, before he ran away. The circumstances of his contract with Mowry seem to indicate that he had been tied to the business longer than that. Whatever the case, it was Mowry he was working for in 1820.[16]

Downingtown was a small village of scarcely forty houses and fewer than 300 inhabitants, but its many inns attested to its importance as the halfway point on the turnpike between Lancaster and Philadelphia. At Downingtown the pike crossed the Brandywine River on an elegant three-arched stone bridge, then ran down the broad Chester Valley to the east before turning south to climb out of the valley at Paoli. Traffic was extremely heavy in both directions. Pittsburgh wagons and small coaches were often found standing three and four deep waiting to get through the toll gates, and the dust, one traveler said, was so thick you could not see objects twenty feet ahead of you. Stages for Philadelphia stopped every day; if an apprentice were not too busy, he might hobnob with half the world.[17]

---

15. Brown's petition, preserved in the Lancaster Historical Society archives, Lancaster, PA, reads: "The Honorable the Judges of the Court of Common Pleas of Lancaster County... the sixteenth day of September 1818: the Petition of Samuel Brown respectfully represents that he is now in actual confinement in the jail of said county, having been committed on execution at the suit of Christian Kauffman for the recovery of twelve dollars... that he offers to deliver up to the use of his creditor all his property... [and] prays to be allowed the benefit of the several acts of Assembly of the Commonwealth of Pennsylvania made for the relief of insolvent debtors." Written below this is the notation "no property but the tools of his trade." His debt totaled over $350 including $50 in judgments against him. For more on the early nineteenth century economy see Appendix D.

16. See letters of A. Henderson, D. Henderson and Ellen Allanson to S. J. Brown cited; also J. F. Williams "Memoir of Joseph R. Brown" in *Minnesota Historical Collections* III: 201 (St. Paul 1880).

17. C. W. Heathcote *History of Chester County Pennsylvania* 171 (1932); see also J. T. Faris *Old Roads Out of Philadelphia* (1917).

Young Joseph's duties would have consisted of assisting the journeymen printers, probably by inking the heavy pads and helping lower the press, as well as scrubbing up, making deliveries and running general errands – onerous work, to be sure. The work day was long, 5 A.M. to 7 P.M. with an hour off for breakfast and one for lunch, leaving twelve hours for toil. He also began to learn typesetting – tiring and time-consuming work in those days when every tiny letter was set by hand, letter by letter, line by line, in a metal "stick" and just as laboriously broken down and each tiny letter replaced in the typecase. Once learned, never forgotten: he was able to demonstrate his skill for James M. Goodhue at the *Pioneer* in St. Paul thirty years later. Working for Mowry would have been an education, whatever else it was. The anti-Federalist editor had a considerable reputation as a Democratic-Republican journalist. He had enough influence to obtain the public printing in the fall of 1820 when he left Downingtown for the new capital at Harrisburg.[18]

Meanwhile, his print shop was a great place to learn about the rest of the world's doings. Exchange papers, the news service of the time, were received daily from Philadelphia, New York and Washington. In them was reported news of the great western adventure authorized by Secretary of War John C. Calhoun. One could read in the winter of 1819–1820 of General Henry Atkinson's exploratory expedition up the Missouri River and the push up the Mississippi by Colonel Henry Leavenworth to the mouth of the St. Peters (now Minnesota) River where American troops were maintaining a precarious toehold in Indian country at the very edge of the British dominions. What the newspapers hadn't reported was the awful news from those expeditions: hundreds of men dead of land scurvy, terrible suffering from the cold and lack of provisions, soldiers shot and scalped by Indians practically within sight of their barracks. Due to the impossibility of getting dispatches out during the winter, that grisly information didn't make it back east until April. Perhaps if it had, Joe Brown would have had second thoughts about joining the army, for he had begun to think seriously about running away.

Joseph and his master had not hit it off well: Mowry was a hard taskmaster, Joseph willful and impertinent. One family story is that Joseph ran away because he was whipped for some trifling incident and was generally treated harshly by his master. But it is clear from the advertisement placed by Mowry in the exchange papers that his apprentice's flight was not a spur-of-the-moment thing, but rather the result of careful calculation. One fine spring day Joseph was sent to deliver papers to the taverns down the valley. It was his opportunity and he seized it with both hands, absconding with his master's horse and possibly some cash he had collected as well. Riding until he or the horse could go no farther, he pulled up at the Buck Tavern, eight miles north of

---

18. Mowry's first venture was *The Temperate Zone* in 1808, which later became *The American Republican*. His career is discussed in John S. Futhey *History of Chester County Pennsylvania* (1881).

Philadelphia, and there caught the stage. Soon he had disappeared into the second-largest city in America.

Mowry was understandably angry when he worded his notice and so perhaps may have been guilty of some exaggeration, but after all the advertisement served no purpose if it didn't describe the fugitive fairly accurately:

$10 REWARD!!

"RAN away on the 22nd inst. an apprentice to the printing business named:

Joseph R. Brown

aged about 17 years and has about 3 years to serve. He was sent with papers from this office down the valley, and I have ascertained that he rode to the Buck tavern, and there took the stage for Philadelphia. He had on a roundabout [short jacket] and pantaloons of brown kersey net, dark imperial cord vest, coarse grey twilled overalls, faced with leather, all part worn, but decent. He is rather small of stature, light hair, eyes and complexion, talkative, pert in his answers, impudent in his manners, smokes segars, fond of liquor and much addicted to swearing when in company. One of his ankles is a little crooked, and the toes of both his feet turn out. His hat was considerably worn, but as it is expected he got money into his possession, he will probably buy a new one. He is not to be believed in any tale he may tell to screen himself from difficulty.

"The above reward will be given for confining him in any jail, and all persons are forbidden to harbour and employ him under the penalty of the law.

"Printers are respectfully requested to republish this advertisement for the good of the craft, and the favor will be reciprocated if necessary.

"Downingtown, March 23, 1820 C. Mowry"[19]

So we have our first description of Joseph R. Brown, and we know a little about how he acted, although the picture may be rather overdrawn. After all, Mowry did want his apprentice back despite his myriad faults, for the award offered is very generous. But Joseph was on his way west, whether he had planned it that way or not. He couldn't return to his family; aside from the flogging he could expect, he would quickly be returned to his master. Besides, his family may not have been reachable. Sometime after Samuel extricated himself from his debtor's cell, he packed up and moved to Erie County in northwestern Pennsylvania,

---

19. *Lancaster Journal* Apr. 14, 1820. Although he was said to enjoy a cigar occasionally, Brown in his adult years appears to have conquered the other vices exposed here, becoming a temperance man whose strongest epithet was "By George." See T. M. Newson, *Pen Pictures of St. Paul, Minnesota and Biographical Sketches of Old Settlers* 204 (St. Paul 1886). S. J. Brown told William Watts Folwell (interview Mar. 9, 1910, Folwell notebooks) that an axe-cut had severed a cord, causing Brown's foot to turn out; apparently, it was a childhood accident. The crooked ankle gave Brown his Indian name "Siharmi" (pronounced seeha-kmi), which has the meaning Crooked Foot in Dakota.

hundreds of miles across the Allegheny Mountains. By 1821 he was living in Fairview (now Girard) township in Erie County and preaching in Girard Hollow, and he may have been there earlier.20 Samuel Brown had nearly acquired a farm near Girard when he died in 1828, apparently of injuries sustained many years earlier in a fall from a horse. True to form, he was deeply in debt; his widow got a small amount of property and his creditors got sixteen cents on the dollar.21 Joseph never saw his father again, a circumstance he sincerely regretted in later life. But in 1820 he couldn't go home, so he set his face towards Philadelphia.

He may have thought to hire out to another printer (as many had done before him), but it would not be easy to find work in Philadelphia where thousands were unemployed – up to 90 percent of the workers in some industries, according to the *Niles Register* – and Mowry's advertisement, reprinted widely, rendered that course dangerous in any case. He may have tried living by his wits, but his meager funds would soon run out and the exceptionally cold spring would make living on the streets extremely uncomfortable, not to say fraught with peril. Then there was the ever-present possibility that he would be spotted and imprisoned. In March of 1820 the Fifth Regiment was still recruiting in Philadelphia for service on the northwestern frontier, and notice of this in the papers may have drawn him to Captain David Perry's recruiting rendezvous; he may even have known Lieutenant William Downey, Perry's recruiting officer and a Lancaster native. Many Lancaster County boys were in the Fifth; perhaps some were Joseph's friends. And if he needed anything else to sell him on an army career in the far west, there was the inducement of a blue-and-white bandsman's uniform with cockaded hat and sword, for Perry was looking for boys to play the fife and drum. And in the end joining the army was his only logical recourse: in April of 1820 he signed up for the $6 cash bounty and a safe berth.

Captain Perry should have required a release from his father or guardian, minimum age for army service being twenty-one, even though by custom this did not apply to boys recruited for musicians. But Captain Perry was extremely lax in such matters, preferring to rely on boys who had no relatives likely to make trouble. That may be why he waited until the last minute to sign up his musicians. At least six of his recruits are

---

20. "In 1821 Samuel Brown, a local preacher, formed a class in Girard Hollow with himself and wife, a Brother Shrives and wife and several others" says Samuel Gregg in *History of Methodism* 189 (1873). It is noteworthy that John Shriver was Samuel's biggest creditor in 1828. Samuel Brown is also said to have started the first Sunday School in Girard in 1824 in W. G. Smeltzer, D.D. *Methodism in Western Pennsylvania 1784–1968* 779 (1969). However, Lydia Ann Carli, born in 1818 "at Columbia" says they moved to Erie when she was seven; it could be that part of Samuel's family was left behind while he established a new home. Samuel bought land in Erie in January of 1826 (Deed Book B 589, Recorder of Deeds Office, Erie County Court House, Erie, PA).

21. Case "Pioneer Days"; Report of the Auditors on the Estate of Samuel Brown deceased, Apr. 9, 1830, File 17719, Probate Office, Erie County Court House. Samuel's family lost the farm; wrote Lydia "He kept all his accounts in his head... [then] died suddenly and took his accounts with him.... We had one payment to make on the farm and mother knew he had lent that sum to some friend, but who she did not... The law allowed us one span of horses, one cow and seven sheep. One of the horses laid down and died and the cow followed suit" (Carli to Brown May 20, 1902). The farm was sold by the sheriff Oct. 3, 1829 (Treasurer's and Sheriff's Deed Book A 107, Erie County records).

listed in the company muster rolls as having joined May 1, 1820, obviously a date of convenience as it begins a pay period. Among these are Joseph R. Brown and four other teen-aged boys destined to become musicians.[22]

The recruiting office was closed April 18 and by May 1, 1820, the great adventure had begun. Joseph R. Brown and the other 130 recruits collected at Philadelphia were on their way west. Brown was a private, pay $6 a month and $12 bonus (half of it in his pocket), in the United States Infantry.

---

22. Muster rolls and post returns, Fifth Regiment, 1818–1820, AGO, NARG 94; Lieutenant William Downey, account with Second Auditor #4123, May 30, 1820, and Records of Paymasters 1820, both in GAO, NARG 217. Brown's actual enlistment record is missing, either lost by Perry or removed from the Second Auditor's files when suit was filed against Perry by the government in 1821 for recovery of his recruiting advances.

Map 2 The Far West of 1820. Rivers and lakes were the highways west of the Alleghenies. Wisconsin, Iowa and Minnesota were still Indian Territory, and there were few settlements save army posts and fur trade locations west of Detroit.

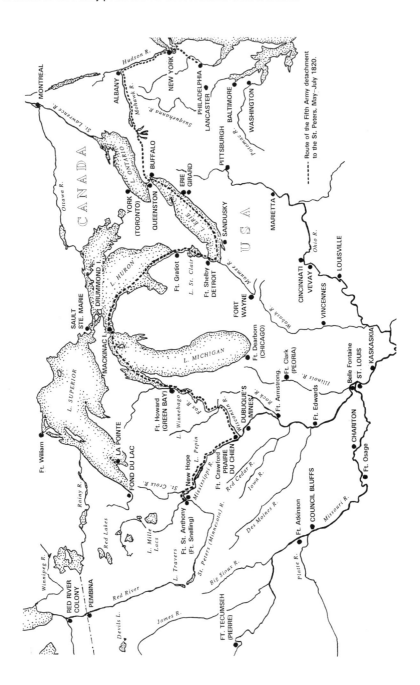

CHAPTER II

"THIS 'OLD HOSS' WAS THAR..."
JOSEPH R. BROWN

On July 7, 1820, the hot, muggy weather broke with sudden thunderstorms and high winds sweeping over the bluffs. At Fort Crawford, just north of the straggling village of Prairie du Chien, commanding officer Major Peter Muhlenberg and Captain Perry sorted out the 183 recruits for the Fifth Regiment in the rain. They were a sorry lot: only half had uniforms and accouterments, the rest made do with civilian dress of varying degrees of serviceability. Thirty-four of the men (mostly sick and unable to travel further) were mustered into Companies A and I at Fort Crawford that day. Forty-seven others were detailed to reinforce Fort Armstrong downstream on Rocky Island (Rock Island, Illinois). Joseph R. Brown and the other boy-musicians remained temporarily at the fort, waiting to proceed upriver to the regimental headquarters at the mouth of the St. Peters (now Minnesota) River.[1]

Figure 1 Fifer at Fort Snelling

Joe Brown was ducking raindrops at the edge of the known world, that is, the world known to citizens of the United States. Although the land west of the Mississippi had been traversed by French and British traders for many decades, it was terra incognita to the United States Army. The commencement of the War of 1812 had prevented thorough American exploration of the Louisiana Purchase. Even though skirmishes during that conflict had taken place on the Mississippi at Prairie du Chien (then Fort Shelby), American troops had

---

1. Meteorological information from Surgeon Generals' reports, now in U.S. Weather Bureau Climatological Reports, NARG 27; troop information from inspection reports, post returns and muster rolls, Forts Crawford, Snelling and Armstrong, AGO.

not ventured across the upper river. After the war, Fort Crawford, built on the site of Fort Shelby in 1816, became the marshaling point for a military venture into Indian territory. From this point in the fall of 1819, the Fifth Regiment under Colonel Henry Leavenworth had pushed some 270 miles into Indian country to the mouth of the St. Peters River where a cantonment was hastily constructed in the face of an early winter. Due to the severity of the weather, the inadequate accommodations and tainted provisions, almost half the men had died or become incapacitated over the course of the winter. Joe Brown's detail was badly needed to relieve that decimated force struggling to establish a toehold in the country of the Sioux.[2]

Figure 2 Fort Crawford and the village of Prairie du Chien. Sketch by Seth Eastman. Wis. Hist. Soc.

The place where Joe Brown found himself on July 7, 1820, was a typical frontier fort. Facing a sluggish backwater of the Mississippi, Fort Crawford sat on low prairie, subject to inundation in times of high water. The defensive works consisted of rough-shingled barracks of horizontal timbers arranged in a hollow square, their twenty-foot-high backs forming the defensive wall. The spaces between the buildings were filled with palisading, fortified gates and two blockhouses strategically placed in opposite corners. There was plenty of room for the new men to get out of the rain; the fort had been built to hold five companies, not, however, comfortably. When the sun came out again and the temperature soared to

---

2. Incredible as it may seem, the Fifth Regiment had only 357 men at its three posts; there were 64 effective at Fort Crawford, 23 at Fort Armstrong and the other 170 manned Cantonment New Hope, the new post at the St. Peters. There had been forty deaths at the latter post alone over the winter where at least forty men were perpetually on sick-call. For more on the military/political situation, see Appendix B.

95° the airless rooms with their single tiny windows became stifling and the mosquitoes unbearable.3

The sixty-four men stationed at Fort Crawford were exceedingly happy to see the reinforcements. They were still jittery from the Indian scares of the preceding spring and summer, and now nervously guarded two Winnebago warriors who had shot and scalped two men from the garrison at Fort Armstrong in March. The Indians had been stirred up, some said, by Robert Dickson, for four decades a prominent British trader on the upper Mississippi and most recently notable as commander of the British forces that had taken Fort Stephenson on Lake Erie. During the war Dickson had recruited the Indians of the Northwest to the British cause. In May, however, he had used his influence to help American Indian Agent Nicholas Boilvin arrange a parley with marauding Winnebago at the Prairie and to convince the Indians to turn over the murderers to Colonel Leavenworth. The two were now in log chains in the none-too-secure guardhouse and the garrison fervently wished they were elsewhere, preferably standing their trial in St. Louis. Dickson, whose activities during the war with the British seemed to have been conveniently forgotten, had ingratiated himself with Colonel Leavenworth and by June had returned to the St. Peters where he furnished the new Sioux agent, Lawrence Taliaferro, with a census of that nation.4 For the moment the threatening Winnebago were being kept at bay, not so much through intimidation from the United States Army as by the Sac and Fox (Mesquakie), who were well-disposed toward the Americans and no great friends of the Rock River Winnebago. John W. Johnson, Yankee in charge of the United States trading factory at the Prairie, still railing against the British traders there whom he saw as a constant goad to the Indians, not to mention threat to his business, wrote in June that "for the time being at least the Indian storm has blown over."5

---

3. The fort and its inadequate siting (it was overlooked by high ground and did not even command the Mississippi) is described as it was in 1817 by Stephen H. Long in *The Northern Expeditions of Stephen H. Long: The Journals of 1817 and 1822 and Related Documents*. Lucile M. Kane, June D. Holmquist, Carolyn Gilman, eds., 88–91 (St. Paul 1987).

4. Major Morrill Marston to Adjutant General, Mar. 20, 1820, AGO LR NARG 94; Major Lawrence Taliaferro Journal 1820, Jul. 7, 1820, Taliaferro papers, MHS. Dickson, a Scot and for more than thirty years a trader in the upper Mississippi Country, had an ascendancy over the Sioux, Winnebago and Menominee Indians unequaled by anyone of his time. Dickson's "stirrings" among the Indians were well known: unable to trade under an American license or move freely in United States territory (he had been arrested in 1817 for supposed infringements), he planned a trading post at the grand forks of the Red River in Lord Selkirk's grant, and had been engaged for several years in persuading the Sioux of the Mississippi to resettle there in what it was presumed would remain Canadian territory—had, in fact, convinced several bands, including part of Little Crow's, to move. While the army officers obviously welcomed the aid of Colonel Dickson, the eastern press took the more alarming view; on Jun. 10, 1820 *Niles Register* (Baltimore) printed an item entitled "A Speck of War" which commented on the Fort Armstrong murders, attributing them to the presence of British traders, notably the "celebrated Dixon." For more on Dickson see Louis Arthur Tohill "Robert Dickson, British Fur Trader on the Upper Mississippi: A Story of Trade, War, and Diplomacy" (Ph. D. dissertation, University of Minnesota: 1926 MHS)

5. John W. Johnson to Thomas L. McKenney, Superintendent of Indian Trade, Jun. 28, 1820, OIA LR, NARG 75. The government factories, initiated in 1796 in the South, attempted to win the allegiance of the Indians and control the fur trade by providing goods to them at fair prices. They could undercut private traders, but their American-made goods were thought by the Indians to be inferior to British goods

Joseph R. Brown had arrived at Prairie du Chien after a journey of more than 1,000 miles in less than twelve weeks. He had left Philadelphia in late April with Captain David Perry and Lieutenant William Downey and their last party of recruits for Fort Mifflin on Tinicum Island, just south of that city, where the detachment was being assembled. Space in that fort was at a premium as the Third Artillery Regiment that garrisoned it had also been recruiting, and many of the new men had to be housed in tents or crowded into the "bombproofs" dug into the walls. Room for most of the Fifth's recruits had been found on Province Island at the mouth of Darby Creek in the ill-kept buildings of the lazarette, or quarantine station, which may have dated back to Dutch times. The boys likely had better quarters; Captain Perry would have kept them under his eye. But in any case they didn't remain at Fort Mifflin long. Final arrangements for the trip west were made on April 27, and shortly afterward the detachment left for New York. At Fort Gibson, on Governor's Island in New York harbor, they joined a contingent from the Fifth's other recruiting station in Boston, commanded by Major Sullivan Burbank, and picked up some artillery recruits bound for Detroit. By May 2 Joe Brown and 180 other new soldiers had begun their great western adventure crammed into a sloop bound up the Hudson River for Albany.[6]

Leaving Albany on the fifth of May for Buffalo, they traveled on shank's mare through Schenectady and up the Mohawk Valley to Utica, heading west over the old route that would be followed in two years by the Erie Canal. By May 18 they were at Williamsville, just outside Buffalo. They were loaded on the schooner *Erie* at the port of Black Rock on the Niagara River, along with their supplies, casks of salt and a load of planks destined for Detroit, then their ship was pulled by a "horned breeze" of ox teams upriver to the lake. *Erie* made Detroit in eight days, where they touched briefly to pick up Captain Perry (who had traveled in style on the lake's first steamboat *Walk-in-the-Water*), then sat becalmed about thirty miles up the St. Clair River, waiting for the strong south wind necessary to make headway against the river's current. There they sat for nearly a week, tormented as much by boredom as by the clouds of mosquitoes that rose from the marshes on either side. It was a week enlivened only by the stir caused when a couple of the new men jumped ship (they were caught at Detroit, where else could they go?), but finally the wind shifted and *Erie* shot out at last over the rapids at the head of the river onto the broad

---

supplied from Canada. Also the credit system, which had become entrenched in the fur trade, undermined their success; the independent traders could advance goods to the Indians, keeping them in perpetual debt, while government factors could give goods only in exchange for peltries. Traders put up fierce opposition, ganging up to form a "wall" about the factory and using any means—threats, cajolery, bribery—to prevent Indians from approaching it. The factory system was abandoned in 1822. (Edgar Bruce Wesley *Guarding the Frontier: A Study of Frontier Defense from 1815 to 1825* 31-50 (reprint Westport, CT 1970).

6. Major Josiah H. Vose to Secretary of War, Jan. 4, 1820, and Surgeon General Joseph Lovell to same, Aug. 31, 1820, OSW LR main series, NARG 107; William Linnard to Quartermaster General, Aug. 14, 1820, OQG consolidated correspondence, NARG 92; Major Twiggs to Adjutant General, Jan. 27, 1820, and Colonel House to same, Apr. 27, 1820, in AGO LR; William Downey account #4123 with Second Auditor.

expanse of Lake Huron. From there it was clear sailing to Mackinac Island, entrepôt and headquarters of the western fur trade since French times, which they cleared June 10 bound for Green Bay. Three days later they had coasted the Door Peninsula and arrived at Fort Howard, an outpost three miles up the Fox River.[7]

At last the recruits could get out of the stinking ship in which they'd been trapped for three weeks! But the forty-man bateaux into which they loaded their supplies were just as crowded, if sweeter-smelling. In went tents, blankets, barrels of pork and flour, cartridges and kettles. The strange flat-bottomed boats were ostensibly propelled by eight men pulling at oars; however, on the rocky whitewater Fox River it seemed they were more often moved by pushing and pulling, wading waist-deep in icy water to "track" them up the rapids. They were following one of the great trade routes west, once an Indian trail, used by French explorers and traders for more than a century and a half. Hundreds of tons of Indian trade goods came this way from Mackinac every year and thousands of dollars worth of valuable furs went back in the spring. As yet, the American presence was unfelt here. Beyond the last shanty of the French Canadian and halfbreed settlement that straggled along the river above the fort lay Indian country. A few miles up the river the detachment passed several large Indian villages, relatives, it was said, of those Winnebagoes who had murdered the soldiers at Fort Armstrong. Desertions became a thing of the past.

Near the portage into the Wisconsin River, the boats had to be forced through immense beds of wild rice which tended to obscure the channel altogether; then bateaux and equipment were dragged over the short, muddy portage (with the aid of an old Frenchman and his oxen), and the troops re-embarked on the broad Wisconsin. Unhappily, the sluggish river was filled with sandbars and planters – half-submerged logs that could take the bottom out of a boat – and low water made the going tedious. Instead of resting their oars and floating on the current, they frequently found themselves slogging along in the shallows to lighten the boats.

All in all it took Captain Perry's detachment nearly three weeks to make the trip across what is now the state of Wisconsin. After so long a journey, they must have heaved sighs of relief as they threaded their way through the last of the shifting sandbars and wooded islets to emerge on

---

7. Vouchers for the march to the Niagara River are in file #4888, Second Auditor's records, GAO; further detail is supplied in the "Court Martial of George Wilson", file C37, Records of Advocate-General, NARG 153. The ship may be traced through the *Detroit Gazette* May 25 & Jun. 2, 1820; and the manifest of *Erie*, Captain Miles, May 20, 1820, bound from Black Rock to Mackinac, papers of U.S. Customs, Mackinac, Michigan, microfilm in MHS. The contingent twice met an expedition led by Michigan Territorial Governor Lewis Cass; this exploring party passed the troop ship as they paddled their north canoe from Detroit to Sault Ste. Marie on June 2, later visited the cantonment at the St. Peters on their return trip down the Mississippi. The expedition is described in Henry Rowe Schoolcraft *Narrative Journal of Travels Through the Northwestern United States*, Mentor L. Williams, ed. (East Lansing 1953).

the mighty Mississippi. Three miles further and they were being welcomed gratefully by the garrison at Prairie du Chien.[8]

Prairie du Chien – a miserable assemblage of decrepit log cabins and fur company warehouses, known colloquially as "the Prairie" – was the last vestige of civilization Joe Brown would see in his travels, if civilization it could be called. It was an old settlement; long a gathering place for the Indians of the river valley, it had been a resort of French fur traders from the seventeenth century. Descendants of these Indians and traders now occupied most of the two dozen or so log buildings clustered along the riverbank on a single street not 800 yards long and farmed the long, narrow French-style fields that ran back from the river on the broad prairie.

The Prairie's business was the fur trade. James Lockwood, agent for the American Fur Company of New York, kept his office and warehouse here, as did his fierce competitors Jean-Baptiste Bertholet and Joseph Rolette, agents for David Stone of Detroit. Nicholas Boilvin's Indian agency nestled up to the fort at the north end of the village near the store of Wilfred Owens, who did a brisk business selling tobacco and whiskey and other necessities to the soldiers. There were almost always Indians encamped nearby.[9] Even in July, the furs shipped and the corn planted, the village drowsing in the hot sun waiting for autumn when Indians by the hundreds would again come in to make credits for the winter hunts, it was a fascinating place. In a few years Joe Brown would get to know it and its colorful inhabitants very well indeed.

It is 270 miles from Fort Crawford to the mouth of the St. Peters River. The traveler on the Mississippi today can see what Joe Brown saw in 1820, for the magnificent scenery along the wild and beautiful river valley has changed very little in the last 150 years. The valley is still lined with fantastic crags and bald, rocky bluffs, the shifting river still bordered with beautiful prairies set amid shaggy wooded islands – although its treacherous, sandbar-studded channel has been tamed somewhat by several dams and the Corps of Engineers. Only the fires are gone, immense fires set by hunters or lightning that every summer burned the prairies treeless, lit up the night sky outlining the bluffs and filled the air with smoke.

---

8. Specific information on this route can be found in Captain Henry Whiting's "Journal of the March of the Fifth Regiment to Prairie du Chien 1819," a report in the Office of the Chief Engineer, NARG 77, and in "Charles C. Trowbridge's Journal" Ralph Brown, ed., in Minnesota *History* Dec. 1942, 345 ff, describing the route in reverse as taken by Cass' party in August 1820. The bateaux were constructed at Fort Howard for use by detachments traveling to the Mississippi; see Colonel William Whistler to Colonel Smith, Dec. 12, 1819, and Colonel Smith to General Jacob Brown, Dec. 16, 1819, both in OSW LR.

9. Not until the mid-1830s did Americans settle at the Prairie in sufficient numbers to turn it into a respectable town; by that time the Indians for whom the trading establishments existed had been removed to reservations in Iowa. For descriptions of the old village see Long *Northern Expeditions* 92; James H. Lockwood "Early Times in Wisconsin" in *Wisconsin Historical Collections* II: 134–150 (reprint Madison 1903).

Map 3 The vicinity of "The Entry" and Fort Snelling at the confluence of the St. Peters (Minnesota) and Mississippi rivers in the early 1820s. Compiled from army maps of the 1820s and 30s in the Fort Snelling map collection, Minn. Hist. Soc.

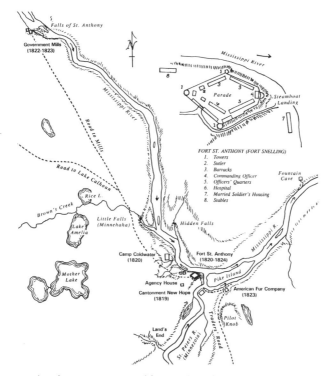

Many travelers' accounts testify to the river's wild beauty, but Joe Brown was more of a pragmatist than they; he and his companions found the river more work than romance. It was a struggle for the tired men to force their heavily laden boats upstream against the wind and current. When rowing wouldn't do, they poled. When poles failed, they used cordelles to winch the boats along, tying their ropes to trees along the bank. It rained, sometimes for three days at a stretch; alternately, it was hot and humid. The only signs of life were a few Indian villages, some quite sizable, whose inhabitants were curious and disposed to be friendly toward Americans, and the occasional abandoned-looking trader's hut marking the mouth of a wooded tributary stream. Finally, on the sixteenth day they passed the lodges of Little Crow's band of Mdewakanton Sioux under the sheer white sandstone cliffs of Dayton's Bluff, where now stands the city of St. Paul, and a little further on, with joyful shouts of relief, found soldiers from the cantonment felling trees for the new fort. After just nine more miles of pulling at the oars, Joe Brown came in sight of his new home.**10**

---

10. This trip is described in detail in Stephen H. Long "Voyage in a Six-Oared Skiff to the Falls of Saint Anthony in 1817" in *Minnesota Historical Collections* II: 9–34 (reprint St. Paul 1889).

Figure 3 Artist's conception of Cantonment New Hope, the log fort constructed in 1819 at Mendota, across the Minnesota River from the present Fort Snelling.

At first view, it was uninspiring. Cantonment New Hope lay close to the water on the right (southwest) bank of the St. Peters about two miles from its mouth, in what had perhaps the autumn before seemed a protected area close to good water, but had in summer proved to be a stagnant marsh infested with mosquitoes. Between the fort and the channel of the Mississippi lay a low brushy island and slough. (The site today is on a backwater of the river in Fort Snelling State Park; the St. Peters, now the Minnesota River, flows today in a new channel to the southeast.)

The fort into which the new recruits were ushered showed signs of its hasty construction the preceding fall. Four shedlike buildings were arranged in a rectangle as at Fort Crawford. Each landward wall had a gate with a defensive platform over it; on the north-facing river side a fourth opening had been left to bring in supplies, but its defensive blockhouse had never been built. In truth, none of the buildings had been finished: winter had descended early and it had been impossible to obtain suitable lumber and shingles. Each room meant for quarters was equipped with a small window and a door, but only half had stone fireplaces and many had no floors. After spending a miserable winter in these buildings and in makeshift shelters rigged on the boats, most of the command moved across the river in May. There, on a commanding eminence about a mile up the Mississippi and near a good cold-water spring, they built an unfortified camp of bark-covered log huts for the officers and tents for the men, a more healthful if less adequately protected site. Camp Coldwater, as they named this cantonment, was in any case meant only for temporary quarters while the permanent works were constructed on the cliff at the confluence of the rivers. But so far nothing had been done toward that end, and by July it was obvious the command would spend at least one more winter at New Hope; therefore, a detail was hard at work rendering those quarters habitable for the coming winter.11

Except for the carpenters, only a few officers and one company remained in the log fort, sharing quarters with the new Indian agent, Lawrence Taliaferro, and the surgeon, Dr. Edmund Purcell. The new recruits were issued equipment and clothes and on July 25 were mustered in, divided among the seven companies occupying the post. Most of them were sent across the river to Camp Coldwater to join their companies. It is probable that Joe Brown stayed at New Hope for the rest of the summer with his new outfit, Major Sullivan Burbank's Company D.

Their sole neighbors were fur traders. On Pike Island across the river stood the trading establishment of Jean-Baptiste Faribault, an independent from Prairie du Chien. Faribault had driven a herd of cattle and horses for the garrison up from Prairie du Chien and pastured them on the island. The Prescott brothers, Philander and Wright, clerks for sutler Louis Devotion, had a cabin nearby on the riverbank and were busily erecting a warehouse two miles upstream on the opposite side of the St. Peters at a place called "Lands End."12

By August, Joseph R. Brown was "learning music" – so noted on the muster rolls – under the tutelage of Drum Major John Schelinski and Fife Major Bernard Curry. Military regulations authorized two principal musicians for each company, at that time designated Fifer and Drummer. Musicians received a dollar more per month than a private, but other musically inclined soldiers could be in the band, as Private Joe Brown was, although they received no extra pay. Colonel Leavenworth felt keenly that a good band was a morale-raiser. Even though there was no appropriation he had managed to acquire some band instruments, as well as books for the post library, by using the assessment against the post sutler's sales. In some regiments, the band was formed up as a separate company and issued distinctive uniforms – a red coat and epaulets; at Fort St. Anthony (as this outpost came to be called), it is harder to tell what the practice was because the musicians remained in their own companies and band uniforms as such were not issued. However, they were acquired in some way, for at a later date we find a note that old band uniforms were being sold. From correspondence we know that the fort definitely had a much-appreciated band in 1822 that may well have been organized a year or two before, but it is difficult to imagine that Colonel Leavenworth's musicians managed many band concerts that first year. 13

---

11. Vose to Colonel Henry Leavenworth, Oct. 1819; Colonel Josiah Snelling to Major General Edmund P. Gaines, Apr. 10, 1820; both in AGO LR.

12. Faribault, a Canadian, had traded at the St. Peters area since 1802; see H. H. Sibley "Memoir of Jean Baptiste Faribault" in *Minnesota Historical Collections* III: 168, 179 (St. Paul 1880). Philander Prescott's account of the fort and the first winter spent there is in Donald Dean Parker, ed., *The Recollections of Philander Prescott, Frontiersman of the Old Northwest*, 1819–1862 30 (Lincoln 1966).

13. Leavenworth to Colonel Parker, May 14, 1820, OSW LR Main Series; Orderly Book Company E Fifth Regiment Jan. 12, 1826; Colonel Samuel B. Archer, to Adjutant General, Apr. 25, 1824, AGO LR; in this letter, concerning a fifer who deserted after being beaten by the Fifth's adjutant, Platt Rogers Green, Archer states that there was a band at Fort St. Anthony in July of 1822. Interestingly enough, Archer was looking for a Joseph Brown who was a witness to the fifer's beating on July 4, 1822. For army life, see

Joe Brown's status as a bandsman meant his life differed a great deal from that of the average private. His duties, as well as his age, exempted him from the ordinary daily routine. He wasn't even issued a musket at first, although that omission may be attributable to the fact the command was short of weapons and ammunition. However, musicians weren't expected to stand guard duty and were excused from routine company drill and camp fatigue, as well as from the onerous "hay parties" and "wood parties," attendance at which was a part of every other soldier's life. They drilled with the other musicians, practicing the music, drum beats and signals out of earshot of the rest of the garrison. Company musicians were expected to attend all parades and drum beats, including reveille, breakfast, dinner and evening roll calls, evening band concert, retreat and tattoo – although it is unclear whether a youngster "learning music" would be similarly constrained. While the presence of professional musicians in a frontier outpost of tents and log cabins may appear frivolous, their function was important. They served as sort of an alarm clock for the post, for all the day's activities were signaled by drum beats. While the timing differed somewhat from post to post and season to season, generally the morning whiskey drum (½ gill per man)

Figure 4 Jean-Baptiste Faribault, Minn. Hist. Soc.

was at 10 minutes to breakfast roll call, which was at 8 A.M., and a half-hour later the signals were beat for fatigue parties to commence work, then sick call and so on through the day. Another whiskey drum sounded at 10 minutes to dinner roll call about 2 P.M., and sometimes for the sutler's whiskey later in the afternoon (spirits were thought to give strength and protection from disease; it would be several years before the daily whiskey ration would be replaced by the seemingly inadequate coffee and sugar ration). Each day and night the orderly drummer and fifer stood ready to beat any special calls – to summon the men to arms or to quench a fire. Fifing was added to many of these calls, and the full band played

Francis Paul Prucha *Broadaxe and Bayonet: The Role of the United States Army in the Development of the Northwest, 1815–1860* (Madison 1953).

for the evening concert, to welcome and send off dignitaries and probably to impress the visiting Sioux and Chippewa.[14]

Joe Brown's only discussion of his early army career was printed in 1856 in the *Henderson Democrat*, and it appears he took some liberties with the facts. He says:

> "When the northern frontier was first formally taken possession of by our good Uncle Sam, this 'old hoss' was *thar...* We blowed the fife for the call of the troops to the first dinner they ate after their landing at the mouth of the St. Peter. We assisted at the erection of the first building erected at the first cantonment and we shoveled sand for the foundation of the first stone building erected in Fort Snelling. We were in the first party that lumbered on the Rum River."[15]

He was demonstrably not with the first troops, although it is perfectly true he was with the troops that built Fort Snelling, that is, the stone fort, and he may have shoveled sand for this later construction. Work began in earnest on the stone fort only after Colonel Josiah Snelling came north to take command of the regiment in late August of 1820 bringing his family with him. Fifty-one men were detailed cutting logs, splitting planks with the broadaxe, burning lime and quarrying stone from the limestone bluffs in the nearby river valley. This work would occupy up to a quarter of the troops for the next three years, but Brown was not likely among them: during his entire army career he never drew any extra duty pay (meaning he was never on special duty detail for ten days or more, which would have entitled him to fifteen cents a day extra pay). The first pine timber was cut on the Rum River by a detachment sent up over the winter of 1821–1822.[16] But J. R. Brown was present in his company February 28 and April 30 during the time the detachment was on the Rum, so if he was at the logging camp it was for a relatively short time and not as a

---

14. Vose "Extract from Post Orders 1823–1827, Fort Armstrong" in Orderly Book Company K Fifth Regiment, Burton Historical Collections, Chicago, microfilm in MHS, gives details. See also *General Regulations of the Army* 32 (Philadelphia 1821). The band is mentioned as playing funeral dirges in Ann Adams "Early Days at Red River Settlement and Ft. Snelling: Reminiscences of Mrs. Ann Adams 1821–1829" J. F. Williams, ed. in *Minnesota Historical Collections* VI: 95 (St. Paul 1894).

15. *Henderson Democrat* Apr. 17, 1856. In a letter to Henry H. Sibley written in January, 1856 (misdated 1855, Sibley papers, MHS) Brown also stated that he came to the St. Peters in 1819 and that he accompanied the Colonel to the Rum, St. Croix and Chippewa (Wis.) rivers in search of antiscorbutics intended to counteract the scurvy. This is patently untrue as Brown was not in camp during that first winter and Leavenworth left the command in September, 1820. However, Colonel Snelling could have sent a detail that included J. R. Brown to lay in a supply of "hemlock tea" for the following winter, 1820-1821, especially since the army had paid dearly to procure it from Joe Rolette at Prairie du Chien in 1819–1820.

16. Col. Josiah Snelling to Adjutant General, Apr. 10, 1822, AGO LR; also see Parker *Prescott* 32. Post returns and paymaster's records reveal that the men who built the fort were on extra duty. Their lot was hard, as it was for most common soldiers until 1833; wrote one disgusted man (he was elsewhere, but he might well have been at Fort Snelling), "I never was told that I would be called on to make roads, build bridges, quarry stone, burn brick and lime, carry the hod, cut wood, hew timber, raft it to the garrison, make shingles, saw plank, build mills, maul rails, drive teams, make hay, herd cattle, build buildings, etc." (Quoted in Prucha *Broadaxe and Bayonet*).

member of the logging party; he might have been sent up as an express or as an orderly to an officer.

Joe Brown's education in Indian ways began almost the instant he set foot at the St. Peters. Just three days after Joe Brown arrived at New Hope, the governor of the territory, Lewis Cass of Michigan, and his exploring party appeared with a contingent of Sandy Lake Chippewa, having taken the northern route through Lake Superior and the St. Louis River to the Mississippi via the Savannah River portage and, after exploration of its headwaters, descended the Mississippi. On the first day of August, Cass and Taliaferro brought the two historically inimical nations together at New Hope for a "peace treaty," toward which neither Sioux nor Chippewa were much inclined. Only a few of the Sioux chiefs would condescend to smoke the pipe of peace with their enemies. Cass and Taliaferro did what they could to get the parties to agree to a truce, and the next day the Chippewa left for home without causing any incidents. Colonel Leavenworth, however, seized on the occasion to keep the Sioux assembled in council, with the purpose of getting them to cede a tract of land on the south side of the river for a military reservation. The Indians were liberally entertained with food and firewater, with the result that one respected old chief, Magasan (White Bustard), was stabbed by a comrade practically at the agent's (and Joe Brown's) front door at New Hope. "This unpleasant affair," Taliaferro reported to Leavenworth, "was caused, doubtless, by an anxiety to obtain the chief's whiskey," and he begged that no whiskey be given to the Indians "unless it be through their proper agent."[17]

Figure 5 Lawrence Taliaferro, Indian Agent at the St. Peters. Minn. Hist. Soc.

---

17. Taliaferro to Leavenworth, Jul. 30, 1820, quoted in Edward Duffield Neill "Occurrences In and Around Fort Snelling from 1819 to 1840" in *Minnesota Historical Collections* II: 103–104 (reprint St. Paul 1894); See also "Autobiography of Major Lawrence Taliaferro" in *Minnesota Historical Collections VI*: 234. (St. Paul 1894) Taliaferro (pronounced Tolliver) was personally known to President James Monroe, who commissioned him Indian agent for the Upper Mississippi in March 1819, when he was just twenty-five. He held his post for twenty years, through six administrations—a tribute to his honesty, integrity and dedication to duty—and got on well with later commandants. He was extremely vain and convinced of his own importance, but these attributes probably commended him to his charges. The agent, although young and undeniably arrogant, understood from the start that the more familiar the Sioux became with the soldiers, the less they would respect either the government or him as its agent. See William Watts Folwell *A History of Minnesota* I: 141–142 (revised St. Paul 1956) and Roy W. Meyer *History of the*

The Sioux of the neighborhood had unrestricted access to the cantonment and were to be seen almost daily in summer, being attracted to the area by the presence of their traders and their "father," the Indian agent, although in the fall most bands abandoned their summer villages,

Figure 6 Fort Snelling was begun in 1820 and was essentially complete by 1823. Watercolor by Seth Eastman in Minn. Hist. Soc.

moving south and west to their hunting grounds. It was Governor Cass' opinion that the Indians of the St. Peters had been spoiled – since the war presents had been handed out willy-nilly in an effort to win their allegiance – although the fault was not entirely that of the United States agents. More than 120 years of contact with British traders and before them the French had taught the Sioux to covet the white man's goods and they had developed a taste for his "milk," that is, whiskey. Some traders used whiskey indiscriminately to create an advantage in the trade. Taliaferro was well aware of the dangers inherent in providing the Indians with liquor but also realized that it was expected as a good-will offering from him as the official representative of their "Great Father" in Washington; it was necessary to bestow whiskey and other gifts on the Indians if the Americans hoped to wean them from their British ties. For the most part, the Sioux who lived near the fort were generally friendly toward their American neighbors. Other Indians in the Mississippi Valley presented continual problems.**18**

Santee Sioux: United States Indian Policy on Trial 35–36 ff (Lincoln 1967) for more about this interesting character.

18   The Sioux, who had been pushed from the Mille Lac area by the Chippewa, lived chiefly in and south of the Minnesota River Valley and west of the Mississippi; their traditional enemies occupied northern Minnesota and Wisconsin, leaving a dangerous 'no-man's land' between.

The boat that arrived on September 15, 1820, carried the news that a soldier at Fort Armstrong had been "shot, scalped and tomahawked" by Winnebagoes, making the third murder in the Wisconsin area that fall. Three days later came word that the Sisseton and Wahpekute Sioux of the Upper St. Peters had murdered two Fur Company employees near the Missouri. Summoned by Taliaferro, the Sisseton came to New Hope and at a council September 30 promised to deliver up the murderers, leaving two hostages. These, however, were carelessly allowed to escape; after that the Indians refused to come in or discuss the matter.

Things stood at stalemate when Taliaferro left for Washington in October. But on November 12, to everyone's surprise, a large body of Sisseton, faces painted black, arms gashed as a token of grief, and singing the death song, appeared outside the fort with the murderers – or to be more accurate, one murderer and the aged father of the other, who had offered himself in his son's stead. Their friends and relatives made a great show, firing guns, whooping and yelling, running to and fro. The garrison was back in winter quarters at New Hope; for most of the men, who had little experience with Sioux customs and were only too ready to believe in an uprising, it must have been terrifying, even with a solid palisade between them and the frenzied-seeming crowd. With cannon at the ready, Colonel Snelling opened the gates and let a delegation in.[19]

The Colonel later described the scene as it was witnessed by the garrison, including Joseph R. Brown:

> "A procession was formed... and marched to the centre of our parade. It was preceded by a Sussitong bearing the British flag; the murderer and devoted chief followed with their arms pinioned and large splinters of wood thrust through them above the elbows, to indicate as I understood their contempt of pain and death. The relatives and friends followed and on their way joined them in singing their death song. When they arrived in front of the guard the British flag was laid on a fire... and consumed; the murderer gave up his [British] medal and both the prisoners surrendered... The friends of the prisoners were fed and then returned home peaceably."[20]

For Joe Brown, it was an impressive introduction to the Sioux and brought home the vulnerability of this small garrison hundreds of miles from any possible assistance. Their isolation was emphasized all the more by the reality of an unforgiving climate for which they were ill prepared, although little could have prepared natives of the eastern seaboard for

19. Taliaferro to John C. Calhoun, Secretary of War, Oct. 1, 1820, and General Alexander McComb to same, Nov. 18, 1820, OSW LR main series; Snelling to Adjutant General, Nov. 10, 1820, AGO LR. Colin Campbell, brother of Taliaferro's interpreter Scott, who had been raised among the Sisseton, was sent by the agent to reason with them; subsequent events can give rise to the thought that Campbell may have exceeded his instructions by threatening the removal of all traders from the Sisseton. The capitulation of the Indians seemed to come as a surprise to Taliaferro, who would never have connived at such a plan.

20. Snelling to Calhoun, Nov. 13, 1820, OSW LR main series. This scene is also described in Parker *Prescott* 33–34 and Neill "Occurrences" 105–106.

winter on the northern prairies. Cold weather set in early; snow fell on October 14 and continued to fall through November, stopping work on the new barracks which Colonel Snelling had so enthusiastically started in mid-September. The river closed November 26, preventing further supplies being brought up and effectively shutting the garrison off from the rest of the world. One last batch of reinforcement troops, a squadron made up of convicts, chronic deserters and other desperadoes, just made it up before the ice cut off communication. With the exception of one company that was able to occupy the new quarters at Fort St. Anthony, the troops settled into the old cantonment at New Hope for what proved to be a long and unusually severe winter. The regiment was short of practically all materials, including clothing, shoes, pots and pans, and also ammunition, an oversight that could easily prove fatal. Colonel Snelling commented on the regimental return in January: "The ammunition (what little we have) appears by the marks to have been put up for the Northwestern army and is literally good for nothing."[21] Much of the powder had been used for blasting rock. Even food was at a premium; once the river was blocked, the only way to get supplies was to haul them up on the ice by French *train* (a wheelless conveyance pulled by a horse or ox). The cattle which had been driven up over the summer starved in the deep snow and biting cold. There was no fresh produce.

The Fifth was feeling the pinch in other ways, too. When paymaster Captain Benjamin Larned finally arrived in June of 1821 with the first pay the men had seen since the summer before – Brown and the other new men had never been paid other than half their bonuses – it proved to be not specie, but shinplasters, notes on defaulting banks, which had been approved by the Paymaster General. The men had to take the notes, and so, of course, did the sutler, Louis Devotion, who had been selling to the men on credit for eight months. Disgusted with this, and with the limits placed on his profits by the army, Devotion quit. When he reached St. Louis, he found he could get nothing for the shinplasters for most of the banks had failed; whereupon, as his epitaph was written by his clerk Philander Prescott: "Mr. Devotion commenced drinking, and his whole business went to destruction by the lawyers." He died the following fall a broken man.[22]

The lack of sutler's supplies hurt as much as the lack of military issue. In addition to spirits and tobacco, the post store provided coffee, tea, candies, sugar, soap, salt fish, razors, smoking pipes – small pleasures that brought variety to the soldier's monotonous existence. The men were expected to keep their tack neat and clean, yet the army issued no means for doing so. Varnish, whiting and blacking, brushes and brooms all were purchased from the sutler. It was more than a disappointment when the new sutler didn't show up for a year after Devotion left: it was a real hardship. A small store of goods was sent up from the Prairie in the

---

21. Purcell, report for 1821, SGO, NARG 27; Fifth Regiment Company B returns, Jan. 31, 1821; Snelling to Adjutant General, Oct. 6, 1820 and Apr. 10, 1822, AGO LR; to Calhoun, Nov. 13, 1820.
22. Parker *Prescott* 49.

spring, but for the most part the men who couldn't afford to send to St. Louis for their wants did without.23

The situation became truly desperate during Joe's second winter at the St. Peters. One boatload of ammunition and accouterments had arrived in early summer, but the quartermaster's clothing boat was stopped by the ice in November and remained stuck below Lake Pepin while the men suffered through another cruel winter with inadequate clothes. Some, including Joseph R. Brown, eked out their inadequate uniforms by purchasing damaged and discarded clothing (left by the dead and deserted); Joe bought a rifle coat for $1.60 ¾ at a general auction held in October. But by December he was without fatigue trousers and shoes. Major Morrell Marston's November report (he was Acting C.O. while Colonel Snelling was in St. Louis) shows that the command was in wretched condition. Company K was encumbered with men "in a slovenly state," and Companies C and E were even worse off. Many muskets were unserviceable, accouterments appeared much worn and the men were destitute of many articles of clothing: no stockings, no greatcoats, no wool overalls and no shoes – in fact, many of the men were reduced to wearing moccasins purchased from the Indians or their traders. He also reported that discipline was lax. Part of the problem was a lack of capable officers: in August Snelling had only four of twenty assigned officers ready for duty, the others being sick, elsewhere on command or never having joined their companies. So many of the men (eighty-five in most months) were on building detail that drills had been dispensed with, as they had had to be over the extremely cold months of the preceding winter. Colonel Snelling was increasingly appalled at the quality of the recruits sent him as replacements – convicts and refuse and foreigners, he called them – who were undisciplined and undependable: "whiskey is their God and Mutiny their watchword," he reported. Morale was correspondingly low. In truth, a growing spirit of insubordination was observable throughout the army, which had begun to undergo severe cutbacks in 1821, and not just at Fort St. Anthony.24

Nonetheless, Fort St. Anthony was not entirely lacking in the amenities of civilization. Since there was no church or chaplain, the women formed a Sunday school class to instruct their children and members of the garrison. Joe Brown could always charm the ladies, and the ladies of Fort St. Anthony were no exception. He joined the Sunday school class, taught by Mesdames Snelling and Clark in the basement of the Snellings' quarters, and soon became quite a favorite. Mrs. Clark's daughter Charlotte was just a little girl at the time, but she remembered Joseph Brown as a "star pupil" in that class.25 Perhaps he was a favorite of hers,

23. Snelling to Adjutant General, Apr. 10, 1822; to Secretary of War, May 6, 1821 OSW LR main series. See also Marcus Hansen *Old Fort Snelling 1819–1858* 87-89 (Iowa City 1918).

24. File #5693 Second Auditor's records 1821; Marston to Adjutant General, Nov. 1, 1821; Lt. Edmund Kirby to same, Dec. 16, 1821; Snelling to same Apr. 10, 1822 and Jan. 1825; all in AGO LR.

25. Charlotte Ouisconsin Van Cleve *Three Score Years and Ten: Life Long Memories of Fort Snelling, Minnesota and Other Parts of the West* 38 (Minneapolis 1888).

too. This doesn't sound like the sassy Joseph Brown who ran away from Downingtown. It would appear that a year or two in the army had already taught him that good manners and social tact would take him further than impudence and pert answers.

There is some evidence to suggest that during his early army career someone influenced Joseph to curb his adolescent brashness and strive to better himself. When he renewed his acquaintance with Charlotte Clark, then Mrs. Van Cleve, in the 1850s, he told her that in addition to her mother and Mrs. Snelling he remembered the wife of Colonel McNeil and spoke of her "in the most affectionate terms, saying that her kindness to him, a mere boy, and her council had had a beneficent influence on his whole life." Where he met Mrs. McNeil, and what she told him, may have to remain a mystery. Colonel John McNeil of the Third Regiment commanded at Mackinac in 1818, had by 1821 moved to Fort Dearborn (Chicago), and was later at Fort Howard (Green Bay), always accompanied by his family. He and Colonel Snelling corresponded frequently about the possibility of conflict with the Indians in the vicinity of the army posts, and it is altogether likely that the McNeils visited the St. Peters (or Prairie du Chien) at some time when Joe was there. However, Brown told his sister Lydia Ann a different story: she understood that shortly after Joseph left home he had got into "an altercation that seemed to change his whole life." Perhaps the truth lies somewhere between: Mrs. McNeil may have intervened on his behalf following some hairsbreadth escape.[26] Certainly Joseph R. Brown's character turned out to be a most temperate one, a far cry from that of the youth given to profanity, "segars" and strong drink. He became noted in later years for his abstinence from liquor (this at a time when drunkenness was condoned by many as a natural state), his gentleness of temper and his aversion to swearing (he preferred instead that mildest of oaths, "By George!"), although he did appreciate his pipe. That this personality was forged in the army and Indian trade is almost beyond belief. Yet Joe Brown was always one who could see where the advantage lay, and at Fort St. Anthony it lay with being well thought of by those in command and their families.

Opportunities for self-improvement that presented themselves were eagerly snapped up by Brown; while in the army he taught himself Latin, Greek and French, or so he told his family. There is no doubt he spoke and wrote French, which was the language of the fur trade and understood by many of the Indians, and this he could have learned from the many traders who frequented the fort. He may also have learned it from the former French soldier, said to have been in Bonaparte's army, who taught French

---

26. Van Cleve, ibid.; J. F. Williams, notes of interview with Lydia Carli, Sep. 20, 1871, in John Fletcher Williams papers, MHS. Colonel McNeil submitted a report on the readiness of the frontier posts to withstand Indian attack, but does not seem to have visited Fort St. Anthony for personal information, relying instead on reports from others. Colonel John McNeil to Winfield Scott, Feb. 6, 1822, OSW LR unregistered series.

to the officer's wives and families.**27** There was no school, but the officer's children were instructed by tutors, as were some traders' sons. William Powell, whose father had been at Fort Douglas (Winnipeg) with Robert Dickson, remembered being brought to the fort in the summer of 1822 in order to attend the school which was kept for the officer's children, and he said that Colonel Dickson's children were left there, too. The first teacher was evidently Benjamin F. Baker, who arrived in August of 1822. In October of 1823 Snelling engaged John Marsh, a Harvard-educated, competent young man, as a tutor for his own children as well as the children of the fort's officers. Marsh is supposed to have tutored the Colonel's eldest son, scarcely two years his junior (more of William Joseph Snelling in a moment), and may have instructed some of the enlisted men in Latin and Greek as well.**28** It is hard to believe Joe Brown ever gained much skill in the classic languages, although he did sometimes sprinkle his letters with Latin tags. Despite his modestly positioning himself as a self-taught man imbued with the liberal culture of the wilderness, Brown must have at times felt the want of a classic education in an age when a "gentleman" was expected to have certain credentials.

The monotony of the winter months during which even drill was impossible was broken by creative pursuits. Even in the early days the soldiers rehearsed and gave plays (more likely, "mellerdramas"), the female parts being taken by the younger boys dressed in girlish garb donated by the officers' wives. This caused a certain amount of merriment as the "women" of the plays seemed, at least to Van Cleve, exceedingly tall and angular, in costumes which were eked out to fit them. Among these willowy youths was Joseph R. Brown. Years later Brown recalled that during the winters of 1821 and 1822 a thespian corps used to murder *Pizarro, or the death of Rolla* in the barracks at the mouth of the St. Peters. He was, he confessed, one of the performers and had "done Elvira" in the tragedy of *Pizarro*, although, as he remembered, his manner of representing the character left something to be desired.**29**

There are hints that from the beginning Joseph R. Brown enjoyed privileges not usually associated with privates. It is difficult to know whether he was protected from some duties and situations (because of his youth, his talents or his friendship with someone influential), or if it can be accounted for by a general lack of discipline at Fort St. Anthony (the

27. Allenson to Brown, Jan. 9, 1871; Adams "Early Days" 352.

28. Parker *Prescott* 47; "William Powell's Recollections" Lyman C. Draper, ed. in *Wisconsin Historical Society Proceedings* 1912: 148-149, 158 (Madison 1913); George D. Lyman *John Marsh, Pioneer* 55, 61–64 (New York 1934). Young Snelling, already a trader, surely did not attend the school, but may have taken advantage of an opportunity to further his classical education. Marsh, unfortunately, did not comment on his pupils.

29. *Henderson Democrat* Jun. 12, 1856; Van Cleve *Three Score Years and Ten* 43. On Brown's revelations, a St. Paul editor commented: "He measures nearly six feet in height and about as much in circumference.... We don't think that even thirty-five years ago he was very delicately formed or strikingly handsome. The idea of his representing tragedy at any time in his life, in any character, strikes us as being sublimely ridiculous, but to attempt the impersonation of a female character... why Brown, this was the most graceless, impudent imposture ever perpetrated." (*Weekly Pioneer and Democrat*, Jun. 26, 1856 [St. Paul])

records of courts-martial shows a sometimes astounding laxness at the St. Peters – men absent overnight without leave, Indian women kept in the barracks, unsupervised work parties out for days). Certain stories seem to connect Joe Brown with Joseph Snelling, and that brings up another intriguing possibility. Musicians were often assigned to duty as waiters or orderlies for officers and their families. Army officers were entitled to servants and got subsistence pay for them, and several officers, including Taliaferro, had brought servants and slaves with them. Since there was no civilian population to draw from at frontier posts, enlisted men were often pressed into service. Fifers, especially, were useful in this capacity, because they were around the post all day, and were exempted from company drill. A fifer is on record as serving Lt. Platt R. Green during the summer of 1822, and among Major Josiah Vose's post orders is one that specifically requires that all extra and daily duty men "except those employed for the private benefit of the officers" attend all roll calls.[30]

There's no evidence, since army records do not show such assignments and he would have received no extra pay, that Joseph R. Brown was employed as an orderly, waiter or even secretary to an officer. But a case can be made to show that he may have served in that capacity to William Joseph Snelling, son of the commanding officer. "Joe" Snelling first appeared at the post in early 1821. He was a young man of great talent, with a taste for adventure and a knack for storytelling. He had received a good education, but unfortunately, led rather an ungoverned life. His studies at West Point Military Academy were cut short in 1821 when he either quit or was asked to leave, and he soon joined his father at Fort St. Anthony. He was then sixteen, the same age as Joe Brown, and was indulged by his otherwise irascible parent in almost every whim.[31] It's only natural that he would make friends with the other boys at the post – and in Joe Brown he would have found a kindred spirit, an enterprising and intelligent rebel. Let us be clear, however, that the evidence for this is circumstantial. Significantly, from the time Snelling appeared in the summer of 1821 through the fall of 1822 when he left the post to become a fur trader, Joe Brown is noted on the muster rolls as "in the band," the only man in the garrison with this notation. He was not yet a company musician (that promotion did not happen until December 1822), but any notation on the rolls would prevent him from being selected for special details. He was needed for some reason, because in the spring when his company was rotated to Fort Armstrong he was kept at the St. Peters by being transferred to Company K. It looks as if young Brown was being made available for assignment to unofficial duties by Colonel Snelling, even, we can postulate, as aide-de-camp to his son Joe.

---

30. Inspector General to Adjutant General, Apr. 25, 1824; Vose "Extract". For details of courts-martial, see records of Advocate-General.

31. Adams "Early Days" 96; Merit Rolls of West Point Military Academy OSW LR unregistered series. Young Snelling was born in Boston Dec. 26, 1804. At West Point he was at the bottom of his class in math and had been since entering the Academy in 1819. He was put on report in November 1820 for "refusing to recite his mathematical lesson," and confined to light prison. He left shortly thereafter.

We know that the two Joes were well acquainted and probably friends. They have long been credited with discovering one of Minnesota's most beautiful resort lakes, Lake Minnetonka, in the early summer of 1822. Even though the army had been in the vicinity for three years, no one had gone as far as the big lake, which is only sixteen to seventeen miles from the fort, but surrounded by hilly and wooded terrain around which early exploring parties probably detoured. Joe Snelling's exploring party was a strange one: it consisted of Joseph Brown, Samuel Watkins (Company C drummer) and a Mr. Stewart (possibly one of the Stewarts – Robert, Thomas, John and William, all underage, three of them company drummers – who joined at the same time as Brown in Philadelphia). This Huckleberry Finn sort of expedition set out to follow Minnehaha Creek, then known as Little Falls Creek, to its source (the creek was a few years later named Browns Creek, not after a teen-aged boy as some have surmised but for Major General Jacob Brown, commander-in-chief of the army from 1814–1828). They apparently didn't explore much farther than Wayzata Bay, camping the second night on "the island in the second lake," and returning home on the third day, driven back by mosquitoes, as one version of the story has it. For some reason, no one ever followed up on this discovery; perhaps their stories of the giant lake were passed off as mostly youthful imagination. The next year, an exploring party led by Major Stephen Long was told of a lake "as big as Lake Champlain" nearby, but they either did not believe it (neither would anyone else with a basic knowledge of geography), or were not interested enough to go and look. The lake never appeared on army maps, although a topographic map of the Fort St. Anthony area prepared in 1823 does show Minnehaha Creek with a correct course. By the time French scientist and cartographer Joseph Nicollet arrived to explore the area in 1836, the presence of a big lake in the vicinity had been entirely forgotten, and so it was omitted from Nicollet's otherwise extremely accurate map of the upper Mississippi basin. The point of this story is not that a military expedition discovered a lake, but that an apparently unsupervised group of boys – all privates – in the company of the commander's son did so.[32] It leads to the suspicion that this was almost certainly not the only such expedition organized by Snelling, but was the only one that discovered something that got reported. And it confirms the use of company musicians as personal attendants.

Remote as it was, the St. Peters got plenty of traffic during the summer months: exploring parties on scientific missions, travelers such as the eccentric Count Giacomo Beltrami, army officers on inspection tours, and, after steamboats began to ply the upper river, civilians attached to the military all made the fort their destination. The summer of 1822 saw the

---

32. The original of this story is in John H. Stevens *The Early History of Hennepin County*, a pamphlet published by the *Northwestern Democrat* of St. Anthony and Minneapolis in 1856, 2–3. James Colhoun, a member of Long's expedition in the summer of 1823, noted in his Journal that the lake had been first known to the garrison twelve months earlier (Long *Northern Expeditions* 283); J. N. Nicollet's map "Hydrographical Basin of the Upper Mississippi River 1843" is available as an MHS reprint (1965 & 1969).

first of an exodus of disheartened settlers from Lord Selkirk's colony on the Red River, which had suffered several years of drought, cold weather and plagues of grasshoppers and rats. Most passed through on their way to the French communities downriver, but a few Swiss families were permitted to stay. Gradually a small community of squatters, including employees of the Indian agent and sutler, grew up north of the fort.[33]

There was a constant coming and going of traders and *engagès* (hired hands). The confluence of the St. Peters and Mississippi, called The Entry, or Mendota (from Dakota *mdote*, a river junction), had long been a staging point for men going up the St. Peters. Now it became an obligatory stop. Each trader entering Indian country must have his goods invoice checked by Mr. Taliaferro and be granted a license to trade by that gentleman if one had not been procured elsewhere. As they returned with their loaded mackinac boats in the spring they were stopped again to be closely questioned about the disposition of the bands on the upper river. Many of those who passed The Entry in 1821–1822 were later to be Joseph R. Brown's companions and competitors in the fur trade – Hazen Mooers, Dennis Robinson, Duncan Campbell, Louis Provençalle, Jean-Baptiste and Alexander Faribault, François and Narcisse Frénière, William Dickson, Joseph Laframboise and François Labathe were among those licensed by Taliaferro that year. Most of these men had traded for British firms before the war, switching allegiance after; in fact, many of the French Canadians had been born in the country and so were American citizens. Some wintered as far west as the James River and Devils Lake, and their stories, as they returned to their rendezvous in the spring, must have been wonderful to hear. Joe Snelling listened as avidly as Joe Brown to their tales of the Indian camps; many of these stirring accounts were immortalized in Snelling's best-known book *Tales of the Northwest*.[34]

In the discharge of his duties as he saw them, Taliaferro felt obliged to do battle constantly with these traders, most especially those agents of the American Fur Company whom he considered to be no better than British agitators. All traders came under his censure, however, for the use of "spiritous liquors" as an article of barter. Whiskey was not allowed in Indian country except that required for personal use of the trader and his boatmen (who would not paddle or portage without it). However, the amount they required was prodigious – boatmen were allowed a gallon of whiskey a month – and with so great a quantity of ardent spirits going into Indian country it was impossible to control the illegal traffic. This tendency of the traders to be on the wrong side of Mr. Taliaferro did not prevent them from getting on well with the officers and men at the fort.[35] They were, in fact, welcomed visitors who brought news from downriver

---

33. Thomas Douglas, Earl of Selkirk, had in 1811 established an agricultural colony of Scots and Irish on a Hudson's Bay Co. grant on the Red River (near present Winnipeg). In 1821 a group of Swiss joined the colony, but terrible conditions there, exacerbated by Selkirk's death the same year, caused many of the Swiss to leave for the U. S.

34. Taliaferro licenses 1821, OSW LR Main series.

35. Meyer *Santee Sioux* 42.

and often carried personal belongings and messages for the members of the garrison. Their knowledge of the Indians of the upper St. Peters and Mississippi made them invaluable sources of information and they were frequently pressed into service as emissaries of the military in negotiations with the Sioux. In the course of their trading activities they took in exquisite examples of Indian art – carved pipes of red catlinite, embroidered moccasins and vests, bear claw necklaces, fancy bows and quivers, painted deerskins, buffalo robes and much more – which were greatly desired by the officers as well as by visitors to the fort.

The small coterie of officers' wives tried to bring as much graciousness and civility as possible to the desolate place that was Fort St. Anthony. Traveler and trader alike were invited to take tea or spend an evening in conversation with the officers and their families and were entertained with style and decorum. Henry Sibley (who did not arrive at the St. Peters until 1835) was told the story of a tea party held by Captain George Gooding and his wife, Lucy, in July (of 1820 or 1821 it must have been, for Gooding left in the fall of 1821) to which the traders Joseph Laframboise, Alexander Faribault and François Labathe were invited. When Mrs. Gooding asked if he would take more tea, the only reply Labathe could make in English was "Tank you, madam." The waiter, interpreting the remark as an assent, took the cup and handed it to the hostess to be replenished. Labathe, following Sioux custom, could politely leave no food or drink unconsumed. After downing seven cups of hot liquid on a steamy day, Labathe's politeness gave way to desperation and he blurted out *"Laframboise, pour l'amour de bon Dieu, pour quoi ne dites vous pas à madame, que je ne'n veut point davantage?"* ("Laframboise, for the love of God, why don't you tell madame that I do not want any more?")**36** Sibley may have had that story from Laframboise, who was a great jester and never let poor Labathe forget his gaffe; or there is just a remote possibility that the oh-so-helpful waiter was Sibley's friend Joseph R. Brown, who was almost certainly employed in some such capacity by Colonel Snelling in 1821 and would have enjoyed telling the story.

The summer of 1821 marked a turning point in the Indian trade on the St. Peters River. Hoping to crowd out competition from the growing number of shoestring trading outfits threaded along the upper Mississippi, the American Fur Company opened an office in St. Louis, and the following year circumvented the most effective of the competition by buying out Oliver Bostwick and David Stone, placing Bostwick in charge of the St. Louis office. Hereafter the goods going into Iowa and up the St. Peters – the western department – would come through St. Louis; the warehouses at Mackinac would supply only the northern department. At the Prairie the firm of Bertholet and Rolette (actually only Rolette, as J.-B. Bertholet had retired to a small farm on Mackinac) had proved a stiff

---

36. H. H. Sibley "Reminiscences of the Early Days of Minnesota" in *Minnesota Historical Collections* III: 247–249.(St. Paul 1880)

and unscrupulous competition for Lockwood. The company entered into an understanding with Joseph Rolette, the upshot of which was that within the year Lockwood had been jettisoned and Rolette left in sole control of all trade from the St. Croix to the Illinois lead mines, from the Red Cedar of Iowa to the headwaters of the St. Peters. Ensconced in the center of his empire at the Prairie, "King" Rolette soon proved to be a bite too big for even the Fur Company to swallow.[37]

Far away to the north, events were taking place that would have an even more profound effect on Brown's life. Pressures from the Americans, the death of Thomas Douglas, Earl of Selkirk (who had colonized and kept the Red River colony together) and merger with their archrivals, the North West Company, brought sweeping changes to the Hudson's Bay Company. In January of 1822 Rolette's clerk, Alexis Bailly (pronounced Bay), who had driven a herd of thirty or forty cattle to the Selkirk settlement at Pembina the preceding summer under Rolette's contract, snowshoed into the fort on his way back to the Prairie. He brought with him news that the newly reorganized Hudson's Bay Company would no longer supply the trading post at Lake Traverse or trade with the Sioux. This was good news to Taliaferro; the post had long been a thorn in his side because it was so far inside U.S. territory and posed a direct threat to American authority. Robert Dickson, who had planned on trading with the

Figure 7 Joseph Rolette, American Fur Company agent at Prairie du Chien. Wis. Hist. Soc.

Sioux on the Red River and had, in 1821, moved his family to Lake Traverse, well inside the U. S. boundary, was left out in the cold. The head of the newly amalgamated trading firms, Sir George Simpson, wanted nothing to do with Dickson or the Sioux trade, nor did he wish to invite an open clash with the United States over the disputed Red River territory. The Selkirk settlement on which Dickson had pinned his hopes was dissolving. Several members of the ill-fated colony, sensing an opportunity, also passed The Entry that January on their way to St. Louis: Scots Kenneth Mackenzie, William

37. Hiram Martin Chittenden *The American Fur Trade of the Far West* I: 319–322 (reprint Stanford 1954); David Lavender *The Fist in the Wilderness* 302, 308–309 (Albuquerque 1964). Joseph Rolette was born in French Canada and had been in the fur trade from (probably) 1797, had worked on the upper Mississippi for Murdoch Cameron and Robert Dickson. He was Dickson's lieutenant in the War of 1812 and took part in the British attack on Fort Shelby (Fort Crawford). Returning to the Prairie in 1815, Rolette formed a partnership with Jean-Baptiste Bertholet and traded undisturbed by American authorities. To the Indians he was *Zica*, the prairie grouse, named for the way he sped about from post to post. To John W. Johnson, American factor at the Prairie, he was an avowed British subject, a whiskey seller and "a person of very loose principles." (Johnson to McKenney, May 25, 1820, OSW LR Main series.)

Laidlaw and Daniel Lamont declared they intended to become American citizens and were looking for an American company to back them with trade goods. They undoubtedly picked up the passports Colonel Dickson had requested for them and himself earlier in the winter via an express from Lake Traverse. Joseph Renville, a Sioux halfbreed who for several years had managed Dickson's trade at Lake Traverse, also applied for a passport, but did not appear that spring, possibly because he had heard that Colonel Snelling was thinking of arresting him for his traffic in illegal spirits. Colonel Dickson himself came down later on his way to Washington City.**38** Something surely was afoot.

When the Scots returned in the fall with licenses from the Superintendent of Indian Affairs at St. Louis, William Clark, goods from Stone and Bostwick of St. Louis and a keelboat ostentatiously named *Clear the Way*, they called themselves Tilton and Company after William P. Tilton, one of the concern's American principals (since they were not yet U.S. citizens, they required genuine Americans to front for them). Unofficially they were known as the Columbia Fur Company, a clear indication that their goal was to tap the fur-rich Rockies. Not wishing to take on the intense competition on the lower Missouri, they planned to headquarter at Lake Traverse, transporting their equipments from thence to the upper Missouri via Robert Dickson's old trade routes. Mackenzie, still a British subject and former employee of the North West Company, was not so well known in the United States that he couldn't appear as the company's agent; Lamont, also a relative newcomer, and Laidlaw, who had been Selkirk's farmer, were ostensibly "boatmen." Dickson, who it cannot be doubted was deeply involved in the new company, kept his name out of it altogether for obvious reasons – he was too well known as British. His eldest son, William, born in United States territory and thus an American citizen, was licensed for a station on the Sheyenne River. Renville, being *persona non grata* in the United States, had to be covered on Duncan Graham's license.**39** For some reason this switch of suppliers,

---

38. Taliaferro Journal Dec. 25, 1821; Snelling to Adjutant General, Jan. 13, 1822, AGO LR. Selkirk and Dickson had good reason to think that the Red River basin would fall within British territory: the Red River was included in the Hudson's Bay Company grant to Selkirk and many thought it was not a part of the Louisiana purchase of 1803. In 1818 the northern boundary of the United States was definitely located at the forty-ninth parallel, although for years there was much uncertainty about the exact location of the boundary. See William E. Lass *Minnesota's Boundary with Canada, Its Evolution since 1783* (St. Paul 1950).

39. Lavender *Fist in the Wilderness* 335–336. Joseph Renville is often given as the organizer and principal behind the new company; however, J. R. Brown stated that Mackenzie, Laidlaw and Lamont were the managing partners (Brown to Sibley, Jan. 3, 1856). It is inconceivable that Renville could command $15,000 credit at St. Louis (even the Hudson's Bay Company would not credit him!), or that the Scots, all relative newcomers to the upper Mississippi and British subjects would have the connections to do so. It is a fact that two Americans, William Tilton and S. S. Dudley were the stated partners, but they appear to have played little role in the company. The driving force behind what came to be known as the Columbia Fur Company was probably Robert Dickson. Dickson had headquartered at Lake Traverse after the war trading with the very Indians the Columbia company proposed to serve; his clerk had been Joseph Renville, formerly a captain in the British volunteers. For five years, as Lord Selkirk's agent, Dickson had attempted to recruit the Indians and traders of Wisconsin and southeastern Minnesota to an experimental settlement on the Red River, a plan that began to fail when the upper Red River basin was definitely determined to be within the United States and that was doomed by the death of Selkirk and the decision of the Hudson's Bay Company not to trade with the Sioux (Tohill "Dickson" 88–96). However, in

from British to American, with the same cast of characters, seems to have satisfied Taliaferro; apparently he felt the Scots' new company (Britons they might be, but they were "gentlemen") was preferable to what he thought of as the lawless American Fur Company (men of "mean principles and low origin") or perhaps he hoped the competition would help keep the others honest.**40** He may also have been swayed in their favor by Colonel Snelling whose eldest son was eager to spend a season among the Sioux.

It is somewhat surprising that when Mackenzie arrived back at the St. Peters in the fall of 1822 he signed on Joseph Snelling to be his clerk at Traverse des Sioux. Of course he knew that Snelling was particularly interested in the Sioux and had turned his talents to learning their language and collecting Dakota lore, beliefs and stories, as well as articles of Indian fabrication. Snelling is said to have been a friend of J-B. Faribault's eldest son, Alexander, who was about the same age but already a licensed trader, and it is not hard to imagine Snelling (and maybe Joe Brown) hanging about the Pike Island camp, dogging the traders' footsteps. Joe Snelling spoke passable French (it was his best subject at West Point), which was the *langue du pays* of the fur traders and their engagès. He was very green. Yet we can be reasonably sure that the traders of the upper Mississippi, nearly all of whom were British citizens or had been for years employed by the British, would do all in their power to accommodate the son of the American Colonel who literally held their passports in his hand.

So before proceeding to Lake Traverse with his boat, Mackenzie installed young Snelling at the Columbia Company's supply post at Traverse des Sioux, some eighty miles up the St. Peters, where several of the trading firms kept their depots. At this point where the river began to get very shallow the *pièces*, that is bales of trade goods, were generally transferred from boats to carts to be hauled the rest of the distance over the prairie. No doubt there were experienced hands with him. Snelling was there to learn the trade, but also to acquire knowledge of the Indians and their way of life. He had been asked to provide some type of report – possibly a census of the Wahpeton and Sisseton – to the Indian office (during the winter his father, who was in Prairie du Chien, wrote to Governor Cass to promise an early answer from Joseph, who, he said, was

---

1820 Dickson was talking of trade in a country which did not interfere with the Hudson's Bay Company (Selkirk papers Vol 7: 6823, University of Winnipeg, microfilm in MHS); in early 1821 William Dickson wrote from Lake Traverse "Since we have been here, we have always lived without any trade, but I believe that we are going to commence this year." (William Dickson to John Lawe, Apr. 18, 1821, *Wisconsin Historical Collections* X: 140–141. Madison, 1888) Evidently his father had conceived of a way to reenter the trade. While the Scots were in St. Louis, Dickson was in Washington, speaking with President Monroe and Secretary of War John C. Calhoun. It is a fact that William Clark issued the licenses shortly after Dickson returned from Washington that summer with letters for Boilvin and Taliaferro, and an unofficial commission to use his influence to help the agents settle the disputes among the Indians. His name couldn't appear on a trading license without jeopardizing his bona fides. At least, this is one guess as to Dickson's plans. It should be remembered that those plans were revised when Robert Dickson died suddenly in 1823 and the mantle passed to his able second, Kenneth Mackenzie.

40. Taliaferro Journal Mar. 27, 1827.

busy arranging his collection).**41** If the Scots knew their new clerk was reporting to the Indian office, presumably they did not care – their plan seems to have been to stay on the right side of Cass and Taliaferro, who, in any case, would concentrate his efforts on the traders of the American Fur Company.

No doubt Joe Brown would have liked to have gone along. In fact, he was probably as well-acquainted with the circle of traders on the St. Peters and as knowledgeable about the fur trade as Joe Snelling, but he was not, in 1822, in a position to change careers. So while Snelling was away, Brown pursued his musical career. In December of 1822 he was promoted to musician, good for another dollar a month pay, and became Company K's fifer. A short time later Company K was ordered to Fort Crawford. They left in the dead of winter, traveling on the ice to the Prairie, but their fifer did not go with them. We can only speculate on why Brown stayed behind when his company left in January, although several ideas present themselves: he may have been wanted for the band until new recruits could be obtained in the spring; he may have been on furlough (although necessarily a short one as he reported present February 28), in which case he would have been free (with permission) to join young Snelling; he may actually have "ascended the Rum River" with that winter's lumbering party, assigned to one of the officers with the party (such duty would not have appeared on the extra duty roster). For whatever reason, Joe Brown stayed "on command" (detached duty) at Fort St. Anthony until the first of May 1823, and when he went down, presumably on one of the army keelboats, he was treated to the startling sight of the stern-wheeler *Virginia*, first steamboat to make it to the St. Peters, just above Lake Pepin.**42**

Brown spent the next eighteen months at Fort Crawford. The place had been built of green timber in 1816 and had not improved over the years. In fact, it was showing definite signs of falling in by 1823. The preceding spring the Mississippi had risen eighteen feet above flood to cover the floors of all the buildings to a depth of several feet. General Winfield Scott's inspection in late 1824 found the place "scarcely habitable." There were only two companies at the post, at times numbering as few as forty-five men, and little for them to do. The soldiers seemingly staved off boredom by frequenting the houses of ill repute and the shops of whiskey sellers, to the detriment of morale and discipline. The problem of keeping the men from ardent spirits became so acute that commanding officer Colonel Willoughby Morgan complained that he could not prevent a great part of the garrison from being in a constant state of inebriation, even the guards and sentries.**43**

---

41. Snelling to Cass, Feb. 12, 1823 OIA LR. Cass had apparently proposed some commission for young Snelling, for in the same letter his father responded on his behalf that "his circumstances are not such as would justify his rejection of any compensation."

42. Muster rolls Co. K; Brown to Sibley, Jan. 3, 1856.

43. Colonel Willoughby Morgan to AGO, Dec. 19, 1822, AGO LR. See also Snelling to Quartermaster General, Mar. 1, 1824, OQG consolidated correspondence.

From one standpoint, Fort Crawford was a more salubrious post than Fort St. Anthony: whereas the troops at the St. Peters were at the mercy of the weather and the contractors – when crops failed or the supply boat did not arrive, they went without – supplies for Fort Crawford usually arrived from downriver when needed and rations were procurable from local farmers as well. Fur Company agent Joe Rolette operated a gristmill at the head of the Prairie and ran large herds of cattle that he was willing to sell to the army – at a price – and he had, in fact, fulfilled several contracts for beef, wheat and candles (made from venison tallow) and had even supplied Leavenworth with hemlock, supposed to stave off scurvy, in 1820. During the winter of 1823–1824 Colonel Snelling's soldiers suffered on half-rations in their fine stone barracks – although whiskey seemed to be in plentiful supply – but at the Prairie Joe Brown and his comrades were well-fed, if uncomfortably housed.**44** And with Boilvin's agency house, the whiskey sellers and the Fur Company warehouses (Rolette had moved into the old government factory warehouse) nestled cozily up to the walls of the fort, the men of Fort Crawford didn't lack for entertainment of a non-military nature.

Fort Crawford's location at the center of tribal battlegrounds – Sac and Fox south of the Wisconsin River, Chippewa and Menominee north of it, Winnebago pushing them from the east, and Sioux generally claiming the western side of the Mississippi – kept tensions high. Pressed from their traditional hunting grounds by Americans moving into Illinois and Wisconsin, the Indians clashed often, but white fears rose more quickly when whites were killed. By the summer of 1824 there had been several "outrages" on the Mississippi and Missouri and alarming symptoms of disaffection among the formerly friendly Sioux of the St. Peters as well. In July, four Prairie du Chien traders ascending the river were ambushed and scalped near the mouth of the Chippewa River. Nearby were also found the bones of two deserters from Fort St. Anthony. This news sent shock waves through the garrisons. A Chippewa war club found near the scene of the murders was interpreted to be that band's open declaration of war. The garrisons, under orders not to interfere with the Indians, were restricted to using defensive measures only. Colonel Snelling wrote hastily for new instructions, otherwise, he stated, "should the navigation of the Mississippi River be obstructed, I shall... attack any hostile band."**45**

For several months the army moved cautiously, trying to assess the Indians' intentions. Only strongly manned details were sent out; bateaux carrying supplies on the Mississippi went heavily armed. In late August a

---

44. Snelling to Quartermaster General Jan. 5, 1822, Oct. 2, 1824, OQG consolidated correspondence; Adams "Early Days" 95

45. Snelling to Atkinson, Jul. 22, Jul. 25 and Aug. 20, 1824; Atkinson to Snelling Aug. 3, 1824 (copy), all in AGO LR. The Secretary of War gave Snelling no limitations "except the actual commencement of hostilities, which will be avoided without the express direction of the government" (!) and General Edmund P. Gaines' order specified "no hostilities except in self-defense." Calhoun to Snelling, Sep. 25, 1824, OIA LS NARG 75; Gaines to Jacob Brown, Aug. 5, 1824, AGO LS. Some civilians of the Prairie took the view that the murders had been motivated by a personal quarrel, since Barette, one of the men killed, had previously clashed with one of the Chippewa while cutting timber near the falls of Black River. (Lockwood "Early Times" 149)

Sioux war party butchered (for their horns) an entire herd of cattle being driven to the St. Peters and were feared to have killed the drovers as well. Sioux and Sac clashed once again when a Sac war party from Rock River came upon the dead cattle and were able to ambush the Sioux while they were dancing their massacre. But no further hostilities broke out. The Chippewa murderers were eventually delivered up, along with their gory trophies, and the river, lifeline of the army outposts, seemed safe enough.[46]

At Fort Crawford nineteen-year-old Joe Brown proved his worth and won his corporal's stripe sometime during the summer of 1824, probably in July, when the post returns show his company short one musician and full-strength on corporals. Apparently the possibility of Indian ambush seemed remote at the end of October when Brown and the other teen-age musician Thomas Stewart were given three-week furloughs and ordered to report at the end of the period at Fort St. Anthony. Did they canoe the river alone? Or did they take advantage of the armed guard on one of the commissary's supply boats? In any event they arrived safely at the fort, now called Fort Snelling, having been renamed by General Scott to honor its intrepid commander and builder. On November 5, the muster rolls tell us, Joseph R. Brown returned from furlough and was transferred into Company H along with his buddy Stewart. All that was necessary for Joe Brown now was to last out the winter and be mustered out in May, his five-year hitch up, and it seems that for a while, at least, this was his plan. After his promotion to musician, presumably in the spring of 1823 when the mails could once again get out and before he reported to Fort Crawford, Brown wrote to his family to tell them that he'd joined the army, was a fifer and was due to get out in 1825, at which time he would come home.[47] Since his family did not seem to know about his promotion to corporal or his tour to Fort Crawford, he may not have written again. Something, as we shall see, had altered his plans.

For his remaining stay at the St. Peters, Joe Brown found a new niche as hospital attendant. When Dr. Purcell died in January, 1824, Joe was listed as hospital steward. However, in March the duties of hospital steward and acting surgeon were taken on by a versatile sergeant named Perrin Barker who first arrived at St. Peters in November of 1821 in the capacity of bandmaster, transferring to hospital a year later, and Joe Brown became the hospital attendant. These two amateurs ran the hospital for three months, and if Philander Prescott's story is correctly dated, must have performed at least one gory amputation during their tenure. According to Prescott, a Sisseton chief, Daniel Lamont's father-in-law, was being held hostage at the fort until the Sisseton made reparations for cattle killed the summer before. The chief was shot while attempting escape, the rifle ball shattering his arm. Prescott says an amputation was

46. Snelling to Atkinson, Jul. 22, 1824; Snelling to Quartermaster General, Aug. 16, 1824, OQG consolidated correspondence; Thomas Forsyth to Vose, Sep. 8, AGO LR, and to Secretary of War, Jun. 2, 1824, OSW LR main series; Schoolcraft to Cass, Aug. 31, 1824, OIA LR Michigan superintendency.
47. A. Henderson to S. J. Brown, Jan. 19, 1871.

undertaken by the sergeant of the hospital: they tied the wounded man to a table and took off the arm while the old stoic took no more notice than if they were cutting away a piece of leather.**48** He doesn't say how the operation affected the hospital attendant.

Brown remained assigned to the hospital through May of 1825. Presumably there were no more amputations. Perrin Barker was discharged "for debility" April 28 and, possibly with a view to a new career in medicine, took the amputation kit with him. Before he left, Sergeant Barker performed one other service: as Acting Surgeon he signed Joseph R. Brown's reenlistment papers.**49**

Reenlistment? Yes, indeed, something caused Joe Brown to change his mind about returning home. He had decided to stay in Indian territory, and to stay one had to be an employee of a licensed trader or on the military payroll. He knew enough traders, but with no experience would one take him on? Can we doubt he tried? He might have been talked into another hitch by Barker or Colonel Snelling with promise of employment in the hospital, because he reenlisted February 1, three months before his time was up and just about when he took up his hospital duties. (Incidentally, the reenlistment paper provides our second description of Joseph R. Brown: at age twenty he was five-foot-ten, had light hair and complexion and blue eyes. He gave his occupation as "laborer" – he couldn't put "soldier" on the form because he was still under age!) But it's likely he had a better reason to stay on. Because in the early part of June he took a two-week leave to make a trip downriver to Prairie du Chien where he married Miss Helen Dickson.

---

48. Parker *Prescott* 73-74. Brown and Barker may have had some help from John Marsh, the schoolmaster, who was being instructed in medicine by Dr. Purcell when he died; Marsh was very interested in Sioux customs and language, was acting as subagent while Taliaferro was away over the winter of 1824–1825 and had an Indian wife. He was only about five years older than Joe, was without doubt his friend and probably his teacher. Lyman *John Marsh* 60, 75, 80.

49. Snelling enlistments, account with second Auditor, GAO.

CHAPTER III

Helen Dickson was seventeen, a vivacious mixed blood, educated, well traveled – and the daughter of the notorious Robert Dickson. Her mother was Totowin, or Elizabeth Winona, a sister of Wakinyanduta (Red Thunder), powerful leader of the Pabaksa (Cuthead) Yanktonai. Born in Canada, she had traveled with her father to his far-flung trading posts at Prairie du Chien, Mackinac, Drummonds Island, Sault Ste. Marie, Green Bay, Pembina, Lake Traverse and perhaps even to his family home near Queenston, Upper Canada, close by Niagara Falls. Her father evidently thought a lot of his eldest daughter and had sought to give her a good education. She had been confirmed and schooled by the Catholic missionaries at Pembina and had been tutored along with the officers' children at Forts Snelling and Crawford. During her sojourn at Prairie du Chien she became a favorite of one of the captain's wives, and could pick her beaus from among the dapper young lieutenants. For the past winter she had been visiting (and maybe attending school) at St. Louis where there would be opportunities for her to be introduced into French society, perhaps with a view to finding a husband among the scions of the old fur-trading families.1

Despite her prospects and her family's best efforts, she decided to marry Joseph R. Brown. It can be surmised that she met Joe at Fort

---

1. Helen (also known as Ellen—her given name was probably Hélène) was born in 1808, baptized at Prairie du Chien in 1817 and given first communion on Christmas Day 1820 at Pembina (records of baptisms, St. Gabriel's parish, Prairie du Chien; J. R. Brown vs. Helen Brown, October 1833, in Civil Case files, series 24, U. S. Circuit Court, Iowa County, Michigan Territory, WHS Regional Research Center, Platteville, Wis.; and *Documents Relating to Northwest Missions 1815–1827*, Grace Lee Nute, ed.: 285. St. Paul 1942.) Her uncle Wakinyanduta had led a Sisseton band before being chosen leader of the Pabaksa Yanktonai about 1814; however, one descendent said that Elizabeth Dickson was of Wahpeton descent (Alfred Coe to Louis Tohill, Aug. 25, 1924, Tohill papers, MHS). Since these nations intermingled a good deal, she may have been of mixed descent and was almost certainly part white as evidenced by her fair skin and name (Totowin or Ixtatotowin means Green Eyed Woman). Madame Dickson's brother, called Dickson's Brother-in-law, was a member of Wabasha's band of Mdewakanton on the Mississippi and several members of the family, including Helen, collected as Mdewakanton halfbreeds under the 1834 and 1837 treaties. Whatever her actual genealogy, her accepted family ties related her to Waneta and several powerful Sisseton and Wahpeton chiefs. See Appendix A for more.

Snelling; Dickson, in the spring of 1822, had left his younger children there to obtain an education while he took his wife back east – Helen would then have been about fourteen, her brother Thomas ten and her sister Mary eight. The following year the Colonel removed Helen, "then a young lady grown," to the Prairie ostensibly to further her education but most likely in reality to scotch a budding romance with a presumptuous private. It will be remembered that Joseph R. Brown transferred to Fort Crawford in May of 1823 – not in the winter when his company went, but five months later, when Helen was removed from the St. Peters. Mary Mooers Brown, who knew Helen as a girl and who was later married to Joe Brown's half brother John, thought that the Colonel had opposed the marriage (as might be expected, Brown being a common soldier of uncertain prospects) and had wanted Helen to marry one of the lieutenants at Fort Crawford.2 However, her father died at Mackinac in August of 1823 and her mother was obliged to return to Canada to collect the pension due her as widow of a Colonel in the British army, taking the youngest children with her. Her eldest brother William was fully occupied with the fur trade at Lake Traverse and beyond on the plains, although it may have been he who tried to assure her future by placing her in safekeeping with friends in St. Louis. But Helen was her own mistress and knew her own mind; even though it may have been against her family's wishes, she wanted to marry Joseph R. Brown.

They were married in Prairie du Chien June 9, 1825, by Helen's godfather, Justice of the Peace Nicholas Boilvin. Although Helen was still in St. Louis on April 29, where she saw the Marquis de Lafayette as he stopped for that one day on his American tour, she could have returned to the Prairie by steamboat anytime in May. Had they made arrangements to meet and already set the date when Helen left? Or did Joe wait to hear she was back before descending the river to claim his bride? Did he talk her into marriage then and there? Whatever romantic notions we care to conjure up could be true. And yet there is always the nagging notion that Joseph Brown desired this marriage not just for the sake of Helen's beaux yeux but also because it allied him to the fabulous Dickson and so might prove his entry into the fur trade (hindsight suggests that once Joe Brown set his mind on something, he would leave no stone unturned in its pursuit). It was a whirlwind wedding trip for Joe, leaving no time for a honeymoon. The young couple was back at the St. Peters in mid-June. A substantial wood barracks had been erected on the river landing below the fort in 1821 to house married soldiers (it also served as a wash-house –

---

2. Powell "Recollections" 194, 158; John R. Case "The First House in Hastings," *The Hastings Gazette* Jan. 1, 1926. Powell says that Dickson took his wife to England in 1822 to be presented to the king and court, which cannot be true, as his whereabouts that summer in Washington, at Prairie du Chien and on Drummonds Island is well documented—he simply did not have the time. Perhaps a statement that he was going to Queenston was misheard.

very handy, as many of the soldier's wives earned rations and pay as laundresses). This barracks was probably the newlywed's first home.3

Brown returned to Company H with a corporal's duties, no longer on the rolls as hospital attendant. After Barker's departure, Edward James, Assistant Surgeon from Fort Crawford, was transferred to Fort Snelling and Brown was relieved of hospital duties – at his request? Or was he mistrusted? Much equipment had disappeared during Barker's tenancy and the hospital books were in a "deranged state." Corporal Brown must have applied himself elsewhere, however, for by November he had earned the rank of third sergeant and another dollar a month in pay. Helen celebrated the occasion (or so it seems, for it was November 3, the same day as Joe's promotion came through) by going shopping. She visited the American Fur Company store at New Hope, a new establishment opened that fall near the site of the old cantonment by Rolette's clerk, Alexis Bailly, to buy eight yards of Gros de Naples (a silk cloth) at $2 a yard and one yard of green gauze at $1, paying $10 cash, balance on account. If this is Helen – the entry is simply "Mrs. Brown" – she spent more than two months of Joe's pay for a fancy dress. "Mrs. Brown" surely was the wife of someone who could be counted on to pay or Bailly wouldn't have run a balance. No other non-com or officer at the fort was named Brown and no trader named Brown was located at the St. Peters at this time either, so Mrs. Brown is almost certainly Helen. It's intriguing to conjecture where she got the $10 cash and where she wore the dress. What's even more interesting is that Sergeant Brown received no pay between August of 1825 and July of 1826, yet paid off the debt February 3, 1826.4 It may be possible for a soldier and his wife (receiving board, room and clothing allowance) to live on $84 to $96 a year, but not by buying $16 dresses. The transaction suggests that Brown had another source of income.

It does not require too great a stretch of the imagination to visualize the twenty-year-old Brown beginning to do some trading (maybe "bargaining" would be a better word) with the Indians who were always to be found nearby, and likely with the Selkirkers and French Canadians as well.

If he were to acquire a choice item cheaply, he could easily turn a good profit selling it to one of the officers who collected such things. Daily observation of the upper river traders would have furnished him a basic knowledge of the mechanics of the business; for capital he had only to sell his liquor ration to another man (other soldiers were known to sell their clothing, pilfer stores, have skill at cards and loan money at usurious rates – we even have examples of men cutting wood "for their own

---

3. Index to Crawford County, Wisconsin, marriages 1816–1846, Vol. I: 19, WHS Madison; Coe to Tohill, Aug. 25, 1924. The barracks is mentioned in Snelling to Jesup, Apr. 23, 1826, OQG consolidated correspondence.

4. Dr. Benjamin F. Harney to Surgeon General Oct. 2, 1825, SGO LR; Alexis Bailly St. Peters Day Book 1825, Bailly papers, MHS; records of paymaster, Fort Snelling, AGO. Bailly's daybook shows that many officers and non-coms and their wives patronized the store, but credit was extended to few privates.

emolument") or perhaps talk the sutler into advancing goods. If he did indeed have quarters separated from the fort, it would have been easy to run a little business on the side, and he had, of course, an invaluable contact in his brother-in-law, William Dickson. Brown apparently had a knack for languages and certainly by this time was conversant in French and passable in Dakota (his wife, after all, was probably more comfortable speaking Dakota, her mother's tongue, although she may have been quite fluent in English as well). He had by nature the perseverance, intelligence, skills and imagination to excel in the fur trade; what he needed was the lucky break that would give him the chance to prove it.

Figure 8 Kaposia, Little Crow's village, showing winter skin tipis and summer lodges of bark, by Frank B. Mayer. New York Public Library, Rare Books and Manuscripts Division.

Let's digress for a moment to see where Alexis Bailly fits into this narrative. For the past two seasons Bailly had wintered on the St. Peters, working for himself in partnership with James Lockwood of Prairie du Chien. In 1825 he came to the St. Peters to open a new store and depot for Rolette on the south bank of the river across from Fort Snelling.[5] This location had been chosen not only to be handy to the fort but also to put pressure on the Columbia Fur Company, whose lower depot was two miles upriver at Lands End. In three short years the Columbia men had caused the American Fur Company great financial pain. Bailly – young,

---

5. Alexis Bailly was born in December of 1798 at St. Josephs, Canada; his father, Joseph, was a French Canadian fur trader and his mother, part Ottawa. He saw service during the 1812 war and first appears on the record in 1818 working for Bertholet and Rolette out of Mackinac. He later moved to the Prairie where he was Rolette's clerk from January of 1821 through June 1823, was a partner in Lockwood and Bailly for two seasons, then rejoined Rolette. During the winter of 1825–1826 he married Lucy, the daughter of Jean-Baptiste Faribault, at the Prairie. Although stationed year-round at the St. Peters, Bailly retained his farm and residence at the Prairie. (Bailly affidavit, Winnebago treaty of 1838, OIA Special Files, NARG 75; Elizabeth Thèrése Baird "Early Days on Mackinac Island," *Wisconsin Historical Collections* XIV: 43 (reprint Madison 1910); Crawford County marriages I: 22; Sibley "Reminiscences" 382–383.)

audacious, competitive – was going to try to get the business back. Incidentally, he was also ideally located to keep an eye on Lawrence Taliaferro, who was thought to be favoring the former British traders.

That Alexis Bailly was also a colorful character there can be no doubt. He had been educated at Montreal, from which, said one neighbor, "he returned a few years later a pompous man and a great dandy." His quick temper and predilection for display later earned him the sobriquet, "The Emperor." He had also the French love of fun, illustrated perfectly by an incident related by one of his contemporaries. In 1823, his first season on the St. Peters, Bailly had shown his enterprise by advancing goods to Philander Prescott, then a clerk for the Columbia Fur Company. In the spring of 1824 he took possession of his erstwhile partner's furs but would not take back the leftover goods, which he said were worthless. Bailly kept the profits for himself claiming Prescott still owed him $130. Prescott's principals, Mackenzie and Lamont, were furious but could do nothing to have the debt erased.

When Prescott tried again to get his money back in 1825 Bailly only laughed at him and told him he was "very impudent to talk to him about an old debt that had been settled by cheating a year ago!" Thereafter, Prescott had as little as possible to do with Bailly, always working for his opposition. His opinion was, and remained, "Mr. Bailly is a Roman Catholic by creed but in spirit is an infidel."**6**

Figure 9 Alexis Bailly, American Fur Co. clerk for the St. Peters. Portrait by Theophile Harnel. Minn. Hist. Soc.

It's fair to assume that by 1825 Joseph Brown knew Alexis Bailly pretty well. According to Bailly, they had met in 1823 when Brown was stationed at Fort Crawford and Bailly was James Lockwood's partner at the Prairie.**7** It is evident that Joe Brown must have begun learning the fur trade business while he was in the army through his contacts with Joe Snelling, Alexander Faribault, Alexis Bailly and others. For Bailly, especially, Brown would have been a good understudy. Bailly was an impeccable record keeper with a fine copperplate hand, a punctilious accountant, an astute businessman and as Sergeant Brown may well have noticed, he was a young man who was doing well by using his brains and talents. He had those qualities necessary to be a successful trader – shrewd business sense, aggressiveness, charm, a gambler's tolerance for risk, personal courage – qualities he may also have recognized in Joe Brown. (It is evident from

6. Parker *Prescott* 56–57, 77, 165.
7. Bailly affidavit in J. R. Brown vs. Helen Brown.

Joe's signature on his reenlistment papers that he had already developed the clear, fast handwriting of his adult years, in itself a recommendation for a clerk's position in an era when a good hand was a marketable skill.) It is not too hard to visualize Bailly or one of the other traders taking an interest in young Brown and encouraging him to seek a career in the fur trade. There is nothing in Bailly's extant books that would indicate he had any financial transactions with Brown, except for the usual purchases at his store, but that does not preclude his noting that the young sergeant had an aptitude for driving a bargain. After all, to get a little ahead of the story, Bailly did know Brown's temperament and abilities well enough to hire him without trial a few years later. It is well to keep in mind that Brown's reenlistment was probably motivated as much by his seeing a chance of becoming a trader as by seeing a chance for promotion. It is quite likely he felt he was on to a profitable career.

The winter of 1825–1826 was notable even during this decade of exceptionally cold weather for its severity. Snow came early and often, piling up drifts to fifteen feet. Fierce storms drove the buffalo from the prairies and out of reach of the hunters. Many of the Indians starved or froze to death, immobilized by the deep snows. In April the snowmelt, coupled with spring rains, overfilled the rivers. The ice began to move on the fifteenth in the St. Peters; on the twenty-first it cleared out of the Mississippi, taking with it three boats, Faribault's trading house and outbuildings on the east bank and the barracks at the landing. So sudden was the onrush of water that one soldier, McDonald by name, was trapped in the building and carried away with it. The barracks was evidently not rebuilt, so other quarters must have been found for the married men's families. At the time there would have been room in the fort where only six companies were housed, totaling under 300 men; but by the end of the year two companies from the abandoned Fort Crawford would have to be assimilated, which would somewhat overtax the facilities.[8]

Given these facts, we can see how a curious statement by John H. Stevens in his *Early History of Hennepin County* might well have a kernel of truth in it. Stevens says "J. R. Brown... made the first claim in the precincts of the county, at the outlet of Little Falls or Browns creek. It embraced the land [in 1856] occupied and owned by Ard Godfrey. Mr. Brown selected the claim in 1826. He never made any improvements of moment and abandoned it in 1830."[9] It is certainly possible that in the summer of 1826 Colonel Snelling, lacking sufficient public housing for his married soldiers and their families, allowed some of them to occupy private dwellings outside the fort. If so, Brown might well have considered himself to be squatting on a claim. Technically, he could have made a

8. Neill "Occurrences" 114–115, 117; Parker *Prescott* 81; Taliaferro Journal February–April 1826; Snelling to Jesup, Apr. 23, 1826.

9. Stevens *Early History* 2. Brown was certainly one of Stevens' informants, so there is no reason to doubt that the story of the claim came directly from him. Stevens probably assumed that by 1826 Brown was out of the army. Brown's statements for publication, we find, are almost always literally true, although they may suffer from omissions or phraseology that encourages the reader to interpret them differently.

claim anywhere on public land that was more than a mile removed from a military installation. Browns Creek was included in the nine-mile wide strip on each side of the Mississippi from the St. Peters to the falls of St. Anthony ceded to the United States under Pike's 1805 treaty and so was public land. (Although it is unlikely Sergeant Brown knew his legal rights this well in 1826, eight years later he was certainly well informed and may have at that time tried to press such a claim).

The outlet of Browns Creek would not have been such an isolated spot as the distance from the fort would suggest: strung out along the road to the government sawmill and gristmill at St. Anthony Falls, which crossed Browns Creek just above its falls, were the farms of the Swiss émigrés who had come from Red River in 1823 – Abraham Perret (or Perry), Joseph Rondo, Benjamin and Pierre Gervais and Louis Massie – as well as the post's cemetery, gardens, stables and smithy. After that disastrous spring of 1826 refugees began to come in numbers from the Selkirk settlement, driven from their homes by high waters, locusts and imminent starvation. Among them was a Swiss named Fournier, whose sixteen-year-old daughter Dionice took Joseph Snelling's eye. They were married in Prairie du Chien that fall.[10]

Joseph Snelling was still living at or near the fort, still dabbling in the Indian trade. Although he hadn't been licensed since 1823, that fall he became involved in a trading venture with the American Fur Company with goods supplied by Rolette and Bailly. He had worked for the Columbia Fur Company for at least a year, and had acquired "a pretty good knowledge of the Sioux Language, as also of the manners and customs of the Indians," as he told Major Stephen H. Long when signing on to accompany his expedition up the St. Peters and down the Red River in the summer of 1823. Always impetuous, he fought a duel with Lieutenant David Hunter in March of 1826, receiving a wound that took most of the summer to heal. He'd flown in the face of his father's wishes by marrying Miss Fournier, although the Colonel's wrath seemed to be directed more toward Rolette than toward his wayward son. Colonel Snelling, never very fond of M. Rolette because of his sharp dealing and whiskey trading, wrote when he heard of the marriage, "To the many favours I have received from your hands, or rather I may say from your tongue, I find you have added the one of providing me with a daughter-in-law. I assure you I know how to appreciate it." Young Snelling wouldn't or couldn't bring his bride back to live with his family inside the fort. They spent the winter in a drafty cabin at the St. Peters. People said it was owing to cold and privations that Dionice died, probably early in 1827, and not long afterwards William Joseph Snelling left the area for good.[11]

Colonel Snelling's quarrel with Joseph Rolette was decidedly exacerbated by his being drawn into an incident between the

10. Adams "Early Days" 88; Folwell Minnesota I: 216–217; Crawford County marriages Vol. I: 25.

11. Long Northern Expeditions 154–155; Rolette to E. T. Langham, subagent, Oct. 11, 1826, Taliaferro papers; Snelling to Rolette Sep. 27, 1826, OIA LR miscellaneous papers; Adams "Early Days" 97.

representatives of the American Fur Company and the Indian agent. In April of 1826 Lawrence Taliaferro had issued a rather imperious edict banning alcohol entirely within the Indian country. Rolette and Bailly had decided to test the issue. Obtaining a permit for two barrels of whiskey from Nicholas Boilvin at the Prairie on June 30, Bailly boldly took the liquor to the St. Peters, reporting it to the agent there on July 15. Taliaferro flew into a rage and ordered the military to seize the "contraband," which Colonel Snelling did the following day. Bailly sued Taliaferro. The goods, he said, were intended for his boatmen. Taliaferro equivocated, pointing out that Snelling had done the actual seizing. The case dragged on for couple of years before Taliaferro finally settled with Bailly for some undisclosed amount. By then, he undoubtedly realized that a Prairie du Chien jury would never find in his favor, especially since the power he had assumed in banning all ardent spirits "except for and on account of the United States" was indefensible in law. Indeed, Taliaferro had soon backed off and allowed J-B. Faribault to pass with whiskey for his engagés.12 He could also be certain that the government would not support him; if he lost the case, he would have to pay damages out of his own pocket. Neither could Colonel Snelling feel that as a regimental commanding officer he would be exempt from lawsuits over doing what he considered to be his duty – in a recent ruling Lieutenant Colonel Talbot Chambers had lost an "interruption of trade" suit at Mackinac instigated by the same American Fur Company and was held personally liable for $5,000 damages. Colonel Snelling might well be wary.

Sergeant Brown could scarcely have failed to hear of this brouhaha. From the beginning we can suppose his sympathies lay with his friends the traders. In time he would come to abhor the presumptuous authority wielded by "the lords of the north" and the Indian agent; his views would come to match those of Bailly and Rolette, whose outlook was exactly that of any self-employed businessman toward unwarranted interference by the agents of government. Some of the other Indian agents, even the Washington clerk, Thomas McKenney, could see the trader's point of view and wink at certain infractions. Whiskey was bad, but at times its use was necessary to lure furs from Canadian competitors who did not balk at using it. Snelling and Taliaferro remained unbending on the point to the last, making mortal enemies of the American Fur Company traders, who further complained that the Columbia Fur Company was shown favoritism by the agent. The chief contentions were that Taliaferro had used Laidlaw and his men in a quasi-official manner to assist in escorting the upper Sioux to their homes after the great congress of the tribes he had organized in the summer of 1825 at Prairie du Chien; that he had persuaded Colonel Snelling to conduct several search-and-destroy

---

12. "Having led with his chin, [Taliaferro] could expect to have it rapped," comments David Lavender (*Fist in the Wilderness* 474n). Records of the lawsuit are in records of Circuit Court, Iowa County, Michigan Territory, WHS Platteville. Bringing in whiskey for the engagés was perfectly legal, as Rolette knew well. The real snarl was over whether one agent's authority extended into another's jurisdiction.

missions aimed at discovering whiskey in American Fur Company posts while allowing the Columbia Company's boats to pass upriver without even a cursory glance; that he had favored the Columbia men in awarding locations, placing Bailly's men in places inconvenient for the Indians; that he had issued licenses to "foreigners" and even allowed these same foreigners to officially hand out government-issue whiskey. How could this be justified? asked Rolette. When did whiskey become bad in Taliaferro's view?[13] Another year would pass before the American Fur Company would be able dislodge the thorn that was the Columbia Fur Company by the simple expedient of buying them out. Until then the three-cornered dispute wrangled on.

To add to the agents' and military's woes, Indian quarrels had been fanned into flame again along the upper Mississippi in that spring of 1826. The murder of Claude Méthode, a Prairie du Chien halfbreed, and his entire family at their sugar camp on Painted Rock Creek (a few miles upstream from Fort Crawford) gave some of the citizens of the Prairie a scare. While James Lockwood was inclined to think it was done by Fox Indians looking for Sioux, the general belief was that the Winnebago were responsible. Two Winnebago who were taken prisoner over the incident lost little time in escaping from the Prairie's makeshift jail, so insecure it was said to be "locked with a boiled carrot." Members of their tribe encamped on the Prairie remained hostile, many openly threatening the villagers. "It is manifest," said Michigan Territorial Judge James Doty, "that the Winnebago have triumphed over the whites." After some maneuvering, the Winnebago chiefs turned over to Colonel Willoughby Morgan (commanding Fort Crawford) three young men who were declared to be implicated in the murders. Two were locked up, this time in the more secure guardhouse of Fort Crawford.[14]

Relatively more secure might more accurately describe the lockup; the fort and its walls were threatening to fall down. Colonel Morgan had several times appealed to the War Department to authorize the building of a new post, preferably on the heights across the river from the mouth of the Wisconsin River called Pike's Peak. General Winfield Scott approved a survey of the site in 1825, then reversed himself and recommended that the Prairie du Chien location be abandoned entirely. With unusual celerity for the war department bureaucracy and timing that couldn't have been worse, the order for abandonment came in the summer of 1826, at the height of the Winnebago bellicosity. By November Colonel Morgan had transferred his men and the two Winnebago prisoners to Fort Snelling, leaving the then "perilously leaning" fort along with a couple of pieces of ordnance and a cache of condemned muskets in the hands of John Marsh,

13. John Jacob Astor to Secretary of War James Barbour, May 26, 1826, OSW LR main series. For a general discussion of the feud, see Lavender *Fist in the Wilderness* 359–364 and Meyer *Santee Sioux* 40–42.

14. Lockwood "Early Times" 156; William J. Snelling (supposed author) "Early Days at Prairie du Chien and the Winnebago Outbreak of 1827," *Wisconsin Historical Collections* V: 127–129 (reprint Madison 1907); James Duane Doty to Secretary of War, Jun. 1, 1826, OIA LR Green Bay agency; Atkinson to Gaines, Aug. 24, 1826, AGO LR.

now subagent at the Prairie. The Winnebago took the sudden disappearance of the military as a sign of fear and weakness on the part of the U. S. government and became even more bold and insolent, much to the discomfiture of the Prairie's French settlers. By the following spring the seething pot was ready to boil over.[15]

Even though these disturbances continued at the Prairie, traffic on the river remained unmolested and unabated. Over the summer of 1826 many boatloads of goods went upriver to Rollette's American Fur Company posts on the Red Cedar, on the Mississippi at Wabasha Prairie and at the mouth of the Chippewa, as well as to posts on the St. Croix and St. Peters rivers where they faced fierce competition from the Columbia Fur Company. Steamboats chugged up as well – as many as fifteen were recorded by Taliaferro that summer – bringing visitors to the garrison and adventurous tourists determined to see the Falls of St. Anthony, which was fast becoming one of the "must-see" scenic wonders of the west. Further down the Mississippi there was a surge of commerce as scores of settlers flocked to the lead regions of what is now southwestern Wisconsin and northwestern Illinois. The government had opened a portion of these lands to miners. Unfortunately, the lure of easy money had attracted thousands of people who did not confine themselves to the government lands, but spread into the Indians' diggings and even usurped their villages. Encroachment by whites in the lands between the Rock River and Wisconsin River was the greatest source of the resentment and hostility evident among the Winnebago, Sac and Fox.[16] But the conflict did not manifest itself on the mighty waterway; travelers passed safely that summer of 1826.

Among those travelers was Joseph R. Brown, though where he went and what he did, with one exception, must be left to the imagination. At the end of May Brown's company, along with Company E, was ordered to Rock Island to relieve the garrison of Fort Armstrong. The move coincided with a six-month furlough granted Sergeant Brown by Colonel Snelling beginning May 1, 1826. Brown was to report to Major Josiah Vose, commanding Fort Armstrong, and rejoin his company there November 1.[17] Now it is not unusual to find a six-month furlough being granted a man who has served his five years with no apparent furlough longer than three weeks (although where post returns are missing, it is possible that a man could be gone nearly two months and still be present for the bi-monthly muster rollcalls). Quite possibly the extended furlough was part of the bonus awarded Brown for reenlisting back in 1825. Six months was the usual time allowed for a career soldier to return to his

---

15. Scott to Morgan, Jun. 10, 1825, AGO LS; Scott to AGO Nov. 9, 1825, Apr. 22, 1826, Western Department Letterbooks III: 207; Atkinson to Gaines, Nov. 5, 1826, AGO LR.

16. Brown to Sibley, Jan. 3, 1856; Taliaferro licenses 1826, OIA LR; Neill "Occurrences" 112–114, 116. In 1826 there were reported to be 400 to 500 miners on the Fever River near Galena; by 1827 estimates had increased to "rising 5,000" people in the area between the Wisconsin and Rock rivers (*Illinois Intelligencer* [Vandalia] Sep. 30, 1826, Aug. 18 and Sep. 15, 1827).

17. Post orders, Orderly Book Company E Fifth Regiment, #103; muster rolls, Fort Snelling.

home back east for a visit, and there is some evidence that that is what Joe Brown intended to do.

What we know for sure is that he turned in his musket, bayonet and "cap compleat" to Lieutenant Joseph Baxley at Fort Snelling, getting a paper to that effect so he could prove himself to be in good standing with the regiment. On July 9 he was in St. Louis, where he picked up his back pay, $78 owing since August last, from Captain Thomas Biddle, the Fifth's paymaster. Was Helen with him? It seems likely. She was pregnant, but not due to deliver until December. Surely she would want to go with her husband if only to renew acquaintances with her friends in Prairie du Chien and St. Louis. Surely Joe, if he intended to go back east, would want to introduce his new wife to his family. Joe's half sister Lydia Ann believed that he had once tried to return home – she thought it was in 1823 or 1824 – but had had to give up the attempt when he was robbed of his money.[18] Lydia may have confused the year because of the letter he had written home in 1823, and of course she knew no more of the episode than Joe told her. He may have concocted the story of the robbery to explain why he had never gone back to reconcile himself with his family. Or it might easily be the truth. Any attempt to travel overland in those times was hazardous. The country was a wilderness as far east as Detroit, populated by Indians (many quite belligerent), their traders and a sprinkling of missionaries. The rivers – Fox, in Wisconsin, Rock, in Illinois – were the only highways through this vast land, although a man alone might follow Indian tracks from village to village. The settlements that existed were threaded along the major waterways, the Mississippi and Ohio rivers, but even in these places there was no lack of desperate characters who might easily be tempted to take a man's pocketbook. Steamboat captains had their boats guarded at the levees every minute to prevent pilferage or outright theft of their cargoes.[19] Joe Brown certainly went to St. Louis specifically to get his money, taking care that he wouldn't be mistaken for a deserter, but what he did then is lost to us now. For whatever reason he reported in at Fort Armstrong a month early, having presumably taken or sent Helen back to the St. Peters where she remained over the winter. On December 26, 1826, their son Solomon W. D. (surely William Dickson) Brown was born there.[20]

It was decidedly prudent on Joe's part to leave his wife at the St. Peters to have their baby. Not only would she be with friends, she was also safely away from the area of greatest unrest. This was to be Joe's first turn of duty at Fort Armstrong, but he would have known from reports that the situation at that post was never very conducive to domestic tranquillity. The fort provided no facilities for married soldier's families within the

---

18. Records of Paymaster, Captain Thomas Biddle, Junior account with GAO, 1826; Lydia Carli to William Watts Folwell, interview Sep. 20, 1871, in Folwell papers.

19. Parker *Prescott* 106–107.

20. Date and place of birth of Solomon Brown and others of Brown's children are recorded in a Bible (hereafter Brown Bible) once in the possession of Ellen Allanson, now missing. A copy taken by William Watts Folwell is in the Folwell papers, MHS. The completeness of the data indicates that it was written by J. R. Brown; also Folwell comments that the original was in Brown's handwriting.

walls and no safety for them without. What the sergeant found when he arrived was an island only about three miles long; outside the fort the only buildings on it were a stable and four log houses occupied by the sutler and some soldiers' families. A little further away was an enclosure containing several log buildings that housed the trader for the American Fur Company, his family and employees. A large Fox village was visible from the fort just 100 yards downstream on the Illinois shore and four miles south of that, on the Rock River, stood Saukenuk, the Sac's largest village, which could muster 800 warriors and was home to the great chiefs Quashquame and Black Hawk. The Sac were not only the most-feared Indians in the upper Mississippi area, they were the sworn enemies of the Sioux. And Helen was a Sioux.

Fort Armstrong itself was well calculated to resist attack. Situated on the high ground at the downstream end of Rock Island at the foot of Rock Rapids, it commanded the island, the river and the prairies on either side of the Mississippi. There was no wall on the river side for none was needed; the island terminated in limestone cliffs twenty-six feet high. At the southern point of the island stood the commanding officer's two-story house flanked by two ranges of officers' quarters. The barracks formed the two landward sides of the work. Built of hewn timber with shed roofs sloping inward, they presented sixteen-foot backs pierced with two rows of loopholes for musketry to the plain. A stone magazine, three blockhouses with cannons and two field pieces completed the defenses.21

Not long after Brown arrived on the island, as the long days of summer turned into the crisp, cool days of fall, the Sac harvested their extensive cornfields in the Mississippi bottomlands, cached their grain and left on their winter hunts. Each September saw the Rock River Indians move across the Mississippi into northern Iowa to their winter hunting grounds on the headwaters of the Iowa, Skunk and Des Moines rivers, while those from the villages lower down on the river moved into central and southern Iowa and northern Missouri. Their traders, most of whom worked for the firm of Davenport, Farrar and Farnham, agents of the American Fur Company, accompanied them on their winter hunts to be as near as possible to their Indians should they need further supplies and to keep their returns out of the hands of competitors. The hunting grounds changed each year, but semi-permanent posts were maintained on the Missouri River at the Black Snake Hills (St. Joseph) and the mouth of the Kansas River and on the upper Des Moines River, as well as on the Mississippi at Rock Island, the Flint Hills (Burlington) and the Des Moines Rapids (Keokuk).22 Russell Farnham, the Astorian, stayed on the

21. Vose to Adjutant General, Jan. 8, 1825, AGO LR; Forsyth to McKenney, Aug. 28, 1824, OIA LR Prairie du Chien; Stephen Watts Kearny, "Journal of Stephen Watts Kearny," Valentine Mott Porter, ed. *Missouri Historical Society Collections* III: 124–125 (St. Louis 1908); Royal Branson Way *The Rock River Valley: Its History, Traditions, Legends and Charms* I: 81 (Chicago 1920).

22. Long *Northern Expeditions* 100–102; J. W. Spencer "Narrative" *The Early Days of Rock Island and Davenport*, Milo Milton Quaife, ed., 28–29 (Chicago 1942); Forsyth survey of Sac and Fox habits in Forsyth to Office of Indian Affairs, Jun. 1824, OIA LR Sac and Fox; report of Farnham and Davenport to

move among these posts all winter, estimating the furs taken and exhorting the hunters to greater efforts, seldom using the house he had built in the summer of 1826 on the Illinois bank of the Mississippi just across from Fort Armstrong. His partner, Amos Farrar, headquartered at Dubuque's mines where he carried on a small smelting operation as well as the fur trade. Only the third partner, George Davenport, remained with his family at Rock Island. Although Davenport, once a soldier, had done considerable business with the fort's commissary and had once been sutler, his presence was an annoyance to Major Vose, who had tried unsuccessfully for several years to have him removed from the island. Vose's complaints centered around the nature of Davenport's operation, which attracted Indians to the island, and his employment of "worthless characters [who] procure liquor and furnish the soldiers and purchase their clothing." Davenport's contention was that he was on ceded land within the jurisdiction of Pike County, Illinois, and he therefore had the right to vend spirits and make a preemption claim. 23

Thomas Forsyth, agent for the Sac and Fox, had predictably gone back to St. Louis for the winter, not to return until the Indians reappeared in April. He had no separate agency house. Instead, he used quarters within the fort, an awkward arrangement at best. The sutler, William Downey, the same who had been Colonel Snelling's recruiting officer and was well-known to J. R. Brown, lived with his wife in a cabin outside the gates. He dabbled in the Indian trade, as did most sutlers, and in 1824 had planned to go into partnership with John Connelly on Fever River. In June of 1826 he resigned his sutlership, obtained a trading license and by fall was presenting an opposition to the Fur Company on Rock River. The new sutler was to be former Captain George Gooding, but as it is doubtful he took up his duties that fall, the post was probably without a sutler over the winter. Downey evidently kept his residence and farm on the island over the summers; both he and Davenport pastured cattle, cut hay and probably stockpiled wood for steamboats on the island.24

Once the Sac and Fox had left the vicinity to go on their fall hunts, the Winnebago came boldly in. Many of these lived fewer than fifty miles up Rock River where stood the village of Wabokieshiek (White Cloud),

---

the Secretary of War 1831, quoted in Frank Edwin Brandt "Russell Farnham, Astorian" in *Transactions of the Illinois Historical Society* 1930 224–225 (Springfield 1930).

23. Brandt, "Farnham" 214, 223; Vose to Adjutant General, Jan. 8, 1825, to Atkinson, Feb. 2, 1825, AGO LR; George Davenport to Secretary of War, Sep. 3, 1825, OSW LR. Davenport, an Englishman, had become an American citizen, joined the U.S. army and fought against his former countrymen. In 1816 he moved with the Eighth Regiment to the Des Moines Rapids as an agent for army contractor William Morrison. He built a trading post, farm and warehouse at Rock Island in the spring of 1817, was sutler at Fort Edwards for several years before returning with the troops that built Fort Armstrong and proved an invaluable aid in subduing the Winnebago during the post's first harrowing years. In 1822 he began trading for the American Fur Company, a few years later joined forces with Russell Farnham.

24. Extract from Post Orders Fort Armstrong, Jun. 6, 1826. Downey was licensed at the mouth of the Macquoketa River but may have moved into Illinois as he presented an opposition to Davenport on the Rock River in 1827–1828 (Farnham to Pierre Chouteau Junior, Feb. 7, 1828 in Chouteau Collection, Missouri Historical Society, St. Louis), was likely in the same area the preceding season. In the summer of 1828 there were still complaints of the inconvenience caused by Davenport and Downey keeping livestock on the island. (Major Gibson to Adjutant General, Aug. 26, 1828, AGO LR).

sometimes called Prophet. Major Vose's orders that fall reveal a nervousness at the proximity of the warlike Winnebago:

> "The season of the year is now arrived, when it is important that the fort should be put in the best possible state of defense... We know that there are a very large and unusual number of Winebago Indians in our vicinity and we have reason to believe the[y] will remain near us during the ensuing winter... [They] have stated that the only object of there coming here is to procure game... We must not however trust to their promises – and we know also that the Winebago are more savage than any Tribe of Indians in this part of the Country."

Vose's orders are clear. Preparedness will be the key: no party of less than three armed men will be allowed outside the fort, precautions against fire will include opening a hole in the ice each night, cartridge boxes will be kept filled, gun crews will drill regularly and their commanders are to act in case of attack without waiting for orders.[25]

There are reasons for nervousness. The fort is desperately understaffed. Major Vose must make do with two lieutenants and an assistant surgeon for officers. In event of an attack, Lieutenant William Alexander is to direct the cannon crews in the blockhouses, Major Vose will direct the crews of the six- and twelve-pounders on the parade and Lieutenant C. C. Hobart will command the remaining men. Sergeant Brown will take charge of the two disposable guns, to see they are kept clean, the ammunition dry and all in readiness; in case of attack he is to report directly to the commanding officer with the musicians of Company H for instructions. Sergeant Brown is now first sergeant in Company H and the post's Acting Sergeant Major. As such he functions as duty officer for Major Vose. The Acting Sergeant Major's duties consist of making out company details, receiving the morning report and serving the commanding officer in a clerical capacity (at Fort Armstrong for sure Brown's penmanship was appreciated). A further order directs that "the acting Sergeant Major will report to the commanding officer at the orderly hour, and immediately before the beating of the whiskey drum in the afternoon." Charged with the duties of an officer (with none of the pay), Sergeant Joseph R. Brown had gone about as far as he could go in the army of the 1820s.[26]

When the expected Winnebago troubles did materialize, they came not at Fort Armstrong but at Fort Crawford, and the perpetrators were not the treacherous Rock River bands but the relatively friendly Winnebago from bands on the Black and Bad Axe rivers. Yet by coincidence, Joseph R. Brown found himself in the middle of the Winnebago War. The egg that

---

25. Extract from Post Orders Fort Armstrong, Oct. 30, 1826, order 38. Major was not alone in his assessment of the nearby Indians. According to John Marsh, "The principal traits which distinguish Winnebagoes from other Indians are their haughty spirit, their great ferocity, their unanimity and their deep-rooted aversion to the American people" (Marsh to Atkinson, Jul. 30, 1827, AGO LR).

26. Extract from Post Orders, Fort Armstrong, orders of Jun. 18, 1826 and May 20, 1827.

hatched the war was an "unfortunate incident" that happened at Fort Snelling that May of 1827, and although Brown wasn't directly involved in it, it nearly cost him his life. The inexplicable part is what Brown was doing there at all.

He was on furlough again in May and June of 1827. We know he traveled up the river to Mendota where he probably saw his six-month-old son for the first time. Then he left for Lake Traverse where William Dickson was collecting the Columbia Fur Company's credits. What his purpose was can only be guessed at: he may have escorted Helen to see her family or carried a message from the Indian agent or simply have been engaged in some trading business with William Dickson. In any case, he was at the Columbia Fur Company's post when a serious dust-up occurred at Fort Snelling between the Sioux and some Chippewa from Sandy Lake, an episode that had serious repercussions for Brown. The Chippewa delegation had come to see the agent and were being hospitably feasted by the Sioux when their hosts turned and fired upon them, killing two and wounding several. Exasperated that they had so blatantly flouted his guarantee of protection for all tribes in the vicinity of the fort, Colonel Snelling ordered those who had acted so treacherously brought in for punishment. Four Mdewakanton men from the village of Ruyapa (Eagle Head) on the St. Peters River were eventually delivered up and were turned over by Colonel Snelling to the Chippewa for retribution. The four were summarily shot and brutally mutilated before the eyes of their friends. The executions took place on the twenty-ninth and thirtieth of May. Many of the Sioux were incensed at Colonel Snelling's cruelty in turning the malefactors over to their enemies, who then meted out the predictably savage punishment. Colonel Snelling felt justified in his actions, but the Sioux were incensed, and, as the colonel noted, "one of the persons shot has many powerful friends and relations, who have determined to avenge his death, and although it was an affair between the two nations the consequences may ultimately fall on us."[27]

Despite general grumbling and dissatisfaction, the Sioux departed the fort peaceably enough, but when the news got to the upper villages there was much wild talk. Joseph Brown was still at Lake Traverse when the news arrived; to get back he had to run a gauntlet of hostile Sioux. At Lac qui Parle he found the relations of the men who were shot "running about in every direction with the warpipe, stating that they knew they could do nothing with the fort, but that they could cut off straggling men and destroy the cattle, etc." Brown, known to be connected with the army, was in some jeopardy. He later wrote of the incident: "I was then at Lac Travers and on my return narrowly escaped being killed by their relations at Lac qui Parle, at Traverse and the Six's village [Shakopee]." He reported the situation to Taliaferro on June 19. The agent with his customary sangfroid noted that the Indians were "much exasperated,"

27. Snelling to Atkinson, May 30, 1827, AGO LR; Taliaferro Journal May 28, 29, 30, 1827. For a highly colored account of the affair, see Wm. J. Snelling "Running the Gauntlet" in *Minnesota Historical Collections* I: 362–373 (reprint St. Paul 1872).

adding that "as a fair statement of the matter reaches them, their hostile feelings will subside."[28]

Before feelings did subside, the lower Sioux did their best to stir up the Winnebago to join them in sending war parties against the Chippewa. Some 400 Sioux, according to reports Rolette had received, had accepted the war club and were advising the Winnebago to do the same, with the intention of launching a simultaneous attack at the Prairie and at Fort Snelling. Fortunately the plan came to the ears of the respected Chief Wabasha, whose wiser counsels prevailed. But other troublemakers convinced the Winnebago that the prisoners that had been delivered to the Chippewa at the St. Peters had been not Sioux, but those Winnebago who had been incarcerated for the Méthode murders the previous year. This talk was believed in Prairie du Chien and in Red Bird's camp on the Black River.[29]

Figure 10 Sioux encampment at Big Stone Lake. Drawing by Samuel Seymour, a member of Stephen Long's 1823 expedition. Maryland Hist. Soc.

As Joseph R. Brown descended the river to Prairie du Chien toward the end of the month of June, the ugly temper of both nations living along it became evident. Two army keelboats left the St. Peters the day after Brown with armed men aboard because they had been stopped by the Sioux on the way upriver. On board one of the keels was Joe's old friend Joe Snelling. Presumably Brown could have ridden down on one of the keels as well, but he chose to go alone in a bark canoe, a much faster way to travel and, as it turned out, a lucky choice. We can probably assume from the circumstance of the canoe that he was alone, that he had again left his wife with their infant son at the St. Peters. Helen's mother appeared at the St. Peters just a week later – she must have been at Lake Traverse with William while Joe Brown was there – and undoubtedly she stopped to see her new grandson before continuing on to visit other relatives at Wabasha's village.[30] Why Joe didn't travel with her and her

28. Taliaferro Journal Jun. 19, 1827; Brown to Sibley, Jan. 3, 1856.
29. Rolette to McKenney, Nov. 18, 1827, OIA LR Prairie du Chien; Snelling "Early Days" 143.
30. Taliaferro Journal, Jul. 1, 1827; Brown to Sibley, Jan. 3, 1856; Snelling "Early Days" 144–145.

bodyguard of Wahpeton warriors leaves room for speculation. Rumors of war were rife along the river and, in fact, it was widely believed that there was a conspiracy afoot to attack the garrisons and the miners on Fever River with the object of driving the whites from the area. There were, however always rumors flying, and so far they had turned out to be groundless. They were apparently discounted by Joseph Brown.31

Brown broke his journey at Wabasha's village, located on the wide prairie where now sits the city of Winona, the one place where he might feel it safe to do so. The Sioux of Wabasha's band were still friendly toward the whites; moreover, he was married to one of their relatives. If he hadn't been made sufficiently wary by his trip down the St. Peters, the warning he received at Wabasha's village would have persuaded him to proceed with caution. At Prairie La Crosse he was hailed by a small party of Winnebago, but put them off by calling out that he would camp round the point. Prudently not waiting to see if they would follow him, Brown paddled all night. By daybreak he was out of the area of immediate danger and by dinnertime on the twenty-seventh of June he was safely in Jean Brunet's tavern in Prairie du Chien.32

The news soon burst upon them that horrid murders had been committed by several Winnebago just three miles from the village. Three men, Wanigsootshkau (The Red Bird), Wekau (Sun) and Chickhonsic (Buffalo Calf), had entered the home of Registre Gagnier in a friendly manner and without warning opened fire, killing Gagnier and Solomon Lipcap, a discharged soldier who lived with the Gagniers. His wife and their ten-year-old son had managed to escape, running to the village to summon help. When the rescue party arrived back at the cabin they found the two men dead – mangled and scalped – and an infant daughter scalped, but alive. The story of these murders reached Brown while he was eating dinner at Brunet's. Soon other villagers came to the tavern, afraid to stay in their homes. It transpired that the same Indians had been at Lockwood's house, where they were scared off by old trader Duncan Graham, before proceeding to Gagnier's more isolated cabin in McNair's coulee. Mrs. Lockwood fled to Brunet's as well. The frightened company ran to the old fort to get the wall and swivel guns and the condemned muskets, which they desperately tried to repair and load. A breastworks was thrown up around the tavern and the guns dragged into position. James Lockwood, who had been some way up the Wisconsin River en route to Green Bay when the express sent by subagent Marsh caught him and apprised him of the danger, quickly returned to find the villagers

---

31. Colonel Atkinson was aware of a plot, although somewhat after the fact, that the Winnebago had been a party to for some nine months, which was to raise an uprising. His information was that the end of June was the time fixed upon and that the next full moon would see the miners attacked and driven from the country. Subagent Marsh was also told that the uprising would be at the full moon and that parties would go to the St. Peters to kill Mr. Taliaferro and others found outside the fort (Marsh to Atkinson, Jul. 30, 1827; Atkinson to Gaines, Sep. 28, 1827, AGO LR).

32. Brown to Sibley, Jan. 3, 1856.

totally panic-stricken, "each commanding, none obeying, but every one giving his opinion freely."**33**

About sunset on July 1 the beleaguered citizens were horrified to witness the keelboat *Oliver H. Perry*, one of those which had so recently left the St. Peters, arrive riddled with bullet holes and carrying two dead and four wounded. It had been attacked near the mouth of the Bad Axe River the preceding evening by a large body of Winnebago led by The Red Bird and, running aground, had been badly shot up. The second boat, with young Snelling aboard, passed the same spot at midnight and was also fired upon, but with no fatalities. The episode at Gagnier's was murder, perhaps the result of a grudge. The attack on the boats was war. Stricken with fear, the villagers decided that the fort, however dilapidated, was a better refuge than the tavern. The guns were dragged back and dirt was thrown up around the palisade to prevent the logs being set on fire. Jean-Baptiste Loyer and Duncan Graham set out for Fort Snelling for reinforcements. As Snelling's troops prepared to depart for the Prairie one soldier wrote, "The whole country appears to be in commotion."**34**

Brown's furlough ended June 30, so it is doubtful that he remained at the Prairie long enough to witness the keelboat disaster. It would have been wisest to leave immediately after the murders were reported to carry the news below, but he may have remained long enough to help the citizens with the fort's guns (he was, after all, the man who was charged with care of the field pieces at Fort Armstrong). Knowing the danger on the river, might he have feared for his friends' lives and waited to see the boat in safely? No, because the attack on the boatload of thirty armed men was totally unthinkable, a thing that no one could foresee happening, as it was not believed the Indians were gathered in force. Given this thinking and the necessity of warning those downriver, it's most likely Brown continued on to carry the news to his post at Rock Island, arriving ahead of the official dispatches.

Report of the uprising spread like wildfire. The keelboat *Oliver H. Perry*, with the wounded and dead still aboard, arrived at Galena, Illinois, on the Fever River on July 4 and a "scene of the most alarming and disorderly confusion ensued." There had already been several scares in the mining area – lonely travelers robbed and insulted, one party fired upon at the Rock River crossing, some miner's huts broken into and the contents despoiled. The intelligence that a general uprising was in progress was the last straw for many of the "suckers" in the mines and they fled the country

---

33. Lockwood "Early Times" 162. The Gagnier murders are also discussed in Snelling "Early Days" 145–146 and Thomas McKenney "The Winnebago War" in *Wisconsin Historical Collections* V: 199–201.(reprint Madison 1907)

34. Lockwood, ibid. 163; extract of a letter from W. J. Snelling to Colonel Snelling, Jul. 3, 1827, included in Snelling to Atkinson, Jul. 20, 1827 in AGO LR; James Engle to mother, Jul. 9, 1827, James Engle papers, MHS. There is a much-expanded version of the facts in Snelling "Early Days" 147–150. Some confusion exists about the dates of these events, but most writers agree that the boats were attacked on June 30. They did not arrive at the Prairie until late July 1. Of the earlier murders, Atkinson in his report says they occurred on June 26, Marsh says June 27 (Marsh to McKenney Jul. 10, 1827, OIA LR Prairie du Chien) and Joe Snelling says June 28. Of these the only eyewitness was Marsh. Later writers tend to compress the events.

in droves. Some retreated only so far as Galena, where fortifications were thrown up and preparations made for war. By September the *Illinois Intelligencer* could report, "All business at the mines is suspended, some of the stores are closed and everything is at a stand... Three months since it was supposed that there were rising of 5,000 men employed at the mines – the estimate now is only about seven hundred."[35]

Massive military efforts were undertaken to squelch the uprising. Colonel Snelling sent four companies from Fort Snelling to re-garrison Fort Crawford. Major Vose at Fort Armstrong could spare no men, but supplied arms to the Committee of Safety at Galena for its defense. At the end of July, General Henry Atkinson arrived at the Prairie with a full regiment from Jefferson Barracks, south of St. Louis, after stopping briefly at Galena. The Indians had moved their families to safety at the Koshkonong Lakes near the headwaters of Rock River, leaving scouting parties of warriors to keep an eye on the movements of the whites. These raiders were magnified into hordes of bloodthirsty savages, poised for attack. "We have been so confident here of an attack," wrote a Prairie du Chien soldier, "that posts have been [as]signed to the officers and men and there is no doubt we shall make a powerful resistance." In August General Atkinson moved against the Winnebago with thirteen companies and a mounted troop of volunteers from Galena led by Missouri militia general Henry Dodge, freshly arrived at the mines and seeking to make a name for himself. Faced with overwhelming odds, The Red Bird put up no fight. He and three others surrendered September 8 at the Portage; two more were given up a few days later.[36] The Winnebago war was over.

Despite the rather quiet end to the Winnebago disturbance, strife continued unabated between Sioux and Chippewa, Sioux and Sac, often dragging in the allied Winnebago, Fox and Menominee. Many bands were afraid to set out on their winter hunts, spooked by roving war parties.

In the midst of these disturbances, a major change had taken place in the organization of the fur trade. Beset by financial difficulties, Mackenzie and Laidlaw had sold out in the middle of July to the American Fur Company, agreeing that the Columbia Fur Company would vacate the entire Mississippi and St. Peters rivers to Rolette's Upper Mississippi Outfit. It should have been a good year for the American Fur Company and would have been, too, if it hadn't been for the unsettled state of the country and for the in-fighting that went on between the rival factions – Rolette against Mackenzie, Rolette against Farnham and Davenport, Farnham and Davenport against Cabanné of St. Louis. The unfortunate result of their schemes and distractions was a harvest of furs considerably smaller than expected. Farnham reported poor results from the Des Moines and Missouri; at Rock Island Charles D. St. Vrain – in charge of

35. Daniel M. Parkinson "Pioneer Life in Wisconsin" in *Wisconsin Historical Collections* II: 329 (reprint Madison 1903); *Illinois Intelligencer* Jul. 21 and Sep. 15, 1827. The miners acquired the name suckers, it is said, because like the migratory fish they arrived in the spring and departed in the fall.

36. Engle to mother, Aug. 4, 1827, Engle papers. See Atkinson report to Gaines, Sep. 28, 1827, AGO LR.

the post over the winter while Davenport paid a visit to his homeland, England – wrote in early 1828 that his post on the Rock River would not return half the usual furs.[37]

It would take a good man to make that post pay, to encourage the Indians to hunt instead of fight and to meet the stiff competition provided by encroaching settlers and independent traders. Before the year was out Farnham and Davenport had found their man... Joseph R. Brown.

37. Lavender *Fist in the Wilderness* 380, 388–389; Farnham to Chouteau, Feb. 7, 1828.

Map 4 The Upper Mississippi country about 1828 when Brown entered the trade, showing general areas occupied by various Indian nations, key trading posts, Indian villages and settlements.

CHAPTER IV

It was not the best of times to be embarking on a career as a fur trader. In fact, the 1828–1829 season would turn out to be one of the worst in recent memory, especially discouraging after the astonishing spring of 1826 that had seen record-breaking quantities of furs taken out of the northwest. It started out cold and got colder, but no snow came, so game could not be tracked and many lakes froze to their bottoms. Thousands of muskrats, the staple of the upper Mississippi trade, died in their lodges that winter, severely limiting the hunters' take.[1]

More important, the Indians did not hunt. An exchange of blows by Fox and Sioux bands early in 1828 resulted in a state of near war for the rest of the year. A halfbreed Fox chief named Morgan had started the troubles by attacking a Sioux camp; the avenging Sioux, missing their Fox targets, fell instead up on some Sac Indians, killing a chief and stealing some horses. And so it went. "The unfortunate blow by the Fox," wrote Rolette to Pierre Chouteau Junior (new manager of American Fur Co. interests in St. Louis) in early 1829, "has deranged the hunt of 600 Indians." Earlier in the winter George Davenport had reported that troubles between Sioux and Fox bands were keeping the Indians from their hunts on the upper Des Moines. "Our whole dependence rests on this [spring hunt of 1829] and the outfit on the Mississippi," he wrote, adding that "if this war continues our trade on the Mississippi will be worth nothing as the Indians cannot hunt any distance from the river, and on the river every settler trades skins."[2]

The settlers were a growing problem. Although the mining area had cleared out during the uprising of 1827, within a year the miners were coming back, hope of riches overcoming their fears. A tentative settlement with the Rock River Indians was all it took to lure settlers into the valley. A ferry was established at the site of Dixon in the spring of 1828, facilitating travel on the overland route from Peoria on the Illinois to

---

1. Rolette to Robert Stuart, Jun. 14, 1829, American Fur Company papers, copy in MHS; Lavender *Fist in the Wilderness* 379.

2. Rolette to Stuart, Mar. 8, 1829, loc. cit; Rolette to Pierre Chouteau Junior, Dec. 19, 1828, George Davenport to Chouteau, Feb. 16, 1829, Chouteau Collection, Missouri Historical Society, St. Louis, copies in MHS. In 1829 the American Fur Company's western department, headed by Ramsay Crooks, consisting of Rolette's Upper Mississippi Outfit and Farnham's Iowa Outfit, transferred all interest to Pierre Chouteau Junior & Co. in St. Louis. The Fur Co. supplied all the foreign connections and capital, Chouteau the management.

Galena on the Fever River, which had become the chief shipping point for the upper Mississippi. People began to pour into the country. The Indians had little choice but to give way under the pressure. Early in 1829 Alexander Wolcott, agent at the embryo Chicago, found it necessary to relocate his Rock River post from the Grand Detour (near the ferry) to a place further north, because the Indians in that quarter had had to move to hunting grounds higher on the river.3

Technically, the land east of the Mississippi had been ceded to the United States by the treaties of 1804 and 1816, with the proviso that the Indians could live on it until the government wished to sell it. Now the government wished to sell it. The first treaty had been obscurely worded and misunderstood; the second confirmed the cession, but was repudiated by some of the bands who professed not to have realized they would have to move. Even then some of those party to the treaties reneged, saying they had not meant to sell, that no one could sell the bones of their forefathers. It was inevitable that they would clash with the incoming whites who understood that the land had been ceded and was available to homestead and develop and who feared and protested the continued presence of Sac, Fox and Winnebago thereon. Although these tribes built summer villages to plant corn and squash, theirs was still essentially a hunting and gathering culture. They did not understand how the land could belong to individuals, as the incoming settlers claimed, and resented being pushed from their hunting grounds. The Indians complained bitterly to their agent Thomas Forsyth. "They compare a white settlement in their neighborhood to a large drop of raccoon grease falling on a new blanket," reported Forsyth. "The drop at first is scarcely perceptible, but in time covers the whole blanket."4

But trade in this transition area was not yet paralyzed, and the fluid situation may have given Brown the chance he was looking for. In 1828 Farnham and Davenport had no one to send to the Rock River post, a post from which, in any case, they could not have expected great returns. It would be more a case of maintaining a supply line to their Winnebago until such time as they would be provided for by treaty and their debts (it was to be hoped) paid off by the government. Sergeant Brown lost little time in convincing George Davenport that he could handle the job.

Brown's move to become a licensed trader may have been precipitated by an order from General Atkinson in March of 1828 to concentrate the Fifth Regiment at Jefferson Barracks, the new headquarters post for the northern frontier, which had been built a few miles below St. Louis. This move was understood at Fort Armstrong to be a temporary one, preliminary to an exchange of posts with the First Regiment at Mackinac and Chicago. By May 5 the two companies from Fort Armstrong had completed the transfer. The rest of the regiment from Forts Snelling and

3. Alexander Wolcott to Cass, Mar. 7, 1829, OIA LR Michigan superintendency; Way *Rock River Valley* 139, 146–148.

4. Chas. J. Kappler *Indian Affairs, Laws and Treaties* II: 74-76, 126-128 (Washington 1904); Forsyth to Cass, Survey of Sac and Fox Habits 1822.

Crawford moved at about the same time. Brown couldn't have been at Jefferson Barracks a week when he applied for a discharge.[5]

If the decision to move the regiment hadn't been made, Joseph R. Brown might well have finished out his term of service. Presumably by 1830, when he was due to get out, approaching civilization would have rendered a soldier's uniform unnecessary as a passport to most of the upper river country. He had a position of some importance at Fort Armstrong, and probably could have become Acting Sergeant Major of the regiment. Colonel Snelling had departed for Washington City the preceding winter (never to return to the regiment, as it happens, for he died there suddenly), leaving Major Vose in charge, so Vose had the opportunity to fill the post. But Brown applied for a discharge. His later explanation of why he left the army was that he had attained to the highest rank he could expect to attain under existing regulations.[6] That reason was for public consumption. His real reasons were more complex: he wanted to remain on the upper Mississippi where he had developed connections, where his wife's relatives lived, where he had prospects for employment – the imminent move would carry him far from his accustomed habitat. Then, it is hard to avoid the assumption that he was also engaged in some local enterprise that he did not want to leave.

It is clear that Brown had at least tentatively contracted to work for Farnham and Davenport before his company left Rock Island in May. It may have been Charles D. St. Vrain – long an American Fur Company trader in the area and manager of Davenport's store while he was away – who decided to take on the untried Brown. Certainly Joe had little or no opportunity to sell himself to either of the partners that spring: George Davenport had been absent for the better part of a year and was still on his way back from Europe in May; to all appearances Russell Farnham, who had spent the fall in St. Louis and the winter canvassing his posts on the Des Moines, returned to his chief depot at Fort Edwards (near Keokuk's village at the mouth of the Des Moines) and came up to Rock Island only briefly, if at all, that spring.[7]

Since there is no file to be found containing Brown's application for a discharge, we can't say for sure when he applied or who recommended him or, for that matter, if he had prearranged for an early discharge as a condition of reenlisting. However, on June 8, 1828, P. H. Gault, Acting Assistant Adjutant General, signed an order at Cincinnati releasing Sergeant Joseph R. Brown from the service "on furnishing a substitute without expense to the United States." He must have had a ready candidate: his discharge is dated July 1, yet the order could scarcely have been received by Major Vose much before June 15, given the slowness of the mails at the best of times. This method of discharge was quite common; some men were only persuaded to reenlist by receiving a certificate entitling them to be released at any time upon securing a

---

5. Atkinson to General Roger Jones, Mar. 10, 1828, Atkinson Order Book, Order #12 Mar. 24, 1828, AGO LR; Orderly Book Company E Special Order #60, May 5, 1828. The First left Jefferson Barracks September 10 for Green Bay and Mackinac; Companies A and I were detailed to Fort Dearborn at Chicago.

6. Orderly Book Company E May 29, 1828, Regimental Order #24; J. R. Brown to Alexander Ramsay, Oct. 21, 1861, draft in Brown papers.

7. Brandt "Farnham" 225–226.

substitute. Technically, Brown had to find a man of equal rank and capabilities to take over his duties. In actuality, the substitute he procured was enlisted as a sergeant, but shortly thereafter demoted to musician, so a certain fiction may have applied.[8]

So Joseph R. Brown was out of the army in July of 1828, maybe had already left the regiment, for the June 30 report shows him "sick in quarters," which could be another polite fiction. He returned to Rock Island that summer. At this time he presumably had Helen and his son Solomon with him (if they had not rejoined him at Fort Armstrong earlier). Once he was on Davenport's payroll his family would be afforded more protection – Brown would have an interpreter and several boatmen generally nearby. Brown probably spent part of the summer building his family a cabin and opening up a small farm, not on the island but across the river on the Iowa side. (William Powell, formerly Robert Dickson's clerk, remembered once staying overnight with Brown at his farm on the western bank of the Mississippi near Fort Armstrong.)[9] Antoine Leclaire, long a trader and interpreter for the Sac also lived on the right bank and by 1827 Davenport had a flatboat that he used to ferry pack horses, cattle and goods for the trade between the island and the Iowa shore. It can be assumed he had a trading house or warehouse there for convenience as well. Even though the trading season did not begin until fall, there was plenty to do over the summer months. Davenport kept milk cows, horses and oxen on the island; there was hay to cut, wood to stockpile for sale to steamboats, crops to hoe and harvest. In August Davenport wrote to his partner (with his own picturesque spelling), "Manager run away from Rock Island the other day he was tired of working and wanted to get to sum place whear thier is nothing to do but get drunk. I am determined to make evrey man thats under my controul work for his wages. I have had three stacks of hay made for our Oxen & horses and have them Building a house for them selves to live in, the old house having fallen down. I brought up Lemrey [Lemoureau?] – Clark and one other man to make hay for my private use. after thay had got stacked about twenty-five Tons, the Beaver Son thought proper to set it on fier and Burnt it all up."[10] Brown apparently had charge of the establishment opposite the island, a convenient site for keeping a eye on the river traffic as well as breaking ground for crops (although much of the area was a slough), making hay, cutting timber or even operating the ferry.

Certainly Brown was not the first soldier to interest himself in the fur trade after departing the service – many men had done so, often by way of the sutlership or store clerk at an army post as Davenport, Downey and Gooding had done. He may have been one of the first to be entrusted with an outfit at a main post his first season out. But it is a fact that in the fall of 1828 Joseph R.

---

8. Orderly Book Company E Jun. 8, 1828; muster rolls Company H. See Atkinson to Adjutant General, Feb. 10, 1828, for the certificate supplied by another sergeant who applied for early discharge "as he would not reenlist without such a pledge," AGO LR.

9. Powell "Recollections" 158–159. This cabin may well have been on the site of Second and Scott streets; at least there was an unoccupied cabin there in 1835, before the townsite was settled, that did not belong to Antoine Leclaire. This site is opposite Fort Armstrong, west of Leclaire's claim. See Harry E. Downer History of Davenport and Scott County I:48, 141, passim (Chicago 1910).

10. Davenport to Farnham, Aug. 19, 1828, quoted in Brandt "Farnham" 227.

Brown, late of the U. S. Army, took a load of trade goods up the Rock River to conduct a winter's trade near the Winnebago village about fifty miles upstream. He was in charge of a post that had been suffering hard times because of its proximity to the troubled area of the lead mines. Yet George Davenport thought this inexperienced youth (he was just twenty-three) would be able to cope with the situation and be able to carry on a trade with the Winnebago – the edgy tribe whose animosity that winter so intimidated Joseph M. Street, the new Prairie du Chien agent, that he felt he should warn Taliaferro, "I like them not... All is not right with the Winnebagoes – the nation is sore."**11** Davenport had little hope getting much return from the Rock River that season, probably was using the post to keep in contact with the Indians while a provisional treaty for cession of their lands was worked out and as a testing ground for his new man. In November he reported resignedly to Chouteau, "There is neither Indians or Muskrats this season in Rock River." The letter reveals that it may have been an afterthought by Davenport to staff the post at all. He says "I have sent J. R. Brown to take charge of the house in Rock River and shall send Jno. K. Forsyth [another new man, son of the agent] to the upper part of the Ioway River... In looking over the license I find our establishment on Rock River has been omitted being put in the license... and also J. R. Brown's name."**12** One has to assume from this letter that J. R. Brown's name would not be unfamiliar to Chouteau.

Brown's trade was mainly with the Winnebago, although he may also have done business with the nearby Sac and Potawatomi – Farnham mentions the Sac were supplied from Rock River. Winnebago is a Siouan language, and may have been passably intelligible to Brown, but he would have had with him a man who could not only interpret but who also knew the country, the Indians and where they could be found. Davenport had traded with these Indians for more than a dozen years and had pioneered the supply route via the Illinois and Rock rivers as early as 1815. In an uncompleted history of the fur trade which Joseph R. Brown commenced in the 1850s he noted that "the first goods brought to Rock Island by any other channel than the Wisconsin was brought by Mr. George Davenport from the Illinois River and were furnished by a Mr. [James] Morrison residing on that river and used in the trade with the Winnebagoes in the valley of Rock River."**13** Brown knew that from Davenport himself.

It might be well to take a look at what Brown's life as an Indian trader was like. Brown had hired on as a clerk at an annual salary plus provisions, with outfit and personnel furnished by the company. With more experience, he might go into partnership with one or more other traders for a percentage of the profits and/or losses, or he might set up as

---

11. Joseph M. Street to Taliaferro, Jan. 27, 1828, Taliaferro papers. Nicholas Boilvin, long-time agent at the Prairie, drowned in 1827 and was replaced by Street, who seems to have been somewhat appalled at first sight of his new charges.

12. Davenport to Chouteau, Nov. 17, 1828, Chouteau Collection.

13. Fragment titled "Notes for Hist. Society" in J. R. Brown's handwriting in Martin McLeod papers, MHS.

an independent trader, buy his goods from whomever would sell to him and sell his furs where he would, taking all profit and loss for himself.

Figure 11 Typical trader's cabin, based on contemporary accounts and drawings. Brown's cabin at Olivers Grove is described as being a one-story log house with one window and a plank door, having several outbuildings and a dugout in the hill behind it for powder.

In any case he would need at least one voyageur working for him as guide and interpreter, several more as boatmen (up to fourteen for a lake canoe, fewer for a mackinac boat) and if the post were remote a blacksmith would be required to repair guns, traps and carts. Winterers' staple food was corn, in the form of meal, larded with strips of pork fat or other grease for energy and flavor. In the case of the engagé or boatman this, along with a tot of rum when the work was done, constituted his entire diet. Clerks did better. Their standard contract called for flour, sugar, coffee, tea and tobacco, although not necessarily of the best quality. For variety they would catch fish, hunt game and purchase meat and vegetables from the natives.

Their wintering house was generally of hewn logs with a plank door, no windows and only a mud-and-stick fireplace in one corner to provide heat and cooking facilities. In the colder regions one or two men could be kept busy all winter chopping and hauling wood to feed the inefficient fires. Depending on the size of the post, there could be two or three of these cabins – one for the clerk, one for the men and one for a storehouse – or there might be one long partitioned house. In the more dangerous areas the cabins would be surrounded with a stockade into which the animals could be driven at night for protection. However, in some places where the Indians feared to allow any type of permanent establishment the clerk had to make do with an Indian lodge. Some posts were quite elaborate and were used for many seasons; others were changed from year to year as the Indians changed their hunting grounds. But since 1824, when the Indian agents were given discretionary powers in assigning locations, they had tended to remain fixed.

Trade outfits were standard, varying only in the kinds and styles of trinkets preferred by each band. The basics were blankets and yard goods – strouds (a heavy red or blue woolen), calicos and plaids, cottons, scarlet cloth. Iron tools and equipment had become necessities to the Indians. They required kettles, axes, knives, needles, fishhooks, rifles, traps and rat spears to live. Each trader also carried a good stock of pretties and trinkets such as mirrors, feathers, combs, beads, hawk bells, vermilion, quills, earbobs, brooches, silk handkerchiefs and top hats to attract new customers and encourage the hunters.**14** These goods – especially traps, guns, ammunition and warm clothing – were advanced to the hunters on credit in the fall in exchange for a specified numbers of furs to be returned as payment in the spring. The successful trader had the ability to judge his debtor's character accurately and press him to hunt diligently, a hardy constitution capable of withstanding heavy work and enduring much privation plus a strong personality capable of keeping the respect of the Indians and halfbreed engagés alike. The price of negligence or misjudgment was at best nothing to show for seven or eight months' work and at worst a knife between the ribs or a ball whizzing past one's ear. It was a life for which Joseph R. Brown was singularly fitted.

Despite the severity of the cold that winter, despite the lack of game and Indians to hunt it, despite the competition in the immediate neighborhood and George Davenport's dire prognostications, Joe Brown managed to collect a reasonable return in furs his first season, which speaks volumes for his talents. Want of snow, besides restricting the hunts and freezing out the rats, provided problems in the spring as well. There was little meltwater to swell the rivers, and the rocky-bottomed Rock River in particular proved impassable for loaded canoes. Come April Brown was still stuck, causing Farnham to despair, "On account of the low water we have received none of the packs from Rock River, Flint Hills or the mines [Dubuque]." Worse, there was no prospect of the Indians making a spring hunt to help make up for winter losses. They were simply afraid to hunt their traditional lands. The Winnebago from Rock River generally came down to the Mississippi while the Sac and Fox were absent in Iowa, but this winter they had retreated further up the Rock to the Koshkonong Lakes region near its head. By April it was obvious that the Indians were not going to expose themselves any further in enemy territory and were withdrawing to their summer camps at the headwaters

---

14. For a vivid account of the daily life of a trader's clerk, see Parker *Prescott*, especially pages 129–131, 139–144. For more on the mechanics of the fur trade, see Appendix C. Prices in 1828 were falling, indicating a depressed economy on the river. Three-point blankets (the heaviest) were $8, strouds $7, tomahawks 1.50, scalping knives 50¢. A gun could be had for $15, but a good rifle would cost $30. Furs held their value: Davenport got $1 for deerskins, $3 for bear or otter, $6.20 a pound for beaver. Muskrats (inevitably called rats), the staple of the trade, brought only 25¢ each. George Davenport Rock Island Ledger 1826–1830, in Davenport papers, Augustana College special collections, Rock Island.

of the river. Farnham had to tell Chouteau they had had a poor season and "all our flattering prospects for a hunt [have] entirely failed."[15]

Brown eventually got his furs down, probably the hard way by packing them out, and accompanied them to St. Louis where Chouteau ran a large sorting, storing and shipping operation. It was imperative that these undressed skins be graded and shipped from the Mississippi country before the really hot weather set in. The Fur Company would suffer a double disaster if the few packs that had come out deteriorated before reaching market. Even shipping on the Mississippi was made difficult by the low water; boats such as the steamer Rover, which had gone aground above Rock Island, simply had to wait for high water to float them off. Brown, Davenport and the other company clerks apparently suffered no hindrance to their passage back upstream on the steamboat Red Rover, as they arrived back at Rock Island in mid-July.[16] Although trade in general had been poor for the season – Rolette estimated that his outfits alone had lost $20,000 through the Sioux/Sac–Fox wars, no small sum – Brown had done at least as well as could be expected on the Rock. He'd earned a better location, so was moved for the 1829–1930 season to the Flint Hills, a trading house near the mouth of Flint River on the site of Burlington, Iowa. This location, between Farnham's store at Keokuk's village and Rock Island, was an important depot for goods going into Iowa and served several Sac and Fox villages along the Mississippi. More than $5,000 worth of merchandise passed through this house each season. With more than thirty employees to chose from, Farnham and Davenport evinced a certain confidence in Brown by placing him at the post.

It appears Brown spent a good deal of the summer of 1829 at the Flint Hills, opening up a farm for the Indians. It may have been that Davenport hoped to avoid further tribal conflict by demonstrating the value of resettling in stable agricultural villages on the Iowa side of the river. In exchange for annuities, which decreased their dependence on hunting, the Indians had agreed to relinquish their homelands in Illinois, but when the time came to move they stubbornly refused to leave. The Indians had been told the government meant to sell their lands in the spring, and it was widely believed when the Sac left on their winter hunts that they would not return to Illinois. Several settlers moved into the Indian houses at Saukenuk during the winter. But in April Black Hawk led his people back to Saukenuk and drove the newcomers from the lodges. The usurpers retaliated by letting their cattle into the Indian cornfields. Obviously something would have to be done to induce the Sac and the related Fox, to leave their old homes on the east bank of the river. Brown's farming project at Shokokon village may have been designed to lure the Indians into opening new cornfields in the fertile bottomlands of Iowa. Both Sac and Fox traded at the Flint Hills and so by this example both might be

---

15. Farnham to Chouteau, Apr. 3, 1829, Chouteau papers.
16. Davenport Ledger, Jul. 20, 1829.

induced to form permanent settlements.**17** Since most traders depended on the Indians for provisions, the idea of ensuring a food supply through nearby Indian farms also makes sense. The idea may have been Brown's or someone else's; but that summer Brown was working for the American Fur Company, and whatever he was doing it was with Farnham and Davenport's blessing and probably at their behest.

Thirty years later Brown remembered that summer a little bit differently. In a letter to William Welsh he explained how he taught the Indians agriculture:

> "Previous to the Black Hawk War, I traded for the American Fur Company at Flint Hills, now known as Burlington, Iowa. The Sac and Fox with whom I traded were the most warlike and restless of the north-western tribes, and their prejudices against the habits of the white were not lessened by the treatment they received from the settlers east of the Mississippi River.
>
> "Appanoose [The Grandchild], the son of Tiema, a Fox Chief, was my sworn friend, or according to the Indians, my brother; I had thought a great deal upon the subject of Indian improvement, and determined to try upon him the plan I had adopted as best calculated to change the habits of the Indians.
>
> "I opened the subject to Appanoose, using such arguments as suggested themselves to interest him in the project. As I possessed his confidence and spoke his language, my arguments made the desired impression... The final result was that he cleared and fenced a ten-acre lot, which he and his wife dug up and planted in corn, potatoes, turnips, etc.
>
> "I had furnished the axes, hoes and seed, and subsisted the family until his planting was completed, but could not afford to subsist them longer, and he had to return to the chase; but he attended to his crop and the yield provided him a wagon, a cow, and many articles of clothing for himself and family, besides furnishing an abundance of corn and potatoes for his subsistence during the winter.
>
> "The success of Appanoose induced other Indians to settle around him and go to work, and when I left, three years afterwards, there were over two hundred acres under cultivation in the Flint creek bottom and some twenty families living in good comfortable log houses."**18**

This letter is a carefully worded effort from an expert lobbyist and although it undoubtedly contains facts they may be suspected of embellishment. Brown could have spent part of three summers (1828, 1829 and 1830) at Flint Hills, but as he was demonstrably elsewhere for much of that time he could not have been putting the effort he describes

---

17. Spencer "Narrative" 15–17, 23–26, 38; John H. Hauberg "The Black Hawk War 1831–32" in *Transactions of the Illinois Historical Society* XXXIX : 99–102 (Springfield 1932). Treaty provisions may be found in Kappler *Laws and Treaties* II: 74–76, 126–128

18. Brown to William Welsh, April 13, 1869, printed in *Journal of the Rev. S. D. Hinman Missionary to the Santee Sioux Indians and Taopi by Bishop Whipple*, William Welsh, compiler, 64–65 (Philadelphia 1869).

into agriculture. Also he forgets to indicate that the Fox and Sac Indians were already part-time agriculturists and knew very well how to clear land for cornfields (in fact, the United States had had a "pattern farm" opposite the site of Montrose in Illinois as early as 1804 to educate the Sac and Fox in agriculture). The Indians lived in semi-permanent villages: the Fox band headed by Tiema had had a summer village at the mouth of Flint River, a few miles north of the trading post, from at least 1821.[19] The idea of "ownership" of individual fenced plats may have been Brown's contribution to their tradition.

It was not really in Brown's or the Fur Company's interest that the Indians abandon hunting for farming – quite the contrary, although in many cases the bands were able to offset some credits with the yearly cash allotment. But it did no one any good if the Indians starved, for as Brown indicated, it fell to the trader to provision the families of those who hunted for him. Over those dismal years the Indians came to depend more and more on their traders; Russell Farnham was persuaded that if he had withdrawn his support "many must have perished with cold & Hunger for we furnished almost the entire supply of clothing, utensils, & ammunition."[20] There was little game left in Illinois in any case, and much competition from the whites who were entering the area. But before the Sac and Fox could be induced to hunt, they must first be distracted from going to war on the settlers as they had on the Sioux. A good first step would be to form new settlements away from both parties of belligerents, luring the Indians with promise of a year-round trader to see to their needs. That might have been Davenport's plan. Unfortunately the Indians maintained a single-minded preoccupation with thoughts of revenge and those who, like Appanoose, could be talked into giving up the warpath remained in the minority.

We catch sight of J. R. Brown a couple of times in the fall of 1829, thanks to visitors at the Flint Hills. This post was practically the only stopping place between Rock Island and Fort Edwards and, as might be expected, there was plenty of traffic. In addition to his interpreter, François Labisseure (Brown's spelling of the name), and several engagés and their families who were always at the post, Brown often had the company of other Fur Company traders who worked the upper Des Moines and Skunk rivers: his books show he did business with Jean Baptiste Clausé, Joseph Cotté, Baptiste Berthe, Maurice Blondeau and others. Accounts from two visitors otherwise unimportant to this narrative give some insight into the difficulties traders faced during this period.

Andrew S. Hughes, agent for the Iowa, came across Mr. Brown of the American Fur Company at his Flint Hills post in early September. He also found there a large party of Sac and Fox collected "some for the purpose of starting out on their fall hunts and others for the purpose of raising a war party to go against the Sioux." Hughes had with him an Iowa chief

---

19. Jacob Van der Zee "Fur Trade in the Eastern Iowa Country from 1800 to 1833," *Iowa Journal of History and Politics* XII: 491 (Iowa City 1914).

20. Farnham to Chouteau, Aug. 1, 1830, quoted in Brandt "Farnham" 227–228.

named Big Neck who had become embroiled in a shooting back on the Grand River of Missouri. Hughes had pursued the Indians to the plains south of the Iowa River where he met Appanoose who helped him secure Big Neck and his party and then guided them to Brown's trading post at the mouth of Flint River. Here the Iowas balked, alarmed by stories circulated by the assembled Sac and Fox that they would be killed. "Mr. Brown and Mr. Labussire who were present used every argument they were capable of," reported Hughes, "but the Indians still persisted in their refusal." Brown furnished plenty of provisions while the parleying went on, and at last Hughes convinced the Big Neck to accompany him to St. Louis to meet with Superintendent of Indian Affairs William Clark. Brown and Labisseure were not so lucky with the Sac and Fox Indians left behind: the war party had proved more attractive to them than the hunting party.[21]

Many of the Indians were still hanging about when Lawrence Taliaferro passed downriver on his way to St. Louis in mid-October, talking of war parties and getting up courage by raiding the white settlements for horses. At the mouth of the Iowa River Taliaferro came across a large Sac war party headed by Pashapaho (The Stabbing Chief) dancing the scalps of three Sioux – said to be a boy, man and woman – killed at the very gate of Rolette's post at the forks of the Red Cedar River (near present-day Nashua, Iowa). Two days later he met Joseph R. Brown at the store at the Lower Yellow Banks (now Oquawka, Illinois), who, doubtless somewhat startled by the news, accompanied Taliaferro to the Flint Hills. "Here, through his family and himself," says Taliaferro, "I obtained all the information as to the affair recently at the forks of Red Cedar. Mrs. B. had seen the scalps and thought one of them to be her uncle's – brother-in-law of the late Colonel Robert Dickson." How that must have shaken up Helen, to have the gory trophy – probably with identifiable ornaments – pushed under her nose! They told her they had dried and eaten the hearts of their victims. She had also learned that the war party had actually dared to approach within thirty yards of Rolette's trading house, threatening to attack the hands within their little picket work. Desperate, the men had finally repulsed the attackers with buckshot, wounding several. The episode was disquieting because generally the Indian wars had not involved direct attacks on white establishments, although the circumstance of Rolette trading with the hated Sioux in territory disputed by the Sac and Fox may have made the Stabbing Chief's hostility to the American Fur Company at least understandable.

What preserved Helen from attack isn't clear: the chiefs of the Sac and Fox had told Taliaferro they couldn't restrain their young men from taking the warpath. Brown was aware the Sac planned to send several war parties against the Sioux over the winter, but didn't seem especially worried about his own part-Sioux family. Taking time to counsel with the Sac encamped at Flint Hills, Taliaferro spoke through Labisseure to

21. Andrew S. Hughes to William Clark, Oct. 11, 1829, OIA LR Missouri superintendency.

"warn them of the approaching storm that must inevitably burst upon them if they continued their wanton and outrageous and infamous attacks upon the Sioux." Taliaferro was justifiably angry and considerably appalled that the Sac would complain to him of the wounds received at the hands of Rolette's men. "You went to war you say against the Sioux. Why did you not go where they were encamped – why did you go where you were certain to find white people[? Y]ou got by it what you deserved and may be thankful that it is no worse... if I were your agent you would find hard times... You have heard what I did with the Sioux for wantonly killing some Chippeways near my house. I will tell you one thing for your comfort – If I were your agent I would now adopt the same plan with you!" Their response was not the least bit encouraging. Incensed at the injustice of the government apparently taking the side of the Sioux, one Sac chief made a thinly veiled threat: "It is wrong for the white people to fight with other Indians against us." Summarizing this exchange, Taliaferro reported to his superiors, "War parties and nothing else is now talked of among these people. They say: we cannot hunt this winter, therefore we will now be compelled to fight the Sioux." Some Sac also brazenly asked the men on Taliaferro's keelboat if there were any Sioux on board. Having delivered his "very severe talk" to bands already in the mood for retaliation, Taliaferro righteously proceeded downriver leaving Joseph R. Brown and a handful of French Canadians and halfbreeds to deal with any repercussions. Brown was well aware of the Indians' habit of saving face by extracting an eye for an eye; he also understood that the injured party felt justified in hitting anyone handy, not necessarily he who had mortified him. Taliaferro's speech had done nothing to ease tensions. Apprised of the general temper of the Indians, Davenport could only remark, "Trade looks bad."**22**

In 1829 an era was ending in the Mississippi valley. The process of settlements overtaking Indian lands had been slow but inexorable. By the summer of 1829 the mounting pressure from white settlers and the powerful interest of the Fur Company had come together to demand the extinction of Indian title to those lands east of the Mississippi and the cession of other lands west of that river. The Indians would be resettled in the still-virgin lands of western Iowa and Nebraska. While the United States government's motives may have been largely benevolent and paternalistic, the Fur Company and the Indians themselves were driven by economic necessity. It was simple: the Indians owed the Company money for goods advanced on credit, more money than they could ever hope to repay. Locked in a closed economy, Indians and traders were totally dependent on each other. The goods the Indians needed to survive, especially the Northwest guns and British woolens, were procurable only from their traders; skins and peltries, their only salable commodities

22. Taliaferro Journal, entries for Oct. 16–20, 1829 and draft of letter to Indian Office Oct. 20, 1829, same volume page 133; Davenport to Chouteau, Nov. 11, 1829, copy in OIA LR St. Louis superintendency. For trading locations see *History of Chickasaw and Howard Counties, Iowa*, W. E. Alexander, ed., 191–192 (Decorah 1883).

except for food, were of value only to the fur companies that were prepared to sell them in New York and England. In poor years the traders still had to supply the goods – and even food – to keep their Indians alive to hunt again. Civilization, in the form of white incursions into Indian lands, always diminished the Indians' ability to pay their debts, a fact well known to the traders for the American Fur Company. Liquor was the chief culprit, but competition with newcomers for hunting and living room, dwindling resources and interruption of traditional ways took their toll. Most of the time the tribes recognized their debts and considered them just, but after so many poor years the collective debt had become too great for individuals or the tribe to recoup. At last they had no recourse but to alienate their homelands for the money to pay off their traders and to start afresh in a new land further west.

Most of the Sac and Fox land east of the Mississippi and south of the Wisconsin rivers had already been ceded. The Indians were warned to move off in 1828 and the land was put up for sale the following year. The remaining Indian lands east of the river were ceded by the Winnebago in a treaty drawn up in the summer of 1829 that relinquished the lead mines to the squatters. The Winnebago treaty provided for the repayment of some traders' credits – mostly to Rolette and the Green Bay traders – and settled a good annuity on the tribe, but simply dispossessing the Sac and Fox of lands already sold did nothing to ease their debt obligations. Something else must be done.

It was precisely for that reason Superintendent Clark called a convocation of the Sac, Fox and Sioux at Prairie du Chien in the spring of 1830. The War Department, which still embodied the Office of Indian Affairs, saw this as an opportunity for a grand council of all the tribes of the upper Mississippi. After several months' delay, representatives of the Sac and Fox, Santee Sioux, Omaha, Iowa, Otoe and other Missouri tribes convened to make a treaty that set a precedent by establishing a separate reservation in the "far west" to be used for resettling the Indians. The treaty provided for cession of a reserve stretching from the Des Moines River to the Missouri that would be held for the Indians by the government and to which they could remove, and also for a forty-mile-wide strip in northern Iowa from the Mississippi to the Des Moines which was to remain neutral ground between Sac and Sioux.[23] Rolette's post would have to be removed from this no-man's-land.

In addition, the Sioux were induced to set aside a tract of land for the halfbreeds of their nation, a fifteen mile wide strip on Lake Pepin from Red Wing's village to Wabasha Prairie that within a few years would prove a bone of contention, lying as it did in the way of settlement of the Minnesota area. The article creating this tract was apparently inserted in the treaty to mollify certain traders connected with the Sioux by marriage – Bailly was at the bottom of it according to one contemporary – in return

---

23. Kappler, *Laws and Treaties* 300–302, 305–307.

for their cooperation in getting the Indians to the treaty site.24 Otherwise the traders gained nothing in the way of compensation (Taliaferro took credit for balking their efforts), save that small annuities to be paid every year for ten years were settled on all the tribes present.

Small comfort to Farnham and Davenport. Although they seem to have considered the Sac and Fox annuity money theirs (they were, in fact, doing a cash business with the Sac), and its yearly delivery into Chief Keokuk's hands merely a formality, they still had unpaid claims that according to Farnham amounted to $52,000. In August of 1830 Farnham put his case to Pierre Chouteau Junior in St. Louis, the letter obviously written to be passed on intact to whatever government official could do the most good. He says in part:

> ". . . I have great fear, such is the amount of the accumulated debt, that even if peace were now restored, the Indians would not be able to pay it off out of the proceeds of their Hunt, after providing for their own current necessities. Seeing their desperate condition, they have repeatedly offered to pay the debt by a cession of land... [T]hey have expressed an entire willingness to cede to the Unt. States a part of their lands west of the Mississippi (a fine Region abounding in minerals) and to stipulate a part of the purchase money by the government to the extinguishment of our debt... [C]onsidering the present embarrassed state of the Indians and the danger of ultimate loss I have entered into an express agreement with their chiefs & leaders to Receive in full payment the stipulated sum of forty thousand dollars, which will barely cover the prime cost without a cent of profit."25

It was all neatly arranged for the commissioners, but this money demand, coupled with a high annuity demand by the Indians, led them to take no action for a while. Meanwhile, the refusal of the Sac and Fox, guided by that stubborn-minded old man Black Hawk, to remove west of the Mississippi precipitated a war, which, if we may get a bit ahead of the story, broke out in the summer of 1832. It was not until Black Hawk, Prophet, the Little Stabbing Chief and others had been taken hostage and a great many of their people slaughtered that the Indians were forced to leave the Illinois country. They were ushered out by a rather generous treaty that included a direct payment of $40,000 to Farnham and Davenport as well as annuity payments of $20,000 per year for thirty years. In return the Sac and Fox agreed to cede all their remaining lands in

24. Folwell *Minnesota* I: 158–159, 322–323. It was Folwell's belief that the movers were certain Sioux halfbreeds who expected to be given patents in fee simple enabling them to sell the land, but were balked when neither President Jackson nor President Van Buren would issue the patents. Folwell's information came from William Quinn, son of Patrick Quinn, government interpreter for later Sioux treaties; Quinn believed the prime mover was Bailly, along with Augustin Rocque, Oliver Cratte, Joseph Buisson and other influential halfbreeds. Folwell Notebook, Aug. 9, 1904, in Folwell papers, MHS.

25. Farnham to Chouteau, Aug. 8, 1831, quoted in Brandt "Farnham" 228. Farnham and Davenport claims in the report of November 1831 showed a capital employed of $33,000 to $60,000 per year, credits extended over seven years totaling $136,768.62 and a balance owing of $53,269.88 "which we do not consider desperate" (Ibid., 222, 224).

Iowa (with the exception of two sections reserved for their old interpreter Antoine Leclaire on the right bank of the Mississippi at the Rock Island rapids).26 This time they went quietly.

At the land sales in the fall of 1829 both Farnham and Davenport had purchased considerable acreage in Illinois (a circumstance that did not exactly endear them to their Sac and Fox customers), much of it as deputies for the settlers coming into the area. When the Iowa lands opened up in 1832, George Davenport continued to acquire property on that side of the river too, eventually owning most of what is now downtown Davenport, Iowa.27 Joseph R. Brown might also have figured as an early settler of that city; he had his farm, or at least a claim cabin, on the site. He returned to that farm in the spring of 1830 after disposing of his furs and settling his account with George Davenport. He was feeling flush enough to make several purchases, including six yards of cotton sarcenet, some embroidery silk, a couple of silk handkerchiefs, and for himself a round jacket and a "hatt" – maybe he was outfitting himself for the Sac/Sioux treaty that was originally supposed to have been held that spring. But perhaps that treaty falling through convinced him that it would be many years before that site would be worth anything as a claim. In the spring of 1830 Joseph R. Brown was ready to quit the Sac and Fox country. He could have had several reasons to make the move. It was evident the Indian wars would continue, making it increasingly difficult and dangerous to trade in Sac territory, and Brown's small band of agriculturists would scarcely repay the trouble. It was equally evident that should the Indians agree to move, the future trading sites would have to be away from the river, on the Missouri or the upper Des Moines, and no doubt Brown could look forward to being transferred to the Upper Missouri Outfit, when for whatever reasons, perhaps personal, Brown wanted to remain on the upper Mississippi. There was, of course, an ever-present danger to Brown's family as well if he remained in Iowa; the episode of Helen's uncle's scalp being dangled in her face could well have served as a warning – it was time to go. On May 7 he closed out his account with Davenport and on July 20 he was back in the shadow of Fort Snelling, purchasing yard goods, ammunition and provisions at Alexis Bailly's store. Brown had found a way to return to the St. Peters; he had come to an agreement with Bailly for a one-year clerkship at $360 per annum, not a bad salary for a relative newcomer to the trade.28 His interest in a claim in what would become downtown Davenport Brown sold, as he later said, "for a box of cigars."29

---

26. Kappler, ibid.

27. Franc B. Wilkie, *Davenport: Past and Present* 145 (Davenport 1888).

28. Davenport Ledger Apr. 2, 7, 16 and May 7, 1830; Bailly Ledger Jul. 20, 1830, Bailly papers. As a wage comparison, at the time a common soldier was paid $72 a year, the government interpreter $150, blacksmith $180, Indian subagent $500. Philander Prescott, an eleven-year veteran of the trade, was hired by Rolette as a clerk the following year for an annual wage of $400.

29. The story of Brown "giving away" his interest in Davenport crops up in several forms in published accounts; the original is probably J. O. Barrett *A History of Traverse County: Browns Valley and Its Environs to 1881*, 7 (reprint edition, no date), which places the sale in 1833–1834. The first recorded transaction in what would be Davenport was the purchase in 1833 by Antoine Leclaire of a

Bailly was undoubtedly at Prairie du Chien that summer of 1830, furthering his interests, while Brown settled his family in at the St. Peters. Perhaps this was the summer he built a claim cabin near Minnehaha Falls, for we really have no clue where he lived. It was near enough Mendota that he was often in the store, sometimes bringing in choice furs such as bear cub, martin and otter, sometimes outfitting himself with a new frock coat and crepe tie, a red sash, new shirts and a capote (a kind of poncho with a hood that could be pulled up in foul weather) made for him by Mrs. Faribault. From transactions Joe and Helen made at the store we can begin to see how they lived, what they did, how they dressed. Purchases of bombazette, velvet, ribbon, satinet and embroidery silk seem destined to make finery for Helen and four-year-old Solomon: they were back in "society" again, and must have clothes suitable for visiting. More mundane acquisitions include calico and flannels for shirts, fishhooks, needles, pins and a brass thimble, shaving soap and a case of razors (these cost Joe as much as fifty pounds of pork!), hair brush, tooth brush, tobacco tin, borax and soda powders, woolen stockings, gloves and a red cap. Ready-made clothes were seldom purchased – either Helen was an accomplished seamstress or the Browns were affluent enough to pay others for sewing. To some extent everyone in the Indian territory dressed "a la hunter": smoke-tanned buckskin shirts, wolfskin caps, elkhide moccasins purchased from the indigenous people were popular and practical for hunting and traveling and gave a colorful effect when embellished with an ornamented powderhorn and minkskin bullet pouch, a short-handle axe tucked into the bright woven sash or belt.[30] But in public clerks of the American Fur Company were businessmen and garbed themselves and their ladies appropriately. It sent a clearer message of their dignity and importance to their Indian clients. Indeed, for a halfbreed to be accepted in the white community (with remarkably little prejudice), he or she had only to don "white" clothing and adopt the habits of white society. Many other items in daily use were without doubt bought or traded for from the fort sutler, steamboat passengers, Indian artisans and other traders.

Sometimes the notations in Bailly's ledgers and notebooks raise more questions than they answer. In September Brown is cryptically credited $12.00 for "feeding three men for working a hole." Clearly Bailly's men, but what was the hole? A mining project? A root cellar or storage pit? The latter is a possibility because Brown appears to have planted vegetables that summer – potatoes and corn – that he sold to Bailly. Fresh produce was a rare luxury in a monotonous diet composed chiefly of salt pork and cornmeal, and Brown seldom wasted a chance to plant. It's evident from

---

disputed claim west of his reserve which may have included the old Brown farm. (Can we guess that one of the disputants purchased the property from Brown, the other squatted on what he thought to be unclaimed land?) The city of Davenport was laid out by Leclaire and Davenport, among others, in 1835 (Downer *History of Davenport* 141–142).

30. This description of an 1827 settler in the mining area from John H. Fonda "Early Wisconsin," in *Wisconsin Historical Collections* V: 227 (reprint Madison 1907). See also Sibley "Reminiscences" 260, 264.

his accounts that he spent part of the summer hunting and fishing, or at least trading for meat and peltries, and improving his habitation until winter credits could be made.31 Meanwhile, a plot was hatching.

After several disastrous seasons, Rolette had asked first Taliaferro, then Prairie du Chien Agent Joseph M. Street, to change his location at the mouth of the Chippewa River, (this post opposite the mouth of the river on the present site of Wabasha had been Augustin Rocque's for several years) to a new site on the River aux Embarass (Zumbro River) because he was apprehensive of the Chippewa becoming "troublesome" in the former location. In fact, he excused himself, he had had to move Rocque and (John?) Reed, the traders licensed for that location the season before, to a station below the mouth of the Chippewa for that very reason. Taliaferro sent approval of the change to Superintendent Clark, and Rolette's man Joseph Labathe was licensed for the Zumbro. In the meantime, Bailly had gone downriver to procure goods for his winter's trade and, of course, learned of the change. He arrived back at the St. Peters October 28, after stopping at Point au Sable to make credits with some of Red Wing's band (Wakute, Shooter, was the new chief, old Tatankamani, or Walking Buffalo, having died in 1829), and by October 30 had persuaded Taliaferro to issue Joseph R. Brown a license for the mouth of the Chippewa. As soon as possible Brown was on his way.

Given the lateness of the season, it is likely Brown moved into Rocque's old buildings on the Minnesota side of the river or into a former wintering house on Beef Slough. One might think that if Rolette's men found the spot unprofitable, not to mention uncomfortable, Brown would also have a hard time there. And so he did. He had little time to make credits with Red Wing's band before they dispersed for their winter camps in the Big Woods west of the river and few of the Sioux would hang about for fear of Chippewa incursions. Bailly invested $1,500 capital in the venture, and the year's effort returned only $1,000 in salable peltries, plus an unrecorded amount of unpaid credits and leftover goods.32 Rolette was furious because at least part of Brown's returns were at Labathe's expense and because Bailly was trading out of his territory as defined in their agreement of 1828. According to the terms of that agreement Rolette would have to split any losses Bailly might incur, and that would include Brown's outfit. So Rolette had the privilege of paying for his own competition. He protested to Street, who tentatively queried Taliaferro: "Mr. Rolette was complaining that though you had removed the trading location from the mouth of the Chippewa River and directed no license to be given there, you had yourself licensed Mr. Bailly who had a trader there. Is this correct? He so seldom tells the truth I pay little attention to what he says." Taliaferro had to admit it was the truth and the next year

---

31. Bailly St. Peter Daybook, various entries 1830, and Ledger 48–49, 70–71, both volumes in Bailly papers.
32. Rolette to Taliaferro, Sep. 10, 1830, Taliaferro Journal 1830, 125, 128, Taliaferro papers; William Clark, Report on Licenses Issued, Sep. 8, 1831, and Taliaferro, Fur Trade Returns for 1831, OIA LR Missouri superintendency.

reinstated the post for Rolette.33 But Bailly pulled Brown out anyway in April. They had more important plans.

Brown had done all right for himself in his first year back at the St. Peters. His personal expenses totaled $90 less than his earnings from salary and sale of furs and vegetables. He'd possibly taken some loss on the outfit, certainly didn't clear enough to pay his and his men's wages, but Bailly could hope to recoup the lost credits in the years ahead. The Mdewakanton were a good risk, such a good risk that Brown a few years later bought those uncollected credits from Bailly, along with others against the bands led by Little Crow and Wabasha, to try to turn them into cash himself.34 The winter had been extremely cold, the snow excessively deep, hampering the hunters; an early break-up put an end to the trade. By the end of April Brown had closed up his trade and on the twenty-ninth reported in at the St. Peters, accompanied, it would appear from Taliaferro's journal, by a part of Wabasha's band who stopped to pay their respects to the agent.

Bad blood there might be between Mr. Bailly's traders and the agent – exacerbated when Indians "made drunk from liquor received of Mr. Bailly" burned down the council house in August of 1830 – but relations between the traders and other residents at Fort Snelling seem to have continued to be quite friendly. That Brown had some cronies there is made plain by an article he wrote for the Minnesota Pioneer in 1850:

> "On the fifth of July, 18 years ago [1831], Mr. Joseph R. Brown and others brought a 2-pounder down from Ft. Snelling with a supply of powder and provisions and celebrated Independence Day in the mouth of the cave which is now christened Fountain Cave, 2 miles above St. Paul. They discharged their gun once within the mouth of the cave, but as the discharge loosened some of the sand and rocks in the arch of the cave, they did the rest of their firing out of the cave. [They] proceeded to explore the cave with a lighted wax candle ... Mr. Brown thinks for a distance of nearly a mile, when they reached a precipitous water fall. Here their candle burnt out, and as matches were then, if invented, but little used, they had no means with them of lighting another candle, and after long retrogression reached again the mouth of the cave and the light of the sun."35

---

33. Bailly and Rolette had a 50/50 split of profits and/or losses for three years from 1828. Memo of Agreement, Feb. 12, 1828, Bailly papers; Street to Taliaferro, Feb. 7, 1831, Taliaferro papers. Although Wabasha was named for the Mdewakanton chiefs of that name, they did not live there. Wabasha's band had originally lived on the upper Iowa River, but at this time were chiefly at Prairie aux Ailes near the site of Winona; they wintered on the Root, Upper Iowa and Red Cedar rivers. Red Wing's band lived on the west side of Lake Pepin at Red Wing and Point au Sable; in winter the bands moved inland on the Cannon, Zumbro and Whitewater rivers, but also hunted Wabasha Prairie opposite the mouth of the Chippewa and Beef rivers (the Beef, or Buffalo, River then entered the Mississippi just below the Chippewa) and their delta, Beef Slough, so called because of the buffalo that wintered there. The upper end of the prairie had long been a trading site.

34. Credits claimed under 1837 treaty with the Sioux, Bailly's and Labathe's certificates of agreement and transfer of balances to Joseph R. Brown 1831 and 1832, OIA Special Files.

35. *Minnesota Pioneer* (St. Paul), Jul. 11, 1850.

The cave, which still exists in the bluff of the Mississippi not far from Randolph Street in St. Paul, fortunately had a stream running through it. Otherwise our heroes might never have found their way back to the entrance.

Brown's stopping place for the summer of 1831 may very well have been Olivers Grove, now Hastings. There are a couple of reasons to think so. John H. Stevens understood that Brown had abandoned his claim at the outlet of Minnehaha Creek in 1830 and when in 1832 Brown officially moved his location to Olivers Grove it is clear that there was already some type of establishment there. In fact, Olivers Grove had been used by traders of the American Fur Company for a decade or more as a dropping-off point for goods – mostly whiskey – smuggled cross-country to the St. Peter's River above the fort to avoid passing the fort and the agent. John Marsh, then subagent, had remarked on this phenomenon as early as 1826, as if it were common knowledge, "If [the boats] are met below the Pine bend [whiskey] will be found on board. I believe it has been the custom of the traders to smuggle whiskey at that place and introduce it into the country either across the land to some place between Pinneshon's (Bloomington) and Six's village (Shakopee), or to carry it by the fort in canoes at night."[36]

Another reason for placing Brown at Olivers Grove as early as 1831 is suggested by an article on early Minnesota agriculture written in 1860. The editor, L. M. Ford, states that J. R. Brown told him that "In 1831 he... had a crop of wheat where now stands the town of Hastings" and that good timothy hay was also raised by him at Hastings. Some writers have refuted this possibility, deeming it unlikely wheat was ever grown at Hastings; but this statement is definitely attributed to Brown, and while he may have misremembered the date, it is not likely he forgot the location of his farm.[37] There's another small suspicious-looking fact: in April of 1831 a splinter group from Little Crow's band, headed by Nasianpa, Early Riser, sometimes called the Grand Soldier, moved away from Kaposia village (then located where St. Paul's railroad yards are now) and settled at the Pine Bend, a few miles above Olivers Grove. This could have been a struggle for power within the band, but it could also have been a "Brown faction" that had been promised a trader at the new location if they would break away from old Cetanwakamani – Little Crow – who sided with the agent in being opposed to the whiskey trade.[38]

That's a lot of maybes, offset by the fact that there was no trading location established at Olivers Grove. A cabin there would be easy to spot from the river and Taliaferro would lose no time in descending on its

---

36. Stevens *Early History*, 2; John Marsh to E. T. Langham, Sep. 15, 1826 in Taliaferro papers. Olivers Grove had been a convenient holding point for boats going upriver since 1819 when Lieutenant Oliver was wintered in there on his way to New Hope with the supply boat.

37. *Minnesota Farmer and Gardener* I:2, Dec. 1860, L. M. Ford and J. H. Stevens, eds. (St. Paul). John Case ("First House at Hastings") did not believe that Brown raised wheat south of the river and offered as proof the statement of Joseph McCoy, brother of Brown's second wife, that he was "quite sure Joe Brown never did any farming at Hastings." Joseph McCoy, however, was not born until 1834.

38. Taliaferro Journal, Apr. 30, 1831.

owner. The location was, however, in ceded territory, being within the nine-square-mile cession at the mouth of the St. Croix River specified in Pike's treaty of 1805, and thus open to settlement, although nobody ever seems to have dragged out that argument. One could assume Brown had it in reserve; he was certainly aware of the provisions of that treaty five years later when he moved back to the vicinity of the fort.

One place Brown did not spend that summer was at Lands End, although this notion has become well established. The trader at that location was one William Brown, another American Fur Company employee, placed there for the 1831–1832 season to keep an eye on Bailly. The error arises from Taliaferro's habit of referring to both traders simply as "Mr. Brown," although sometimes he distinguishes "Mr. J. R. Brown a trader from Chippewa River" and "Wm. Brown from Devil's Lake."**39** It was the latter who in July took over the trading house at Lands End for the American Fur Company. And why did Rolette feel he had to put another trader in just two miles from Bailly? The simple reason was that Bailly – along with J. R. Brown, Jean-Baptiste and Alexander Faribault, Louis Provençalle and Joseph Laframboise, among others – had set up a strong opposition to the American Fur Company right where the old Columbia Fur Company had proved such an annoyance, on the St. Peters.

---

39. E.D. Neill seems to have initiated this mistake with his account misread from Taliaferro's Journals in "Early Days," 125.

Map 5 Trading locations and Indian villages in the St. Peters region 1830-1832. Dotted lines show cart routes, some no more than Indian trails, used to take goods to the trading posts.

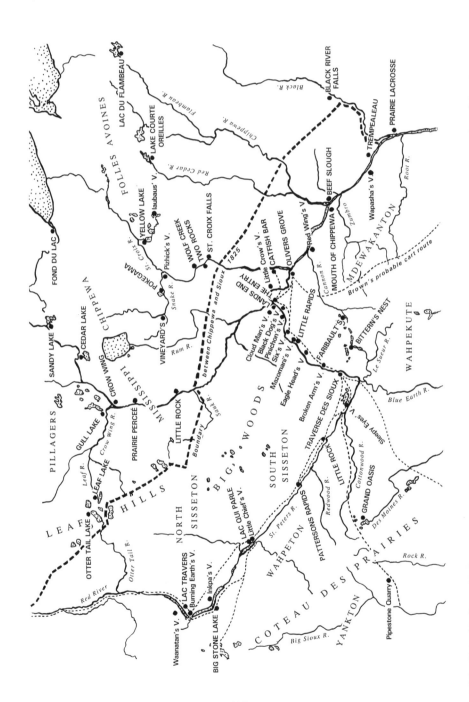

CHAPTER V

"A Mr. Howard from New York arrived today in the express boat," noted Taliaferro in his diary April 26, 1831. "He is engaged in the Am. Fur Company's service."[1]

Seeing Mr. Hiram E. Howard make for Bailly's post must have convinced the agent that the newcomer was an emissary of J. J. Astor. In reality, Howard was an agent of Cephas Mills and Company of New York. Mills and Company had decided to see if money could be made in the northern fur trade, and so sent Howard to examine the prospects. By luck or design, he fell in with Mr. Bailly.

Howard had with him about $3,000 worth of Indian trade goods with the promise of much more, and Bailly took to him immediately. Bailly told Howard that he had had enough of the American Fur Company and of Joseph Rolette, who was in charge of all its Upper Mississippi trade, in particular. He didn't, of course, mention his indebtedness to Rolette, or that his contract was up for negotiation: as Mills sadly remarked later, "He studiously concealed his views." Within two days Joseph R. Brown arrived from the Chippewa to settle up his accounts with Bailly. He immediately joined the coalition and within a week negotiations were complete.

Bailly painted a rosy picture of the possibilities of making a breach in the Colossus' wall of traders, but he was shrewd enough to see that it was going to take a big effort over several years to make an opposition pay. Their plans (at least as Bailly developed them) were awesome: Mills and Company would agree to supply $300,000 capital over a four-year period and Bailly would supply the know-how, based on ten years' experience with Rolette and the American Fur Company. The first year they would need $30,000 to establish a toehold on the St. Peters, St. Croix and Cannon rivers with the Sioux and on the Mississippi and Snake rivers with the Chippewa. They would out-price Rolette, go after all the business they could get, use whiskey if they had to. The second year they would double their efforts and capital, extend posts north to Leech Lake, Sandy Lake, Leaf River and Red Lake, and west to Lake Traverse, Devils Lake,

---

1. Taliaferro Journal 1831 64.

the Sheyenne and James rivers. Heavy losses would be inevitable and expected while they built and expanded the trade. By the third year, with $100,000 worth of goods, they would be at the Yellowstone, by the fourth year at the Rockies! Profits and losses would be shared equally.2 Some of the best AMF traders could be induced to join them: Joseph Laframboise, Louis "Lablanc" Provençalle and the Faribaults were also disgruntled with Rolette's high-handed ways, and each had a loyal following of Indians. Bailly's plan was to strangle Rolette's St. Peter trade before he knew what had happened.

Obviously more goods were needed, and quickly. They made a deal with Alexander Culbertson, sutler at Fort Snelling, to buy out his stock and his trading establishment for $4,000; Culbertson would work for Bailly and Company. When the mailboat left May 3 Howard was on it carrying a memorandum for $15,000 worth of goods for Cephas Mills and Lewis Lyman, partners in the concern, to deliver in August; he stopped at the Prairie to purchase a small additional supply of merchandise.

Secrecy was, of course, useless. Rolette soon found out and rushed to meet the opposition, hiring men at any price and hurriedly making a trip to the St. Peters in July, where he installed William Brown at the Lands End post. But Bailly, according to old-timer Philander Prescott (who watched the proceedings that summer with some amusement), had stolen a march on Rolette, getting most of the best traders before the Company knew what was going on.3 In August Rolette made a whirlwind trip up the St. Peters to Lac qui Parle and Lake Traverse to size up the situation and muster his troops. He knew Bailly could hurt him.

While Rolette reconnoitered, Joseph R. Brown and Alexis Bailly left for the Prairie. There Brown met three men who were persuaded to join the opposition: Bernard W. Brisbois was the grandson of Rolette's old political rival Michel Brisbois and sheriff of Crawford County; Miles Vineyard and James B. Dallam were inexperienced in the Upper Mississippi trade, but had good family connections and apparently some political clout. They may have been chosen to add an aura of legitimacy to the operation and so to influence Joseph M. Street, Indian agent at the Prairie, to issue licenses. After outfitting several oxcarts at the Prairie to bring up Bailly and Company's merchandise (read "whiskey"), these three and Brown drove them through to the St. Peters, where they arrived September 18. Whether or not this was the first trip through by land with carts, it was an unusual enough proceeding to call for comment by Taliaferro.4

---

2. This, at least, was Bailly's understanding; the partners in Mills and Company did not seem to think they would be engaged in a losing business, although they apparently accepted the increased capital for the first year's operations. What Howard thought or conveyed to his principals is anybody's guess. Bailly vs. C. Mills & Co., Civil case files 1823–1836, U. S. Circuit Court, Iowa County, Michigan Territory (plea of breach of covenant), WHS Platteville.

3. Parker *Prescott* 129.

4. Taliaferro Journal Sep. 18, 1831. None of Brown's companions had held licenses in their own name, but were probably not inexperienced traders. Brisbois, twenty-three years old, belonged to one of the Prairie's oldest families and held a not-unimportant political appointment (to which he returned). James Dallam's brother John had some interest in the 1830 Winnebago treaty. James Dallam was later

They would have taken "Rolette's Road," which left the Mississippi near Painted Rock Creek, tracked west on the highland between the Turkey and Upper Iowa Rivers, then turned north to cross the latter near the present state line (Rolette had used this route for years to supply posts on the upper Red Cedar and Des Moines rivers). Somewhere south of Mendota the barrels could be taken off and sent to a point upriver of the fort, while the blameless merchandise went on to Bailly's warehouse.

It was a sensational season. Bailly's men were there first, making the credits. Philander Prescott, sent to oppose Alex Faribault at the Bittern's Nest (probably Lake Elysian on the headwaters of the Le Sueur River), was too late with too little: ". . . [Faribault] had got there long before me and... had given the Indians all a credit and started them off again, so when I got there, there was not an Indian to be seen." Rolette's instructions were to undercut Bailly at any cost. According to Prescott, they sold goods for anything they could, "even if it was half price only of the value of the goods we would sell, to keep them from going to the opposition; and of course, they had to sell at the same price or they could not get any trade. When we could not do anything else, we used to induce each other's men to run off, and we would do all the mischief we could to injure the trade for each other."[5] Prescott was probably right in his belief that the Sioux got more goods from the American Fur Company in the 1831 season than they had received in the three years preceding: "Everything they asked for, even large quantities of liquor was given them." Bailly's other posts did equally well in Sioux territory – J.-B. Faribault at Little Rapids, Louis Provençalle at Traverse des Sioux, Alexander Culbertson at Lac qui Parle and Joseph Laframboise on the headwaters of the Des Moines near Lake Shetek faced little opposition.

Rolette had expected trouble in his territory and had risen quickly to meet it. But Bailly's strike into Chippewa country seems to have caught the agents of the Company's northern department sleeping. This may be laid to his subterfuge of procuring licenses from Joseph M. Street in Prairie du Chien (who had no business issuing them) instead of from Henry Schoolcraft, Indian agent at La Pointe on Wisconsin's Madeline Island. Street sent along the traders' bonds explaining, not very satisfactorily, that Bailly was so late returning from St. Louis that he could not send to Schoolcraft's agency for licenses in time enough to get his men to their wintering grounds. "I should not, even under these

able (despite his association with Bailly) to get an appointment as subagent for the Chippewa in 1835, and was elected to the first Wisconsin Territorial Legislature in 1836. The Vineyard family, originally from Kentucky, were prominent in the Platteville area. Miles W. Vineyard was appointed to the same subagency on Dallam's resignation (there was another appointee briefly between them), later moved to Grant County, Wisconsin, where in 1839 he was appointed Auctioneer by Governor Dodge. His brother was James R. Vineyard, a member of the Wisconsin Territorial Legislature from 1836 until 1842, who shot Charles P. Arndt in the Council chambers over an argument involving the appointment of Miles for Sheriff of Grant County. See "Autobiography of Bernard W. Brisbois," manuscript in MHS, and Bernard W. Brisbois "Recollections of Prairie du Chien" in *Wisconsin Historical Collections* IX: 288 (Madison); for appointments see *Territorial Papers of the United States* XXVII, John Porter Bloom, ed., 57, 88, 226, 960, 1185 (Washington 1969).

5. Parker *Prescott* 130–131

circumstances, have taken it upon myself to grant the licenses," Street wrote to Schoolcraft, "but that I had had the pleasure of... becoming acquainted with you during the short stay which you lately made... from which I have presumed I could do so without its being regarded as an improper interference."6

Bailly's first plan seems to have been to take on William Aitkin, whose Fond du Lac Outfit controlled the trade from Sandy Lake north to Lake Winnipeg. But Bailly found he was short of goods; instead of a $30,000 outfit he had only two-thirds that amount of merchandise from Mills and Company and some of that did not arrive from the east until November. Prudence dictated that he not face such a formidable opponent as Aitkin, who had been trading in that country since 1822, with inadequate goods. So he sent Dallam, whose license was for Gull Lake, only as far as the Prairie Percée (near Little Falls). He made up no outfit at all for Brisbois, who had been licensed for Sandy Lake, keeping him instead at The Entry to handle the local business. But on the St. Croix he set up a strong opposition to the traders supplied from Lac Courte Oreilles and spared neither goods nor strong spirits. Lyman Warren, American Fur Company agent for the Follesavoine and Chippewa of northwestern Wisconsin, glumly reported that winter that a trader from the Mississippi had entered the St. Croix River and introduced whiskey among the Chippewa of Snake River. It was Joseph R. Brown.7

Brown's post was strategically located in the St. Croix valley about five miles above the upper dalles (Taylors Falls) at a place called Two Rocks or The Granite Rocks. There, at the head of a ten-mile stretch of intermittent rapids, the river valley broadens to embrace a wide prairie on the west bank – the perfect site for a trading house, except for its proximity to Sioux territory. Bailly issued Brown $3,000 worth of goods, a hefty percentage of his stock, which was split between Brown at Two Rocks and Miles Vineyard, who wintered for Brown "near Pokegama, on the Snake River." This branch house was probably at the junction of the Portage (Groundhouse) and Snake rivers, not far from Warren's trader Thomas Connor at the south end of Lake Pokegama. Brown and Vineyard did serious damage to Connor's trade, as can be seen from Robert Stuart's complaint to the Secretary of War in the spring: "Our traders of Lake Superior have just arrived with very bad returns and this principally owed to most severe opposition from Prairie du Chien and St. Peters. The traders of these places had large quantities of whiskey and the consequence is a heavy loss to our people who had none. I do not understand how the Indian agent of either place could issue licenses."8

---

6. Joseph M. Street to Henry Schoolcraft, Sep. 5, 1831, OIA LR, Michigan superintendency

7. Among other supplies, Bailly purchased twenty-seven kegs of alcohol at Louisville that fall. Inventory Book Bailly papers, MHS; Henry Schoolcraft Report... 1832, OIA LR Michigan superintendency, and William Clark, License Report 1832, OIA LR St. Louis superintendency. For traders' locations, see Special File #145, Bailly affidavit Jun. 24, 1839, OIA.

8. Robert Stuart to Lewis Cass, Jun. 6, 1832, OSW LR main series. Brown's post was pinpointed by Henry Schoolcraft's party as being on the west bank and less than a mile above the [Dobney] rapids. See Henry Rowe Schoolcraft "Exploratory Trip Through the St. Croix and Burntwood Rivers," reprinted in

The opposition plagued Aitkin on the Mississippi too. He cried to Henry Sibley, Robert Stuart's clerk at Mackinac, "We are annoyed all over the country by opposition, but after the HB (Hudson's Bay) Co., our worst neighbor is Baillies people as they are well supplied with high wines which always bears a predominant sway in the Indian trade." Aitkin also fretted that he had lost business because his prices were too high, a result of having to pay more for goods brought in through Mackinac. "They undersell us and say they are doing a good business," he lamented.9

Another complaint against Brown surfaced the following May. Cetanwakamani, Chief Little Crow, informed Taliaferro that Brown had not left his wintering posts on the St. Croix, but actually was encouraging the Chippewa to plant corn and remain with him there over the summer. This, he said, would keep the Chippewa about the area, hunting and destroying game on Sioux lands, and he was certain this would lead to renewed difficulties with these ancient enemies. Brown was indeed engaged in agricultural pursuits. In his letter to Welsh he discussed his progress with the Snake River Indians:

Figure 12 Cetanwakamani (He Shoots Pigeon Hawks Walking), Chief Little Crow when Brown was at Fort Snelling; his son, Wakinyantanka (Big Thunder) succeeded as chief of the Kaposia band ca. 1834. Portrait by Henry Inman. Minn. Hist. Soc.

"Flushed with my success with the Fox Indians, I determined to see what could be done with the Chippeways, and during the winter selected two men to experiment with. Having induced them to commence work, I furnished tools, seeds &c, and subsisted them and their families until the planting was completed. The crops were well taken care of, and gave a good yield and the failure of the [wild] rice crop in the fall made the corn, potatoes, pumpkins and turnips very valuable to the Indians and probably saved many of the little band from starvation during the winter. The next spring... twelve families planted about one hundred acres."10

Faced with the possibility of Indian warfare (he was quite right to be alarmed, for by August there was a full-scale clash), Taliaferro

Schoolcraft's Expedition to Lake Itasca: The Discovery of the Source of the Mississippi 84, 219, 271 Philip P. Mason, ed. (1958). An 1825 treaty had set a dividing line between Sioux and Chippewa territory which crossed the St. Croix at the Standing Cedars, at the bend of the river a few miles below Taylors Falls. Neither nation was inclined to respect this artificial boundary and clashes were frequent.

9. William Aitkin to Sibley, Feb. 10, 1832, AMF papers, microfilm in MHS.

10. Welsh *Taopi* 67

reproached Bailly, telling him that he thought the chief was right and that the St. Croix posts ought to be abandoned, and not just for the summers, but permanently. Bailly's temper rose. Taliaferro faithfully copied down the tantrum in his journal: "He stated in the course of his observations that he had a mind to kick the chief – or would kick him if he troubled him much – that he had no right to object to him having a trading house on the St. Croix and that it did not concern him. He, Mr. Bailly, supposed that the chief wished him to pay tribute for the privilege of going through the country to the St. Croix, but that he would be d – d if he would do that for a blanket or a keg of whiskey."[11]

The blast to Bailly's sweeping ambitions came with the arrival of Hiram Howard back at the St. Peters in early summer. Warily Howard informed Bailly that his principals were disenchanted with the fur business and wanted out of the contract. They were even willing to take the entire $5,000 loss. Bailly tried to hold them to the contract, reminding Howard that they'd never intended to make money the first year, that Mills had agreed to a four-year venture and that he had conducted his end of the business accordingly. Finally, Bailly magnanimously decided he would agree to the dissolution, provided he could return to Rolette with advantageous terms, even though, as he said, he would be mortified to do so. Howard and Bailly descended to the Prairie to see what terms could be made.

It seemed that things were going to go Bailly's way. Rolette was only too eager to buy out A. Bailly and Company's assets, would even pay liberally to see an end to the competition. Bailly's new contract with Rolette provided a partnership with William Brown to trade for the American Fur Company at The Entry on a 50/50 basis. Bailly was to run the store, Brown to do the legwork (and very likely to keep an eye on Bailly, whom Rolette did not trust one inch!). Finding that Bailly had been taken back by his old employer with better terms than he had had when he left, along with the knowledge that Bailly had pocketed a note on Rolette for $6,600, led Mills and Company to believe they had been victims of "a gross fraud." They were sure of it when Bailly and Rolette filed a bill of complaint against them, hoping to recoup more of Bailly's losses.[12]

Even though Bailly had only three-quarters interest in the new firm of Bailly and Brown, his reinstatement with the Company was thought to be quite a coup. "Mr. Bailly, to keep him quiet and from inducing other oppositions coming into the country, was made chief clerk for the Minnesota River. Mendota was made the main depot for the whole Minnesota trade," wrote Philander Prescott, who was rankling somewhat at Bailly's good fortune and his own assignment to a post with dismal prospects on the Coteau des Prairies.[13] Rolette spent the summer rounding up his stray sheep. Laframboise was given a post on the Big Sioux, the Faribaults and Provençalle kept their old locations. Dallam

---

11. Taliaferro Journal May 27, 1832.
12. Bailly/William Brown agreement May 10, 1832, in Bailly papers, MHS; Bailly vs. C. Mills & Co.
13. Parker *Prescott* 133.

took a post on the Sheyenne River; Brisbois, somewhat disgusted with the way things had turned out, went back to the Prairie and his old job as sheriff.

Joseph R. Brown cut loose from the Company to trade as an independent and made a deal for goods from Bailly and Brown at 50 per cent advance. He anticipated that no license would be issued for the upper St. Croix River, so made plans to move his operations to Olivers Grove. Apparently the news that there would be a trader at Olivers Grove caused two of Little Crow's headmen, Nasianpa and Wakanojanjan or Spirit Light (usually called by the whites Medicine Bottle), to leave Kaposia with parts of that band to establish new villages at the Pine Bend and on Grey Cloud Island. This defection irritated Little Crow no end and appears to be the real reason he wanted Brown removed. Henry Schoolcraft heard all about it when he visited the St. Peters at the end of July. In his conversations with Cetanwakamani, Schoolcraft learned that Brown's location had been changed to the mouth of the St. Croix and that the chief was unhappy with the arrangement. "He spoke against the location of any trading post on the St. Croix which should be fixed so near the lines as to bring the Sioux and Chippewa into contact. He also stated reasons why a post at the mouth of the St. Croix, which is exclusively in the Sioux country, was not necessary," Schoolcraft reported. "He wishes to keep his band together and... requested me to stop at his village and to use my influence in persuading his people to live in one village, and not to continue as they now were, in two distant villages which were not, in consequence, fully under his control."**14**

Taliaferro was away downriver, so Schoolcraft busied himself with hearing the full extent of the allegations against Joseph R. Brown and Alexis Bailly. He was appalled: "No doubt can exist that each of them took in, and used in their trade, a considerable quantity of whiskey," he wrote to Joseph M. Street, advising him to issue no license for the St. Croix or its mouth while Taliaferro was gone. Brown, however, already had his license. As soon as Taliaferro was out of sight, he had approached Captain William Jouett, commanding officer at Fort Snelling and acting agent in Taliaferro's absence, with representatives of Little Crow's recalcitrant bands from Pine Bend and Grey Cloud Island who requested that a trader be situated conveniently for them. Captain Jouett had issued Brown a license for the mouth of the St. Croix "at the request of the Indians concerned."**15** Brown had begun to move his equipment, goods and family as soon as he returned from the Prairie at the end of June; by the end of July Two Rocks was deserted.

On his return trip to La Pointe, Schoolcraft came across the notorious Brown himself, descending the St. Croix with several canoes in company with some Frenchmen and their Indian families. "We examined his papers to determine whether he had been legally licensed and caused a search of

---

14. Schoolcraft Report... 1832.
15. J. R. Brown to Lewis Cass, Jun. 17, 1836, copy in Sibley papers MHS. Brown's account with Bailly, including a complete record of his trade goods, is in Outward Invoices, Bailly papers.

his canoes in quest of whiskey," he reported. None was discovered. Thoroughly annoyed, Schoolcraft revoked Brown's license for Two Rocks for its unexpired time and made a point of burning Brown's abandoned log buildings at the head of the rapids.16 These pyrotechnics bothered Brown not a bit. His claims under the 1837 treaty show that he continued to trade with Snake River Chippewa through 1833 and 1834, possibly from the branch house at the mouth of Wolf Creek, six miles upstream from Two Rocks on the left bank of the river, probably the location known years afterward as Brown's Island.

He continued to entice the Indians to remain in the vicinity through opening farms at Pokegama, the mouth of the Snake River and at Pikgonagon or Yellow Lake. A member of Schoolcraft's party had noticed the cornfields belonging to the village of Pizhick, The Buffalo, located at the mouth of Snake River, and thought they looked "tolerably good," and commented on the corn and pumpkins at Yellow Lake. Brown's revelations to William Welsh indicate he paid little attention to the agent's injunction: "… [At Pokegama] the population more than doubled. Had my means been adequate, I could have had fifty farms started the third year after I located there."17

In the summer of 1832 an incident occurred which had some ramifications for both Bailly and Brown. Joseph Rolette, with singularly bad sense (because the Black Hawk War had stirred up high feelings among the Indians all along the Mississippi) had started sixteen kegs of high wines north by keelboat.18 Taliaferro was not around, but Captain William Jouett, tipped off by someone, met the boat at Lake Pepin, and after a bit of a scuffle, arrested two Fur Company traders, Hazen Mooers and Louis Provençalle, and confiscated the spirits.

This episode caused Bailly much merriment; he gleefully reported on it in August to Street: "There has been some consternation among those nations who have not yet joined the temperance societies… caused by the seizure of some whiskey in Messrs. Mooers & Leblanc's boat; it has completely prostrated all their hope of drunken frolics, and they cannot be made to comprehend that it's all for their benefit. How your friend Rolette will relish the seizure of his whiskey and the retention of one of his boats in no very favorable weather uncovered is more than I can possibly tell."19 Sure enough, several of the barrels were damaged. Rolette suspected, and with good reason, that Bailly was responsible for alerting the authorities to the shipment of spirits. The two had had a running feud from the 1820s that had flared up again during Bailly's opposition, leaving them generally not on speaking terms. Moreover, despite his questionable trade activities, Bailly seemed to be on friendly terms with Fort Snelling's commanding officer. For Bailly, Rolette could only lie in

16. Schoolcraft *Expedition* 81, 84.
17. Douglass Houghton Journal reprinted in Schoolcraft *Expedition* 271; Welsh *Taopi* 64. For Brown's branch house see W. H. C. Folsom *Fifty Years in the Northwest* 123 (St. Paul 1888).
18. High proof alcohol that would be diluted at the destination and flavored with anything handy.
19. Bailly to Street, Aug. 3, 1832, Street papers, microfilm in MHS.

wait. But he could, and promptly did, sue Captain William Jouett and Lieutenant Jefferson Vail, who had aided in the seizure, contending that they were not in Indian country when the raid occurred. The case proved quite a setback to Rolette when the court ruled in favor of the defendants. But it also made Captain Jouett more cautious of interfering with the Fur Company's commerce; his defense had cost him two trips to Mineral Point and Prairie du Chien at his own expense with no indication that the War Department would defend similar actions in the future.[20]

Mooers was lucky his goods had not been seized along with the high wine barrels. He was allowed to proceed so that the Indians in his trading area at the headwaters of the St. Peters and Red rivers would not suffer for want of supplies. With Mooers were his family and several engagés – including James Dallam en route to the Sheyenne – and Helen Brown. A pause here. Almost no mention has been made of Helen Brown and her son Solomon for the very good reason that almost nothing is known about them. Except for that one instance when Taliaferro reported her at the Flint Hills, we don't even know if she accompanied her husband to his posts. Although they had been married for seven years, she had borne Brown only the one son, which can be construed as an argument that they did not live together long. It is plain that the marriage fell apart after the first few years, but neither ever spoke of the reasons. Bernard Brisbois once gave it as his opinion that although Helen "was partially educated, she did not turn out well." How well he knew her we can only guess, but she was his neighbor at The Entry while Joe was trading on the St. Croix. Alexis Bailly, who must have known the facts, said Helen left Joe in the summer of 1831 and went voluntarily into the Indian country, never to return. Brown, in his suit for divorce, said she had abandoned him to take up residence near Fort Snelling where she lived a "lewd and unchaste" life. Those statements were sworn to provide grounds for divorce, and so are marginally true, in fact if not in spirit; the truth was, Brown had a girlfriend on the St. Croix, a part-Chippewa named Margaret McCoy, daughter of his foreman, Francis McCoy. Whether this new *femme* had provided the final straw or Helen had found a more amenable mate cannot be learned now.

Brown resolved his domestic problems by sending Helen back to her relatives in Canada, incidentally beyond the bounds of Michigan Territory, where he intended to divorce her. She may have gone voluntarily, but she didn't necessarily go happily. Mary Mooers, Hazen's daughter, recalled that voyage in the summer of 1832: "I remember how Helen cried on the way up the river on the keel boat. I remember her well, and that she was a fine looking young woman." Her tears were likely not for Joe Brown, but for her son, whom Brown kept with him, no doubt through genuine affection, but also because of the boy's expectations as a halfbreed of the Sioux. Young Solomon was given over to the Baillys to board while Joe

20. Rolette to Bailly, Feb. 13, 1832, Bailly papers; Schoolcraft to Street, Jul. 25, 1832, Street papers; Joseph Rolette vs. William Jouett, Civil Case files, U. S. Circuit Court, Iowa and Crawford Counties, Michigan Territory; Jouett to Adjutant General, AGO LR.

attended to his post, although according to Philander Prescott, who also boarded his son there, Lucy Bailly was a "miserable, vengeful" woman, "remarkably fond of whipping other people's children." Helen apparently soon shook her skirts of Brown; on the way to Mooers' post at Lake Traverse she took up with Dallam and is said to have commented that "she did not know what Mr. Dallam had done to her but she believed that she liked him as well as she ever had liked Mr. Brown."

In 1832 a divorce required an act of the territorial legislature or a lawsuit; neither process was swift. Grounds were few – adultery, insanity, desertion. A year later Joseph R. Brown journeyed to Mineral Point to bring suit against his wife for desertion and adultery. His application was heard at the October 1833 term of the Michigan Territorial Circuit Court. Since the defendant had not appeared, the case was put off until the following year while Helen Brown was advertised for (by tacking up a notice on the courthouse door in Mineral Point – Helen had probably never been in Mineral Point in her life). Helen having failed to appear again in 1834, Brown testified that his wife had left his house in the month of June 1831, first going to Fort Snelling on the west side of the Mississippi and remaining there for about one year, then leaving that place for Lake Traverse and the Whitewood (James) River "where she has resided, as he is informed and believes, ever since" and further that she has since leaving "committed numerous acts of adultery with divers persons." His attorney, Thomas P. Burnett, presented depositions of those who could swear to her bad conduct and the marriage finally ordered by the court to be "dissolved, annulled and set aside and entirely held for naught." It goes without saying the divorce was a put-up job, the flight of the defendant up the St. Peters a prearranged farce.**21** Helen's cooperation may have been enlisted; it would have been best if she agreed not to return for several years and presumably she also desired to be free to marry again. Possibly Brown had dropped a word to Jim Dallam as well; according to the deponents, he played his part well. In any case, Brown returned from Mineral Point in October of 1834 a free man.

Meanwhile, an opportunity for Solomon had come along that was eagerly seized by his father. In 1825 the government had instituted a school for the children of the Choctaw nation near Great Crossing, Kentucky. The school had been expanded over the years to include enrollment of the halfbreed offspring of other tribes; since 1831 at least three Sioux boys per year had been authorized at the Choctaw Academy. The boys' education and board was paid for – all the parents need furnish

---

21. Case "First House in Hastings;" Parker *Prescott* 150–152; "boarding and lodging of your boy $26.50" in Bailly Miscellaneous Accounts, 1832, Bailly papers; affidavits in this and preceding paragraph in Joseph R. Brown vs. Helen Brown. Helen recovered from her marriage to Brown, returned to the Minnesota area married to Moses Arconge, a French Canadian who had worked for Mooers. They had at least two children, were divorced some years later. Helen Brown Arconge ended her days near Greenwood, South Dakota. Brown had likely known his attorney, Thomas Pendleton Burnett, from 1829 when Burnett was subagent at the Prairie. An up-and-coming politico, Burnett became district attorney for Crawford, Iowa, Dubuque and Des Moines counties in 1834 and was elected to the Michigan territorial council in 1835, and to the first Wisconsin legislature in 1836, although he was not seated. (John R. Burgman, ed., *History of the Bench and Bar of Wisconsin* II: 180 [Chicago 1898].)

was clothing and transportation to Kentucky. In the fall of 1833 Major Horatio Grooms, the new subagent, was given permission to select three students from the St. Peters. Brown jumped at the chance, outfitted his seven-year-old with new clothes and two pairs of brogans and sent him off to Kentucky with the Major and William Campbell, son of Taliaferro's interpreter Scott Campbell. Prescott's oldest son, also named William, was supposed to be the third, but his Indian relatives kicked up such a fuss the boy was left behind.

Although the school had been visited by Grooms and was painted by him in the most glowing colors, life there proved to be harrowing for some of the students. The contractor, Senator Richard M. Johnson (soon to be Martin Van Buren's running mate), was a penny-pinching sort who had made the academy a fine instrument for milking the government of its Indian Education Fund while denying his charges adequate food, blankets and medical attention. Bailly's two boys, who were entered in 1834 along with William Prescott, returned to say that they had but one meal a day and were beaten, but since this accusation served to return them to their home it could have been somewhat overstated.

Privations were a fact of life on the frontier. However, Prescott's son died at the academy in late 1835. And Solomon Brown, perhaps not as robust as some of the boys, died there on the fifteenth of October 1836. In his report, supervisor Reverend Thomas H. Henderson explained the death by saying that Solomon Brown "was sent to the school a poor, afflicted child, upon whom three years attention by the best and most skillful physicians had been spent without success." Whether this satisfied Joe Brown is hard to say; he looked into the matter and visited the academy in 1837 when he made a trip back east, but what he learned he kept to himself. After all, many children – sometimes whole families – died of contagious diseases in the nineteenth century. Brown was aware his son was sickly, may have had a premonition that he would not live long. Discussing his family situation in a letter in October of 1836 to Henry Sibley, he wrote "My boy ... might die before he came of age."**22** Two weeks later Solomon Brown was dead.

Brown's move to Olivers Grove in the summer of 1832 had been carefully studied. A comment in the Reverend William T. Boutwell's diary that the traders "carry [their whiskey] from the Mississippi across by land to the St. Peters," makes it clear the location was well known to be in use as a convenient site for landing the liquor barrels. There the contents were put in smaller kegs suitable for transport; the gentle grade and high prairie behind the grove made it easy to leapfrog the kegs by cart to a point upriver of the fort to avoid inspection. Old settlers remembered where

22. Horatio Grooms statement for 1834, Thomas H. Henderson reports Oct. 31, 1834, Jan. 1, 1836, Jan. 23, 1837 in records of the Choctaw Academy, OIA LR Schools; Parker *Prescott* 150–151, 154, 162, 248; Brown to Sibley, Oct. 4, 1836, Sibley papers. Philander Prescott evidently did think the academy culpable: "My son, whilst he was sick, had no nursing at all, and when he would cry for water, the old brute of a Negro woman would whip him for crying for water and food. I never shall forgive myself for sending my boy off to school amongst strangers."

Brown's cabin stood, visible from the river, a little way up the slope in a grove of white and bur oaks. The one-story cabin was built of logs with a door of boards and a window on one side of the door that could be closed with a wooden shutter. Dug into the rocky hillside behind it were storage cellars, possibly used as powder magazines.

The trees that gave Olivers Grove its name stretched northeast from Brown's house along the bank of Lake Rebecca and the plateau above the river; bordering the river were meadows and small lakes ringed by sandbars that supported hazels, willows and maples. It was a pretty place, but the area was said to be shunned by the Sioux, who thought the lake they called Matowakan, was haunted, a circumstance that may have recommended the place as being reasonably secure for Brown's operations.[23] It was soon to become notorious.

While there was probably some type of structure at the site when Brown arrived in 1832, he necessarily put a lot of effort into the place over the next two years. Purchases from Bailly of plank, glass, hinges, padlocks, hasps and staples indicate improvements were being made on an ongoing basis. Although descriptions are lacking, we can imagine cabins for the engagés, livestock shelters and storehouses were nearby. In the fertile flood plain Brown planted grain, vegetables and timothy hay. His dairying operation provided an excess of milk and butter to sell at Mendota. In addition, he had a herd of swine running wild in the bottoms, several span of oxen and a riding horse or two (Bailly sold Brown horses and pigs, wrote a cattle deal with him in 1833, sold him chickens in 1835). Over the winter Brown put his men to fishing through the ice for sturgeon (he sold 1,825 pounds of sturgeon to Bailly in the winter of 1833) and chopping wood for sale to steamboats in the spring. He also put a small crew to work on the upper St. Croix cutting pine logs.[24]

Joseph R. Brown has always received credit for being Minnesota's premier lumberman, based on his cutting of logs on the St. Croix in 1837. But truth to tell, his first documented efforts at lumbering took place over the winter of 1833–1834. He planned to bring out a log raft on the St. Croix that spring, although what he intended to do with it is not clear. Wherever he planned to sell it, at Fort Snelling where wood was always needed or to one of the steam mills downriver, he would have needed a steamboat to tow it up the Mississippi or through Lake Pepin. Where he got his knowledge of logging and rafting is another mystery. Since Joseph Rolette, Jean Brunet and other Prairie du Chien entrepreneurs had been cutting and rafting lumber (mostly illegally) from the Black and Chippewa rivers from at least 1828, men skilled in cutting and rafting logs were readily available at the Prairie. Brown's letter to Bailly in the spring of 1834 makes it clear that it was pine timber he was after, not firewood:

---

23. William T. Boutwell Diary Jul. 25, 1832, in Boutwell papers, MHS; Case "First House in Hastings" and "Pioneer Days."

24. See various JRB accounts for 1832–1835 in Bailly Personal Memorandum Book, Day Books and Miscellaneous Accounts in Bailly papers.

"Please send me by Roberts... all the flour you can possibly spare (not exceeding a barrel). I would also thank you to loan me your X cut saw and to let me have two axes until I get mine from Snake River... Do try and let me have some flour, as I will require it in getting out my raft. I will start next week for Snake River... Packs I have none, unless it is of sturgeon."25

Brown's activities did not pass unnoticed: at Yellow River Charles Wulff Borup, trading for the American Fur Company's Northern Outfit, penned a letter to agent Schoolcraft at the behest of Chief Iaubaus (Little Buck) of the Follesavoine. The Indians, he said, flatly refused to let any whites cut logs on their land and Iaubaus had complained that "logs have been cut this winter – 1833-1834 – by one Big Knife called 'Brown' without asking our permission, nor have we received any remuneration whatever in lieu of those logs which he and his men called Joseph Lagru and Raphael [probably Ralph Reaume] have cut and taken off this spring."26 If any arrangement of payment had been made by Brown it was probably with Pizhick's Snake River band of Chippewa, but since he had also made credits with some Pikgonagon Indians, Borup was understandably anxious to keep Brown out of his territory.

We'll pick up that thread later. Meanwhile... In the spring of 1833 Bailly prodded his former opposition traders to collect everything they could from the Indians who had their credits in hopes of keeping losses at a minimum. Before he left, Taliaferro had been incensed to find Alex Faribault and others at Cloud Man's village near Lake Calhoun removing guns, kettles and even knives. He wrote pompously in his journal, "I caused the Indians to retain their guns and kettles, they living in rather a dangerous place." That goods given on credit actually belonged to the traders never entered Taliaferro's head. Determined to put a stop to what he called "this increasing evil," the agent issued a public notice in July of 1833 forbidding the traders to take back their loaned property and declaring them "out of government protection" if they attempted to do so. Understanding full well the implications of Taliaferro's edict, some Indians developed rather a saucy attitude towards traders who tried to collect credits, even becoming bold about killing and stealing livestock.

Prescott put his finger on the chief trouble: the Sioux had been spoiled by their fat year during the competition. Brown and Bailly were much tighter with their goods, and coupled with this the hunts in 1832–1833 were poor, as game was scarce and the buffalo had moved far out onto the

25. Brown to Bailly, Mar. 6, 1834, Bailly papers. Timber was scarce at St. Louis, especially pine, which could only be procured on the Mississippi's northern tributaries. Ninian Edwards, owner of the Alton (Illinois) steam mill had made a point of needing pine logs from the upper Mississippi and some crews were cutting for him on the Black and Chippewa rivers under contracts with the Chippewa (Ninian Edwards to Cass, Sep. 30, 1831, OIA LR Chicago superintendency). That his activities were illegal surely did not bother Brown; he may have known that Jean Brunet had been arrested heading upriver with a log crew and "edge tools" in 1829, had sued Agent Joseph Street and Major Stephen Kearny and was awarded $1,200 damages by a Prairie du Chien jury (Civil case files, Iowa and Crawford counties).
26. Iaubaus et al. to Schoolcraft, Apr. 30, 1834 (misdated 1833), OIA LR Michigan superintendency, microfilm in Bayless Library, Sault Ste. Marie.

prairie away from the Mdewakanton wintering places. Also many of the Sioux of the Mississippi were much swelled with their prowess during the Black Hawk War (they claimed to have destroyed nearly 200 Sac at the Bad Axe in August), and now they flexed their muscles against the Chippewa and their traders alike. Said Bailly summing up the season, "They now menace our lives with as little remorse as they formerly did that of our stock." He had a point. In October Joseph R. Brown was attacked while attempting to collect debts due him by Red Wing's band – the Indian came at him with a knife but his aim was deflected when a bystander knocked the assassin's arm. Brown was saved, but J.-B. Faribault wasn't so lucky. Just a few weeks after the first incident Faribault was stabbed in the back while shutting the door of his post at the Little Rapids (Chaska) by an Indian to whom he had refused credit. The blade penetrated his lung and very nearly killed him. Bailly, outraged and practically incoherent, wrote to Major John Bliss, Jouett's replacement, detailing these incidents and others as well and declaring that Taliaferro's public notice had the effect of giving the Indians license to steal: "How could we compel an Indian to pay a debt when he knew he could refuse with impunity?" He said he had applied to the agent and had received only the laconic reply that "as he had done, so must he run the risks."27

By this time, the Bailly-Taliaferro feud had gone too far for compromise. The agent was determined to remove Bailly from the Indian country and he soon got his chance. He was convinced the chief whiskey purveyors were supplied by the American Fur Company – he named Hortabis, Mooers, Labathe, Rocque, J. R. Brown, Provençalle, Renville and the Faribaults in a letter to Superintendent Clark in March. William Brown, who had also been a thorn in the agent's side wasn't on the list, but perhaps the agent knew he was quitting the St. Peters trade for Milwaukee, having had enough of Mr. Bailly himself. Fanning the fire, Little Crow and his son Wakinyantanka, Big Thunder, (who became chief on his father's death late in 1833 or early in 1834) came to Taliaferro frequently with their grievances, mostly directed at Bailly and J. R. Brown. "The traders are talking bad about you and call you many hard names," Little Crow told the agent, who malevolently recorded every insult in his journal.28

Taliaferro knew that he would not be able to get away with closing the Mendota post, but he could at least put a crimp in the whiskey traffic by removing the location at Olivers Grove. To this end he sent a letter to Brown June 8 that, as Brown remembered it (the original is gone), stated the agent's intention of abolishing the post the next year and thereafter issuing no license to trade between The Entry and the mouth of the Chippewa. Brown, after reading the letter, handed it to Bailly who demonstrated his disgust at the contents by "applying it in a vulgar manner to his person." Then he handed it back to the Indian who had

27. Taliaferro Journal May 24, 1832; Bailly to Major John Bliss, Jan. 1, 1834, Bailly papers.
28. Taliaferro to Clark, Mar. 15, 1833, copy in Taliaferro papers; Taliaferro Journal Jun. 22, 1833.

borne the message with the remark, "Your father [the agent] is a fool for writing such a letter and you, Nasiampah, are a greater fool for being the bearer of it." This ill-advised act of choler on Bailly's part gave Taliaferro a reason to request Bailly's removal.

The charge: treating the government in contempt in the person of the agent in the presence of Indians! To Taliaferro, this was the ultimate outrage. He would not let it pass. Brown and Philander Prescott, who had also been present, were later asked to provide certificates attesting to Bailly's words and actions. Brown gave it, as he said, under the impression that his license to return to the Indian country depended on his giving it. While Taliaferro remained agent undoubtedly it did.29

Tempers boiled as the summer wore on. At the August annuity payments the agent was personally harassed by Rolette and his emissaries whom he thought felt disposed to cut his throat! Troubles continued even after Taliaferro departed for warmer climes in September. Aside from the stabbing incidents much livestock was wantonly slaughtered by the Indians – Brown had lost most of his swine according to Bailly, and wagons had been stopped and the goods stolen. Said Major Bliss, reporting the traders' claims for depredations that winter, "Many of the traders here have the reputation of being quite unpopular with the Indians and will probably remain so."30

With the spring came Taliaferro and the renewal of complaints from Wakinyantanka against Brown's operation. In early June he told the agent: "There is a white man (J. R. Brown)" – the parentheses are Taliaferro's – "at the Olive Grove (bend in the river) near St. Croix who has a farm and his cattle are running over our lands and scaring off what deer we were in the habit of hunting and also fencing in our old encamping grounds where [we] always place our lodges to fish for our families. We wish him removed as his house is of no use to us in the trade." He went on to predict that Brown would make his houses and fields larger and cut all the timber to sell to steamboats, as he had done for some time. The burden of this grievance seems to be that if the wood is of use to Brown, it should be of equal value to the Indians. In other words, Wakinyantanka would like to be paid for it. According to Brown, Wakinyantanka had no more right to interfere in that part of the Sioux land than a Yankton would have had; his hunts were made on the upper St. Peters and his trade was with the fort sutler, Mirie, who was a clerk for B. F. Baker. Brown accused the agent of putting Wakinyantanka up to this calumny. The true reason for the complaint, said Brown, was that B. F. Baker was a "protégé" of the agent's and if Brown were removed all the trade from the Pine Bend bands of Nasianpa and Wakanojanjan must necessarily come to him.

29. Taliaferro to Clark, Jun. 10, 1833, and Journal, Jun. 22, 1833; Brown to Cass, Jun. 17, 1836.
30. Taliaferro to Elbert Herring, Aug. 20, 1833, in Taliaferro papers; John Bliss to General McComb, Jan. 11, 1834, OSW LR main series. Rolette publicly accused the agent of defrauding the Indians and made charges of improper conduct against him: see Rolette vs. Taliaferro, complaint in suit, Special File #12, OIA.

Brown, of course, had a lot more at stake than his fur trade business. Moving his establishment was going to cost him a great deal of money, at least $5,000 he estimated. He'd put a great deal of time and trouble into the buildings and crops and had let the Indians run up indebtedness, expecting to remain there several years. Also he felt he would be at a disadvantage selling his produce if he were to move to Wabasha Prairie as requested by Little Crow. Nonetheless, on June 10 Taliaferro sent a letter to Brown stating that he was abolishing the post, giving him until November to harvest his crops and remove his belongings. Brown went to the agency to plead his case, taking with him several Indians of the Pine Bend band who also remonstrated with the agent, citing the inconvenience of having to travel to The Entry for their goods and pointing out that any damage done to the game near Olivers Grove interested them alone, not Little Crow. All, of course, to no avail. Brown believed that he was being made to suffer as a result of the ill-will Taliaferro bore Alexis Bailly being extended to those concerned in business with him. To Secretary of War Lewis Cass he wrote that his only recourse was to act toward the agent in much the same way the Indians did toward an evil spirit, that is, to worship him not out of respect, or for any benefits they expect to obtain thereby, but to prevent his doing them harm.31

On the thirtieth of June, 1834, Congress passed a new Indian Intercourse Act which prohibited liquor in any form and for any purpose whatsoever within Indian territory and gave the Indian agents great discretionary power in dealing with abuses of this law. On July 11, even before he could have had official notice of the Act, Taliaferro moved against Bailly. Apprised that Bailly was even then enroute from the Prairie with several boats, some containing whiskey destined for Indian country, he sent subagent Horatio Grooms and a detail of soldiers to intercept him. Grooms was to proceed first to Olivers Grove "and cause a thorough search to be made of J. R. Brown's trading house both within and without for whiskey." If Grooms met the boats above Olivers Grove, he was to examine them, then proceed to Brown's and overhaul that establishment. In vindication of this action, Taliaferro noted in his journal – evidently a draft for his report – that Bailly was given to corrupting the Indians and accused him of introducing some ten or fifteen kegs of whiskey into the country that summer alone. This had resulted in "the Indians drunk and some of our people from the St. Croix on their way to this post on business... insulted by the Sioux at Oliver Grove and very near three of them to loosing their lives." In addition, he stated, much of the whiskey found its way to the soldiers at the fort by means of Mr. Brown and his hired men. Brown and Bailly were both away, as he knew full well, so Major Grooms would have a free hand at discovering any contraband.32

Grooms didn't turn up anything at Brown's, but Scott Campbell, one of Taliaferro's employees, did a week later. Campbell brought in the heads

---

31. Taliaferro Journal Jun. 10, 1834; Brown to Cass, Jun. 17, 1836.

32. Taliaferro to Grooms, Jul. 10 and 11, 1834, in Bailly vs. Taliaferro, complaint in suit, Special file #175 OIA; Taliaferro Journal Jul. 12, 1834.

of two whiskey barrels he said were found in the woods near Brown's, along with the news that Alexander Faribault's cart had been there a day or two before to take off the whiskey in portable kegs – the tracks were quite fresh coming and going. Alarmed by the raid on Brown's, the smugglers sent the younger Faribaults, Oliver and David, to Lake Pepin to warn the ascending boats, but they were too late. Horatio Grooms had found the keelboats about ten miles below the fort, with Bailly on board, along with Moses Arconge, Louis Lablanc, Vital Guerin, Peter Parrant and Joseph Laframboise, and had confiscated six barrels of whiskey. Bailly promptly and characteristically sued the agent for trespass, stating in the complaint that in the fray he had been "greatly bruised, hurt and wounded," and after some nine years managed to get a judgment against him, but the practical and short-term effect was to give Taliaferro a reason for refusing Bailly a license, not only for Olivers Grove, but for the post at Mendota as well. In fact, he went so far as to attempt to obtain an order from the Indian department for Bailly's expulsion from Indian country altogether.[33]

One factor that militated against Bailly was that the American Fur Company no longer wanted him at the St. Peters. Ramsay Crooks, taking over the reins from an ailing John Jacob Astor, was adamant that there should be no liquor introduced into Indian country by any of his employees. Bailly's troublesome ways were no longer to be tolerated. "I deem it of great importance to get rid of him," wrote Crooks to Rolette, "and we never can consider ourselves safe so long as he has any control over the trade of our people."[34] In the matter of Bailly, Rolette found himself in the unusual position of siding with and supporting the agent. Taliaferro eventually turned the confiscated whiskey over to Rolette in return for his bond that Rolette would defend him against all suits on account of the seizure, a move that gives rise to the thought that Rolette may have been the whistle-blower. Crooks was astounded when he heard that Rolette was defending Taliaferro. Bailly also thought the coalition, as he put it, "most unnatural"; to explain Rolette's conduct, he told the Indian office that "it was the result of a bargain with Major Taliaferro: Rolette wanted me out of the Indian country and it would gratify Major Taliaferro."[35] Bailly kept the case dragging on through the courts by suits and countersuits until Rolette's death in 1845 allowed him to win by default.

When Ramsay Crooks came out to Mackinac that August a new partnership was formed. There an agreement was signed between Crooks, Rolette, Rolette's clerk Hercules Dousman and Robert Stuart's young clerk, Henry Hastings Sibley. Sibley had had charge of the Mackinac office for five years and had impressed Crooks with his reliability and

---

33. Taliaferro Journal Jul. 17 and 18, 1843; Bailly vs. Taliaferro, OIA Special file #175.
34. Ramsay Crooks to Rolette, Dec. 20, 1834, American Fur Company Letterbook Vol. I in New York Historical Society archives; microfilm in MHS.
35. Bailly to Elbert Herring, Jul. 29, 1835, OIA Special File #12.

good business sense. He was made Chief Agent for the American Fur Company trade at the St. Peters.[36]

The only problem was how to get rid of Bailly permanently. Even though Taliaferro had refused to renew Bailly's license, Major Bliss, as acting agent while Taliaferro was absent, waffled and granted it and also gave Brown a license for a new location at the mouth of the Chippewa. Bliss defended his actions to Superintendent Clark by saying that his partial acquaintance with the whole matter would not let him determine if he would be justified in refusing them.

Bailly had already demon-strated that he didn't need the American Fur Company to obtain trade goods, so it was paramount that he be bought out and thus prevented from forming another opposition. To this end Henry Sibley went to the St. Peter in late October, stayed with Bailly over the winter, and by May had arranged to purchase Bailly's entire interest in the four fur posts he controlled. That spring Bailly and his family left Mendota for the Prairie where he still retained property. He later moved to the Halfbreed Tract on Lake Pepin and soon established himself on the site of Wabasha.[37]

Figure 13 Henry Hastings Sibley, who replaced Alexis Bailly as chief clerk for the American Fur Co. at the St. Peters in 1835. Portrait by Thomas C. Healy. Minn. Hist. Soc.

Meanwhile, Brown was still a source of anxiety for the officers of Fort Snelling. Over the winter he had moved his stock, not to the mouth of the Chippewa on Lake Pepin, but to the somewhat protected bottom-lands on the east bank of the Mississippi, only a mile or so north of the fort (in the vicinity of Hidden Falls).

In April of 1835 he was found to be building a log house there, well within the cession described in Pike's treaty, and thus, according to Brown, upon the public lands. There were plenty of other squatters on the reserve: refugee families from the Red River had even been encouraged to settle there because their livestock and gardens helped

---

36. Agreement Aug. 15, 1834, copy in Dousman papers. The Company got 50 percent of the profits, took all losses; Rolette had 25 percent, Dousman 15 percent and Sibley 10 percent plus a guaranteed salary of $1,200 per annum.

37. Bliss to Clark, Sep. 30, 1834, OIA Special File #12; Sibley to Crooks, Nov. 1, 1834, copy in Sibley papers. See also Theodore C. Blegen *The Autobiography of Henry Hastings Sibley* 24–34 (Minneapolis 1932).

provide food for the garrison. The military had not disturbed Alexis Bailly, who had a considerable stock of cattle, horses, swine and sheep, not to mention land under cultivation, directly across from the fort's landing at Mendota. But Brown's just-out-of-sight location, that was exceedingly handy to the garrison (there was even a cartway down the cliff to a landing where one of the Red River colonists, Louis Massie, formerly an employee of Robert Dickson, kept a boat directly across from Brown's new edifice), and Brown's reputation as a whiskey-seller made this a situation the army couldn't tolerate.

Figure 14 Hercules Dousman, partner with Sibley and Rolette in the St. Peters Outfit. Minn. Hist. Soc.

Major Bliss sent Lt. McClure to instruct Brown to leave and return to his licensed location; Brown replied he would not leave the reserve and his man, Ralph Reaume, when ordered to stop building, said he was only bound to obey orders from Mr. Brown. Brown repeated his refusal to Major Bliss, saying he had a perfect right to settle upon any public lands one mile or more distant from any U. S. fort and he was going to uphold that right. "He then notified me that he abandoned his trading post at the mouth of the Chippewa. I am informed that he has brought on a large stock of cattle and also that he has been previously advised by counsel that heavy damages would be awarded for any forcible removal," wrote Bliss to Major General E. P. Gaines, commander of the western department of the army. Nervously, he asked for a ruling; he was unsure of his powers since it was patent that the Indian title to the land had been extinguished and it also seemed that only the President had the power to employ military force in removing intruders from public lands. Brown was undoubtedly aware, probably through T. P. Burnett, that a similar incident had taken place at Fort Howard in 1825; John P. Arndt, operator of a tavern on the opposite bank, had been arrested, along with his ferryman and customers. They brought suit against the officer of the day in Judge James D. Doty's court at Green Bay and were awarded a $100 fine. (Doty had since become a member of the legislative council of Michigan Territory – in which Brown resided – and had made a reputation upholding citizen's rights in conflicts with military authority. An early resident of Prairie du Chien, Doty was one of Burnett's oldest friends.)38

Bliss received formal authorization to remove Brown in September, but before Brown's rights could be put to the test, the issue was decided in another way. On June 17, 1835, Joseph R. Brown signed an agreement with Henry H. Sibley to work for the American Fur Company's Western Outfit.39 By September he was on his way to a new post at Lake Traverse, near the headwaters of the St. Peters River, and for a few years relative peace and harmony reigned at the St. Peters.

Figure 15   Old Columbia Co. post at Lake Traverse (rebuilt by Brown in 1835) showing Sioux scaffold burial, foreground. Drawing by Samuel Seymour in 1823. Minn. Hist. Soc.

38. Bliss to J. McClure, Apr. 13, 1835 and McClure to Bliss, Apr. 15, 1835, enclosed in Bliss to Gaines, Apr. 30, 1835, AGO LR. As attorney for the American Fur Company, Doty had served as counsel for both Rolette and Bailly when their liquor shipments were seized. Judge Doty defined his principles in 1831: "When I came to this District all power was in the hands of the army and the Indian traders. In establishing a civil jurisdiction I was brought directly in contract with them, and the sole question was, whether the Laws should prevail, and all the members of society be brought within the rules prescribed for its government. The courts are established, and the army is dissatisfied." (Alice E. Smith *James Duane Doty: Frontier Promoter* 93 [Madison 1954]. For more on Doty and Burnett, see especially pages 72–73, 90, 153.)

39. Cass to Bliss, Sep. 3, 1835, OSW LS; Brown/Sibley agreement Jun. 17, 1835, Sibley papers.

CHAPTER VI

"A SERIOUS DIFFICULTY WITH THE INDIANS AT LAKE TRAVERSE."
SAMUEL POND

The bed of the St. Peters was filled with clamshells set edgewise that tore at the moccasins and bare feet of the men struggling to move the cumbersome mackinac boat upstream. Slowly they inched her up, taking half-loads at a time, sometimes in the shallowest parts of the river taking the heavy bales on their backs and stumbling upstream afoot over the bars of rock. Never again, vowed Brown, would he attempt to take any boat upriver further than the Traverse. The sinuous river, dwindling in the heat of summer, had barely enough water to float a canoe, let alone a six-ton boat. Even after leaving half the goods at the Little Rock they still had to lighten the load frequently to drag the boat over places where the water was not more than six inches deep. They had departed July 30 from The Entry; by August 15 they had succeeded in gaining Patterson's Rapids, where Renville was supposed to meet them with oxcarts for the last leg of the journey to Lake Traverse.

No Renville. An express sent to Lac qui Parle to inquire what had delayed them was informed that an invoice was wanted so he should know how many carts to send. At last, wrote Brown to Sibley, "the squire" coming to the conclusion that all the carts were enough, and having no more to send, the transportation was provided and only nine days were lost. It was not, Brown might have reflected, an auspicious beginning for this new venture.[1]

It should have been obvious to anyone who knew either of them that Joseph R. Brown and Joseph Renville Senior would not be likely to get along in joyous harmony. Renville, who since the War of 1812 had lived in this country in the style of a medieval baron, surrounded by a bodyguard of fierce Wahpeton soldiers and exercising absolute control over relatives and retainers alike, was not about to have his orders questioned by any brash young upstart the Fur Company should elect to send into his bailiwick. Brown was not disposed by nature to put up with the old man's autocratic ways, much less take orders from him. In theory, all they were required to do was cooperate. According to his agreement with Henry

---

1. Brown to Sibley, Sep. 28, 1835, Sibley papers; Taliaferro Journal Jul. 30, 1835. The Traverse, or Traverse des Sioux, was a fording place on the St. Peters a few miles below the present city of St. Peter; the trading location called Little Rock, or Petite Roche, was northwest of present New Ulm near Little Rock Creek; Patterson's Rapids was a short distance above the mouth of the Redwood River.

Sibley, Brown was to run the Lake Traverse post; his was the responsibility for the equipment, supplies and men. Renville, long an independent, had agreed to operate the Yankton Outfit for the Fur Company for 50 percent of the profit or loss, handling all transactions with the Indians.2

It was clear to Brown from the moment he arrived at Patterson's Rapids that the arrangement was not going to work, but he decided to submit to the situation for a short time, confident that when Sibley made his inspection tour in a few weeks he could get him to adjust matters. Meanwhile, he blew off steam in a letter to Sibley, which, in six closely written pages, managed to detail the grievances, notice the scandal, give a business report, forecast the returns and tell Sibley of what was needed to make the Yankton Outfit successful!3

All things considered, Renvilles notwithstanding, Brown realized he was lucky to have this opportunity. When he was evicted from the post at Olivers Grove he was over $2,000 in debt to the old concern (J. J. Astor's American Fur Company; the reorganized business under Ramsey Crooks was generally called the 'new concern'); the proffered post at the mouth of the Chippewa had little potential and during the last season he had run up more unpaid credits and another $328 in debts while taking out almost no packs.

Bailly had gotten out with his feathers ruffled but his finances in good shape, as Sibley had been required to buy him out lock, stock and leaky old barrel. And, in that summer of 1835, Brown had been in more danger than he realized of being evicted from the reserve; in Washington, Secretary of War Lewis Cass had referred the matter to President Jackson whose directive was that the intruders should be removed and the law enforced. Brown had given up the only license Major Taliaferro would consider issuing to him and had no prospects for a post, unless he cared to follow Bailly below. Sibley provided the best possibility for employment. And Sibley, searching about for someone competent to straighten out the books of the upper posts (Crooks in desperation to make sense of their accounts had written to Sibley that he doubted the traders of the upper St. Peters had any system of business, but maybe he could ascertain how they contrived to destroy time!) found just the man in Brown.4

In return for absolution of his debt, Brown signed on with the Western Outfit as clerk and trader for four years with a salary of $150 per annum and provisions – his contract specified the grub he was entitled to: two barrels of pork, three barrels of flour, five pounds of tea, ten pounds each

2. Agreements, Sibley and Rolette with Joseph Renville Nov. 6, 1835, and with J. R. Brown Jun. 17, 1835, Sibley papers.

3. Brown to Sibley, Sep. 28, 1835. Separate books were kept for each trading venture and outfit names changed from season to season. Sibley's St. Peters Outfit was part of Rolette's Upper Mississippi Outfit. Joe's Yankton Outfit was a part of Renville's Western Outfit.

4. Lewis Cass to John Bliss, Sep. 3, 1835, OSW LS; Ramsay Crooks to Sibley, Apr. 18, 1835, AMF Letterbook (New Concern) I, AMF papers, New York, microfilm MHS. Brown updated and consolidated the trade account books kept at Lake Traverse by Mooers and earlier traders; see "Commissioner's Report: Ramsay Investigation," U.S. Senate Document 61, 33rd Congress, 1st session 238 (1854).

of coffee and sugar and one keg of lard. The contract also required that Brown obey the lawful orders of the legally authorized agents of the Western Outfit, and that meant deferring to Renville in the trade. This he said he would do, but the system broke down when Renville and his son Joseph Junior declined to spend any time at the post, leaving Brown to deal with angry customers who would not understand that he had no power to issue credits himself. Brown saw right away that "there is great likelihood of my having all the work to do, and should there be a failure … I shall be blessed with the censure, whereas if the equipment does well, it certainly cannot be attributed to my exertions." He also took exception to Renville's system of issuing credits to every Indian willy-nilly as a method of preventing them from killing his cattle – an early example of paying for protection. Apparently it worked, Brown noted to Sibley, as no cattle had been killed, although old age had toted off a horse. But, he said, the credits are made so high that if the Indians do not hunt and earn enough to pay in the fall they cannot be credited further in the winter "and then the farce will commence."[5]

Figure 16 A typical trader's fort on the western plains. The trader and his interpreter parley with a Sisseton hunter. Brown's Lake Traverse post would have looked much like this. Drawing based on Brown's and Sibley's descriptions, sketches of other western posts and excavations at Ft. Renville, Lac qui Parle.

Brown's post was on the southeast shore of Lake Traverse, about five miles north of the present town of Browns Valley, and from his description of the age and deteriorated state of the buildings may have been the very place William Dickson had headquartered for the old Columbia Fur Company. For some years past Hazen Mooers had run the post for the

5. Brown to Sibley, Sep. 28, 1835.

American Fur Company, but in 1835 Mooers joined Benjamin F. Baker as an independent trader and moved his establishment to the Little Rock, leaving the Lake Traverse post to be covered by Renville from Lac qui Parle.6 Fearful of the quarrelsome nature of the Sisseton and Yankton, the builders had enclosed the houses within a stockade of substantial oak pickets, pierced with portholes for muskets and fortified with blockhouses at opposite angles. Except for delegations of three or four chiefs, Indians were never allowed inside; all trading was done through an opening in the massive doors, which was closed up at the end of the day. This palisade was not large enough to protect all the livestock, so earlier traders at Lake Traverse and Lac qui Parle had learned to live with having horses and oxen shot down in their presence. "[They] are unable to obtain any redress and perhaps even dare not reprove those who have done it," declared Thomas Smith Williamson, missionary at Lac qui Parle.7

When Brown moved in, the log buildings were exceedingly dilapidated, their sod chimneys crumbling, their roofs covered with grass. Half were unfit for any use, he told Sibley, neither were there stables or fences that could be called by those names, a situation that would quickly have to be rectified if they were to provide protection for the cattle and horses during the severe winter months ahead. On all sides stretched treeless prairies, in places blackened by fire and strewn with the bleached bones of buffalo, relics of the immense kills made by the Yankton in former years.8 Wood was scarce. The fort's firewood had to be brought in from a small stand of trees in a sheltered ravine a mile and a half distant. The logs of which the place was built must have been laboriously dragged from the Coteau des Prairies, the ridge of rock and glacial debris rising out of the prairie some fifteen miles to the west that divides the watershed of the Missouri from that of the Minnesota River and Red River, which flows north to Hudson Bay. A large Yankton village, headed by Waanatan (Little Charger), was located on the west side of Lake Traverse in the summer; other bands – Yankton, Sisseton and Wahpeton – had summer camps near the two big lakes that straddle the continental divide and on their islands. From Big Stone and Traverse lakes, and from the many small lakes and swamps on the coteau, they gathered muskrats by the thousands, as well as beaver, otter, fisher, raccoon and fox. Over the winter the Indians dispersed to the Sheyenne and James rivers, often wintering as far away as Devils Lake or "The Place Where They Cut Bows" (Jamestown), following the buffalo herds which were their chief source of wealth, as well as of food and shelter. And, since the buffalo were also the Fur Company's source of wealth (they would take out nearly seven tons of hides, 135 hundred-pound packs, the following spring), the traders must needs follow the

---

6. For location of this post see Grace Lee Nute "Posts in the Minnesota Fur Trading Area" in *Minnesota History* XV: 377–379 (St. Paul); Parker *Prescott*, n155; George W. Featherstonhaugh *Canoe Voyage Up the Minnay Sotor* I: 391 (reprint St. Paul 1970).

7. Blegen, *Sibley Autobiography* 193; Thomas Smith Williamson to David Greene, Aug. 5, 1835, ABCFM papers, copies in MHS.

8. Brown to Sibley, Sep. 28, 1835; Featherstonhaugh *Canoe Voyage* I: 383–384, 389.

Indians. To be closer to their clients, the company had placed a branch house two days' march from the main post on the Sheyenne River. At this branch house and the main post were stationed about a dozen men, mostly French Canadians, serving an area encompassing more than 10,000 square miles.[9]

On his arrival at Lake Traverse, Brown found that in addition to repairing the buildings and bringing in the hay and getting his equipment off to the Sheyenne station in steadily worsening weather, he had to deal with problems of a more domestic nature. In residence in the cabin reserved for Joseph Renville was Madeleine Winona Crawford (usually called Winona, which means first-born daughter, although her Indian name was Mazardewin, Tinkling Iron), widow of Renville's brother, Victor Renville (Ohiye), who had met his end in a raid against the Chippewa near Baker's post at Crow Wing in 1832. She had been taken as a second wife, in time-honored Sioux tradition, by the squire himself, but this acquisition by a man supposed to be a devout Catholic and, indeed, neighbor of a missionary station, was the cause of great scandal. "The squire has been presented with and forced to accept of a second better half," wrote Brown to Sibley with tongue in check, "so that he may now be considered to consist of three halves, two better & of course the other mediocre, or probably inferior. Although this is an affair that causes him a great deal of uneasiness, as it will give bad ideas to his children, etc., still *entre nous*, he took good care to make the application early last summer and arranged the whole forcing part of the business with the dame & her relations. She is his brother's wife who was killed by the Chippeways, and according to law in such cases made & provided belongs to him." Renville, however, very wisely felt that he could not have his two femmes in the same camp and so had stationed Winona Crawford at Lake Traverse and his other wife, Mary, a sister of Big Thunder, at Lac qui Parle.[10]

Brown might laugh at Renville, but he was far from immune to the blandishments of the fair sex himself, and indeed, had got quite a reputation back at The Entry, which evidently he did not bother to notice or correct. While trading with the St. Croix Chippewa in 1831, he began living with Margaret McCoy, a mixed blood of Chippewa and French Canadian parentage from Red River (Margaret was often called by the diminutive Mary, and sometimes referred to as Cecille, presumably a pet name). Having been stung once by an unhappy and perhaps bitter marriage, Joe Brown had no intention of making Margaret McCoy his wife, not even when he found out as he was preparing to move to Lake Traverse in the summer of 1835 that she was pregnant. He would not take

---

9. Brown to Sibley, Jan. 25, 1836, Sibley papers; Williamson to Greene, Aug. 5, 1835.

10. Brown to Sibley, Jan. 25, 1836; Thomas Hughes *Indian Chiefs of Southern Minnesota*, 53, 112 (reprint Minneapolis 1969). Victor's role in leading a Sioux war party to the Chippewa camp on the Mississippi was well known. Taliaferro (according to his Journal) had been instrumental in persuading Dr. Thomas S. Williamson and Alexander G. Huggins to locate their Indian mission at Lac qui Parle to help keep an eye on the Renvilles.

her along, giving as his excuse that she, a Chippewa, would be in mortal danger there, which was quite probably true. He left her with her family – her father, Francis McCoy, was in charge of Brown's goods at The Entry – even cautioning Sibley at one time "not to give anything to McCoy's daughter on my account." This heartless-seeming attitude earned him some censure; George Featherstonhaugh, an English explorer visiting Fort Snelling that September, heard and cheerfully repeated the gossip: "Mr. Brown, the Sergeant [French] says, is a gay deceiver amongst the Indian fair. First he married after the Indian fashion a half-breed young lady, a daughter of a Col. Dixon, then became tired of her. He connected himself with another half-breed, a daughter of one McCoy, a trader. They had both of them lived with him here, but casting off the second he got such an exceedingly bad character for abandoning his women and children that he had found it convenient to move away to some distant part of that country. The probability is that he also has two or three wives in the United States."**11**

When Featherstonhaugh arrived at Lake Traverse, on a geographical reconnaisance mission for the U.S. government, he quickly tumbled to the *ménage à trois* he found there. The scandal about Renville and Winona, who was serving as Brown's cook, did not escape him: "I rather think she makes Mr. Brown's cabin her home when Renville is not here. But Mr. Brown, who is cursed with a restless penchant for ladies is notoriously engaged in trying to persuade her young daughter to live with him as his wife and offers her all sorts of presents to persuade her, but hitherto in vain." Mr. F., with his quick analysis of character and situations and his bad taste in writing it down, made enemies everywhere, and Brown was no exception. While accepting Brown's hospitality, he commented on the coarse way he lived – "a few broken plates placed on a very dirty board, with some coffee and maize cakes to correspond" – and grumbled about the hardness of the floor and unsuitability of the water for washing. Brown seems to have urged him to move on. Mr. F. had been playing up to Winona and had given both her and her daughter presents. Says Featherstonhaugh of Brown, "He saw that the women had commenced their intrigues and was annoyed by it. As long as he had been the only person there, things went on quietly and he could take his own time to carry out his plans of domestic happiness, but the arrival of my party had awakened amongst the women all their love for finery and intrigue and it

---

11. Brown to Sibley, Oct. 4, 1836, Sibley papers; Case "First House;" Featherstonhaugh Journal, 109, 113, microfilm copy in MHS (it is interesting to compare this manuscript with the published *Canoe Voyage* 385–387 to see the change of sense in the rewriting some months later). Featherstonhaugh is generally said to have been pronounced either "Fanshaw" or "Furstonhaw." Although Mr. F. was widely criticized by contemporaries and later historians—Edward Duffield Neill even went so far as to call the work "remarkable for its vulgarity" and the author "devoid of the instincts of a gentleman"—he was a keen and careful observer and often caught the character of his subjects, perhaps too well for their liking. Philander Prescott held a similar opinion of Brown's character: "Mr. Brown had left his first wife, a Sioux half-breed, Miss Ellen Dickson, and married a Chippewa half-breed. He got a divorce from her on the flimsy excuse that he wanted to go to trade with the Sioux Indians and he was afraid they would kill his wife... and married a Sioux half-breed whom he lives with up to this time, and as many more as he likes." (Parker *Prescott* 171).

was evident that things would get in a mess of some kind or other if we staid." Mr. F. beat a strategic retreat.12

Figure 17 Susan Frénière, third wife of Joseph R. Brown. Picture in author's collection.

Deplore, if you will, his bad taste in publishing it, but Featherstonhaugh had hit the nail on the head. The fifteen-year-old maiden whom Brown was so leisurely pursuing was Susan Frénière, the child of Winona's first marriage to Narcisse Frénière, who had been born in this very post on Christmas Day 1819. Narcisse had abandoned Winona (or she him) shortly after the girl was born and had taken a new femme from the James River Yanktonai band with whom he wintered, fathering at least four more children, half siblings to Susan.13 What Mr. F. did not know was that Narcisse was actually on Brown's payroll that season, but had been discreetly assigned to the Sheyenne camp (Featherstonhaugh had extracted quite a lot of information, but not that tidbit, from Narcisse's twin, François Frénière, who was serving as Brown's interpreter).

Susan was well worth pursuing. She was petite and graceful as a deer, so slender that a man's two hands could span her waist. Her oval face had the high cheekbones of the Dakota and this, with her black hair and shy black eyes, gave her more of the appearance of her mother's people than her father's. She spoke only Dakota with fluency, although she could

12. Featherstonhaugh Journal 108, *Canoe Voyage* 387. Although Brown's promiscuity was snickered at by some of his contemporaries, he seems to have been no better or worse than most. For a trader, a woman was an economic necessity as well as an important link to the Indians with whom he traded. She was his cook, managed his house in his absence, made moccasins and clothing, prepared skins, gathered wild food and watched over the garden; a man who did these things for himself would be laughed at by the Indians and by his employees. In return, the woman gained a certain prestige and her family a means of support. Many of these "arrangements" were as enduring as any marriage: Philander Prescott, for example, lived with his Indian wife for fourteen years, finally marrying her in a church ceremony. Lawrence Taliaferro had an Indian wife and two daughters whom he openly acknowledged and Henry Sibley also took an Indian wife who bore him a daughter, Helen, but these men later married white women and the Indian "wives" were discarded discreetly, if painfully. For more, see Blegen *Sibley Autobiography* 39, Parker *Prescott* 56.

13. Narcisse and François were employed by Hudson's Bay Company clerk John Bourke at the Lake Traverse post in 1819–1820. The night Susan was born all the engagés and many of their Indian friends got royally drunk. In 1820 the Frénières went over to the American opposition at Big Stone Lake. Bourke relates they sent for their wives that next December; possibly Winona elected to remain at Lake Traverse with Victor Renville. John P. Bourke Journal of Transactions in the Sioux District 1819–1820, Dec. 26, 1819, and Upper Red River Journal 1820–1821, Nov. 13, Dec. 2 and 7, 1820; both volumes in Hudson's Bay Company papers, Winnipeg.

converse in French. Her Indian name was Hinyajicedutawin (Soft Scarlet Down) and she was a direct descendent of old Tatankamani (Walking Buffalo) who had been Chief Red Wing when Joe Brown first came to the upper Mississippi. Her mother was the offspring of Red Wing's daughter Mazadehdegawin and Lewis Crawford, a long-time British trader on the upper Mississippi and trusted ally of Robert Dickson. Although of Mdewakanton heritage, she was also related to the Sisseton of Lake Traverse where she was raised, through an aunt who had married into the family of Wambiupiduta (Scarlet Plume), chief of the Sisseton village at the foot of Big Stone Lake, and by extension to the powerful Yankton chief Waanatan, who was married to this aunt's daughter. Her half brother, Gabriel Renville, born in 1825 to Winona and Victor, had ties through his father to the Little Crow band. So, although the exact importance of these kinship ties is difficult to assess and, to give him credit, Brown was probably less interested in Susan's lineage than in her fresh beauty, but if he wanted to ally himself to the Sioux through dynastic lines, he could hardly have picked a better consort.**14**

Brown's domestic arrangements were considerably furthered through an accident which took place during Sibley's inspection tour in mid-October. The arrival of Sibley's entourage had created rather a festive air about the post. The men got up a pistol shooting competition, perhaps in deference to Sibley, who was known to be a crack shot and an avid sportsman. Joseph Renville had brought with him a pair of fine British dueling pistols, but being unused to their hair triggers he unfortunately shot before he was ready and the wild shot hit his niece, who was standing with a bevy of women and children gathered to watch the sport. They carried her into Brown's quarters, but there was little they could do for Susan except stop the bleeding and wash the wound, for the ball had passed right through her groin. Sibley immediately rode for Lac qui Parle to find Thomas Williamson, who was the only person with medical training west of Fort Snelling, and sent him to the aid of the injured girl.

---

14. Narcisse Frénière and his twin brother François had traded in the Lake Traverse area for several decades for the Hudson's Bay Company, the Columbia company and the American Fur Company. They were probably sons of Charles Jacques Frénière, employed as a trader by the General Society (Michilimackinac), who was married to a daughter of the Yankton chief Takokokipixni (Who Fears Nothing). Narcisse (called Cekpa, Twin) had families by at least two Yanktonai women. Winona Crawford, born about 1805, was called Madeleine by the French Canadians, later took the name Abigail—probably her baptismal name. Her Indian name Mazardewin is translated by some as Ringing or Tinkling Iron, by her grandson Victor as Iron Ring (the "r" in her name represents the guttural, so is pronounced maza-'hde-win). She moved with her mother to the Big Stone Lake area when Crawford abandoned them (he also had children by a Prairie du Chien woman, Pelagie Lapointe, and in 1806 married Sophie Mitchell at Mackinac where he remained, starting another family). Mazadehdegawin remarried and Winona's half sister, Julia Hazatainwin, was born near the coteau in 1813. Winona's second marriage to Victor Renville, produced two daughters that did not live past childhood and one son, Tiwakan (Spirit Lodge) or Gabriel Renville. Victor's mother was a sister or parallel cousin of Cetanwakamani (Little Crow I) and his father a General Society trader named Joseph Rainville. This genealogical material is compiled from "Proceedings of the Court of Inquiry Against Joseph Ainse" *Michigan Pioneer and Historical Collections* XV: 543–546 and "Reply of Joseph Ainse" in same XXIII: 644; Hughes *Indian Chiefs* 87-88, 122; Winona Blanch Allanson *Indian Moons* 7–8 (St. Paul 1927); S. J. Brown to Doane Robinson, Mar. 12, 1921 and Jul. 28, 1904 in Robinson papers, SDHS; BIA records, Goodwill, SD; Victor Renville "A Sketch of the Minnesota Massacre," *Collections of the State Historical Society of North Dakota* V: 251, 254, 270 passim. See also Appendix A.

The wound infected and for several weeks, Susan was very ill indeed, but at last Dr. Williamson's ministrations proved effective. A month later Susan was pronounced by Williamson "nearly well." While she convalesced, Brown had a opportunity to work his wiles on her. By spring Susan had yielded and was living with him as his femme.15

There were no *mangeurs du lard* – pork eaters, common canoemen – among the men at Lake Traverse and beyond. They were *hivernants* (winterers), seasoned veterans, indefatigable at canoeing and portaging bales and trusted to go *en derouin* – which meant following the Indians to their remote winter hunting grounds with a limited amount of trade goods to secure the peltries on the spot. Brown's man at the Sheyenne, an Englishman named James Clewet, was only twenty-five, but had been in the Dakota country for three years with Hazen Mooers. With him at the winter station were the Frénière brothers Louisan and Narcisse, the latter described by Brown (who was well aware of his relationship to Susan) as untrustworthy and worse than anyone but the Renvilles – "and that is saying a great deal!" – although he thought Louisan a good man to have. The third brother, François, served as Brown's interpreter and "as he is trusted with nothing he will answer very well." The rest of the crew, a mere half dozen plus Joseph Robinette, the blacksmith, seem to have been no better or worse than Brown expected.16

Farmers, however, they were not. Brown brought energy and drive to this post and he insisted that his men work as hard as he. There was hay to make, winter wheat to plant, a corral and barn to build, fence to mend, wood to chop. ("We burn 2½ to 3 cord a day," wrote Brown to Sibley in January, requesting that he furnish the outfit with stoves for economy, indeed for necessity; "I will admit they cost money, they are heavy for transportation in carts and in fact I will admit almost anything to satisfy you," he acknowledged, if he could be relieved of the burden of cutting wood and hauling it more than a mile, a process requiring three men full time. "I am satisfied that with the stoves two men beside the blacksmith is all that is necessary for this post," he wrote, adding that the timber would last twice as long. He didn't get them.) Soon the heavy labor, and Brown's way of keeping his men at it, caused much grumbling among the help. Brown even went so far as to take a man that Renville had sent up to

15. The story of the shooting is in Blegen *Sibley Autobiography* 37–38; Taliaferro remarks in his Journal, Oct. 30, 1835, "Joseph Rainville accidently shot his niece." Williamson to Sibley, Nov. 25, 1835 (misdated 1825, misfiled in Sibley papers as 1836): "I went to Lake Traverse about three weeks ago to see the unfortunate girl. I found her quite ill in consequence of the matter not getting sufficient vent." Folwell (*Minnesota* I: 198–199) states that Williamson was a graduate of the Yale Medical School, had practiced medicine nine years before becoming a minister of the gospel. He was appointed missionary to the Dakota in 1834, had arrived at Lac qui Parle in July 1835.

16. Brown to Sibley, May 6, 1836, Sibley papers; for more on Clewet (sometimes Clewett) see John Fletcher Williams *The History of the City of St. Paul and of the County of Ramsey, Minnesota*, 88–89 (St. Paul 1876); for the derouin (called by Brown "durwin," sometimes "derouine" or "drouine," derived from *courir en derouin*) see Reuben Gold Thwaites "A Wisconsin Fur Trader's Journal 1804–1805" in *Wisconsin Historical Collections* XIX: 200 (Madison 1910).

repair traps at the blacksmith's shop and turn him to his own work, an event that rankled Renville the more as the traps remained unrepaired.[17]

Another bone of contention was the quantity and quality of provisions. It may have been Brown's personal conviction that a diet of corn was adequate for the engagés or a result of attempts to cut expenses or stretch provisions, but by the start of Brown's second season at Lake Traverse complaints had reached Sibley that Brown was stinting his equipments in provisions, especially flour (although it was Sibley himself who demanded that Brown "try to reduce the expenses of the Yankton Outfit within reasonable bounds"). Of course, Brown had confidently expected to produce some flour from the wheat grown at Lake Traverse over the summer, but that hope had proved futile. "It is true," he wrote to Sibley, "that you had supposed that I would make flour with a corn mill and sift it through a sieve that grains of wheat will pass without touching, but the birds have taken upon themselves to save me that trouble." The Frénières were the chief complainers. According to Brown, they had a great idea of their abilities and were convinced the company could not dispense with their services. "I gave them," he told Sibley, "what I have wintered with frequently and what I conceived to be a just proportion. Narcisse told me when I was making his equipment that you had promised him three barrels, but as I did not believe him I did not give them. He also told me he was not subject to my orders in any way."[18]

Narcisse might refuse to interpret for Brown when asked, but in general Brown's orders were obeyed, not because he was liked, but because he was respected and even feared. Renville had tried to get Brown's men to disobey him with no luck. "The men listen to Mr. Brown it seems," he wrote to Sibley. "They pay attention to him and do not refuse to obey him."[19] There is no doubt that Brown was willing to compel obedience if necessary. At one time Sibley had had to warn Brown not to use force, an order which Brown ignored in his second season at the post when faced with a balk by one of his men who wished to go with the winterers and not to remain at Lake Traverse "for fear of eating corn." Brown explained the situation to Sibley: "When the day came for the outfit to go I kept a couple of Indians to aid me… as I had understood the other men of the outfit intended to interfere. They, however, got wind of the Indians and the affair was settled by my disobeying your order of last year and bruising my thumb in striking him with my pistol."[20] Brown's ability to mobilize adherents among the Indians may have rivaled that of Renville, but it is certain he did not generally ingratiate himself with the French Canadian engagés. Even by the end of the first season his men were showing a mutinous temper. Brown advised Sibley to hire a new crew for the summer and send them up with the goods "as work has

---

17. Brown to Sibley, Jan. 25, 1836; Renville to Sibley, Jan. 8, 1836, in Sibley papers.
18. Brown to Sibley, Oct. 4, 1836. As Sibley remembered it, the ration issued to the common man in those days was 2 ounces tallow and 1 quart hulled corn per day (Sibley "Reminiscences" 246).
19. Renville to Sibley, Jan. 8, 1836, Sibley papers. Translated from French by authors.
20. Brown to Sibley, Oct. 4, 1836.

frightened those here. They will go to the Sheyenne, but this place they do not like."[21] Evidently the idea of spending the summer farming was too much for them.

Part of the problem stemmed from the business arrangement with Renville. The Lac qui Parle trader lost no time complaining about Brown's conduct to Sibley, and deliberately fostered some of the ill-feeling among the engagés by telling them that Brown was mistreating them. To Sibley, however, Renville piously wrote that he had always told the men to listen to Mr. Brown in the works of the farm. But in the same letter he complained that "Mr. Brown does not work for the business of the outfit; he works only on his farm instead of aiding us in the business. He has hurt us much in having had permission to lock the gates of the fort, as the Indians come in by night as well as day with their furs and it offends them very much and they are terribly angry with him." Joseph Renville, Junior and Brown had had some words about the arrangement that resulted in Brown locking up the supplies from the Renvilles as well as from the Indians. "You know," said Renville *père*, "that according to the agreement my son is in charge of the Indian trade and he gives the orders for that; but it seems that affairs are much changed and Mr. Brown is in charge of everything. He has forbidden the men to obey my son in anything under threat of losing their pay... [He told us] he was obliged to watch us, and that if all did not seem well he had the order to take everything into his own hands."[22] Brown, for his part, complained that the lack of auspicious success in the trade was entirely ascribable to bad management by the Renvilles: they had not provided enough lead for the spring hunts and young Joseph, indeed, had not been present in the spring to extend credits. Brown acknowledged to Sibley that he should not have allowed things to degenerate to that point: "You will probably say (at least I say myself) that I should have taken means to prevent this. But my orders not to interfere in the trade held me back." In March, Sibley in desperation had authorized Brown to credit the good Indians, but by then, as Brown reported, the spring hunts were lost.[23]

Frustrations Brown may have had during his first season at Lake Traverse, but by May he had made it through the winter and was looking forward to starting down with the returns. The hunts had been poor, partly because the severity of the winter had driven many Indians to the brink of starvation, and partly in consequence of an Aricara raid that had destroyed fifty lodges of Sioux.[24] At least there had been good progress on refurbishing the fort itself. Despite some of his men falling sick and some refusing to work, he had been able to erect the body of a building 50 by 18 feet and another 15 by 22 feet, and planned by summer to complete

---

21. Brown to Sibley, May 6, 1836, Sibley papers. It is likely that Brown's adherents were relatives of Winona and Susan, not a soldiers' lodge like the Kit Fox Society that guarded Renville's post.

22. Renville to Sibley, Jan. 8, 1836. It should be noted that all Renville's correspondence was in French, and, since he did not write, had to be transcribed by someone to whom he could dictate. This system can certainly lead to misunderstandings. (Translations by author.)

23. Brown to Sibley, May 6, 1836.

24. Taliaferro to William Clark, Apr. 30, 1836, Letterbook 1836–1839, Taliaferro papers.

a barn and stable, fence forty acres and plant all the seed he had brought. By the time the men came back from the Traverse with the wagons needed to remove the packs and a wheelwright to refit the carts, he expected to have the place in tolerably good shape, his spring wheat, corn, potatoes and peas planted. But, he warned Sibley, "If ever I am caught to pass another year as I have done this... I believe you will catch a weasel asleep."**25**

Under the circumstances, his complaint was probably justified. His orders were to see that the outfit sustained no loss, but at the same time he was not to interfere in the trade, which left him half the time where he could do neither the one nor the other. The insuperable problem, from Joe's point of view, was the Renvilles. "Make what argument you will, at St. Peters they will promise anything you will ask and once here they will do what they please in spite of you," he cautioned Sibley, adding that he would not remain there another year under the present arrangement, or, for that matter, any other arrangement concerned with the Renvilles. "Send me anywhere else, to Petite Roche, to Devil's Lake, to hell if you wish, and I will not murmur... but never while I have legs to escape will I pass one month in the same fort with one of that family."**26** Sibley had to capitulate. There would be nothing but trouble if Brown and the Renvilles, *père et fils*, were not separated. He would give Brown sole control of the post.

But would Taliaferro license Brown? News of Brown's difficulties at Lake Traverse had preceded him to the St. Peters, brought by some of the remote chiefs of the Yankton and Sisseton, who complained of Mr. Brown to their agent and asked to have him removed. But even Taliaferro could see that they had been put up to it, and that their complaint that Brown would not give them free access to all his apartments was frivolous. "I find that <u>mal</u> councils have proceeded from Jos. Renville Sr." he confided to his journal, "and that he alone in all human probability is to blame." But this did not make Taliaferro any less reluctant to license Brown. There was still Schoolcraft's charge that Brown was selling whiskey, Brown's difficulties with Major Bliss "and other matters requiring explanation." However, the agent found after investigation – and Brown's signature on the certificate condemning Mr. Bailly – that Brown might apply for a license to trade at Lake Traverse, contenting himself with merely warning Sibley that as the Indians had protested and threatened to take their business to the traders on the Missouri, he would not be responsible for anything that might happen to Brown at that post.**27**

As to the business of Brown's encroachments on the reserve, Taliaferro had heard all the evidence bearing on what the army had deemed a serious case and found the law and the rights and privileges of the post were no longer being infringed upon. After all, there were some ten to twenty other squatters on the reserve, including Sibley with his fine new stone house

25. Brown to Sibley, May 5, 1836.
26. Ibid.
27. Taliaferro Journal Jun. 8, 17, 30, 1836; Taliaferro to Sibley, Jul. 22, 1836, Sibley papers.

and warehouse at Mendota; in the agent's opinion "all must pass free, or all condemned."**28** Buisson, who had had charge of Brown's cattle, had removed to the Halfbreed Tract on Lake Pepin and Brown, hesitating to send the cattle with him, placed his herd in Sibley's care. Many cattle had died over the winter – Brown lost seven, Sibley seven, Taliaferro three – and Brown considered selling his remaining stock to Oliver Cratte; he wrote to ask Sibley to try to get $100 for them. For the moment, the rights of the army versus those of the settlers remained at stalemate.

Before JRB left the St. Peters that summer of 1836, he had one more obligation to take care of, and that, inexplicable as it may seem, was to marry Margaret McCoy. Now this effectuation, as he later explained to Sibley, was the furthest thing from his mind when he arrived at The Entry in June. But waiting for him was a letter from his brother (probably John Wesley) that informed him that there was an inheritance waiting for him, or more precisely, for his children. His godfather, his Uncle Thomas (Henderson?), under the impression that Joseph was dead, had left $2,000 in trust for his children upon their coming of age if any could be found within ten years. Brown, anxious to get this inheritance for his offspring – he would, of course, supervise its use – decided to marry Miss McCoy to legitimize their baby girl Margaret, born at St. Peters the preceding November 14. Officiating at the ceremony was the good Dr. Williamson, who seems to have been a bit fuddled about the parties to this whirlwind marriage, for he was not sure what name to fill in for the bride on the certificate. Brown realized that ten-year-old Solomon might not survive "and then the money would go to a public school" and rationalized that by marrying Margaret he would be able to collect for at least one child. He told Sibley wistfully, "I want to go for my boy in the spring, who Mr. Bailly informs me is very miserable," but he never did, for by the end of the year he knew that Solomon was dead. "Others have different views of the marriage ceremony," he philosophized, "but I think the good it will do the child will balance the sin and that will square the account. I do not care what others may think of my motives for marrying. I would as leave they would think it was through sentiment or folly (perhaps it was) as not. But I can never acknowledge her as my wife. I will get the child when old enough and that is all the intercourse I can have with her hereafter."**29**

Sterling sentiments they are, though somewhat tarnished by later events. For whether he knew it or not, Susan Frénière was then four months pregnant with his child. And although Susan was the woman Brown at the moment desired and the woman with whom he would contentedly spend the rest of his life, he was sufficiently enamored of McCoy's daughter to continue to live with her off and on while he was at the St. Peters (he would undoubtedly see it as a necessity). She would, in fact, bear him another child, Mary, born in 1838. She had, he said, agreed to divorce him whenever he wished, but as we will see this desiderata was

28. Taliaferro Journal Apr. 9, Jun. 17, 1836.
29. Brown to Sibley, Oct. 4, 1836 (second letter); in Williamson's Account Book, ABCFM papers, the bride's name was filled in, presumably later, with a different ink.

not easily effected. Without doubt his new wife understood that Brown could not take her with him into Sioux country, and probably also knew (or surmised) that he had a woman waiting at his post. She may have contented herself with the status and material benefits conferred on her by the marriage. We can hardly believe Brown revealed his duplicity to Susan when he returned to Lake Traverse, although she must soon have found out, for many of the men from Lake Traverse and Lac qui Parle went below that summer and could hardly have avoided hearing the gossip. Sibley presumably was aware of these machinations and took Mr. Brown's protestations with a grain of salt. In any case, he was hardly in a position to complain; he, too, was living with a Mdewakanton girl, Red Blanket, (by whom he later had a child, then "put aside" when it suited him to marry a woman from back East).

By the time Brown returned to the post in mid-July, things there had become hot enough to cause him to forget his domestic dilemma. Mandan from the upper Missouri had overrun the northern part of Yankton territory, coming as close as the "elbow" of the Sheyenne, where in June a battle had taken place that resulted in the deaths of nine Sioux and eight Mandan – a small fraction of the total deaths that summer. War parties had become common. Some of Brown's men who had been sent to the Yankton camp to procure *tareau* (dried buffalo meat) had seen some thirty Mandan, and even though they were not personally threatened or molested "fear drove them home in a sweat" without the meat. Yankton and Sisseton hunters dared not venture far from their villages. "They, as may be supposed, have not much room to move," wrote Brown to Taliaferro, assessing the situation he found on his return. Full-fledged war had not yet broken out solely because Waanatan wished to negotiate a rescue of Yankton prisoners held by the Mandan. Waanatan had learned that the agent contemplated a visit to his village and replied (Brown translating his words and enclosing them in his letter to Taliaferro): "I would advise you not to come next summer unless well attended, for you will meet Mandan war parties, and if you do come, do not interfere with our war... [D]o not stop us from revenging the disgrace they have put upon us."**30**

Given the fluid situation, it was not easy to decide where to set up the branch houses. Brown was in favor of Devils Lake, which he felt was the only wintering spot the Yankton could use, as no other place attracted sufficient animals to subsist the Indians through the winter. He thought he could get good returns there, especially now that William Aitkin had removed his post from Pembina, which meant that the Red River halfbreeds might turn instead to Brown for supplies and to sell their peltry. But to Sibley the dangers in so far-flung a post outweighed the advantages, particularly since, as Brown reported over the summer, 500 lodges of Otoe and Assiniboin had moved in there, and these nations were also at war with the Yankton. At length Butte Pelée (Bald Hillock) and a

---

30. Brown to Sibley, Jul. 19, 1836, Sibley papers; Brown to Taliaferro, Jul. 19, 1836, enclosing Waanatan to Taliaferro, copied in Taliaferro Journal 1836 156.

place near the elbow of the Sheyenne were chosen over Brown's protestations that no Indians would winter there. But the sudden descent of an early winter put an end to both the hostilities and the hope of a profitable rat hunt. Cold weather froze the lakes on the coteau before the rats made their lodges; what rats were left were impossible to get at – alternate freezing and thawing had left the lakes neither hard enough for spearing holes nor liquid enough for canoes. And so the Indians left for their winter lodges without taking any furs – "they are as poor as snakes," wrote Brown to Sibley at the end of November.[31] In his newsy letter he somehow failed to mention that he now had a week-old baby daughter, born to Susan on November 21 and named Lydia Ann after his sister.

Brown was expected to provide a lot of his own provisions (by raising crops and buying meat from the Indians) and, if possible, to supply the downriver posts as well to alleviate the terrible labor required to bring anything up the river. In the fall of 1835 he had furnished corn to Williamson at Lac qui Parle, and he sent the remainder of his parched grain, some eighty-five bushels, to Oliver Faribault at Little Rock the following year. At that time he estimated his new corn crop would come to at least 200 bushels. Another much-valued commodity that came from the west was meat – tareau, pemmican (a mixture of jerked meat, fat and berries) and tallow (for candles). Over the winter of 1836–1837 Brown bought nearly two tons of the stuff from Yankton hunters. He sent 500 pounds to Mendota at Christmastime, and could get a lot more, he wrote to Sibley, if he had horses to trade. The *gens libre*, the Red River halfbreeds, always had plenty of tareau, but would not travel so far south as Lake Traverse to sell it unless they could get horses in exchange; horses were essential to these buffalo hunters of the plains and were one commodity not available to them through the Hudson's Bay Company. They would also trade fine peltry for horses, Brown thought. But stock was hard to get to Lake Traverse and hard to keep. The beasts suffered much from the long, cold winters and Brown's few horses were quite worn out by arduous trips across the prairie with little or no feed to be found. Also good-looking animals acted as a magnet for troublemakers among the Indians, who took every opportunity to steal them or even to slaughter them as a means of voicing their displeasure. Brown felt that oxen were preferable to horses for work at the post because the Indians were not tempted to steal them. Yet they also could be killed, as one was that fall by a young man to whom Brown refused credit. "He had his gun broke by another Indian on the spot," wrote Brown to Sibley – no joke, that punishment, to a man who lived by hunting. But losing draft animals meant much trouble in the spring when the loaded carts of furs and skins had to be taken out.[32]

---

31. Brown to Sibley, Nov. 30, 1836, Sibley papers. The elbow of the Sheyenne is the great bend the river makes near Lisbon, North Dakota; the winter camp at Butte Pelée was in the Sheyenne valley north of Valley City.

32. Brown to Sibley, Jul. 19, Nov. 30, 1836; Oliver Faribault to Sibley, Aug. 15, 1836; Hypolite Dupuis to Sibley, Dec. 28, 1836, all in Sibley papers; Williamson Account Book Nov. 25, 1836. The Sioux

As winter closed down with an icy hand, life at Lake Traverse became monotonous – short bitterly cold days followed by long nights lit only by guttering tallow candles and flickering firelight, activities reduced to caring for the stock, cutting wood and counting inventory. Brown must have read and reread the papers Sibley had sent up with the last supply carts in November, bitterly regretted his lack of Cavendish tobacco (with calculated sarcasm he groused to Sibley, "My agreement specifies tobacco, without reference to the quality; at the time that was made I presumed I would not be asked to chew common tobacco that contains enough copperas to poison a horse!").**33** In much of the United States March signals the end of deep winter, but on the northern plains March is the month of the big snows, blinding blizzards that fill the air, blotting out all landmarks, casting up fifteen-foot drifts and catching at the very breath of anyone unlucky enough to be caught in one. Out of one of these northers on March 21, just at dusk, two men on snowshoes, half starved, half frozen, stumbled into Brown's post. They were Martin McLeod and Pierre Bottineau, and they were lucky to be alive.

McLeod, a young Canadian adventurer, had joined up with crusader James Dickson's Indian Liberation Army in Montreal. They'd come as far as the Red River settlement to recruit halfbreeds for the army, after which Dickson (no relation to Robert) planned to cross the plains to the Rockies, descend upon Santa Fé and with the spoils of war set up an Indian free state in California. Unfortunately – or perhaps for the army's sake one should say fortunately – winter and a lack of funds, recruits and equipment had penned them at the Red River.**34** McLeod and two companions, Richard Hayes and a Polish soldier named Ignatius Parys, deciding anything was preferable to sitting forever in Pembina, had persuaded Bottineau to guide them to the United States. As they proceeded south with dog *traineaux* the weather became colder, the snow deeper. After two weeks they had come 200 miles and were short on grub, incredibly thirsty (for snow, McLeod found, could not be swallowed to quench thirst, but must be first boiled and that required starting a fire) and had been several times lost and nearly frozen on the trackless prairie. Then near the Sheyenne River crossing came the whiteout, catching them strung out on the prairie. McLeod and Bottineau survived by digging into the snowdrifts, but Hayes perished, never to be found, and Parys, although alive, was badly frozen. Finding they could not carry him, McLeod and Bottineau made a shelter, collected wood for a fire, killed a dog for food and left Parys there while they struggled on to Brown's.

McLeod enjoyed a week and a half of Joseph R. Brown's company, reading material and hospitality while he recuperated, having dispatched Bottineau and François Frénière with a cart and horses to rescue Parys, in

---

punishment for an act that might harm the band was to despoil the offender's goods by cutting his clothes or tent or breaking his gun, axe or kettle.

33. Brown to Sibley, Oct. 4, 1836.

34. The quest of "General" James Dickson is a story in itself. For a synopsis, see Grace Lee Nute "The Diary of Martin McLeod" in *Minnesota History Bulletin* IV: 351–352 (St. Paul 1922).

vain as it turned out. Parys was found dead; in his delirium he had thrown off his clothes and let his fire go out. They brought his corpse back to Lake Traverse, where they buried him April 2. Then McLeod and Bottineau once again set off for the States. Despite his experience, Martin McLeod remained in the country to become a fur trader. By June he was learning the trade working for B. F. Baker at Mendota.35

Figure 18 Mouth of the St. Croix (now Point Douglas and Prescott) with a small river raft of logs on its way to Lake Pepin. The rafts used sails in good weather but most needed the help of a steamboat to navigate Lake Pepin. Watercolor by Henry Lewis in *Das Illustrirte Mississippithal*.

As soon as he could get away, Brown too headed for The Entry. He was there by the end of May when he gave Taliaferro yet another report of Indian slaughter near the coteau. In mid-June he met with his old clerk Miles Vineyard, now subagent for the Chippewa, to discuss his claims against the St. Croix and Snake river bands – Vineyard was now in the enviable position of being able to certify his own books of Indian credits, which he did for Brown on June 19.36 Then Vineyard left for Leech Lake to collect his charges, for there was going to be a treaty. All the hope and planning of five years was going to pay off this summer of 1837, and Joseph R. Brown was ready.

There had been talk of a settlement with the northern tribes since 1832, when the Sac, Fox and Winnebago lands were vacated, and Congress had voted an appropriation to effect this in 1836. At stake were lands not generally suitable for settlement and farming, but valuable for the pine timber that covered the country from south of Snake River through

35. Martin McLeod Diary, McLeod papers, MHS; published version in Nute "Diary of Martin McLeod" 408–418, 422, and in "Narrative of Martin McLeod" in *Army and Navy Chronicle* Jul. 27, 1837.

36. Taliaferro to Governor Henry Dodge, May 30 and Jun. 18, 1837, in Letterbook 1836–1839, Taliaferro papers; J. R. Brown "Balances Due in Credits June 18, 1837," verified by M. M. Vineyard, OIA LR Wisconsin superintendency.

northern Minnesota as well as throughout much of northern and central Wisconsin.

Plenty of people had an interest in these lands. Brown, as we have seen, was logging as early as 1833 on the upper St. Croix. There had been literally hundreds of people attempting to log on the tributaries east of the Mississippi – the Black, Chippewa and St. Croix rivers – from 1824 on, some with government sanction and some without. When the agents got wind of unauthorized people in the pineries, they called on the military put them off, but there was no way to keep up with the influx. In November of 1836 Lawrence Taliaferro told one Joseph Pitt, who had a boat and men at the falls of the St. Croix and was cutting timber with the consent of the Chippewa, that he must leave, and about the same time he was obliged to put off Benjamin St. Cyr from the Chippewa River pine lands. Despite the law of 1834, which was quite clear that no one would be permitted to cut timber on Indian lands with the chiefs' approbation or no, William Aitkin, Henry Sibley and Lyman Warren convened the St. Croix and Pokegama Indians in March of 1837 to get them to sign a ten-year agreement for timber rights on the upper St. Croix; many others, including William Dickson, had applied for permission to negotiate with the Indians for pine timber in northern Wisconsin. All were turned down.37

Figure 19 Cheever's mills at St. Croix Falls. Franklin Steele was first to see the potential of this site for a sawmill in 1837. Painting by Henry Lewis. Minneapolis Institute of Arts.

Among those who had not applied for permission was Joseph R. Brown. He had simply gone ahead, as he probably had every winter since

---

37. Taliaferro Journal Aug. 11, Nov. 1, 1836, Letterbook 1836–1839 Nov. 5, 1836; William Aitkin to Sibley, Feb. 1837, Sibley papers.

he had come to the St. Croix, sending a crew in to cut timber on Chippewa lands near the St. Croix. Although the southern limit of white pine is generally at the level of Rock Creek, two good stands were available lower on the St. Croix, one on Lawrence Creek and another a few miles north at Taylors Falls. It was there Brown chose to cut over the winter of 1836–1837, stockpiling the logs on the flats above the river west of the falls. For some reason, these logs were never made into rafts. As soon as news of the treaty got out, timber speculators began arriving by the hundreds, among them Franklin Steele, a lumberman from Pennsylvania who came out to the new territory expressly to survey its timber potential. Steele arrived in the summer of 1837 and immediately after the treaty signing he and George W. Fitch started out from Fort Snelling for the dalles of the St. Croix in a bark canoe, trailed by a scow loaded with tools, supplies and laborers (never mind that the treaty was yet unratified). They made two claims on the east side of the falls, and while they were building cabins, four other parties arrived to make claim to the water power. On the opposite bank Steele found "the veritable Joe Brown," as he said, "trading with the Indians, a few rods from where Baker & Taylor built their mill (near the end of the present [1888] toll bridge)." Steele added, "Brown had also cut pine logs, part of which, in 1838, were used by Baker & Taylor, but most of them were burned by forest fires on the ground where they were felled." Calvin A. Tuttle, who came to St. Croix Falls in 1838, thought that Brown had been cutting the preceding winter on the Taylors Falls flats, that is the flood plain between the dalles and the falls. He estimated that Brown had more than 200,000 board feet of pine logs on the ground, apparently abandoned by him after the fire.38

Although it was next to impossible for Brown himself to have been on the St. Croix over the winters he spent at Lake Traverse, he could easily have had a crew there; with experienced loggers, he had no need to be on the spot. Steele's mention of trading makes it even probable that he still had a branch house at Taylors Falls, which was not so very far from his old Two Rocks location.

Brown never attempted to prove a claim on the site, although he may have retained an interest in the trading house – the trader on the spot in 1838 was one Robinette, possibly Joseph, who had been Brown's blacksmith at Lake Traverse. When Jesse Taylor and B. F. Baker arrived that summer to make a claim to the west side of the water power, they found a bark shanty with Robinette in possession and were required to

38. Folsom *Fifty Years* 82-83, 92, 96, 303; Newton H. Winchell *The Geology of Minnesota* II: 405 (St. Paul 1888). Tuttle says the man holding Steele's claim was one Lagoo, likely to be the Joseph Lagru (variously Lagrew, Lagroo, Lagros, Lagris and also known as Joseph Sansfaçon Senior) who was cutting for Brown in 1833 and who had worked for him most intervening years. Sutler Samuel Stambaugh provides the reason for this frantic logging activity: "Pine boards are now selling at Galena, St. Louis and the intermediate towns at Sixty dollars per thousand feet! And one-twentieth part of the demand cannot be supplied." According to Bailly, pine planks were actually brought to Galena from Wheeling on the Ohio to finish dwelling houses. (Samuel C. Stambaugh to Harris, Oct. 6, 1836, OIA LR Wisconsin superintendency; Alexis Bailly to Senator L. F. Linn, April 1836, George W. Jones papers, Iowa State Historical Society, Des Moines).

buy him out. In truth, the country was quickly filling up with would-be lumber barons, and although Pizhick (Buffalo) had chased out one crew, by May of 1838 there were some 200 individuals engaged in preparing rafts of pine timber to descend the St. Croix and Chippewa rivers, and by October the estimate was 500.**39** Clearly something would have to be done to prevent a reenactment of the troubles northern Illinois had seen in the late 1820s and early 1830s.

Bailly had probably expressed the frustrations and temper of the upper Mississippi country most accurately in 1836 when he advised a member of the Senate:

> "A few years back the labour of a few Lumbering parties operating with whip saws was sufficient to supply the wants of that market, but now that the country is settling with a rapidity unexampled in the history of our country it requires greater supplies... Several attempts have been made to obtain the sanction of the department with the permission of the Indians to establish mills in the Pine Country. All have been refused with a single exception, a merchant by the name of Lockwood... his supplies are very limited and at enormous prices... Is it to be expected that a population like that of the valley of the Mississippi above St. Louis to suffer for want of Lumber because a few miserable Indians hold the country?"**40**

Pressure for a treaty was also coming from the agents of the American Fur Company who were hoping for a quick settlement of their outstanding Indian accounts. To this end it was desirable to hobble Major Taliaferro, because it was well known that his enmity toward AMF traders would cause him to disallow any and all claims put forward. Sibley appealed to Ramsay Crooks to do what he could to prevent Taliaferro's appointment as special commissioner, suggesting instead that Henry Dodge, new governor of Wisconsin Territory, be appointed. As for the agent, he averred, "The wavering and uncertain measures of the incumbent make him all but despised by the Sioux who do not hesitate to speak of him (& sometimes to him) in the most contemptuous terms." Another snag was that the Astors (the old concern) were not using their influence to press for old claims. Hercules Dousman had in desperation left for New York to enlist what help he could find on behalf on the upper Mississippi traders.**41** Also interested in a treaty – and with perhaps more political influence to bring to bear – was Fort Snelling's sutler, Samuel C. Stambaugh, one-time editor of a democratic newspaper in Lancaster, Pennsylvania, and good friend of James Buchanan. Since his arrival at the St. Peters in 1835, Colonel Stambaugh had been attempting to acquire or

---

39. Folsom *Fifty Years* 303–304; Taliaferro to Dodge, May 18 and Oct. 1, 1838, OIA LR Wisconsin superintendency. Along with timber cutters and rafters came millwrights; within a year or two mills were sawing at Steele's claim (St. Croix Lumbering Company), B. F. Baker's claim (North West Lumber Co.) and at Fall Creek, a few miles below the dalles (Marine Lumber Co.).

40. Bailly to Lewis F. Linn, April 1836, George W. Jones papers, Iowa Hist. Soc., Des Moines.

41. Sibley to Ramsay Crooks, Dec. 24, 1836, quoted in Blegen *Sibley Autobiography* 60–61.

lease the old government mills at St. Anthony Falls, in the full knowledge that when the pineries were opened, the water power would become immensely valuable. He also hoped to capitalize on the tourist trade by erecting a large hotel at the falls.**42**

These high expectations were fulfilled in the summer of 1837. Governor Dodge, as ex-officio commissioner of Indian affairs for the new territory of Wisconsin, was named commissioner to treat with the Chippewa at Fort Snelling; Secretary of War Joel Poinsett would personally conduct negotiations with the Sioux in Washington City. On July 29 an assemblage of Chippewa, estimated by Taliaferro at nearly 1,200, ceded to the United States all interest in their lands east of the Mississippi and south of a line from opposite the mouth of Crow Wing River to Upper Lake St. Croix (about thirty miles south of Fond du Lac). This vast pine land, amounting to fully sixty million acres encompassing much of eastern Minnesota as well as northern Wisconsin, was given up in return for $700,000 in goods and money, payable in twenty annual installments. An additional $100,000 was to be distributed to the halfbreeds of the Chippewa nation, and, much to Taliaferro's disgust, $70,000 was earmarked for payment of the Indians' debts to their traders.**43**

Taliaferro felt the Chippewa had been hoodwinked. In his autobiography he recalled that just as the treaty was about to be signed:

> "Dousman and another Sioux trader entered the agency office in seemingly great haste, asked for a sheet or two of letter paper and... in a few minutes Dousman came and laid the account before the Secretary Mr. [Verplank] Van Antwerp. Commissioner Dodge looked at this afterthought account of $5,000 and told interpreter Peter Quinn to ask the Indians if that claim was just for the mills on the Chippewa. The response was 'no,' the Sioux had all the benefit of it, but the chief from Chippewa River said for peace he (the commissioner) might give $500... Nevertheless the $5,000 was interlined in their treaty and a plain fraud traded on the helpless Indians in the name of Bruner [Brunet]."

Taliaferro was so on edge about this treaty that when Lyman Warren and a large body of Pillagers came down from Leech Lake "like so many black devils" to force Warren's claims and burst into the commissioner's tent he actually drew his pistol on Warren. Pugonakeeshig (Hole-in-the-Day the elder, chief from Gull Lake), seizing the moment, cried out "Shoot, my father!" Fortunately, Governor Dodge intervened and quieter

---

42. Stambaugh, who had previously been awarded the agency at Green Bay and the position of secretary to the commission on removal of the southern Indians by the Democrats, was appointed sutler at Fort Snelling in 1835. Sibley and Crooks, who felt the sutler always bore an unfair advantage in the Indian trade and had lobbied for a law to prevent the sutler from trading, first tried to buy out Stambaugh. Sibley finally formed a partnership with him for 50 percent of the profits, Sibley to run the business and Stambaugh to keep out of the way. The agreement led to distrust and recriminations on both sides and both parties breathed a sigh of relief when the appointment was not renewed in 1839. See Francis Paul Prucha "Army Sutlers and the American Fur Company" in *Minnesota History* XL: 25–31 (St. Paul 1966).

43. Kappler *Laws and Treaties*, 491–493; Folwell *Minnesota* I: 159–160.

heads prevailed. But Warren's claims were allowed to the tune of $25,000, as were William Aitkin's for $28,000. Brown, Bailly and other smaller traders also were awarded pretty much what showed on their books, in Brown's case $1,600.**44**

No sooner had the treaty with the Chippewa been signed than preparations got under way for a similar cession from the Sioux. Taliaferro had an appropriation waiting to take the principal chiefs to Washington City to sign the treaty in the presence of their Great Father. In early September about twenty-five chiefs and headmen of the Mdewakanton boarded the steamer *Pavilion* with agent Taliaferro for the trip east. Close behind them were the traders – Sibley, Bailly, Laframbois, Rocque, Labathe, the younger Faribaults, Stambaugh and Joseph R. Brown among others – armed with powers of attorney and petitions, determined to protect their interests. Several of these named had tried to get the chiefs to promise that they would provide for the payment of their just debts as the Chippewa had, but their adjurations had been hitherto in vain. The agent had surprised them by chartering the boat and hustling the Indians off under their noses; there was nothing to do but follow. On September 29, after much skirmishing, a treaty was concluded between Special Commissioner Joel Poinsett and the Mdewakanton by which the latter ceded their lands east of the Mississippi (a cession of relatively useless territory so far as the Sioux were concerned because of its contiguity to the Chippewa lands – only one village, Medicine Bottle's, was in the cession; Little Crow had moved Kaposia village to the Iowa side of the river earlier) for the sum of $300,000 to be invested and paid as an annuity "forever," plus $23,750 in goods and services annually for twenty years, $110,000 cash to "relatives and friends" of the chiefs and headmen and $90,000 for payment of their just debts. It was a good bargain for a strip of land a few miles wide on the east bank of the Mississippi from the Bad Axe to the St. Croix and the triangle of land between the Mississippi and St. Croix south of the Chippewa boundary line – a very good bargain indeed.**45**

It is difficult today to comprehend the importance of these two treaties to the white inhabitants of the northwest in 1837. From the time of ratification, there was no government authority needed to be on the ceded land, no license to trade, no restrictions on selling whiskey or anything else, no bar to harvesting the timber and mineral riches except as the territory of Wisconsin might require. We can only get a glimmer of the vital concern felt for the outcome of the treaties by observing to what lengths and expense people were willing to go to accomplish it, even to letting the next season's trade slide. Joseph R. Brown financed what was in all likelihood his first trip back east (he'd been gone eighteen years) and didn't even look up his relatives. He had more important things to do. For one, he had a great interest in getting the treaty makers to approve

44. Taliaferro "Autobiography" 215–216; Dodge to A. C. Harris Sep. 20, 1837 containing list of claims submitted, in OIA LR Wisconsin superintendency.
45. Kappler *Laws and Treaties* 493–494

payments to traders for their outstanding credits with the lower Sioux. Brown had gambled on this payoff when he bought Bailly's unpaid credits back in 1832; this was his one and only chance to be paid for them and for his five years of trade with the Mdewakanton. It was more than disappointing when trader's claims – originally submitted at $247,848 – were judged to be worth only $90,000. Out of this would have to be paid claims dating back twenty years or more. To his good fortune, when the commissioners arrived at the St. Peters in the summer of 1838 to examine the merits of the traders' claims, Brown's were the first books examined. Although a large percentage of his $5,500 claim was disallowed for overcharges, he did get $2,340, and since his debt to the Fur Company had been absolved in his agreement to work for the Western Outfit, it was his free and clear. In general, Fur Company traders had to settle for about 40 percent of the book value of their claims, and of that much was simply passed on to Ramsay Crooks or the Astors in payment of their debts to the old and new concerns. Brown's other claims for depredations were not allowed, but undaunted he kept pushing for them and may have eventually got some payment – as late as 1848 he was still trying, asking Sibley, then in Washington, to press his claim of $370 for "cattle killed while they were in the hands of Buisson" (prior to 1837) as he had paid Buisson for his share of the loss.[46]

Brown was also eager to promote a new disposition of the 1830 Halfbreed Tract. In August, during the interval between the treaties, Brown, Bailly, Stambaugh and others had improved their time by drawing up a petition for settlement of the set-aside land on individuals – who might then sell it – instead of it being held in common by those who would live on it. Among the entitled halfbreeds making the petition are Solomon Brown (although Joseph was then surely aware his son had died the preceding winter) and Susan Frénière, who was signed for by "her attorney Joseph R. Brown."[47] Despite pressures – and Bailly and Stambaugh had made at least one previous trip to Washington to plead their case – no revision was made in the ownership of the tract, but a clause was written into the Sioux treaty that provided $110,000 to be paid to the half and quarter blood relations of the Mdewakantons. This was almost as good. When it all shook out and the payments were made on the first of October 1838, Brown was $3,000 richer. Through powers of attorney, he collected $750 each for Solomon and Susan, $500 each for his baby daughter Lydia Ann, her grandmother Madeleine (Winona) Crawford and his ward Gabriel Renville, having during the interval between treaty and payment snatched the guardianship of Victor's son from Squire Renville.[48]

46. Claims under the treaty of Sep. 29, 1837, Special File #200, OIA; Brown to Sibley, Nov. 12, 1848, Sibley papers.
47. "Petition of the Half & Quarter Breeds to Joel R. Poinsett..." undated draft in Bailly papers; "Half-Breed Petition for the Survey and Allotment of the Lake Pepin Reserve" Aug. 15, 1837, OIA LR Wisconsin superintendency.
48. Schedule of payments in OIA Special File #200. An affidavit in Sibley's Account Book (Sibley papers) shows that Brown had been duly appointed guardian of Gabriel Renville by the judge of Probate

Mention of Solomon Brown reminds us that Joseph R. Brown had at least one personal reason besides the treaty for making the trip east in the fall of 1837: to satisfy himself about the Choctaw Academy and his son's death there. Brown and Scott Campbell, the treaty interpreter whose son William was still at the Academy, got Joshua Pilcher, Sioux Agent for the Missouri, to petition the Secretary of War for an order to pass by the school with them on his return west. Although he does not name the two men in this letter, Pilcher refers to them as "the fathers of two Yancton boys who were placed at Col. Johnson's school about 4 years since." He asked that the one be allowed to see his son and take him home "if he sees fit," adding, "The father of the other boy (the boy who is dead) is also with me, and I wish to let him accompany me by the school." There is no reason to doubt this is Campbell and Brown. Pilcher received the go-ahead and appropriation October 27 and the entourage could have started back by the first of November. It is to be noted that Brown's insistence on examining the Academy also resulted in his passage paid back home.**49** They would have arrived at the St. Peters about the same time the chiefs did in mid-November. It must have been nip and tuck to get back to Lake Traverse before snow closed the way that winter.

Brown was faced with a certain dilemma. In the face of mounting competition in the St. Croix pineries, he appears to have put in no cutting crew that winter. He may have found his usual crew already signed up with other timber speculators; it is clear he was cramped for time. His contract with Sibley still had two years to run, so while prospects in the St. Croix area brightened, he was committed to what promised to be a tough trading year on the unsettled plains. Unable to take full advantage of the golden opportunities awaiting firstcomers to the ceded land, Brown had to return to Lake Traverse.

At least one of Brown's men had defected; Narcisse Frénière had gone over to B. F. Baker and was licensed at the Butte Pelée. Louis Provençalle Junior agreed to run Brown's branch house on the Sheyenne. Louis was supplied with more than $1,800 in equipment, but both must have known that there was not enough business on the Sheyenne to warrant two houses in opposition there, especially as Narcisse was so well known to the Yankton. The Indians were no better disposed than in previous years, and in addition the smallpox was among them – a fearful decimator that had carried off a hundred of them between Lake Traverse and the James by midwinter. The warlike Yankton and Yanktonai still preferred fighting to hunting, molesting the traders constantly, so much so that the previous

---

Court of Crawford County, Wisconsin Territory. The legality of Brown's guardianship is somewhat suspect at this point; he formally applied for guardianship of Gabriel and his and Susan's children from Crawford County probate court Jan. 6, 1840 (Probate Book B, Prairie du Chien).

49. Joshua Pilcher to Secretary of War, Oct. 20, 1837, and answer Oct. 27, 1837, in OIA LR Schools. Pilcher was actually in Washington to see to treaties with the Sac and Fox and Sioux of the Missouri, which were signed October 28 (Kappler, 495–497). Although kept on the books as Yankton Sioux, the two boys entered by Major Grooms in December of 1833 were Mdewakanton halfbreeds Solomon Brown and William Campbell (Richard M. Johnson to Thomas Henderson, Dec. 7, 1833. Thomas Henderson papers, copies in WHS Madison).

summer Sibley had requested an armed troop be sent to the coteau to bring the belligerents to order.50 Further outrages were expected.

They were not long in coming. The season was still young when Brown experienced what Samuel Pond called "a serious difficulty with the Indians at Lake Traverse" that resulted in Brown being shot, one of his men killed, his teams lost and eventually in the abandonment of the post. Although the facts are difficult to assess at this remove, the story told by Samuel J. Brown, who undoubtedly heard it from his father several times, is probably as accurate as any. According to him the trouble started over a chicken, shot by a Sisseton in mourning for a dead relative who had taken a vow to shoot the first live thing he came across as a means of assuaging his grief. This happened to be Brown's chicken, and might as well have been Brown himself, had Isannapca seen him first. Hearing the shot, Brown jumped up from the table where he was writing, confronted the chicken-killer and, after delivering a lecture on the inadvisability of injuring private property, took away the Indian's gun, saying he could have it back when the chicken was paid for. After working for some time, while Isannapca hung about disconsolately, Brown had a change of heart and to induce him to leave gave him back his gun. A short time later Brown happened to glance up and through the open window saw the man taking aim – at him! He dropped to the floor, but not quickly enough to escape taking part of the charge in the neck and shoulder. (In Sam's story, the gun was loaded with shot, but Alexander G. Huggins, writing from the missionary station at Lac qui Parle that winter, said that Brown had been hit with a ball which penetrated two fingerbreadths under the skin. This is most likely right, because it is probable Huggins' associate Dr. Thomas Williamson was called in to dress the wound.) Down, but not out, Brown gave the war whoop – or at least cried out – which so unnerved the assailant he started to run. Brown's man Demarrais caught up with him, but in his excitement the French Canadian twisted the lock right off his pistol. Isannapca got away unpunished, the unpleasant consequence of which was that his comrades grew bolder.51

There was worse to come. During the winter young Louis Provençalle, Jr., son of the old trader, was killed while on derouin near the James River by one of the Yankton with whom he had come to trade. Louis' man had been sent back for supplies, leaving Louis, his wife and child with the teams. While the trader was out setting wolf traps, he was waylaid and shot by Xunkahaton (The Horned Dog) for no better reason than the Indian coveted Louis' horses. As soon as report of the death was received at Lake Traverse some of Brown's men and a group of well-disposed Sioux gave chase, but they were several days behind and were unable to

---

50. Taliaferro licenses Sep. 30, 1837, and Sibley to Dodge, Apr. 23, 1838, both in OIA LR Wisconsin superintendency; for condition of the Indians, see Williamson to Greene, May 8, 1838, ABCFM papers.

51. Samuel W. Pond "The Dakota or Sioux in Minnesota as They Were in 1834" *Minnesota Historical Collections* XII: 334 (St. Paul 1908); S. J. Brown Notebook, Brown papers; Alexander G. Huggins to Eli Huggins, Feb. 25, 1838, Huggins papers, MHS. Pond and Huggins were both missionaries at Lac qui Parle.

overtake the murderer as he fled toward the Missouri or to recover the horses. The loss of two teams, added to the destruction of other horses and oxen that had been shot or run off during the winter, made it impossible for Brown to get his furs out that spring. He had to swallow his pride and send to Renville for assistance. The old squire sent his sons with carts to help Brown remove his goods, but with all the delay it was June before Brown got everything down.[52] When he arrived at The Entry he learned he wouldn't be going back to Lake Traverse.

Because of the impossibility of getting any communication out of the upper St. Peters country in winter, it had been mid-April before the distressing news from Lake Traverse reached Sibley at Mendota. He immediately made plans to abandon the post. Rolette and Dousman agreed, advocating that they burn all the buildings at Lake Traverse, withdrawing everything from the area, and that they establish no new post for at least a year, for to make the punishment effective, Dousman wrote, "you must leave them no hope whatever." He was also of the opinion that the unsettled economic state below, that is, in the United States, which had been undergoing a rather severe recession in 1837 and 1838, made it imperative that the Upper Mississippi Outfit be curtailed and expenses cut to the bone "to avoid being engulphed in the general ruin about us." To Sibley he emphasized, "it is better to lose a few furs than to run us in debt to collect them."[53] Sometime after Brown had removed the last of the equipment from Lake Traverse that summer the post was razed and fired, and trade was suspended west of Lac qui Parle for several years.

Sibley called removal of their trader "the greatest punishment which could be inflicted upon a band," as indeed it was on the coteau, for the western Sioux were entirely dependent upon the trade for the clothing, guns, ammunition and traps necessary for their survival. Punishment was undoubtedly called for. Sibley had given Brown free rein in the trade and Brown had "got tough" with the Sioux, reversing Renville's appeasement policy, and the Indians had reacted predictably. Brown had a reputation by this time as a "hard" trader – Eli Pettijohn, Philander Prescott's son-in-law, said Brown could get a buffalo robe for a plug and a half of tobacco – but it is perfectly clear that his methods were condoned by the principals in the Western Outfit and that they knew the risks inherent in putting more pressure on the upper bands. Economic necessity caused them to take those risks. Dousman's comment on hearing of the winter's disasters was, "With the exception of the death of Louis, it is no worse than I have long feared."[54]

About the same time as Renville was readying carts to go to Brown's aid at Lake Traverse, Hazen Mooers and his son-in-law Andrew

---

52. Williamson to Greene, May 10, 1838, ABCFM papers; Williamson to Sibley May 29, 1838, Sibley papers; Sibley to Dodge Apr. 23, 1838.

53. Dousman to Sibley, May 6, 1838, Sibley papers.

54. Sibley "Reminiscences" 247; Eli Pettijohn to W. W. Folwell, Jan. 1, 1905, Notebooks, Folwell papers, MHS; Dousman to Sibley May 6, 1838. Dousman figured the Sioux trade for that season to be a $16,000 loss. "It will take all your treaty money to make up this way," he added in his letter to Sibley.

Robertson at their post downstream at the Little Rock had grown tired of losing money and were preparing to leave the deteriorating fur trade altogether. In May Williamson noted "Mr. Moore [sic] has abandoned his houses and expects to leave the Indian trade and engage in some other more lucrative business."**55**

The site he had selected was Chanwakan (Medicine Wood, so called because of an unusual – and therefore "wakan" – beech tree growing there) on the western end of Grey Cloud Island. He had had this spot in mind since the first talk that the land would be ceded, and was familiar with the place and the Indians from trading activities there in 1836 and 1837 with Medicine Bottle's village, so it's likely the move had been planned for at least a year. Whether he and Brown had some understanding previously, or simply got the same idea at the same time, is hard to tell today. But that summer all three families – Mooers, Robertson and Brown – moved to the big island in the Mississippi some eighteen miles below Fort Snelling. Mary Mooers (aged ten at the time) thought all three came together on the same day, but that isn't too likely. It was nearly June when Brown got down with his furs; he probably brought his family down when he returned to remove the rest of the post's goods in July, which agrees with the recollection of Marcelle Courturier, who thought Mooers preceded Brown.**56**

Obedient to the terms of the treaty, Medicine Bottle had moved his band across the river to the Pine Bend bottoms opposite his old village, leaving some large bark lodges on the northwestern end of the island into which Mooers and Robertson moved their families. Brown brought his new family – Susan, pregnant with Angus (who was born in August), and baby Lydia Ann – to the southern shore of the island where a log house had been erected the summer before. According to Courturier, Brown built the house before he moved (it might even have been the location from which Mooers had made his credits the preceding year). This house was located about 250 feet back from the Mississippi, about a mile downstream from Medicine Bottle's new village, and was backed by a

---

55. Williamson to Greene, May 10, 1838. Hazen Mooers was a New Yorker who came west about 1817 and was employed by James Aird as a trader for the American Fur Company at Prairie du Chien. His first wife was Mary Wakanhditaninwin, a Mdewakantan women, by whom he had a son John. Later he married Marpiyarotowin (Grey Cloud), also called Margaret, daughter of Aird and the original Grey Cloud, who was a daughter of Wabasha. Margaret had by her first husband, British trader Thomas G. Anderson, a daughter Jane, who became the wife of Andrew Robertson, and a son, Angus Malcom, who was Sibley's clerk from 1837–1839. Grey Cloud left Anderson and rejoined her people at Big Stone Lake in 1813; he returned to Canada where he remarried after the war. Grey Cloud and Mooers married about 1818, had three daughters, one of whom, Mary, wed JRB's half brother John. See Case "Historical Notes of Grey Cloud Island and Its Vicinity," *Minnesota Historical Collections* XV: 371–372; John Mooers "Memoire of Hazen Mooers," in Minnesota biographical collections MHS; Lyman Draper, ed. "Personal Narrative of Captain Thomas G. Anderson" in *Minnesota Historical Collections* IX; 192, passim.

56. Case "First House"; Mooers' affidavits 1836, 1837, OIA Special File #200; "Last of the Voyageurs; Maxcell Courturier of Grey Cloud Island," *St. Paul Pioneer Press* May 27, 1894. Courturier, then just 22, was hired by Brown in the fall of 1838, later married Brown's daughter Margaret, and was intimately acquainted with events on the island. He had been in the country for years, worked at least one season for Mooers and was one of the men on Bailly's whiskey boat that was seized in 1834. His name, variously spelled Marcier, Marcelle and Maxcel, reflects the pronunciation of the French "r", which is something of a gargle: mahr-say.

beautiful sandy prairie that covered most of the lower island. He was accompanied to the island by Jim Clewet and in the fall was joined by Marcelle Courturier (who had spent the last season working with Mooers), Joseph Bourcier (Brown's chief boatman) and Pierre Felix

Figure 20 Delegation of Dakota in New York ca. 1858, including Akipa at back, left. Others, standing, Stubby Horn, Mazasha (Red Iron), Anpetutokaca (John Other Day), Mazakutemani (Little Paul), Charles Crawford (Akipa's eldest son); seated, Mazomani (Iron Walker), Wamdiupiduta (Scarlet Plume), Sweet Corn, Upiyahdaheya (Big Curly Head). Photo by Fredericks. Minn. Hist. Soc.

(married to François Frénière's daughter Rosalie). All three had been long in the employ of the Fur Company; they built their cabins close by Brown's.[57]

Also with the Brown household, it appears, were Winona Crawford, her son Gabriel, her baby François, (later known as Charles Renville Crawford) and her new husband Akipa (Meeting). Akipa, whose full name was Tacandupahotanka, His Big-voiced Pipe, was a nephew or son of the Wahpeton chief Tankamani or Big Walker. In his letter to Welsh Brown states that he was accompanied to the island by a young man from the Lake Traverse band, "a very influential brave... entitled to wear eleven War Eagles and five Crow feathers," and his wife and child. This was Akipa. Brown goes on:

57. Case "Historical Notes" 372, 374; Douglas A. Birk *Grey Cloud; An Archeological Approach* 27, 31, 76 (St. Paul 1972); "Maxcell Courturier"; Brown Bible. Angus Mitchell Anderson Brown was born on the island August 14; he was obviously named after Robertson's brother-in-law and Sibley's clerk, Angus Malcom Anderson—the middle name must have been Brown's error. About this time Andrew Robertson named the island Grey Cloud after his mother-in-law.

"As I had determined to open a farm for myself, I induced him to locate near me. I had but little difficulty in getting him to cut house logs and, with some assistance from me, he built a comfortable house before winter set in. In the spring he had cut and hauled rails to enclose about twenty acres. With but little assistance he built his fence, and he drove the oxen that plowed his field, one of my men holding the plow."**58**

Figure 21 Akipa or Tacandupahotanka (His Big Voiced Pipe) Drawing by A. Anderson, pub. In Thomas Hughes' *Indian Chiefs*.

Akipa, although he said he did not like white men or their ways, did become a farmer and sold milk at Fort Snelling. Indeed, farms were opened by everyone as soon as possible. Mooers and Robertson soon built good houses and, according to young Tom Robertson who was born on the island in 1839, raised corn, potatoes and vegetables to sell to the fort. Their first crop of wheat was planted in 1839 (although one might wonder if Brown, with his predilection for raising grain, hadn't seeded a crop there earlier – in early 1839 he borrowed a scythe and snath from Sibley, though this might have been for a spring mowing). Eventually they specialized in blooded stock and hogs and did some dairying, shipping their produce, cattle, hogs, butter and cheese to St. Louis by steamboat, and we may be sure Brown followed much the same lines. The island had plentiful grass for grazing stock, especially lush in the marshy area just west of Brown's farm. Brown had also chosen – with his usual acumen – the best steamboat landing. He opened in this convenient spot a store well stocked with goods suitable to the Indian trade, also continued his sideline of selling wood and produce to the boats and "kept tavern."**59**

It's difficult to conceive of a prettier situation. When the Fur Company decided to withdraw from Lake Traverse, Brown was left without a post,

58. Welsh *Taopi* 68. Akipa was hardly Brown's tool, as we shall see. He and Winona had two boys, the eldest Wakaninape (called in French François and in English Charles Renville) was born about 1838 or 1839 and the younger, Tukaniyanke (called Narcisse or Thomas Renville), about 1842. A baby girl born to them died. Both sons later took the surname Crawford. Akipa was a full blood Wahpeton, brother or half brother to the historic chiefs Mazasha (Red Iron) and Mazomani (Walking Iron). He was also known as Joseph Akipa Renville; not related to the Renvilles, he apparently took the name as a mark of respect. Hughes *Indian Chiefs*, 88, 92–94; S. J. Brown to Marion Satterlee Apr. 9, 1915 in Satterlee papers, MHS. See Appendix A.

59. S.J. Brown to W. W. Folwell, July 24, 1908 in Notebooks, Folwell papers; Thomas A. Robertson "Reminiscences," manuscript in Sioux Uprising Collection, MHS; Case "Historical Notes" 373.

but with a year to run on his contract. Although it's not entirely clear how this impasse was resolved, apparently Sibley and Dousman let the contract expire on schedule in June of 1839, making such use of Brown's services as they could in the interim. In July of 1838 Brown was sent to Lake Traverse to retrieve the inventory and other portable goods. At Lac qui Parle he ran across John Charles Frémont and Joseph Nicollet who had set out to explore the coteau and James River, but had precipitously returned to Renville's post for fear of marauding Yankton. He gladly carried their messages back to The Entry. Of the post's $2,500 inventory, Brown left behind only three carts, which were probably rescued by Renville when he went up to burn the place. Because of low water, some of the heavier, bulkier items such as grindstones, snowshoes, an anvil, two ploughs and a corn mill had to be left at the Traverse.**60**

By July 23 Brown was back. He had no outfit at Chanwakan, but did get goods from Sibley and Dousman for the 1838–1839 season. He did some business for he had nearly 2,000 rats and some fine furs to sell Sibley in the spring of 1839. After his contract was up, he was free to sell furs where he wished, and since no license was required to trade in the ceded country, there is no record to tell how much business he did. Although Courturier said Brown was not actively involved in trading after his move to Chanwakan, it is certain he always had at least a finger in the Indian trade.

The villages of Medicine Bottle and Nasianpa were nearby and handy for his Grey Cloud Island location. When the annuities were paid in September, Brown (and every other trader) was ready with a stock of attractive goods. The Chippewa had not been required to remove, so there is the possibility he had a man trading on the St. Croix at Wolf Creek (his branch house was still being used in the 1840s by Alexander Livingston and Louis Roberts) or at the falls. W. H. C. Folsom thought Brown had several branch houses at this time, "one on the upper St. Croix where the Nevers dam is located [1898], one on the St. Peters River, another on the State Park at Taylors Falls," the location noticed by Steele in 1837.**61**

Within a year Brown was free to pursue his own plans, seemingly modest at first, which soon evolved into a scheme to form a political entity in the newly ceded land. If in 1838 Brown envisioned a new county or even a new territory in the northwest, he did not elaborate upon his vision to others. He was aware that with the Indian title extinguished this new land would soon fill with settlers and that these settlers would need towns with steamboat landings, accommodations and access to the interior. And this is where the genius of Joseph R. Brown begins to show itself.

Unlike most of the boomers pouring into the country, Brown was in no rush to grab the prime timberlands or to corral the sources of waterpower for mills. His speculative eye was on townsites through which the tide of settlement must soon funnel. Therefore, he made no attempt to stake a

---

60. Stephen R. Riggs to Sibley, Jul. 16, 1838, John Charles Frémont to Sibley, Jul. 16, 1838; Sibley Notebook, Aug. 23 and Jun. 1, 1838, all in Sibley papers.
61. Sibley Account Books, various entries 1838–1842; Folsom Notebook, Folsom papers, MHS.

Map 6 Grey Cloud Island, Chanwakan, and vicinity after the 1837 treaties.

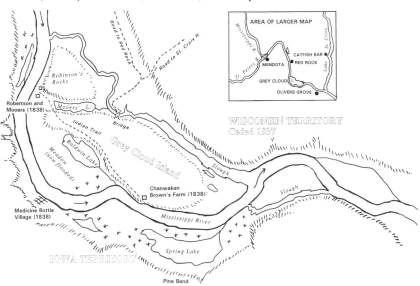

claim at Taylors Falls; it was a site difficult of access to steamboats and an awkward, narrow building site to boot. His first choice was his original claim opposite Fort Snelling, the claim from which he'd been warned off in 1835. That location was for all practical purposes at the head of navigation of the Mississippi (the channel from there to the Falls of St. Anthony being narrow and filled with sandbars) and was blessed with a fine steamboat landing, a spacious levee and access to the gently rolling prairies atop the cliffs. It is almost certain that as early as 1835 Brown had considered this a choice spot for a speculative venture, rejecting (or never considering) the sites later platted as St. Anthony and St. Paul as too difficult to get to and the other possible landings on the left bank of the Mississippi as too swampy for usefulness. It just seemed logical that the great city that would rise in the far north should be centered right there at The Entry, at the head of navigation, the place that had been chosen by Pike in 1805 and that had functioned for years as the natural center of the region. Of the three natural townsites presented by the junction of the rivers – Mendota, Fort Snelling and Brown's claim – only the latter was available for settlement, the other two being still in Indian territory. He began making improvements on it as soon as possible (more on that later); meanwhile, he found Grey Cloud Island an excellent location for farming and stock raising. And just to be sure (since settlement seemed to be concentrating on the St. Croix River) he had his eye on several St. Croix locations as well – at the river's mouth, at the head of Lake St. Croix (where he had placed a warehouse to supply his upriver posts) and on the lake at St. Marys Point near the small halfbreed and voyageur settlement called Catfish Bar (Afton).

For the first time since leaving Rock River Joseph R. Brown was living where free enterprise was permitted. And he had some enterprises in mind, among them a fine grogshop positioned to be convenient to the soldiers at the fort and a ferry to make communication between the banks easy. But first there was groundwork to lay.

CHAPTER VII

"[HE] LAID OUT A TOWN HE CALLED DACOTAH, WHICH HE FONDLY BELIEVED WOULD IN THE FUTURE BECOME A CITY." LYDIA ANN CARLI

The great western immigration had commenced, and if it had not yet reached the St. Peters, it was only a matter of time. Settlers were pouring into Illinois, Wisconsin and Iowa; in 1834 alone more than 80,000 people had shipped from Buffalo for western ports, not counting the thousands more who loaded up family and furniture and drove wagons west by land. Even the recession of 1837 had not slowed the rolling tide. Many of these "movers" came through Chicago, which had been in 1830 no more than a muddy pasture belonging to Fort Dearborn but was by the year 1838 a city of nearly 4,000 souls. Among those eastern emigrants then living in rough, raw Chicago was Joe Brown's half sister, Lydia Ann Carli.

After reestablishing contact with his family in 1835, Brown had even considered joining Lydia Ann and her new husband, Paul J. Carli (described by her as "an Italian, wealthy and educated, an artist painter and accomplished musician, [but] somewhat deficient in business methods"), in embryo Chicago, where it seemed certain a speculator could soon make a killing.1 However, at that time Brown had more debts than cash with which to speculate, and his advantageous agreement with Henry Sibley had wiped out all notion he might have had of leaving the St. Peters area. But through correspondence with his sister he had watched Chicago grow, and although Paul Carli was unable to make money (he had traded his interests in two prime downtown properties for 160 acres six miles up the Chicago River that never amounted to more than a

---

1. Quoted in Augustus B. Easton *History of the St. Croix Valley* I: 8 (Chicago 1909). Lydia Ann, along with an aunt and other family members, joined a wagon train from Springfield in the summer of 1834. Since her father's death in 1828 she had "dodged along any way, picking wool or spinning or doing anything I could get... until I was sixteen and went to Chicago with some friends. There I met Mr. Carli. He was wealthy, of a good family and highly educated. As I never let anything good pass me, I married him—not for love, for I left my heart in Springfield—but I wanted money, and that I got." Paul was running the Eagle Hotel where the party stopped; Lydia Ann went down to the dining room for a pitcher of water, there met Paul who "then and there succumbed," and within six weeks she was his bride. By 1838 Carli had lost his interest in the hotel and in a general merchandise store in downtown Chicago, and had moved to a farm a few miles out of town. (Carli to Brown, May 20, 1902; Carli to Williams Sep. 20, 1871; *Stillwater Messenger* Dec. 19, 1896.) For life in frontier Chicago, see Amos A. Parker *Trip to the West and Texas*, 29–49 (Boston 1836) and Joseph N. Balistier *Annals of Chicago* 1840, 23–25 (reprint Chicago 1874).

woodlot), others had prospered. The lesson Brown had learned watching his old mentor George Davenport grow rich after buying up the land across the river from Rock Island and platting a city there was not lost on him either, especially when he remembered how easily he had given up his own preemption right to the site. Chicago, Davenport, Galena, Peoria, Dubuque – these cities were growing enormously fast because they were staging points for the emigration west, the vortices that drew in every mover, the channels for all provisions, mail and equipment needed for settlement. In 1838 Brown was sitting on a similarly well-placed townsite at The Entry; his prime objective was to secure it for preemption, to hang on to it until the land was surveyed (which he confidently felt would happen within very few years) and came into the market. For this object-ive, among others, he had come to Chicago.

Figure 22   Lydia Ann Carli, Brown's half sister.
Washington County Hist. Soc.

"In 1838 my brother, Joseph R. Brown, whom I had never seen before, appeared at our place. He had... laid out a town he called Dakota, which he fondly believ-ed would in the future become a city," Lydia Carli remembered.**2** Probably she telescoped events, attaching the name of Brown's later townsite to the location he hoped to develop near The Entry, which he called Sintomonee (from *sintomni*, All Over, evidently used in the sense of Known All Over the World) but which was more generally called Brown's Ferry or Rumtown (just as Dacotah became more generally known as Carli's). It's possible, of course, that the name Dacotah (as Brown spelled it) had already occurred to him as the ideal name for the new capital city of the northwest and that he merely transferred the name to the new site on the St. Croix in 1841. He later proposed the name Dacotah for the new territory as well. Brown told the Carlis he hadn't come to Chicago to stay, but wanted to persuade them – and Paul's brother Christopher, who had opened up a medical practice in Chicago in 1837 – to come to the new country with him. He said he wanted to have some of his family around him. More practically, he needed investment capital as well as intelligent, well-educated people whom he could trust to help him run the many projects he had in mind for

2. Easton *St. Croix Valley* I: 8.

156

that country, but these reasons he may have kept to himself. He painted a rosy picture of the great northwest and of the opportunities awaiting those who were lucky enough to get in on the ground floor, offering many inducements to the Carlis to resettle. He told them that he would attend the Wisconsin territorial legislature that winter to get the charters necessary for his townsite – a statement that Lydia apparently interpreted to mean that her brother was a member of that body. But his arguments left them unpersuaded. Paul Carli had determined to invest in another variety store in downtown Chicago and Christopher planned to move on to New Orleans. That part of Brown's plan would have to wait.3

Brown's trip to Chicago that October had another object as well. With him on the steamboat to Galena and on the miserable stage on which he continued the journey to Chicago (over roads so rutted and muddy that the overturning of the coach five or six times was expected) was his ward, Gabriel Renville. Brown had taken a great interest in Susan's half brother, who was an intelligent thirteen-year-old, not much older than Solomon would have been had he lived; perhaps he found in Gabriel a substitute for his lost son. Although young Gabriel had had some lessons in reading and writing the Dakota language in Dr. Williamson's mission school at Lac qui Parle, he was blissfully unaware of the rudiments of English. His guardian planned to change all that. Brown had heard of a school in Chicago that would board the boy and teach him to read and write English. The importance – and privilege – of an education was impressed on the boy. He sat Gabriel down and cut his long hair, a ceremony that more than any other symbolized to the Sioux rejection of the Indian way of life and commitment to the ideal of "white civilization," dressed him in white boy's clothes and, withdrawing $100 from his halfbreed payment money, set off for Chicago with his ward. They couldn't even wait for the Chippewa payment, which had been unconscionably delayed, for they would miss the start of the term. So on October 4 Brown gave William Aitkin his power of attorney to collect for him and the next day left Chanwakan.4

The trip was made with all deliberate speed. By November 5 Brown had returned as far as Prairie du Chien and was preparing to make the last leg of the journey to the St. Peters by land. There he also made certain arrangements for a proposed grogshop and ferry at Sintomonee. He contracted with Hercules Dousman for whiskey to be delivered in the spring, also provided himself with the services of one Henry C. Mencke, an English adventurer, to run the store. His other need was to obtain a territorial charter authorizing him to keep a ferry across the Mississippi between the landing at Massie's house on the east bank and "a point on the west bank about two miles above the mouth of the St. Peters River."

3. Carli to Williams, Sep. 20, 1871; "St. Croix Valley Old Settlers Biographies" (circa 1875), manuscript in MHS.

4. Samuel J. Brown "Biography of Gabriel Renville," manuscript in Brown papers and "Chief Gabriel Renville: A Memoire" in Minnesota biographical collections, MHS; J. R. Brown power of attorney Oct. 4, 1838, in Sibley papers.

This would, he said in his petition to the legislature, be a convenience to the population, which was equally situated on both sides of the river. Indeed the chosen site was admirably situated for the purpose, with a clear river crossing and an easy road up on each side. That it would also be a convenience for the patrons of the grogshop, those hard-drinking soldiers from Fort Snelling, wasn't mentioned. On reflection it will be seen that these two attractions were calculated to give Brown a firmer claim to the location, the grogshop qualifying as a residence and improvement for preemption and the ferry as a legitimate reason to be there.[5] This is not to suggest that the financial aspects of the project were not in themselves attractive: Brown fully expected to coin money at the location.

While at the Prairie, he approached Ira Brunson, representative from Crawford County, about introducing his petition at the next legislative assembly. This Brunson did, but in rather a slipshod manner. A document bearing no signatures, not even Brown's, but instead signed by former councilman Joseph Brisbois "for J. R. Brown," was got up the opening day of the second session of the second legislature on January 21, 1839, and presented to the House one week later. Perhaps because it was such a routine request, even though it uncharacteristically asked for a fifteen-year permit in order to allow the operator time to recoup his initial expenses in buying boats and hiring hands, the petition was returned from the select committee (on which Brunson sat) as a bill. But some undisclosed opposition developed and the bill was postponed indefinitely by the House. Brown couldn't believe it. He had been so sure, he had informed the Fort Snelling commander that his ferry was approved. The following August Major Joseph Plympton was still under the impression the legislature had passed the act: "The Territorial authorities of Wisconsin have, I am informed, granted a ferry license on the Mississippi just above this fort for the purpose of ferrying soldiers and Indians to and from a whisky shop, for most assuredly the ferry is not needed for other purposes," wrote Plympton in his August report.[6]

This disappointing episode presumably taught Joseph R. Brown another lesson that he would not forget. Hereafter he would not trust others to carry the ball, but would himself personally supervise the introduction and management of his bills and petitions. By the next legislative session he was thoroughly organized and would emerge from it as expert a lobbyist as ever graced a seat of government.

Great changes were coming about in the great northwest, partly because Indian territory was being organized. Illinois had come into the union in 1818, Missouri three years later. All of Wisconsin and Minnesota east of the Mississippi were then contained in Michigan Territory, while the land west of the Mississippi was unorganized Indian lands.

---

5. Dousman to Sibley, Nov. 5, 1838, Sibley papers; Petition of J. R. Brown for a ferry charter, Jan. 21, 1839, in papers of the Wisconsin Territorial Legislature: Petitions, WHS, Madison.
6. Petition of J. R. Brown, Jan. 21, 1839; *Wiskonsan Enquirer* (Madison) Feb. 2, 1839; Joseph Plympton to Adjutant General, Aug. 1, 1839, AGO LR.

Map 7 The settlements, and some settlers, near Fort Snelling ca. 1837-39, based on maps drawn by Lt. E. K. Smith in 1837 and 1838.

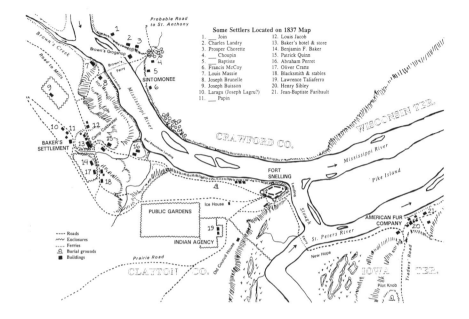

Some Settlers Located on 1837 Map

1. ___ Join	12. Louis Jacob
2. Charles Landry	13. Baker's hotel & store
3. Prosper Chorette	14. Benjamin F. Baker
4. ___ Choupin	15. Patrick Quinn
5. ___ Baptiste	16. Abraham Perret
6. Francis McCoy	17. Oliver Cratte
7. Louis Massie	18. Blacksmith & stables
8. Joseph Brunelle	19. Lawrence Taliaferro
9. Joseph Buisson	20. Henry Sibley
10. Laragu (Joseph Lagru?)	21. Jean-Baptiste Faribault
11. ___ Papin	

In 1834 the section between the Missouri River and Canada was attached to Michigan Territory, and subsequently, in 1836 became a part of Wisconsin Territory.

After the treaties with the Sioux and Chippewa were ratified in 1838, Iowa Territory was created west of the Mississippi with its capital located temporarily at Burlington (since most settlers lived along the river) until a new capital city could be built at Iowa City. Wisconsin's first legislature had met temporarily at Belmont and Burlington, finally settled on a new central location at Four Lakes, soon to be Madison, as the permanent capital.

That part of Minnesota east of the Mississippi came under jurisdiction of Crawford County, Wisconsin, with Prairie du Chien the county seat. Everyone east of the river was compelled to travel to the Prairie for every bit of legal business, even probates. Obviously it would be much more satisfactory if the seat of justice were closer to the St. Peters. A new county, with its concomitant courts, would be ideal. As a stopgap to bring some system of justice to the area, Brown had provided himself with a commission as justice of the peace, probably procured for him by Brunson. All it required was a recommendation from Governor Henry Dodge and confirmation by the Council, which was given February 15, at the end of the session. Henry Sibley, it is true, was already a J.P., but since he lived west of the river in Iowa Territory his commission was for Clayton County and did not extend across the river. Again, the commission provided a not unwelcome addition to Brown's income: at $2.00 per marriage and 25¢ per summons, not to mention 12½¢ per folio of 100 words recorded, Brown could make the J.P.'s fees add up.[7]

Construction on the new whiskey store started as soon as the snow was gone. One of the first boats of the season, *Ariel*, brought up its stock in trade – twenty barrels of whiskey – which were put off at Grey Cloud Island. This commerce did not pass unnoticed by Lawrence Taliaferro, who also noted: "Last winter Mr. B. was at the Prairie and brought up himself 4 or 5 bbls. Here begins what was anticipated when the Sioux relinquished their land."[8] By April 23, the fort's surgeon, alarmed at the increasing episodes of intoxication among the men, pointed the finger directly at Brown and his partners Angus Anderson and James Clewet. Reported Dr. John Emerson:

> "Since the middle of winter we have been completely inundated with ardent spirits, and consequently the most beastly scenes of intoxication among the soldier of this garrison and the Indians in its vicinity... The whiskey is brought here by citizens who are pouring in upon us and settling themselves on the opposite shore of the Mississippi River, in defiance of our worthy commanding office, Major J. Plympton, whose authority they set at naught. At

7. *Wisconsin Territorial Papers: Crawford County* I: 185 (Madison 1841). Justice of the Peace fees were set by law January 17, 1838, in Acts of Wisconsin Territorial Legislature 1836–1838 (First legislature, second session)

8. Taliaferro Journal Apr. 14, 1839.

this moment there is a citizen, Jos. R. Brown, once a soldier in the Fifth Infantry, who was discharged at this post while Col. Snelling commanded, and who has been since employed by the American Fur Company, actually building on the land marked out by the commanding officer as the Reserve, and within gunshot distance of the fort, a very extensive whiskey shop. They are encouraged in their nefarious deeds in consequence of letters received by them, as they say, from Saint Louis and Washington, mentioning that no Reserve would be acknowledged by the proper authority."**9**

The opinion from Washington was no doubt obtained by Wisconsin Territorial Delegate James Duane Doty (a man whom Brown had known since 1823, when he became judge of district court and moved his residence to the Prairie).

Intemperance among the soldiery had always been one of the army's more thorny problems, but it reached new heights the night of June 3 when forty-seven men – two-thirds of the command – were confined to the guardhouse for drunkenness after a spree in the establishment run by Mr. Mencke. Many of these turned up on the sick list, further decimating the command. This particular beano was very much ill-timed, coinciding as it did with Brigadier General John E. Wool's tour of inspection to the post. It may well have influenced Wool to lend strong support to Major Plympton's proposal that a reserve be established for Fort Snelling and all white settlers driven beyond the twenty-mile limit, a position he endorsed in his inspection report. Ultimately, as we shall see, this report swung the scales against Brown and partners. But all aggression was not on one side. The day after the big drunk, some persons unknown paid a visit to "the Hell," as Taliaferro called it, and destroyed at least some of its equipment.**10** Brown, to be fair, was likely not even around when these skirmishes were taking place. He kept out of the daily running of the store, the ostensible proprietor being Clewet and the manager Mencke, but it was well known that Brown had an interest in it and not a few of his employees, including Mencke and McCoy were living on the spot or on the bluff above. He may have remonstrated with the commanding office on June 23 before setting off for a quick trip up to Lac qui Parle, but otherwise was little seen in the vicinity of the fort. By mid-August the whiskey shop east of the river was again in full operation.**11**

Despite Major Plympton's sardonic remarks, there was probably enough business, apart from the garrison and the Sioux, to warrant a ferry on the Mississippi. In January of 1839 a traveler described the area near the fort as consisting of sixty to eighty houses, four of which were framed but the greater number logs, two stores and no tavern – which he seemed to regret. Lieutenant E. K. Smith's 1837 survey found eighty-two people living in Baker's settlement (near the sutler's store and Massie's landing

9. John Emerson to Thomas Lawson, Apr. 23, 1839, SGO LR.
10. Taliaferro Journal Jun. 4, 1839; Surgeon's report Fort Snelling June 30, 1839, AGO records; Taliaferro to Dodge, Jun. 14, 1839, OIA LR, Wisconsin superintendency; John G. Wool to Secretary of War, June 1839, LR OSW.
11. Stephen Riggs to Sibley, Jul. 12, 1839, Sibley papers; Taliaferro Journal Aug. 13, 1839.

about two miles north of the fort), twenty-five on the opposite side at Brown's and about fifty on Sibley's Mendota side, all of whom were unconnected with the military. Even he commented the total seemed low. In addition, there were a number of civilians attached to the fort as servants, blacksmiths, interpreters and the like. Records of the ferry kept by Sibley between the fort's landing and the site of old Cantonment New Hope show a considerable commerce in people, goods, horses and cattle being transferred back and forth. Among his passengers, incidentally, in the spring of 1839 was Tiwakan – Gabriel Renville. Indeed, Joe's ward had stuck it out only a month or two in Chicago before running away. Remarkably, the young man had made the entire 450-mile journey back to Grey Cloud Island on foot in the dead of winter, living on roots and herbs and what he could find on the way. Brown didn't push the school issue again, instead put the boy to work as general factotum and probably took him along on his trip to Lac qui Parle – Brown and Tiwakan both passed the ferry that day coming and going. Thereafter Tiwakan going about Brown's business became a familiar sight at the St. Peters.**12**

The grogshop's undoubted popularity proved its undoing. It was simply too much of an irritant, even a bête noire, for Major Taliaferro and the officers of Fort Snelling to be allowed to exist. These persons, "doubtless after much consultation, came to the praiseworthy determination, by means 'fair or foul,' of breaking up the concern," says a correspondent to the *Wiskonsan Enquirer* who calls himself "Badger" and who, from the writing style and knowledge displayed, can only be our friend Joseph R. Brown. Badger says attempts were made to intimidate the proprietor Clewet by invoking the old bug-bear "military reserve" to frighten him off. Failing that, he says, they employed non-commissioned officers of the army and some French Canadians to go in the night and pull down the house and destroy the property, but this was also unsuccessful "owing it is said to the reluctance of those applied to [of] assuming the responsibility of so wicked an act." As a last resort they went to the Sioux, who at first declined having anything to do with it. Then, according to Badger, the Indian agent convinced The Red Hail to do the dirty work – this he says was confirmed by the Indian who led the party.

He describes what happened next: On a rainy Sunday, the eighth of September, 1839, fifteen or twenty Indians crossed the river to Rumtown and first tried to persuade Mencke to violate his license by selling them liquor (money had been furnished them says Badger). Failing to entrap the wary Mencke, the Indians then commenced to pull off the roof, threatening the life of anyone who interfered. As Mencke was alone, he prudently retired. Going straight to Major Plympton, he asked for help. That officer replied that it wasn't a military matter – for Indian depredations you had to see the agent. So to Taliaferro Mencke went, only to be told, according

12. *Wiskonsan Enquirer* Apr. 13, 1839; E. K. Smith report Oct. 19, 1837, quoted in Williams *St. Paul*, 60; Sibley Account Book; S.J. Brown "Chief Gabriel Renville."

to Badger, that "it was too late in the day, and rather rainy, but that he would assuredly attend to it in the morning!" He finishes, "Meanwhile, however, the poor man's house was partly pulled down and his property destroyed."[13]

This is laying too much at Taliaferro's door. According to his own testimony, the agent wasn't even at home when Mencke arrived with a letter from the commanding officer requesting he look into the matter. Scott Campbell, the agent's interpreter, did make a sortie across the river, but of course found the Indians dispersed. Taliaferro reported to Major Plympton that the demolished house – in a later note this is downgraded to a building having only "a small opening... in one corner of a loose roof" – had some two or more barrels of whiskey and he understood that as the Indians were soon to receive their annuity payment "some of the braves in order to prevent great drunkenness and blood shed among their people proceeded without consultation except among themselves to break up the establishment."[14]

This assuredly did not satisfy Mr. Brown, who typically did not go after the guilty Indians directly, but instead took legal action against the agent. This, if it worked, would produce several beneficial effects: in addition to damages awarded, it would demonstrate to the Sioux that their agent was not invincible, would distract Taliaferro from his current campaign to aid and abet the cadre of army officers bent on enlarging the reserve and would possibly even remove him from the scene altogether (Brown could hardly have known that Major T., sick and tired of the constant harangues at the St. Peters, had actually tendered his resignation some weeks earlier). Carry the battle to the enemy was always Brown's motto.

As for the Sioux, there were other ways to even the score. While Mencke and Clewet were en route to the Prairie to carry out plan one, legal action against the agent, Brown put in claims for the depredations and let it be known among the Mdewakanton that restitution for the damage would have to be made – they could expect the (grossly inflated) amount to be deducted from their annuities, which were due to be paid in September. At a formal council of the chiefs of the lower bands held September 23, with Taliaferro, Sibley, Lieutenant John C. Frémont and several other representatives of the military present, there was much discussion about the amount of money that was being withheld from the payment. During the proceedings The Red Hail rose unexpectedly and said to Taliaferro: "My Father: I have something to say to the soldiers. We went over the river and got some whiskey and then turned the man off – he ran away. If we did this you will have to pay for it. It can't come out of

---

13. *Wiskonsan Enquirer* Dec. 14, 1839. Selling liquor to Indians not in Indian territory was perfectly legal; however, a grocery or tavern license permitted sale of liquor in quantities of one quart or under only. Presumably the raiding party tried to purchase a keg.

14. By October Major T. had a different opinion of the incident: he railed that the trouble had been caused by "the acts of drunken Indians" and intimated that 8–10 gallons of whiskey were taken. Taliaferro Journal, Sep. 8, 21, Oct. 5, 1839 and Taliaferro to Plympton, Sep. 8, 1839, copy in same volume p. 205.

our money. You told me to drive him (Mink) off, so if anything comes of it you must pay your money and not ours." The Red Hail told the council that Mr. Campbell had given him money to go over to get whiskey, all of which Taliaferro of course denied. (Assuredly Lawrence Taliaferro was not the man to stoop to illegally inciting the Indians, but only heaven knows if his interpreter acted always in the agent's best interests.) The agent maintained afterward that the chief had been put up to it and, in fact, had been paid to accuse him by "some people from the other side," a view confirmed by Philander Prescott, whose testimony unfortunately arrived too late for the council. Those accused of instigating the affair were Angus Anderson and Alexander Faribault, both of whom denied knowing anything of The Red Hail's intention until just before the council.[15]

There was worse to come. Taliaferro received a warning to be careful if he went down to the Prairie that fall, because Mencke was there and had threatened to grab him. But Mencke had actually proceeded on to Prairie la Porte (Guttenberg, Iowa), where he was made a special deputy by Clayton County Sheriff John W. Griffith. Clewet was with him and there swore out a charge against the agent, and so a warrant was issued to Mencke to serve on Major Taliaferro. At 6 A.M. on October 5 – this is graphically depicted in Taliaferro's diary – Mencke and Clewet burst in upon the agent (who was ill, and still in his dressing gown), threw him to the floor and with a pistol clapped to his head and a knee on his stomach announced that he was arrested at the suit of James Clewet for trespass and $3,000 damages. They demanded bail of $280, but the agent had it not, nor would the deputy take it from Dr. Emerson or others at the fort. Mencke was all for taking Taliaferro downriver to jail, but the plaintiff had him hold the agent in custody while he went for a blank bond. The agent was allowed to send a note to Major Plympton, who seemed loath to involve the military. Finally at 3 o'clock in the afternoon, after a nine-hour standoff, Plympton dispatched Lieutenant Daniel McPhail with a troop of soldiers to effect a rescue. Mr. Mencke was escorted back across the river on the pretext that the "newly fledged government officer" – Taliaferro's words – was in Indian country without a passport.

Badger took great offense at this summary use of military force to interfere with a civil officer, no matter of how green importation, calling it "an outrage upon the whole community!" Taliaferro, of course, knew who was behind his embarrassment – he noted next day in his diary: "Jos. R. Brown threatens but don't shew himself at the Agency. Brown, Mencke and Cluett are disposed to injure me all possible." Frantically, Taliaferro tried to withdraw his resignation so that he could fight the suit on the spot, as it were, rather than from his home in Bedford, Pennsylvania, and, as he hoped, with the financial aid of the government. "It admits not of a doubt

15. Taliaferro Journal Sep. 23, 1839; Taliaferro to Sibley, Sep. 28, 1839, copied in same volume p. 281. Depositions made Sep. 23, 1839, in Sibley papers. The truth of this matter will never be known. Sibley seemed to be surprised by the actions of Anderson and Faribault and of his father-in-law The Red Hail. For Prescott's view of the affair, see Parker Prescott, 168–170.

but that Joseph R. Brown, Henry C. Menke and James Cluete, all of a notorious stamp for vile conduct in this country, will cause my arrest again, right or wrong," he wrote to Iowa Governor Robert Lucas, pleading that the governor intercede to suspend the acceptance of his resignation "until I can save myself from ruin." Even though the resignation was accepted, the government did render Major Taliaferro some assistance in fighting the suit. Clewet and company pursued the charges until the following summer at least, then apparently let them drop.16 The idea had been to get rid of Taliaferro and by then that staunch champion of the Sioux had gone. After twenty-one years of squabbles he had had enough.

Lawrence Taliaferro was not Joseph R. Brown's only antagonist. The new commanding officer, Major Joseph Plympton, would prove an even more formidable opponent. In the end it was not Brown's whiskey store that clinched his expulsion from the east bank of the river (although some of his contemporaries, Prescott for one, thought so: "[T]he Indians used to go there and get whisky and kick up a fuss. This was the cause of the citizens all being drove off from the reserve – J. R. Brown's whisky shop – for none others kept any but him."), it was his position at the best steamboat landing below the Falls of St. Anthony.17 For it turned out Major Plympton was every bit as knowledgeable about townsites as Brown, and from the moment of his arrival as head of the regiment in August of 1837 he and Brown had clashed. Even before that summer the squatters near the fort had been requested to leave, the reasons given being that their cattle overran the government fields and that they competed with the garrison for firewood. In August of 1837, with Stambaugh (who was anxious to get a toehold at the falls) and Sibley (who had an immense investment in buildings and livestock on the proposed reserve) as their spokesmen, many of the settlers on the west bank of the Mississippi endorsed a memorial to President Martin Van Buren seeking recompense for their improvements if the lands they occupied were purchased from the Sioux as a military reserve.18 No one in their wildest dreams imagined that the reserve would be extended to the already ceded lands on the east side of the river.

Major Plympton from the first interested himself in the squatter's encroachments. In October of 1837 he had Lieutenant E. K. Smith survey the area and draw up a map, which was submitted to the War Department. On being asked to delineate the area he felt was required for military purposes, Plympton transmitted another map the following March on which was marked off a large tract of land west of the Mississippi extending from Nine Mile Creek above St. Anthony Falls south to intersect the St. Peters River above Pinichon's village.

16. Taliaferro Journal Sep. 21, Oct. 5 and 6, 1839; Taliaferro to Robert Lucas, Oct. 7, 1839, copy in same volume 225–226; Plympton to Taliaferro, Oct. 7, 1839, in Special File #12, OIA. Sibley, as Justice of the Peace, was to hold a preliminary hearing of the suit in August of 1840 (writ Aug. 13, 1840, Sibley papers); presumably one or both of the protagonists did not appear and the case was dropped.

17. Parker Prescott 169.

18. Williams St. Paul 59–60.

Map 8 The Fort Snelling Reserve as laid out in March 1838. Based on 1839 survey by Lt. James L. Thompson. The lakes have been given their modern names and several present-day streets are shown for reference.

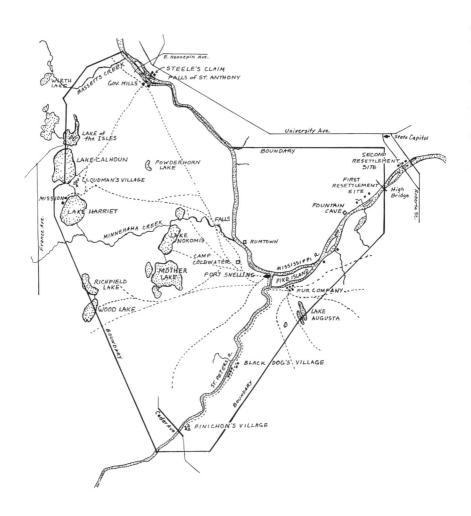

Surprising everyone including Secretary of War Poinsett, embraced considerable acreage east of the river within a line commencing about three miles south of the falls then running east to the Mississippi near Fountain Cave and up that river to Pilot Knob to include the settlement at Mendota within its bounds. Public notice was given July 17, 1838, that everyone residing within the lines so delineated must remove. Some did, probably less from fear of military force than from a desire to secure for themselves the best land for preemption. Let it be understood that much scrabbling for position was initiated by the news brought by the steamboat *Palmyra* on July 15 that the treaty had been ratified and the lands were now open to settlement. Abraham Perret, the Gervais families, Peter Parrant and others had moved even before the official word to the area east of Fountain Cave, which was supposed to be outside the survey line.[19]

The significance of the strange way the reserve was laid out so as not to include the east bank of the river at the falls, but all land below that point, was not lost on Joseph R. Brown. The land above, which included the water power and ultimate head of navigation, had immediately been snapped up by speculators. Among these, wrote Brown to James Doty, Wisconsin territorial delegate to Congress, were the commanding and other officers of Fort Snelling. This combine, he indicated, had also laid claim to another location at the mouth of the St. Croix River (Prescott, Wisconsin) that was admirably situated for the lumber regions of that river. "One great thorn in their side," continued Brown, "was the steamboat landings on the east side of the Mississippi, which would, if left open, render a competition in the commerce of the pine regions feasible." Therefore, he said, they had laid out the reserve to include all the possible landings below their claim for fifteen miles. Colonel Stambaugh, who along with Franklin Steele (his successor as fort sutler) and others had also made claims on the east side of the falls, went to bat for the dispossessed settlers. Stambaugh wrote to Secretary Poinsett in early 1839 to object to the extension of the reserve east and south of the Mississippi and St. Peters rivers because it interfered with the natural development of the ceded land and had been done solely to enhance the value of certain claims. If military force must be kept up, at heavy expense, to preserve the peace between the Indians and settlers, he asked Poinsett, why should the latter be thrown out of sight and sound of that protection? The arguments given by the military, preservation of the timber and removal of whiskey sellers, were in his opinion merely smoke. Brown hit the same point in his letter to Doty: "Any man who will examine that tract east of the Mississippi asked for as a reserve will see that it does not contain any timber of consequence, all the best timber being already cut by the troops; and as for the sale of spirits, it is useless to suppose the distance of two, three or five miles will prevent soldiers from getting it when so inclined."[20]

Naturally, military logic prevailed. Quite possibly General Wool's report swung the balance, and if so Brown and Clewet had only themselves to blame. On October 21 the Secretary of War issued an order

---

19. Smith maps October 1837 and Mar. 25, 1838. For a complete discussion of the reserve question, see Folwell *Minnesota* I: 218–220, 422 and Williams *St. Paul* 60–77.

20. Brown to Doty, Dec. 10, 1839, in *U.S. House Document* 144, "Reservation at Fort Snelling" 26th Congress, 1st Session; Stambaugh to Secretary of War, Feb. 11, 1839, OSW LR. For a history of the various shenanigans used to secure the claims at the falls, see Folwell *Minnesota* I: 452–454.

to Edward James, United States marshal for Wisconsin Territory, to remove the settlers as quickly as possible and to call upon the commanding officer at Fort Snelling if it became necessary to employ force. By accident this letter was missent and was not received by the marshal until February of 1840, a delay that gave the settlers some reprieve. Meanwhile, in early October of 1839 Major Plympton had the reserve area properly surveyed so that the land could be withdrawn from the general land sales, and – lo, and behold – when the lines were run out the reserve was now found to extend downriver of Fountain Cave another two miles! The families who had moved to the cave area, where there was what Brown calls "an inconvenient steamboat landing" that the officers had presumably overlooked, were found to be still within the lines and once again ordered off.21

This was too much. Someone (Brown was surely involved if not the instigator) organized a citizen's group and prepared to fight, being unaware that the Secretary of War's fiat was en route. At a public meeting November 16 at Perret's, with J. R. Clewet presiding and H. C. Mencke acting as secretary (and J. R. Brown pulling the strings), a resolution was produced that detailed the injustices done the inhabitants of the territory through the flagrant misuse of power by the military and provided for a committee, to consist of Brown and Mencke, to draft a petition to the territorial legislature asking for a resolution opposing the extension of the reserve. Brown was named to carry the petition to Madison. This time Joseph R. Brown did not make the mistake of expecting someone else to follow through for him. The petition was duly drafted – it is in Brown's handwriting – and signed by some two dozen of the east bank citizens. Brown was in Madison at the opening of the third session of the second legislature on December 2, 1839. His petitions (there were more, but we'll take the others up later) were introduced by Ira Brunson on December 9 and by December 16 both House and Council had passed a resolution condemning the extension of the reserve to the east bank of the Mississippi. Delegate Doty forwarded all proceedings to Secretary of War Poinsett, noting that the government was preempting land supposedly under the control of the Territory of Wisconsin without its consent, and the matter was duly taken up by Congress the following March, only to die a swift death in committee.22

---

21. Joel Poinsett to Edward James, Oct. 21, 1839 and James to Poinsett, Feb. 18, 1840, both in OSW LR & LS main series. For the new lines see Lieutenant J. L. Thompson "Map of the Military Reserve Embracing Ft. Snelling—done at Ft. Snelling Oct. & Nov. 1839 by order of Maj. Plympton," copy in MHS; Brown to Doty, Dec. 10, 1839.

22. "Petition from the citizens of Crawford County in Relation to the Reservation at Ft. Snelling" in papers of the Wisconsin Territorial legislature: petitions; *House Journal* 1839-1840, Second Wisconsin Territorial Legislature; *U.S. House Document* 144. Signers of the petition were (as spelled therein): James R. Clewet, H. C. Mencke, Abram Perret, Charles Perret, Benj. Gervais, Pierre Gervais, Francois Lerant, Euzeb Lanctot, Charles Mousseau, Vital Guerran, Jos. R. Brown, John Rix, John Müller, John Aitken, Francois D'Zierie, Sam'l Jno. Findley, Anthony Tilor Findley, Pierre Felix, Thomas Jones. Seven other names were added in Brown's and Mencke's hands, but only Charles Bruce Senior placed his X on the petition. The others (who were probably not at the meeting but who were east bank residents) were Francois Bruce, Severe Bruce, Jacque LeFevre, Marcier Courtereir, John B. Dennynier and Charles A. Lousiasse.

In the meantime Marshal James had received his instructions and dispatched his deputy, Ira Brunson, to carry out the law. Brunson soon found warnings were of no use; the squatters would not budge. He called on the military for help and on May 6, 1840, the remaining settlers were put off by force, their goods carried outside and their buildings rendered uninhabitable. This expulsion led many of them to move downriver to the site of St. Paul, which already had a small nucleus of inhabitants and which soon thereafter would become the focus of immigrant and business activity in the region. Badger let off steam again in a letter to the Enquirer dated May 16, 1840, expressing horror at the way the settlers had been treated, especially Pierre Gervais, who even though sick in bed was forcibly ejected into the elements "to die where he was." As to the extent of the reserve, Badger did not see why it could not be enlarged yearly and eventually made to embrace all the government lands in Wisconsin. Deputy Marshal Brunson replied in a later edition to Badger's charges, but even he admitted that it was "a question of doubtful import whether the evil to be remedied [removal of the whiskey sellers] was of sufficient magnitude to justify such a waste of property and outrage upon the feelings of the people removed."[23]

Spearheaded by Brown, the settler's group struggled for years to gain preemption rights to the land from which they had been ejected or, at the very least, to be awarded compensation for their improvements thereon. Many memorials on their behalf were sent to Congress, even so late as

---

23. *Wiskonsan Enquirer* Jul. 8 and Aug. 19, 1840.

1852. In the Martin McLeod papers is a document in Brown's handwriting, contained in the 1849 memorial as introduced, which sets out the lands then claimed by Brown, McLeod and others, Brown's being the quarter section of prairie now south of Morgan and east of Cleveland avenues in St. Paul's Highland Park area plus the two lots fronting the river where the grogshop had been located. But the army outlasted the claimants. When the reserve was finally abandoned by the army and the land released for public sale in September of 1854, Brown no longer was interested in it, for by then the rival metropolises of St. Paul and St. Anthony were too well established, the pattern of settlement too well advanced. It is interesting that in 1855 the German geographer and world traveler, Johann Georg Kohl, remarked that the site of St. Paul seemed to him misplaced, and that "[an] excellent place for a city would have been at the union of two great rivers, Mississippi and Minnesota, where the countryside spreads into a still broader and more beautiful landscape, soil is more fertile, and management of transportation by land and water is easier.' That he inquired about this anomaly is clear, as he says: "I was told that St. Paul's founders originally intended to put their city in the latter place. But Fort Snelling was in the way."[24]

This gets us ahead of our story. Let us return to late November of 1839, when it still seemed feasible that the extension of the reserve might be quashed. When Brown started down on the ice with his dog traineau bound for Madison he was in high good humor. With him he had more than the settler's petition to present to the legislature. William H. C. Folsom, whom he hired in Prairie du Chien to drive him and Ira Brunson to Madison, commented on Brown's large "Black Betty" – a capacious traveling bag that Folsom indicates was the butt of much humor and wit during that trip. The contents of Old Betty, Brown told him, must establish a new county away up in the northwest.[25] In truth, she was stuffed with petitions and not improbably cash. As soon as he received his quasi-official commission as delegate from the about-to-be-displaced settlers, he had penned their petition and at least five others that were, to all appearances, signed at the same time. For several days he must have been exceptionally busy gathering signatures; one petition he notarized himself on November 19. Soon after that date he must have left for Madison.

It would be interesting to know where Joseph R. Brown acquired his legislative know-how and his seemingly effortless style of drafting petitions and bills. Since he had become a Justice of the Peace he had had plenty of practice writing depositions, writs and warrants, and so had learned much "legalese." He could learn much more from the likes of Delegate James D. Doty, Thomas P. Burnett and his old comrades Dallam, Vineyard and Brunson, all of whom were then or had been

24. Undated draft memorial in the McLeod papers; Johann Kohl "Johann Georg Kohl: A German Traveler in Minnesota Territory" Frederic Trautmann, translator and editor, in *Minnesota History* 49/4: 130, (St. Paul 1984).
25. Folsom *Fifty Years* 35; see also W. H. C. Folsom Diary in Folsom papers, MHS.

members of territorial legislatures. But obviously, the knowledge that contributed most to his success was his understanding of people and his ability to get them to do what he wanted them to do. His lobbying skills must have been practically inborn, withal being finely tuned by a decade of dealing with Bailly and Rolette. When he undertook to explain some point to a member, sweet reason held sway and the member found himself persuaded that Joe Brown must have what he wanted. He must have been even then as he was described a few years later by a political colleague, Charles D. Gilfillan:

> "The most remarkable man... who ever appeared in the northwest was Joseph R. Brown... He drew up most of the bills and told the presiding officers how to rule. This he did in no dictatorial manner, but because nearly all members knew nothing about legislation... He had a most infectious laugh and keen sense of humor and was always the center of a crowd. Those people who had been prejudiced against him... after being a few moments in his presence were satisfied that 'Jo, the Juggler,' was not so bad a man after all... He would often laugh in late years over the bad things that had been said of him. He possessed one noble attribute: he entertained no hard feelings towards those who had reviled him. He had a good heart, and would put himself to a great deal of trouble to do a kindness, even to those who had traduced him. He was a well-read man, and wrote and spoke the French language with ease... How he... acquired [his] learning is a mystery to me."**26**

How indeed. Mr. Brown, although not a member of the legislature, seemed to be able to orchestrate its activities. (To keep this in perspective, remember that Madison was then just one year old, a town of fewer than 300 souls including the legislators – thirteen councilors, twenty-six representatives – all of whom with "lawyers and their wives and certain hangers-on, employed and expectants" were crowded into three small unfinished hotels; becoming intimate with those in power presented no problem when you were rooming with them.)**27** The first business after opening remarks and organization was the presentation of Mr. Brown's petitions by Mr. Brunson. This is in itself amazing: weighty matters were before the legislature, matters involving the discredited state banks, a monetary crisis and investigation of frauds connected with the building of the capitol, matters which indeed occupied most of their time during the session. Yet the problems of the few citizens residing in what had until very recently been Indian territory took their immediate attention and the representative from Crawford County took the floor. First read was the petition of the citizens of Crawford County relative to the military reserve at Fort Snelling; second was a petition from the same praying for passage

---

26. Charles D. Gilfillan "Early Political History of Minnesota," *Minnesota Historical Collections* IX: 179.
27. Morleigh (pseud.) *A Merry Briton in Pioneer Wisconsin* 16 (Madison 1950, reprint from *Life in the West...* [London 1842]).

of a law regulating claims upon the public lands, which was sort of an addendum to the former. With the encouragement of immigration as its purpose (a favorite Brown hobbyhorse), this petition asked that settlers be able to secure their claim so that they could not be "jumped" by speculators – a magnanimous gesture on the part of Mr. Brown, for he had, and would, make a good living off settling his neighbors' land squabbles in Justice's Court. His more immediate object must have been to preserve his and other settlers' claims on the reserve in the case they were forcibly removed. But the select committee to which this petition was referred along with the others apparently did not feel that any additional law was required, the preemption act of 1838 being adequate to govern claims, and so did not report or recommend a bill.**28**

A third petition written and carried to Madison by Brown (who was as involved in the issue as Samuel Stambaugh and Alexis Bailly) was that of the halfbreeds of the Sioux asking for the division of their lands on the upper Mississippi, that is the tract on Lake Pepin that had been given the mixed blood relatives of the Mdewakanton, Wahpekute, Wahpeton and Sisseton bands under the 1830 treaty. More than a hundred names are appended to this document, many, however, in the handwriting of Joseph R. Brown, including the entire Renville clan whose names are accompanied by the notation: "by Jos. R. Brown their attorney." Many of these claimants (and their white relatives) had a lively appreciation of the speculative value of this strip of land. They wanted to be able to "turn the mineral and other resources of said tract of land to a profitable account," that is to sell it, and to do that they needed private ownership. Therefore they petitioned the legislature for immediate survey and apportionment of the strip. The select committee quickly reported a resolution charging Delegate Doty to "use his influence to procure passage of a law directing early survey and apportionment in fee simple among the claimants of said tract." On the eleventh the resolution was engrossed, along with that protesting extension of the reserve of Fort Snelling, and the following Monday Governor Dodge signed them both.**29** Unfortunately for the halfbreeds (among them Susan Frénière, Gabriel Renville, Solomon Brown and the Dickson family, including Helen) this resolution got no further in Washington than had the memorials on the same subject sent to the Secretary of War in 1837 and 1838 by Stambaugh. The Indian Office's position was that it was inexpedient to attempt to divide the tract – how could the government be sure that the land would not fall into hands other than the claimants? That was, of course, the point.**30**

---

28. The record of actions on this and following petitions and bills is summarized from Journals of the House and Council, second Wisconsin Territorial Legislature. The original bills, petitions and memorials are in papers of the Wisconsin Territorial Legislature, WHS, Madison. Commentary on proceedings and text of many speeches were recorded in the *Wiskonsan Enquirer*, Dec. 14, 21 and 28, 1839 and Jan. 4 and 11, 1840.

29. Papers of the Wisconsin Territorial Legislature: resolutions.

30. T. H. Crawford to Poinsett, Mar. 7, 1840, copy in Sibley papers, summarizes the history of the tract and concludes that the treaty of 1837 did not contemplate the division of the Halfbreed Tract into sections, but rather that grants could be made to meritorious individuals.

Obstructions from Congress were yet to come as Brown contemplated the success of his political maneuverings in Madison. From Old Betty came yet another petition from the citizens of the northwest, a rehash of last session's petition for a ferry charter. This time, the signatures of more than thirty inhabitants accompanied their request to end the "incalculable inconvenience" occasioned by the want of ferries and praying the legislature authorize four, viz. across the Mississippi at Grey Cloud Island to be run by Andrew Robertson, across the Mississippi at "Rejection" (a bit of fun poked at last session's fiasco) to be run by Joseph R. Brown, across the Mississippi above the Falls of St. Anthony by Henry C. Mencke (if forced, they would move Mencke's whiskey operation to this site outside the proposed reserve) and across the St. Croix at "Battle Grounds" (Battle Hollow at Stillwater) by Hypolite Dupuis, a clerk of Henry Sibley's. All of these proprietors can here be considered stand-ins for Joseph R. Brown.

All was clear sailing this time. The petition was referred, as the others had been, to Mr. Brunson's select committee and emerged four days later as House Bill #4 authorizing certain ferries, the only difference from the petition being that Hazen Mooers' name had replaced that of Andrew Robertson. The charters were first allowed for twelve years, later amended to five, and the bill passed easily December 20, just two weeks after introduction. It passed the Council as well, but not without picking up an amendment adding a fifth ferry charter totally unrelated to the rest of the bill. With this amendment the House could not concur and so Brown watched his bill slip away again, just when success seemed so close.

In the spirit of saving what he could, Brown applied to the Crawford County board of commissioners for a license to keep a ferry across the Mississippi River opposite Massie's landing in Iowa Territory and also one across the St. Croix at the Battle Ground at the head of Lake St. Croix, which requests were granted January 18. (Apparently he left Robertson to look after his own affairs; Robertson wrote to Hercules Dousman asking his help in procuring a charter, received the reply it was too late for that year.) Brown also made the gesture of appearing at the Iowa Territorial Legislature then meeting in Burlington. He must have left Madison soon after his bill was tabled on January 1 (yes, they sat on Christmas Day – a holiday of not much account according to the *Madison Express* – and New Year's Day as well), for he had passed Prairie du Chien, leaving his requests for the ferry licenses with Dousman, and by January 7 was off for Burlington. Unfortunately it was too close to the end of the session to have his ferry petition considered; still, it had been worth a try. Whether he also applied for a license from the Clayton County board cannot be determined. Probably not, it wasn't necessary.**31**

---

31. *Wisconsin Territorial Papers: Crawford County* I: 155; Dousman to Sibley, Jan. 7, 1840 (misdated 1839), Sibley papers. Greater weight would be attached to a law of the territory than to a county charter, but a county authority was better than nothing. Burlington was on the site of Brown's old Flint Hills post; the Wisconsin legislature had met there in 1837 when Iowa was still part of that territory.

When Brown and Brunson went down to Madison that winter of 1839 they had with them a fifth petition, that all-important document asking for a new county to be formed from the northern part of Crawford, but Brunson did not introduce it. Instead – surprise! – Mr. Barlow Shackelford of the Committee on Territorial Affairs was found to be already in possession of a petition from the inhabitants of northern Wisconsin who wished to organize a new county to be called St. Croix. This petition had been got up the preceding May by the loggers of the Marine and St. Croix Lumbering companies, and they had on it the signatures of nearly everyone north of Lake St. Croix – eighty solid citizens who wanted the timberlands north of the Chippewa River and west of the headwaters of the St. Croix to constitute the new county St. Croix with the county seat to be located at Prescott's claim at the mouth of the St. Croix River. Joe Brown pocketed his petition, which defined a much smaller county centered not on the St. Croix but on the Mississippi, with the county seat to be located at Chanwakan (he could hardly propose Sintomonee while the reserve issue was unresolved), and set about to effect some sort of compromise.

House Bill #5, as reported from Shackelford's committee on the thirteenth, was pretty straightforward, as county bills go. The boundaries had been changed to "a line commencing at the mouth of the Chippewa River and running thence a due east course to a point twenty miles west of the Wisconsin River and continuing thence a due north course to the boundary line of the State of Michigan." Election of officers was set for the first Monday in August 1840, and district court for the second Monday in June each year. The duly elected county commissioners were given freedom to select a temporary site for the courthouse until the seat of justice should be determined by law. This was not good. The territory covered by the county was too large and included the mills on the Chippewa and Red Cedar rivers whose owners' interest lay with the Prairie and who, in any case, did not wish to be included in the new county. And from Brown's standpoint the location of the county seat could not be left to chance. Establishment of a civil court was an important part of Brown's scheme to challenge the jurisdiction of the military over the civilian population, and he was determined not to allow the seat of justice to be located on a claim controlled by the syndicate from Fort Snelling.

The proponents of this bill, who had already proved to be a litigious bunch, would see that the court was sited at Prescott's claim on St. Croix where it would be convenient for them unless Brown could conceive a palatable alternative. Brunson waded in and managed to talk the bill to stalemate; on December 18 it was ordered to lie on the table by a slim vote of 13 to 11. Brunson then produced the counterpetition of J. R. Brown and thirty citizens of the southern part of the country in question, crossing out

---

When Iowa Territory was formed in 1838, Burlington was made the place of legislative assembly while a new capitol was built at Iowa City and the Wisconsin assembly moved to the new city of Madison, a speculative venture of J. D. Doty and Morgan Martin.

the part that proposed to locate the county seat at Chanwakan. This, too, was ordered to lie on the table.

Map 9 St. Croix County as laid out by the Wisconsin Territorial Legislature in January 1840, and the county originally proposed by Brown.

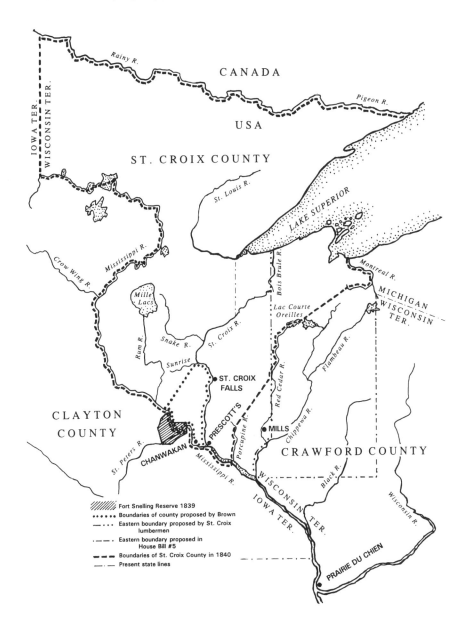

How much the two groups of petitioners knew of each others plans is now impossible to determine. By their petition date (Brown's is undated, but appears to have been signed with the rest in November), the mill people were six months ahead of Brown and had already selected the name St. Croix for the county. Brown's counterproposal may have been conceived without knowledge of the lumbermen's petition, or in answer to it. Their interests differed widely: the lumbermen's aim was to include all the timberland on the St. Croix and Chippewa rivers and their tributaries, while Brown's was to zero in on the site of future immigration – townsites, farmsites and supply points centering on The Entry – and to get a county whose machinery he could manage. Both wanted a convenient court in which to fight their legal battles.

Brown's original petition proposed a county that comprised only lands west of the St. Croix River from its mouth to the Sunrise River (thus excluding the St. Croix Lumbering Company settlement on the east side at the falls) and south of a line from the forks of the Sunrise to the falls of St. Anthony, including most of the settlements but entirely avoiding the timber and mineral lands to the north. He may have reasoned that another county would in due time be made north of his, centering on the falls, and that this would satisfy the mill people, or he may just have misjudged the political acumen of those lumbermen. That both groups of petitioners proposed the same county name would argue that there had been some discussion about the new political entity among the inhabitants of the county. The proposals were competitive. It would appear that Brown was caught off guard.

By Christmas Eve some compromises had been achieved. The bill was revived and sent to a select committee composed of Ira Brunson, Horatio Wells and Thomas Cruson to be pushed into acceptable form. On December 28 they reported a substitute bill (which is, incidentally, in J. R. Brown's handwriting). In this substitute the boundaries of the county have been made smaller, excluding the Chippewa River and most of its tributaries, but still encompassing an immense tract centered on the St. Croix River: its southern boundary is at the mouth of the Porcupine (Rush) River angling northeastward to Lac Courte Oreilles and the Michigan border, then following the shore of Lake Superior to Canada. As for the county seat, its location is to be determined by vote at the first election with this proviso: "The County Commissioners shall not locate the County Seat on any land occupied without the consent of the occupant, nor unless said occupant shall pay into the country treasury not less than $800 for the right of said county to the land." This clause authorized the county to sell its right (under the act of May 26, 1824) to preempt a quarter section of land for a seat of justice. It may be understood as a means of providing the new county with sufficient funds to run its machinery until taxes can be collected, and was undoubtedly so promoted by Brown. It may also be understood as providing the buyer with an ironclad deed to 160 acres of unsurveyed land. Brown intended to be the buyer. At the time he was still unaware that the reserve was being withdrawn from the public land sales and that the settlers were doomed to be put off by law. He may well have amused himself by imagining the awesome sight of the seat of justice rising tall and proud just across the river from the commanding officer's house at Fort Snelling. Whatever the argument, it convinced the House. The substitute bill with its strange seventh clause was found acceptable and was passed by that body 17–6 on January 2, by the Council a few days later.

The small population base of the new St. Croix County precluded having a representative to the legislature elected from that county alone; therefore, two representatives and one councilman would be elected at large from the counties of Crawford and St. Croix. The bill set up voting precincts at St. Croix Falls, Chanwakan and La Pointe, the same precincts that had been set up the preceding summer for Crawford County (there had been political maneuvering all summer in northern Crawford County, resulting in a special meeting of the county board at the Prairie in July to establish election precincts in the newly purchased land; it's not clear whether Brown or the mill people were behind this activity). The election was to be held in August of 1840 so that the county might be organized for the territorial elections which would take place in September. Brown was betting that most of the people at the mills were more interested in their internal squabbles than in politics and that their support could likely be bought with certain concessions, allowing him to run everything else. Though not entirely happy with the product of this travail, he could congratulate himself that the "establishment of a new county away up in the northwest" had gone moderately well.

Joseph R. Brown spent just thirty days at Madison as a lobbyist and came away with nearly everything he wanted, including a divorce from Margaret McCoy. Timing it so as not to prejudice his other petitions, Brown waited until the third week of the session before firing his final salvo. His petition asserted that since the outbreak of hostilities between the Sioux and Chippewa of the St. Croix in the summer of 1839, it was no longer safe for Margaret, a Chippewa, to reside there with Brown and that, in fact, she had only saved her life on one occasion by flight – a statement that might well be true if she was with the body of Chippewa that had been ambushed that July at Battle Hollow, the site of Brown's proposed ferry and a stone's throw from his warehouse on the shores of Lake St. Croix; further, he could not leave his business there without incurring "heavy pecuniary loss" and therefore he and his wife felt their happiness would be better secured by a separation. In view of the circumstances they prayed the legislature would grant them a divorce. A bill to annul the marriage of Joseph R. and Margaret Brown (again, in Brown's handwriting) was reported from committee on December 24 and passed by the House in a close vote six days later. Brown was assured it would also pass in the Council, and so shortly after the New Year left Madison for Burlington to attempt to resuscitate his ferry at Sintomonee. However, opposition to the divorce bill developed in the Council as soon as Brown was out of sight. The general feeling was that they had passed enough divorce bills; such bills took up too much time and were in any case the prerogative of the judiciary. An example was to be made. The bill was referred to the Committee on Judiciary, from which chairman Morgan Martin reported a substitute, now entitled "An Act for the Relief of Joseph R. Brown." One of the more unusual divorce bills ever enacted by the Wisconsin legislature, it granted the divorce provided Margaret Brown get one-third of all property owned by Joseph R. Brown and that the divorce be not final until submitted to the judge of district court for Crawford County and the settlement duly recorded by the register of deeds. The bill became law January 11, two days before the session adjourned.32

Brown had expected some opposition to his divorce plea; his first divorce had undoubtedly taught him some of the pitfalls. Attempting to provide himself with as much ammunition as could be acquired for the battle, he had first tried to get the signatures of Francis and Margaret McCoy, Margaret's parents, appended to an approval of the separation, apparently without success. Pressed for time, he had left Henry Sibley and his new clerk William H. Forbes to draw up a marriage agreement between Margaret Brown and Peter Bouché (a Fur Company employee, said to be of Clayton County, Iowa), to be implemented as soon as the legislature should grant the separation of J. R. Brown and wife. This document was signed and witnessed at the St. Peters on December 18, the same day Ebenezer Childs read Brown's petition to the House – very late, but if Sibley sent it via an express to Madison Brown may have had it in hand for some of the discussion. These documents may or may not have helped promote his case, but as evidence of the far-seeing and imaginative mind of Mr. Joseph R. Brown they are superb. However startling the final version of the divorce bill, Brown had little choice but to make a financial settlement with Margaret. In February he did so, notarizing the deed himself (being, as he noted, the only J.P. within 250 miles). He made one condition, to which Margaret agreed, that he have sole control over the two girls, bearing the expense of their support and education. Margaret was to receive from Brown what she agreed was one-third of all his personal property (there being no real estate), viz., 2 calves, 1 bay mare, 2 breeding sows, a dozen Dung-hill fowl, $375 cash, and the improvements made by Brown on a claim on Red Rock Prairie (sometimes Red Stone Prairie), about ten miles north of Chanwakan on the Mississippi, which may well have been where Margaret was then living. Witnessing this document were Peter F. Bouchea and James R. Clewet, the latter of whom swore that all had been fully explained and interpreted to Mrs. Brown. It apparently seemed a fair settlement to Judge Charles Dunn, chief justice for Wisconsin Territory, to whose district court in Prairie du Chien Brown submitted the documents August 11. Brown's deed of separation from his wife Margaret was duly received, certified and recorded by the register of

32. The bill is printed in the *House Journal*, 2nd Wisconsin Territorial Legislature, 2nd Session.

deeds, and on April 29, 1841 Brown found himself once again a free man.**33**

Returning to Chanwakan in the latter part of January, Justice Brown soon found that his neighbors had plenty of legal business for him to attend to. In late February Philander Prescott came to Brown to accuse Charles D. Foote of claim jumping. Prescott, who had bought out B. F. Baker's stock and had been running the store near Fort Snelling, found himself at loose ends when Baker, ill from consumption, gave up his business in the fall of 1839 to go to St. Louis (where he soon died). Once again out of a job, Prescott had been happy to accept a proposal from Dr. Emerson and other officers from Fort Snelling: they had agreed to furnish him $1,000 to build a house and store and had offered him a one-eighth interest in the land and buildings if he would remove to the mouth of the St. Croix and hold the townsite these speculators had taken up. This he had done, but Prescott being Prescott, he had returned to the St. Peters during the cold months to see his family, and while he was thus engaged the claim was marked over by Foote, a carpenter from the St. Croix mills. Appalled at the thought of what his principals would do to him, Prescott sued to recover the claim. Another popular citizen, Mr. Pierre "Pig's Eye" Parrant, had suffered a similar misfortune; his claim at the Grand Marais (now Pig's Eye Lake) had been taken over by Michael Leclaire whilst he had his good eye turned. These suits required jury trials – the first jury trials to be held in the valley. In March Justice Brown got everybody together to try the two cases at the same time.**34**

Those trials on Saturday, March 7, 1840, must have provided the social event of the season. Just about everybody in the southern half of the county was there, if not as juror then as a witness for one of the four litigants. Forming the gallery – we can imagine the scene – were spectators and interested parties – officers, friends, relatives – all crowded into Brown's barely adequate log house at Chanwakan and overflowing into the yard. Everything was handled in best legal fashion. Constable Edmund Brisette returned the writs and produced the witnesses; at 10 A.M. the jury of twelve was sworn to try Parrant vs. Leclaire. It did not take them long to find for Leclaire and the plaintiff was ordered to pay costs of $36.31, which he did. Now the sagacious student of Minnesota history will recollect that this particular dispute is supposed to have involved a footrace between the claimants. According to the story (actually told by Clewet) Squire Brown, not being able to decide the issue and loving a joke, declared that neither claimant had valid right to the land

33. Contract between Margaret Brown and Peter F. Bouché Dec. 18, 1839 (Sibley's handwriting), copy in author's possession; Indenture Feb. 25, 1840 between Joseph R. Brown and Margaret Brown, Crawford County Deed Book B, Prairie du Chien. Bouché (or Bouchea) probably had no intention of marrying Margaret, although he may have been then living with her. Bouché, William Stitts and Joseph Lagru, all refugees from the reserve, took up claims at the mouth of Willow River in 1840, forming the nucleus of the village that became Hudson, Wisconsin. In September of 1841 Bouché married Louise Bruce, the ceremony performed by Justice Joseph R. Brown. See Brown Docket 1839–1841 Sep. 29, 1841, Brown papers; Folsom *Fifty Years* 159–160.

34. Parker *Prescott* 168–170; Brown Docket Feb. 16, Mar. 7, 1840.

in question and that the one who first staked it out in the presence of witnesses would be entitled to it. Thus commenced the eight-mile race through bogs and sloughs, which was, of course, won by the younger Leclaire. It made a good story (and it's possible Brown threatened the old whiskey-seller with some such debacle), but it's just so much legend. The dispute was properly settled by a jury of their peers, and Parrant, far from leaving the country in chagrin, as the story goes, merely made another claim west of Dayton's Bluff where he remained for several years.[35]

After lunch Justice Brown summoned the jury to sit once again to hear Prescott's complaint against Charles Foote. This case proved not so easy. The jury found, after much discussion, that they could not agree. Brown could only dismiss them and set a new time and venire for a new trial: April 4 at Judd's Mills (Marine). Part of the problem may have been conflict of interest – the jury foreman, George Brower, appeared for the defendant as a witness, as did juryman Francis Nasson, who also helped Foote survey the disputed claim the following Sunday. On Monday an infuriated Prescott sued Foote, Nasson and Alexander McHattie for Sabbath-breaking. Obviously a change of venire was a good idea! (Also Brown was running out of eligible jurors in the southern part of the county.) April fourth saw a new jury of mostly Judd's Mills men impaneled. This time the survey was produced and some charts exhibited, but still to no avail. This jury requested a visit to the premises. So off trooped the whole court by boat to the mouth of the St. Croix where the next Monday the jury examined the disputed ground and after three and a half hours confessed themselves still confounded. According to Prescott this hanging of juries was not by chance, but by direction of Mr. Brown:

> "The Justice would like to see my claim taken from me because the officers had an interest in it, in fact, owned near the whole. Brown felt sore about the whiskey shop being broken up, for it was a source of quite a little income to him, and he would like to see the officers injured in return if he could do anything to injure them. Here it is supposed he done all he could to get a jury that would decide against me, but my proof was too strong, and the work showed too much for any just jury to decide against me. But there were enough always to make a split [jury] and keep me in expense, which had now come to over $200 [actually $150.94½ by Brown's records]."

At last, Prescott and Foote agreed to a compromise, whereby Foote would retain eighty rods fronting on the St. Croix, virtually splitting the claim, and pay costs of witnesses, while Prescott would pay the rest. "This the officers did not like, but it was the best I could do, and so it stood," recalled Prescott.[36]

---

35. See Williams *St. Paul* 147.

36. Parker *Prescott* 169–170, 172–173. Prescott got the claim back in 1842 by re-jumping it. Foote didn't contest the claim, which gives some weight to Prescott's theory that he was put up to the original jumping and was not a legitimate settler.

Until December of 1840, Brown was the only J.P. in St. Croix County. During his tenure (he renewed his commission through 1843) he gained a reputation for sagacity in the dispensation of justice. He officiated at weddings, and, if we may believe Ira Brunson, even at baptisms – surely a bit out of the jurisdiction of a J.P., but in character for Brown. Brunson related that Brown, at the plea of a woman about to lose her unbaptised baby, "with swelling heart and tearful eyes" read the baptismal service and christened the babe, there being no priest in the county. "No one," said Brunson, "was more spiritually benefited than the justice, to whom the recurrence of the occasion always brought serious thoughts."[37]

One of the settlers who had been put off the reserve that spring of 1840 was a former voyageur named Vital Guerin. Guerin relocated to the site of St. Paul, taking over the claim of a man in jail at Prairie du Chien awaiting trial for murder. Murder was nearly done again when Ed Phalen returned to his claim in July after being released by the U.S. district court to find the Frenchman in his claim and cabin. Phalen told Guerin (Clewet interpreting) if he wasn't off in a week, he would come back and put him off. Fortunately for Guerin, he had husky friends to help him stand off the former soldier who, sure enough, made his appearance one week later, shirtsleeves rolled up, axe in hand. Seeing the formidable opposition, Phalen backed off and resorted to the law, suing Guerin in Brown's court. Guerin's position was that since Phalen had been off the claim for six months, he had vacated it; he called Peter (Pierre) Parrant as a witness. Two juries hung and eventually the parties submitted to arbitration, which also failed. But an "amicable adjustment" was made in 1842 and Phalen and Guerin agreed to divide the claim. Phalen soon sold his half and took another claim on the east side of St. Paul, greatly to everyone's relief for the irascible Irishman was not liked among the French settlers in early St. Paul. To see why, we must return to the previous fall.[38]

The murder for which Phalen was held was the first criminal case Justice Brown heard in the spring of 1839. Edward Phalen (sometimes Phelan, Felyn, etc.) was a private at Ft. Snelling, a strapping six-footer who was said to have boasted that he had led a lawless life before joining the army. On discharge in 1838 he took up two claims in the St. Paul area, one of which he held for John Hays, the sergeant of his company, who joined him in his cabin on the side of the bluff (near St. Paul's present civic center) when he got out in 1839. Both unmarried men, they apparently lived together without serious conflict until September 5, when Hays unaccountably disappeared. Suspicion fell on Phalen from the start.

The facts are these. The night Hays went missing, Phalen stumbled into the cabin of another old soldier, William Evans, who lived on the side

37. Ira Brunson "Early Times in the Old Northwest," in *Wisconsin Historical Society Proceedings* 1904 170, (Madison 1905). Except for an occasional visit, there was no priest regularly at the St. Peters until the Reverend Lucian Galtier founded St. Paul's Church in 1841.

38. Brown Docket Apr. 25, 1840. See Williams *St. Paul* 102–103 to compare Guerin's memory of the episode thirty years later. He had forgotten the two hung juries, was sure he had won the case. Phalen paid the court costs.

of Dayton's Bluff about a mile and a half east of the settlement known as Imnijaska or White Rock, sometimes as the Old Cave settlement, now St. Paul. He was wet, hatless, disheveled and clutching a canoe paddle. He said he was looking for a lost calf and had fallen into a creek in the dark, losing his hat. Two young men from the St. Croix pineries, Stephen Scott and John Foy, who were staying the night with Evans, became suspicious (or were urged by Evans to investigate) and left early next morning to get their canoe, which had been beached on the Mississippi a short distance away. They were delayed reaching the river by the arrival of Jim Clewet, Henry Mencke and Pierre Gervais in a heavily laden canoe. This party stopped to sell Scott and Foy a bottle of whiskey and palaver (they certainly had something to talk about; it was just three days after the raid on their whiskey store). The upshot was that Phalen beat them back to his cabin and had already taken out his canoe before they came in sight of his landing, which was about a quarter-mile from his cabin. Scott and Foy watched Phalen return, beach his canoe and proceed up the hill to his cabin. They began to approach his place warily, Foy following Phalen up the path and Scott scouring the bottoms, where he found a trampled place and fresh blood. Questioning Phalen, Scott asked if he might have killed a cow, but was told No, he hadn't lost any stock. When asked Hays' whereabouts, Phalen said he had just put him across the river.

There the matter lay, though some searching took place after Hays failed to return in a few days. Phalen told various stories about how Hays had gone in search of a calf he thought the Kaposia Indians had stolen, once said the calf had returned by itself. He let out that Hays had quarreled with a man from Big Thunder's band and, forgetting his prior story, said that the Indian might have killed the calf. At one point he had gone to Ft. Snelling to get a soldier, Bartholomew Baldwin, and an interpreter to question the Kaposia Indians, whose village was now several miles south across the river from Red Stone Prairie, but they learned nothing. On September 27 Hays' naked body was found by some of Little Crow's band near the old cave (Carver's Cave) on a sandbar, partly in the water, in plain sight. The Indians came to Maj. Taliaferro who sent them to tell their tale at the fort, and soon a detail under Lt. Daniel McPhail and Dr. John Emerson descended the river to investigate. Dr. Emerson testified the body was shockingly mutilated, the face and jaw smashed in; when asked he opined the wounds could have been made by a canoe paddle. Phalen helped identify and bury the body, then went to Mendota where he and Pvt. Baldwin made statements to Justice of the Peace Henry Sibley.

Realizing he had no jurisdiction (the body had been found in Crawford Co.) Sibley gave the affidavits to Justice Brown, who issued a warrant for the arrest of Phalen, sent Mencke to serve it, and convened a preliminary hearing November 1. Based on evidence, Brown sent Phalen for trial in U.S. district court at the Prairie. His reasons were noted in his docket: first, Phalen had not time to travel from Evan's house to his own, take Hays across the river and return before Scott and Foy came up; second, Phalen said he thought an Indian had killed his calf, yet said the blood in the bottom could not be from his cattle – "I consider the affair of the calf to be a fabrication," wrote Brown; third, he tried to stop a search by various stories; and fourth, Phalen acted suspiciously the night he went to Evan's house with the canoe paddle – what was he doing with a paddle searching a calf on land? On November 4 John McCormack was made special constable to take Phalen to Prairie du Chien on the steamer *Detroit*. There Phalen stayed in jail until court was convened in May of 1840.

Although several witnesses – including Scott, Foy and Mencke – turned up, there was no real evidence of Phalen's guilt and the case either was decided in his favor or dismissed by the grand jury – most of the records of the May 1840 session are missing. In any case, Phalen was freed. About a year later Dowan (Singer), a son of Wakinyantanka, was said to have confessed the murder just before he died in a skirmish with the Chippewa. The story may have been a convenient back-formation put out after Dowan's death. The mystery of Hays' death was never unraveled, though public opinion favored a theory that Phalen had something to do with it.**39** So Justice J. R. Brown's first criminal case must be marked "unsolved," the facts now too obscured to ever be fully known.

---

39. Brown Docket Nov. 1, 1839; Taliaferro Journal Sep. 15, 27 and 28, 1839; Williams St. Paul 70–72, 90–93, 102, 145–146; *Wisconsin Territorial Papers: Crawford County* I: 174, 185; U.S. vs. Ed. Phalen, May term 1840 in Witness Book, U.S. District Court, Crawford Co. Wisconsin Territory 1840, WHS, Madison; Newsom *Pen Pictures* 11. Brown's docket has testimony from John Emerson, Daniel McPhail, Stephen Scott, John Foy, Genevieve Gervais, Bartholomew Baldwin, William Evans, James Clewet, Henry Mencke, Alphonse Gervais and Benjamin Gervais and Brown's summation. Foy, Scott and Mencke all were paid for five days as witnesses, but the 1840 dockets (except the Witness Book) and executions have not been found, so it is impossible to tell if a trial was held. The records have been missing a long time: in the 1870s Ira Brunson, then a judge, searched and failed to find them. As recorded in Williams' *History of St. Paul*, public opinion was against Phalen, though there is no evidence he conducted himself improperly or ever showed signs of being violent (Williams' informants may have had axes to grind). Phalen stayed in St. Paul to 1850, taking and selling several claims on the east side of St. Paul (near the creek that bears his name), started for California with another east side settler in 1850 (supposedly to flee a perjury indictment) and was said to have been killed on the journey.

Map 10 Settlements in St. Croix County, 1840-1846. Most of the roads shown were barely passable as late as 1849. The northern route from Stillwater to St. Paul was not laid out until 1847; the route via Morgan's Halfway House was opened in 1848.

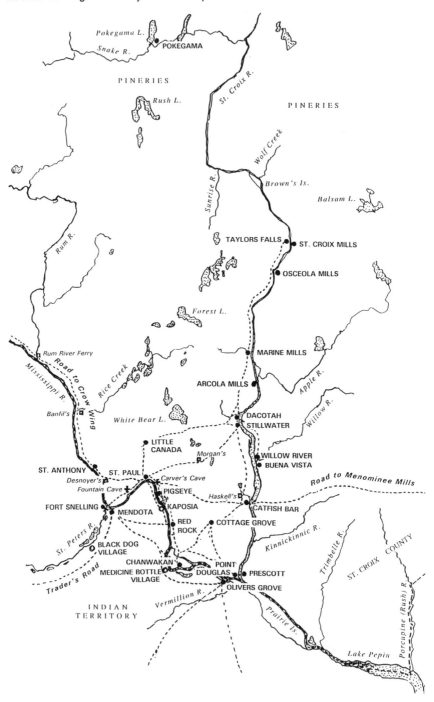

CHAPTER VIII

"AN ELECTION RODE OVER BY THE
CAR OF LOCO-FOCOISM." MADISON EXPRESS, 1842

Dacotah, Brown's new townsite (which he intended to make the county seat and, if possible, the capital of a new territory), was finally located by him in the summer of 1840 at his warehouse at the head of Lake St. Croix near the mouth of Pine Creek (now Browns Creek). Not the best location for a great capital and center of commerce, it was the only practical one available to him for the purpose. And it did possess certain amenities: there was a decent steamboat landing, water power that could drive several mills, a small but level plateau for building with a manageable slope to the bluff tops, and most important, a way out for carts and wagons following the creek valley. That he was locating in the St. Croix valley at all was one of the concessions he had had to make to the people at the upstream mills who did not relish the idea of traveling overland to Chanwakan or any other site on the Mississippi, but who would accept as the county seat almost any site in the valley. He hedged his bet only so far as to acquire a 320-acre claim on the Mississippi near the mouth of the St. Croix from Francis Chevalier, the first deed recorded in St. Croix County, July 5, 1840.[1]

In June of 1840 there was very little to indicate that the new metropolis of the northwest might grow at the head of Lake St. Croix. That month two young adventurers, E. Wolcott and Lewis Hall, found its proprietor, Joseph R. Brown, at the small French Canadian and halfbreed settlement across from the mouth of the Kinnickinnic River called Catfish Bar (Afton) and were invited to accompany him to the Chippewa village and mission station at Pokegama whence he was going to take the federal census, having been made assistant to Deputy Marshal Ira Brunson for that purpose. They stopped one night at the head of the lake "in a dry and picturesque spot" where Brown told his companion he intended to lay out a town, "and he asked me to stay or come back and take an interest with him," reminisced Wolcott. Since he mentions sleeping in his blanket, it is

---

1. St. Croix County Deed Book A in Register of Deeds office, Washington County Courthouse; this deed was by necessity—because there were yet no county officers—recorded after the fact. In order not to seem to be holding two claims, Brown held this claim as guardian for Gabriel Renville.

probable that there was no habitation then on the future site of Dacotah, but only the "warehouse," which may have been no more than a storage cellar, or a bark hut.

Wolcott and Hall did not seem unduly nervous about going into Chippewa country, even though they had ample evidence of the Indian wars then raging up and down the St. Croix. While at Fort Snelling they had noticed a "furious and uncontrollable excitement" among the Sioux that had culminated in a fierce war dance on the flat below the fort. They had been shown the bones and clothing still littering the site of the previous July's massacre of a party of Chippewa at Battle Hollow and casually poked among them looking for souvenirs. The Indians were in a dangerous frame of mind; the preceding year had seen more than 125 deaths from warfare among the Sioux and Chippewa in the ceded land, and 1840 had started out with several more murders. It transpired that the two Chippewas paddling Brown's birchbark canoe had with them, whether known to Brown or not, a grisly relic of one of these encounters – a Sioux scalp that had been taken practically at the gates of the fort and the very one that had precipitated the war dance at Fort Snelling. This trophy, to the horror of the missionaries, set off "the most infernal yelling and whooping and beating of drums" when it was displayed at Pokegama. Ignoring these undercurrents, Wolcott thought the canoe trip an idyll. He slept happily under Mr. Brown's mosquito bar and wolfed down his provisions – flour and salt pork and tea and sugar – supplemented with turtle eggs dug out of the downstream ends of the sandbars, all cooked in a tin bucket. His description of their ascent of the St. Croix presents us with a brief but wonderful picture of Joe Brown's irrepressible good spirits: "And Mr. Brown with his clear, sonorous voice waked the answering echoes of the lonely lake and river, as he sang with the Indians the French-Canadian boat-songs as we sailed."2

They stopped at all the settlements en route for Brown to take the census and do some politicking. At Marine they found sixteen men and one woman; at St. Croix Falls fifty-eight men and two women; at Pokegama two missionary and two French Canadian families and the Indian farmer, Jeremiah Russell. Brown omitted enumerating any whiskey sellers, though he passed several known "trading" sites along the river. Census complete on the seventh of July, he retraced his steps to Catfish Bar, crossing on foot to Chanwakan, and after dispatching Wolcott safely to the fort left to deliver the census returns to Brunson at Prairie du Chien. There were, he found, 351 non-Indian people living in the area between the Mississippi and St. Croix Rivers. Daniel Bushnell, subagent at La Pointe, had counted 458 souls in the settlements near Lake Superior and Brunson found 1,502 people south of the Chippewa and north of the

2. E. Wolcott to Joseph R. Carli, Apr. 29, 1892, manuscript in MHS, published as "Reminiscences of the St. Croix River, 1840," Nancy Goodman, ed., in *Historical Whisperings* 22/4 Jan. 1995. For the Indian affrays of that summer see Return I. Holcombe *Minnesota in Three Centuries* II: 169–175 (Minnesota 1908) and Gideon Pond "Indian Warfare in Minnesota," *Minnesota Historical Collections*: III: 129–138.

Wisconsin rivers.3 Theoretically there should have been perhaps 250 men of voting age in the St. Croix and La Pointe precincts; however, a large percentage of the population were not American citizens, nor could many of the eligible voters conveniently reach their polling places. Even given these facts, the voter turnout at the August 3 special election was dismal. Only 44 votes were cast for the county officers, with an additional 14 ballots given for location of the county seat. A good guess would be that of the three precincts established by the county organic act, only Chanwakan and possibly St. Croix Falls were heard from – if any vote was taken at La Pointe, the returns never made it to the Prairie.

The men who ran for, and won, the new offices were mostly from the southern part of the county, though some attempt seems to have been made to get a balanced slate. Written ballots must have been distributed for the slate of candidates (all of whom ran unopposed) and for Brown's warehouse as seat of justice, because with the exception of a few write-ins and scratch-outs everyone got 44 votes. Apparently fourteen folks voted only on location of the county seat: the final tally was 45 votes for Brown's warehouse at the head of Lake St. Croix and 13 for Prescott's claim at the mouth of the river. Three county commissioners were elected: Hazen Mooers from Chanwakan, Calvin Tuttle, millwright at St. Croix Falls, and Samuel Burkleo of Marine. The three county assessors elected were Orange Walker, Joseph Haskell and Philander Prescott. James Norris was elected coroner and supervisor of roads, Phineas Lawrence county collector, and Joseph R. Brown everything else – treasurer, surveyor and register of deeds. His election to all these offices may have been disputed; he received fewer than the total 44 votes, even though no one else got any. However, all was in order and the returns were certified by the clerk of the Crawford County board August 25.4

The territorial election held on September 28 gave Brown a chance to show what he had learned about winning elections. First, although the new county board did not meet until October, the voting precincts were somehow changed to three that were more manageable: Chanwakan, Red Rock Prairie and Marine Mills. There is a presumption here that the St. Croix mill people were uninterested in the election and did not want a precinct (although at the Pokegama mission they were interested enough to form an unauthorized precinct). The petition that had resulted in St. Croix County had, on evidence, been got up by Walker and others at Judd's Mills – it's likely the signatures of upriver loggers were obtained as they came by that summer with their rafts – so that group may have successfully lobbied to change the polling place to one more convenient. One could assume that when Brown and William Dibble of Marine

---

3. Federal Census, Crawford County, Wisconsin Territory, July 7, 1840.
4. Election returns 1840, Secretary of State's files, Wisconsin Territory, series 211, WHS Madison. Walker was one of the original partners and later sole owner of the Marine Lumber Company; Lawrence was a logger and early river pilot, at this time probably employed logging (Lawrence Creek in Franconia township is supposed to have been named for him; the white pine logs he cut there were floated down and sawed at Marine); Haskell and Norris were first employed by the St. Croix Falls Company, had subsequently opened farms near Lake St. Croix.

delivered the election returns to the Prairie in August they petitioned the county board to establish these new precincts – except that there is no record of such action in the minutes of the county board. How it was done remains a bit of a mystery.

Second, since two representatives were to be selected and four had filed (the others from the Prairie), Brown conceived a simple plan to give himself a better chance to receive a plurality of the votes. He allied himself with the Reverend Alfred Brunson, a Whig, founder of the Methodist missions at Kaposia and Crow Wing, who had lived several years in the St. Croix country before moving to the Prairie to take up law. Undoubtedly he and Brown knew each other. In a special election that summer, Brunson had run for (and lost) Brisbois' vacated seat on the Council, and so was also well known to most of the voters. He was also the father of Ira Brunson, to whom Brown may have owed a favor or two, and Burnett's father-in-law. Brown could assure Brunson all the St. Croix vote simply by putting his name on the same ballot: a vote for one would be a vote for both. Voters who didn't especially like Brown or his Democratic politics (although party politics as a real force were several years in the future) might be attracted to the Reverend Brunson, who would carry Brown with him. Two Democrats had got up a similar ticket at Prairie du Chien but unfortunately just before the election one man died and Brown offered himself as a brother Democrat to the remaining candidate, Theophilus Lachapelle. The ploy was clear, at least after the fact, to William Wyman, Whig editor of the *Madison Express*:

> "The course which Mr. Brown took in this affair is not but should be generally known. He was brought out at the election by Mr. Brunson and his friends and run upon the same ticket. But just before the election the person who was running with Lachapelle died. Lachapelle and his friends had not time to call out another candidate and so placed Brown's name upon their ticket. By this means Brown ran on both tickets in Crawford by which means he obtained an overwhelming majority."

Too true. At the St. Croix Brown and Brunson got all 38 votes, and at the Prairie Brown had 130 of the 156 possible, making a total of 168 for Brown, 106 for Brunson and 88 for Lachapelle.[5] Foresight – and a certain serendipity – had got Joseph R. Brown elected representative to the third Wisconsin territorial legislature.

Before leaving for Madison, Brown had St Croix county board duties to attend to. At the first official meeting of the county board, held in Brown's house October 5, Joseph R. Brown was approved as county clerk by the two board members present – Hazen Mooers and Samuel Burkleo – and was sworn in as treasurer. The board located the county seat on the tract of land at the head of Lake St. Croix bounded on the north by Pine Creek that had been chosen by the voters and according to the directions

---

5. *Madison Express*, Jan. 1, 1842; poll books in Secretary of State's files, Wisconsin Territory, WHS Madison.

in the organic act transferred all right and title in this quarter section to Joseph R. Brown for $800 consideration, which Brown then paid to himself as treasurer, the bank being presumably in his left hand pocket. The commissioners purchased back one-half acre "in the central part of any town that may be surveyed" and contracted with Brown to build a two-story courthouse, stone jail and county offices on the county property, which they would then lease back. Brown as proprietor would be responsible for applying for a deed as soon as the land came into market, as surveyor for determining the tract's metes and bounds, and as register of deeds for recording the conveyance, as he soon did. Their major business thus so satisfactorily taken care of, the county board quickly authorized payment of $30 each to J. R. Brown and William Dibble for carrying the election returns to the Prairie and $2.50 to Clerk Brown for a ledger. As a sop they granted to Philander Prescott ferry permits for the St. Croix and Mississippi rivers at the mouth of the St. Croix, and having done great deeds, the St. Croix County Board adjourned.6

Recommending candidates for other county offices that would be territorial appointments gave Brown an opportunity to reward his friends and appease those who might have had reason to doubt his motives. In December Governor Henry Dodge appointed Brown's running mate, Alfred Brunson, a newly fledged lawyer, district attorney for Crawford and St. Croix; Orange Walker became judge of probate and Phineas Lawrence was made sheriff. The other two appointees were Andrew Robertson, auctioneer, and Joseph R. Brown, inspector – the officer who sees that roads, bridges and ditches are kept up. A bevy of new J.P.'s also appeared: David Hone and Orange Walker at Marine, Jeremiah Russell at Pokegama, James Clewet (who in 1839 had married Abraham Perret's daughter Rose and taken up a claim at the Old Cave settlement) and Joseph Haskell (now a farmer near St. Marys point). All of these offices, though unpaid, were compensated by lucrative fees. A similar pattern in appointments was evident two months later when the Fifth Battalion of Wisconsin Militia was formed in St. Croix County. The officers were, predictably enough, Joseph R. Brown, Major; Phineas Lawrence, Adjutant; James Norris, Quartermaster; and captaining the three companies Hazen Mooers, Orange Walker and Jeremiah Russell.7 It will be noted, whether by desire or design, the fifty-eight men of the St. Croix Lumbering Company are practically unrepresented here, save by agent Calvin Tuttle, who as token commissioner perhaps found it inconvenient to travel to Dacotah for board meetings.

The first session of the third territorial legislature, for which Brown arrived a week late in December of 1840, was a long and vituperative one, lasting the legal maximum of seventy-five days and filled with those trivialities that made Brown despair of getting his agenda accomplished. All but three of the legislators were new members elected under the recent

6. *Wisconsin Territorial Papers: St. Croix County* : "Proceedings of St. Croix County Board" 1 (Madison 1841); St. Croix County Deed Book A.
7. Bloom *Territorial Papers* XXVII: 252, 272.

reapportionment, and they were forced to grapple with a number of contested elections, the resolution of which took up a large proportion of the session. Too, the lawmakers were disturbed in their labors by the lack of comforts in the capitol building, still unfinished thanks to the investigation that the last legislature had pursued into misuse of the building appropriation by the treasurer of the capitol commission, J. D. Doty. Several members wished to remove the capital to some other location, but after days of spinning their wheels they were unable to agree on a suitable alternative (and of course, the clash of vested interests and sectional rivalries among the members had been skillfully utilized by Doty to sell them on locating the capital at Madison in the first place). They eventually authorized $7,000 worth of bonds to complete the drafty building.[8]

Figure 24 James Duane Doty.
Wis. Hist. Soc.

Throughout the session Brown took an active part. While it would be pointless to follow every issue that interested Brown during that session, certain items do stand out. He was nominated to a select committee to investigate the financial activities of U.S. attorney Moses M. Strong, a squib fired by Doty to get back at Strong for uncovering "irregularities" in Doty's land dealings during Strong's tenure as fiscal agent of the territory (although it appeared Strong's conversion of public funds had been badly managed, his honesty was soon vindicated). Brown took a stand in many debates – actually spoke out against another member's divorce bill as being too time-consuming for the House's attention! – introduced a measure to extend the jurisdiction of justices of the peace from being limited to cases involving up to $50 to being able to deal with those up to $100 (which was deemed not the legislature's prerogative and referred to a committee to be memorialized to Congress) and presented a memorial to Congress praying that the jurisdiction of Wisconsin be extended to the middle of Lake Pepin and the Mississippi River. He also served on a select committee to study a bill for assessing

8. Moses M. Strong *Territorial Legislature in Wisconsin* 23–24 (Madison 1870). The investigative committee authorized by the 1838–1839 legislature found that the commission had used the $40,000 appropriation indiscriminately to build hotels, bridges, a sawmill and other amenities to enhance Doty's townsite. The lawmakers elected three new commissioners, but Doty refused to turn over the accounts and the former commission was sued. This left the group with the funds unable to proceed, and the new commissioners with no funds to use. See Smith *Doty* 217–218

and collecting county revenues. On Brown's motion the House adjourned at Christmas for ten days, partly to give the commissioners time to take testimony in one of the election disputes, partly because some members wished to be home at Christmas. Brown appears to have left Madison during this time – whatever his business during the interval, he was still at it on January 4 and did not answer rollcall when they reconvened.

Throughout the two sessions and despite the wrangles, Brown never lost track of his plans for St. Croix County. He had come down equipped with a bill he was able to introduce on Christmas eve, just before the recess, that located three territorial roads in the new county, roads that were a necessity if farmers were to be attracted to the area. The bill described routes from Marine Mills to Grey Cloud Island, passing near Dacotah and Prospect Grove (Norris' settlement, now Cottage Grove), from St. Croix Falls to Marine Mills and from Prescott's ferry to Grey Cloud Island. In addition the commissioners were to locate the best spot for construction of a bridge across the channel separating Grey Cloud Island from the mainland. This bill was amended by adding to it a Council bill that established other territorial roads, and, with Mr. Brown in the chair, was taken to the committee of the whole, where it passed easily on the first day of February, 1841.9

That same week a memorial was read from Theophilus Lachapelle contesting the election in St. Croix County on the grounds that many of the votes given there were illegal, a contention, the author stated, that would be supported by the Honorable Joseph R. Brown, who was cognizant of the facts and who had told the memorialist that full and legal proof could be had to sustain this allegation. Aghast, Alfred Brunson countered with a statement of his own that boiled down to: Lachapelle isn't here in person to press his suit, he isn't presently a resident of the territory (having accepted a job at the Indian subagency on the Turkey River in Iowa) and whether or not there were some illegal votes, Mr. Brown knew that there had been 14 votes for himself and Brunson given at the Pokegama precinct, which had come in too late and were thus not counted. The committee on elections would have nothing to do with what looked to be a long drawn-out fight and "declined expressing any opinion." Since Joseph R. Brown was supposed to know so much about it, the committee recommended he should be authorized commissioner to take testimony in St. Croix County and that "all reasonable expenses be paid." A resolution to this effect was quickly passed by the House, most of whose members had had more than enough disputed elections for one session, and Brown ordered to report his findings at the fall session of the legislature. An interesting concept, that – asking a man to report on his own possible fraud. But with that the disputants had to be content.10

---

9. *House Journal* 1840–1842; House documents series 160, WHS; *Madison Express* Dec. 12, 19, 26, 1840; Jan. 9, 1841.

10. *House Journal* Feb. 13, 1841; Memorial of Theophilus Lachapelle, Feb. 6, 1841, and Statement of Alfred Brunson, Feb. 12, 1841, in documents of the House (3rd Wis. Ter. Legislature, 1st session).

Now there was more behind this turn of events than is apparent on the surface. The election in the fall of 1840 of a Whig to the presidency after forty years of Democratic administrations had awakened new interest in party politics in Wisconsin. Heretofore, Wisconsinites had been given to supporting the candidate they deemed would do them the most good or who had the most personal influence, with little regard to party affiliation. Politics was purely a local affair; residents of a territory could not even vote in a national election. Spasmodic efforts had been made to organize political parties in the territory, but had been largely unsuccessful. However, with President William Henry Harrison came the certainty of a shake-up and a new set of territorial officers. Whigs sensing preferments began declaring themselves, and some people changed sides, among them former Democrat James Duane Doty, who meant to be territorial governor. In the closing days of November, 1840, plans were made to hold the first ever Whig convention in Madison; first signer of the call was the Reverend Alfred Brunson. So now it becomes clear why a man who had been an acceptable candidate last October was no longer favored by the Democrats of Crawford and St. Croix counties, and why Lachapelle's Democratic friends, including Joseph R. Brown, had put him up to contesting the election. Democrats were going to have to do some fancy stepping if they intended to hang onto any advantages.11

They met the challenge quickly. A Democratic meeting was held in Madison on January 18 with Joseph R. Brown acting as secretary. This meeting named Democratic committees for each county – William Holcombe (the new company agent at St. Croix Falls), Hazen Mooers and J. R. Clewet comprising the St. Croix county committee, and Theophilus Lachapelle, Dr. B. O. Miller and Daniel G. Fenton the committee for Crawford – and began making plans for a convention to be held February 11. The delegate to this convention from the St. Croix proved to be Joseph R. Brown, who was also selected a vice president of the convention under president Morgan L. Martin of Green Bay and was called to serve on the nominating committee. The convention was a huge success. Eighty-one Whigs had convened on February 4; 139 Democratic delegates rose to meet the Whig threat on the eleventh and "placed the Democratic party in an attitude of readiness for any subsequent political contests."12 And Joseph R. Brown propelled himself to center stage in Democratic politics through his position in the legislature, a position acquired, as it would turn out, with mostly illegal votes in St. Croix County.

Brown was also the (self-appointed) St. Croix delegate to the territorial temperance convention, which was held in Madison January 22. A territorial temperance society was chartered and Brown was named by

---

11. *Wiskonsan Enquirer* Feb. 13, 1841; Moses M. Strong *History of the Territory of Wisconsin from 1836 to 1848* 347 (Madison (1885); Smith *Doty* 249. Lachapelle was told in effect by his "friends" if he did not contest the election he might never expect another vote in Crawford County (Report of the Commissioner Appointed to Take Testimony Relative to the Contested Seat Occupied by Mr. Brunson, *House Documents 1841*: 30).

12. *Wiskonsan Enquirer* "Extra" Jan. 18, 1841; Strong *History* 349–350.

that body corresponding secretary for St. Croix County. Among the founders of this organization was Alfred Brunson, who delivered an address, and having stated their purpose – to restrain themselves from the intemperate use of intoxicating liquor and to endeavor by moderate means to persuade others to do likewise – the convention adjourned with a rendition of the "Temperance Ode" sung by the choir.[13] There is no reason to doubt Brown's sincerity on the subject of temperance. Even though he had been almost continuously involved in selling whiskey to Indians and soldiers for a dozen or more years, he was himself an abstainer and often spoke out against the evils of a system that allowed certain degraded elements of society to prey upon the hapless American natives. He was able to divorce these personal ethics from business considerations. As have many business owners, he found it was easy to rationalize that he was only taking advantage of a situation that would exist whether he engaged in it or not. But perhaps an alliance with the sons of temperance was not a bad hedge. Never an adherent of any organized religion, Brown may have felt it expedient to ally himself with the moral elements of society in this way.

It had been a long session and a busy one, and as it drew to a close Brown was anxious to get away. Undoubtedly he would have liked to return to Chanwakan as soon as possible to see Susan and his new daughter, Ellen, born January 2. He enjoyed his children and must have wanted to spend some time at home with them, may have worried if Susan and the baby were not doing well. But the prospect of wringing some advantage from the redistribution of power in Washington proved the stronger lure. Delegate Doty was in Washington, actively campaigning for appointment as governor, supported in his quest by prominent Whigs, among them Nathaniel P. Tallmadge, Henry Clay and Daniel Webster, soon to become secretary of state, and also by Ramsay Crooks for whom he had done many favors.[14] And although it was suspected but not officially known at the end of February 1841, the man who would replace Poinsett as secretary of war was Representative John Bell of Tennessee, who had been chairman of the House committee on Indian affairs that had set in train the 1837 treaty negotiations. The last legal day of the legislative session at Madison was February 19; Harrison's inauguration would be March 4. Clearly there was no time for delay. February 18 was clean-up-the-details day; on the motion of Mr. Deming, it was determined that J. R. Brown was entitled to full pay for the week he had been absent in December. On the nineteenth Governor Dodge signed Brown's road bill and several others into law. Asked to wait upon the governor to see if he

---

13. *Madison Express* Feb. 6, 1841.

14. Doty had been acting as an agent for the Astor concern speculating in Wisconsin lands and securing patents for settlers whose claims went back before the 1812 war. In this neither he nor the American Fur Company was disinterested; Astor's tactics were to secure possession of these tracts to the inhabitant, then demand a mortgage on the holding in satisfaction of the owner's debts. Smith *Doty* 45. For the number and birth dates of Brown's children, see Appendix A..

had any more business to lay before the House, Brown declined and quickly left the chamber.15

Brown was probably in Washington City with many of the other traders that March. During that same month he was assuredly in Black Horse and Baltimore visiting his cousins and looking up his mother's sister, and it is highly likely that he took the opportunity to visit Washington as well.16 Everyone who had any hope of power or patronage would be there for the inaugural. The festive celebrations and informal gatherings provided plenty of ways to mingle with the great, to fraternize with the powerful, to promote emigration to the new western county. At the very least Brown would want to urge Doty to use his influence in securing his old Indian claims. In January he had approached Governor Dodge about getting the Chippewa subagency removed from La Pointe to St. Croix Falls to make it easier for the Chippewa of the upper Mississippi to receive their annuities (and, of course, easier for the traders on the St. Croix and Mississippi to collect). His letter outlining the dissatisfaction of the Indians with the government and the possibility the Hudson's Bay Company might capitalize on it had been forwarded to the Indian Office, and no doubt he was anxious to see its effect.17 He had plenty of reason to contrive a meeting with Secretary of War John Bell, with whom he may have been acquainted from the 1837 hearings, to explore the possibility of getting a reversal of Poinsett's ruling on the reserve. Moreover, there was the likelihood of another treaty with the Sioux, the expectation of which had attracted Ramsay Crooks to Washington. Poinsett and Missouri agent Joshua Pilcher had proposed using lands next to the Cherokee on the Neosho River in what is now Oklahoma for settlement of the tribes remaining in the Mississippi valley – Winnebago, Potawatomi, Ottawa, Chippewa, ·Sac and Fox – whose continued presence in proximity to the white settlements would inevitably lead to further bloodshed. Crooks wanted an agreement with the northern Sioux and a pay-off on their debts, a pay-off now necessary to save his failing American Fur Company. This fit in well with Secretary Bell's plans.

For some years Bell had cherished a somewhat utopian scheme to establish a permanent home for the displaced northern tribes that would be forever free from the advancing white civilization. He proposed that land be purchased from the Sioux of the St. Peters for a northern Indian district that would serve as a counterpoise to the southwestern Indian territory and would be separated from it by a belt of settlements in Iowa and Missouri.

---

15. *House Journal; Madison Express* Feb. 27, 1841; Smith *Doty* 249–250.

16. Andrew Henderson to S. J. Brown, Jan. 18, 1871; Ellen Henderson to Ellen Brown, Feb. 6, 1871.

17. Brown to Dodge, Jan. 20, 1841, enclosed in Dodge to T. Hartley Crawford, Feb. 12, 1841, OIA LR Wisconsin superintendency. "The Indians of Lac Superior succeed in getting four-fifths of all the goods," reported Brown, and of course their traders succeeded in getting four-fifths of the annuities paid, which he didn't report. Both Dodge and Brown represented that the Hudson's Bay Company had strong influence over the northern tribes and "could raise an Indian army within our own boundaries." This threat was generally believed and always provoked a strong reaction in Washington when it was raised.

It was widely felt that the lands north of Iowa were too cold and the growing season too short to be desirable for agriculture, so there would be little pressure to reclaim such lands if set aside for the Indians. Bell's choice for the treaty commissioner was none other than James Duane Doty, his collaborator of the previous winter on claims made under the Winnebago Treaty. The death of President Harrison one month after the inauguration thoroughly disorganized the administration; however, the new president, John Tyler, honored Harrison's wishes and confirmed Doty as governor of Wisconsin Territory. Under the territory's organic act this also made him ex officio superintendent of Indian affairs for Wisconsin, but since his authority would not extend across the river into Iowa, he was made a special sole commissioner for the treaty-making. Bell moved quickly. He needed no appropriation because $5,000 had been set aside under the Indian Act of 1840 to provide for purchase of western lands on which to settle the Winnebago. Crooks had made it clear that whatever equipment the commissioner required would be furnished by his agents in the west. Bell's formal instructions to Doty were issued May 22; soon after the new governor was on his way west.[18]

Brown left Washington a month or so before the governor and therefore probably did not know of Doty's commission. He returned by way of Chicago, and at last persuaded the Carlis to move to his new townsite of Dacotah. Paul Carli was in deep financial difficulty. He had given up his Chicago store and his farm in 1839, and moving to Fox River Grove, some thirty-five miles west, had preempted a claim there. He was now obliged to support not only Lydia Ann and their two children, but also Lydia's twice-widowed mother, Mary Hall, and his wife's two youngest brothers, Samuel Fletcher Brown, nineteen, and Nathaniel Brown, thirteen. In September of 1840 Paul assigned his 160 acres on the Fox River to his brother Christopher, perhaps with the intention of moving to Twin River, Wisconsin (at least, one of his creditors went looking for him there). Brown's proposal looked better and better to Paul and Lydia. In the spring they packed up and moved. Paul's brother Christopher escorted Lydia Ann, her mother, brothers and children first to Galena and then by steamboat to Grey Cloud Island where they arrived May 13. Paul came overland driving their horses. Unfortunately none of the animals survived the strain of the journey and the lack of feed.[19]

Joseph R. may also have traveled with his sister and her family. He stopped at the Prairie du Chien post office the first week in May, the week the Indian Queen left with the immigrants on board, and there complied with his commission to give notice to the election contestants as to the time and place where he would take the evidence. He set the time for June

---

18. Bell to Doty, May 22, 1841, OSW LR main series. For background see Smith *Doty* 249–257 and Folwell *Minnesota* I: 457–458. The area that became Oklahoma had been set aside in 1834 for the southern tribes: Cherokee, Choctaw, Creek, Seminole and Chickasaw.

19. Lydia Carli to Williams, Sep. 20, 1871; John Lawe to John Mead, Nov. 5, 1841, Green Bay/Prairie du Chien papers, WHS, Madison; Conveyance Paul Carli to Christopher Carli, Sep. 20, 1840, Franklin Steele papers, MHS; *Stillwater Messenger* Dec. 19, 1896.

21, following on the heels of the first district court, which was slated to be held June 14 at Dacotah. Whilst writing the notices, Brown joked about Brunson's bad fortune with postmaster Joseph Brisbois and Theophilus Lachapelle, who was also present. The notice for the other contestant, left in the Brunson box, was later handed him by the postmaster with the remark that it appeared he was "a gone coon," or so Brisbois later swore. Mr. Brunson was not amused.[20]

There was yet no residence at Dacotah to receive the Carlis, only the shell of an ambitious framed building destined to serve as hotel, courthouse and county offices and behind it a small building of stone for the jail. This much had been erected in Brown's absence by a crew of Frenchmen bossed by Joseph M. Hall, a carpenter who had originally come up to work at the St. Croix mills. Work on the building had apparently stopped, probably due partly to lack of sawn lumber from the mills upstream and partly to most of the builders being off on a raft. Leaving the women and children with Susan at Chanwakan, Brown quickly put his young half brothers and the Carlis to work building a commodious house of tamarack logs, halved together at the corners and chinked with clay. The windowless walls were plastered over with more clay in an effort to make the structure less drafty, which gave the place an appearance not unlike the adobes of lower California. By the end of June all was ready. Joe returned to Chanwakan to fetch the womenfolk. They were loaded into a bateau – the three children aged five, three and six months in the center, Lydia, Mary Hall and their possessions all packed in with six oarsmen – and were rowed up the river to their new home, where Paul and the boys awaited them, arriving June 29. However spacious the Tamarack House, it must have been a bit cramped when everyone moved in, more so when passing travelers were taken in, fed and given a bed (be it ever so crowded, many a sojourner remarked on what a great comfort it was to sleep in a house). All around Dacotah was a wilderness, the nearest neighbors (save the Indians who camped near the creek) the families of Francis McCoy on the point at Bayport and Jacob Fahlstrom, another lumberman-turned-farmer, on the prairie where today is Lakeland. Joseph's family was even farther away at Chanwakan.[21]

While living quarters for the "first family" of Dacotah were under construction, Brown was busy with preparations for the court that would, he trusted, soon be held in the yet unfinished courthouse. That the court would be held at all had to be taken on trust. The circuit judge, David Irvin, had appointed no clerk and, it would seem from what transpired that summer, had had no contact with Brown or anyone else in the St. Croix area. Yet he did appear, perhaps unexpectedly, and he caught Joseph R. Brown by surprise.

20. Report of the Commissioner. . . , 34–36.
21. Easton *St. Croix Valley* 9–13; Carli to Williams Sep. 20, 1871; *Stillwater Messenger* Dec. 19, 1896. McCoy probably also worked on the buildings at Dacotah; he advertised in the *Minnesota Pioneer* (Apr. 28, 1849, St. Paul) as a housebuilder.

Irvin had a choice of three steamboats up: *Chippewa* arrived at Fort Snelling on June 5, *Agnes* on June 10 and *Chippewa* on her second run June 27. With the court set for the fourteenth, he should have been on *Agnes*, but he may have confused the issue by coming by the earlier or later boat. Bypassing Chanwakan, Judge Irvin got off at Fort Snelling, where he was loaned a horse and guide by trader Norman Kittson and directed to the county seat, some twenty miles over a road that was little more than a trail. At Dacotah he found only the two young Browns, a half-dozen French Canadians who assured him they were to be the jury, an unfinished courthouse with sashless windows gaping wide and an unfurnished log house in which to lodge. Although the sheriff may have turned up, there seemingly were no preparations for a court and no Joseph R. Brown.

Map 11 Stillwater. Brown's townsite of Dacotah in 1841 has been obliterated by the relocation and widening of the highway and railroad. Dotted lines show location of modern streets and shoreline; double lines show roads indicated on the 1847 survey.

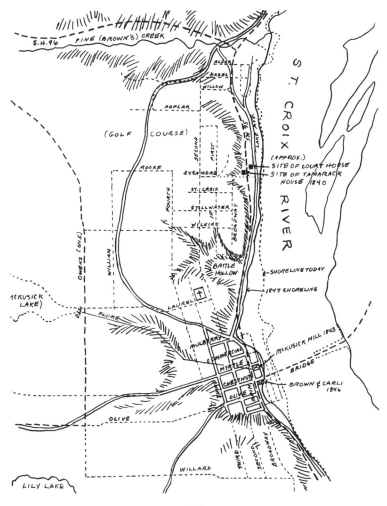

197

Well, so what? Brown had not been appointed clerk, although he had very likely been recommended; Alfred Brunson, the district attorney, had been at the Prairie when Judge Irvin left, and had intended to go up to attend the court; that he did not accompany the judge may have been at the judge's suggestion. Surely Judge Irvin could not have expected to hold a court with no clerk, no prosecutor, no attorneys. His manner suggests that he planned merely to appoint officers, hold preliminary hearings and organize for an official court the following year. At this point the story gets a bit hard to comprehend. The judge was exceedingly put out by having to sleep on deerskins on the floor of "Hotel Brown" and make a meal of venison and St. Croix fish, for which he was obliged to provide his own salt. Certainly he could not have expected much more; he had held court for years at Mineral Point in a ramshackle building at the bottom of a ravine. But the judge, it was said, was an irascible bachelor, a fastidious and parsimonious man who very much disliked to be made to look a fool. For no very good reason, it would seem, except for having been inconvenienced by Brown's absence, the judge refused to wait and left Dacotah the next morning, never to return. Probably he hastened to catch the same steamboat descending the river. Judge Irvin not only never again attempted to hold district court in St. Croix county, but also was instrumental in having this additional court dissolved by an amendment to the county's organic act in April of 1843. He seems altogether to have reacted with uncalled-for choler to what seems a slight imposition. A story that may be apocryphal, but certainly had some currency, is that after he again reached civilization Irvin had delivered to Sheriff Phineas Lawrence papers to be served on Brown, which Lawrence did, presenting Brown with the document and commanding him to "surrender in the name of the United States of America and the immortal God."[22] What brought on this comedy of errors?

A slate of grand and petit jurors had been selected by the county board in June, so it would seem that preparations had indeed been made for a court. There may have even been a criminal case on the docket: Lydia Carli remarked that there was a man incarcerated in the little stone jail that summer, although who he was and what he was accused of she did not know (whoever he was, he saved the county additional expense and himself a long wait by escaping one night when the two watchmen fell asleep). So what happened? Perhaps the best guess is that Brown had taken upon himself the responsibilities of clerk of court without the

---

22. W. H. C. Folsom "History of Lumbering in the St. Croix Valley," *Minnesota Historical Collections* IV: 300 (St. Paul 1902). Prescott told the same story; another contemporary, Henry L. Moss ("Last Days of Wisconsin Territory and Early Days of Minnesota Territory, *Minnesota Historical Collections* VIII: 73), has some variations. Brown presumably passed Prairie du Chien in early May before the judge had arrived there for the May term of district court. Laden with his sister's goods and anxious to complete the buildings, he must have left the details of the June court in someone else's hands, and the someone did not follow through. Whatever happened to Irvin at Dacotah, he adamantly thereafter refused to return, is said to have declared that next time he held court in Dacotah he would provide himself with moccasins, clout and blanket. For more on David Irvin see J. G. Knapp "Early Reminiscences of Madison," *Wisconsin Historical Collections* VI: 378–379 (reprint Madison 1908).

appointment and the punctilious judge would not countenance such gross impertinence. This theory is bolstered somewhat by the papers supposedly served on Brown: What was Brown to surrender, if not the docket and other papers appropriate to the court? Irvin's writ was probably a cease and desist order against Brown. When the organic act was amended, it contained a clause requiring that the "Clerk of District Court of St. Croix County" – whoever that might be since none was believed to have been appointed – "deliver over all dockets, etc." The amended document also allowed the county officers to keep offices at Red Stone Prairie, now Newport, for convenience (they couldn't change the county seat without inviting a lawsuit), while for judicial purposes St. Croix County was attached to Crawford County, a situation that prevailed until 1847 and certainly did not endear Brown to the electorate. Meanwhile, Brown smarted under the flat refusal of Judge Irvin to appoint a clerk or provide for writs and arrest warrants to be issued. By the following year he felt so shackled he appealed to Governor Doty to grant him special authority as deputy marshal or as major in the militia to proceed in the apprehension of criminals. Doty was unable to comply with this request, and was certainly in no position to coerce Irvin, who was an old political antagonist. Not the least of Brown's disappointments was the loss of the hefty fees: Clerk of district court was one of the best-paying jobs in any county.23

There was little time for self-reproach. A letter from Dousman to Sibley dated June 18 contained electrifying news: Doty was appointed sole commissioner to treat with the Sioux and would probably also be authorized to settle with the halfbreeds for their lands on Lake Pepin. Dousman exhorted Sibley to be prepared – "have the interpreters and Indians as much under your thumb as you can" – and to be careful – "all the Loafers in the country will be there." The governor stopped only briefly to talk with Dousman and Rolette before ascending the river to Mendota where Sibley met him July 10. An express letter sent by Dousman must have arrived at Sibley's store about the same time as the boat carrying Governor Doty, his wife and Albert Parris, a clerk the Indian office had sent out to aid the commissioner. Dousman's letter reveals a certain amount of desperation:

> "In treating with the Indians it appears he is not authorized to allow any claims to traders or donations to half breeds... He, however, promises fairly that he will recommend to the Government to make provisions for all just claims on the Indians. On the whole I think it will be our interest to aid him in accomplishing the views of the Government and after conversing with him freely on the subject, I hope you will come to the same

---

23. *Acts of the Third Wisconsin Territorial Legislature: 1842–1843*; (Madison 1843); Carli to Williams, Sep. 20, 1871; Brown to Doty, Jul. 14, 1842, enclosed in Doty to Secretary of War, Aug. 9, 1842, OSW LR main series. Brown was away in June of 1842 when the battle of Kaposia (a Chippewa raid on the Sioux) took place a few miles north of his farm. At his return he took a deposition from the husband of one of the slain women, but wrote to Doty that he felt he had no powers as J.P. to pursue the Chippewa murderers without special authority.

conclusion. I have told him to make you acquainted at once without fear or reserve with all he wants and that you would do what is correct and aid him efficiently. He will want goods for presents and to his men – let him have, of course, all he wants."**24**

What Doty wanted was $10,000 worth of goods for presents. He gave Sibley a voucher for $1,264 for provisions supplied the Indians at the council. He also wanted, and got, the support and intervention of the traders, particularly the Faribaults, Renvilles, Bailly and Laframboise. In return, it was discovered that traders' claims to the amount of $150,000 could indeed be allowed in the treaty.

To all appearances there wasn't $10,000 worth of Indian trade goods north of St. Louis. Only a month previously Dousman had despaired of having enough merchandise to meet the annuities payments. Sibley's stock was also cut to the bone because he had seriously planned to exit the business that season, due to Ramsay Crooks having sold the Western Outfit to Pierre Chouteau Junior. Sibley, Dousman and Rolette had at last decided to go another year with Chouteau, and goods ordered late were even then on the way from Pittsburgh. They would not arrive in time for the treaty, however, and the Indians had to take a raincheck on the presents promised by the treaty makers. Sibley managed to deliver them that fall; but as $10,000 represents nearly the amount of capital invested by the Western Outfit in a normal trade year, it is very doubtful that all of the goods promised got to the signers of the treaty. The whole transaction has the air of a payoff. Sibley did not receive the voucher for $10,000 until the treaty was consummated and Doty was back in Madison, which suggests that he may have there met with some cash. This put both the burden of supplying the war department with proof that the goods were delivered and the risk that the special appropriation needed to repay the money would not be forthcoming squarely on Sibley's shoulders. But Sibley was a man of charm and believability; enclosing his $10,000 draft, Doty urged Sibley "You must go to Washington this winter to aid us in giving the proper explanation," and added that Congress might ask for some certificate from a disinterested party that the goods had been delivered. Even if they didn't recoup the voucher, Sibley and Crooks would consider it money reasonably well invested.**25**

With the help of the upriver traders, the Indians were very quickly gathered at Traverse des Sioux. Colonel Amos J. Bruce, Taliaferro's successor as Sioux agent, was unaccountably absent. The only whites in evidence were the Fur Company traders, a small escort of officers from Fort Snelling and the Reverend Stephen Riggs, who had tagged along from Lac qui Parle with his charges to see they were not taken advantage of. Joseph R. Brown and other independent traders were not invited,

24. Dousman to Sibley, Jun. 18 and Jul. 6, 1841, Sibley papers.
25. Doty to Sibley, Nov. 3, 1841, Sibley papers; Sibley to Crooks, Apr. 2, 1842, American Fur Company papers.

although some of them must have had considerable claims against the upper Sioux. They were paid off in another way: by being given sinecures in the new Indian Territory set forth by the treaty. Brown, if he is not apparent in the proceedings was certainly hovering round the edges (he had even spent $10 on a new bombazine coat for the occasion). Apparently very few others who might have been interested in the treaty had time to make any moves before Commissioner Doty had it signed, sealed and delivered. Despite the official view that the proposed treaty was designed to create an Indian state "devoted to Indian occupation forever," people generally anticipated that it would open up the lands between that Indian state and the Mississippi to the rapidly advancing white population and would as well stimulate a great traffic in goods and services to be supplied to the wards of the government. "Probably much of the purchase which lies in the state of Iowa will be sold to be settled by whites," heralded the *Madison Express*. Secretary of War Bell, in presenting the document to the Senate committee was moved to remark that much of the land acquired, especially the southern and eastern parts of it would be subject to sale at many times the purchase price and would therefore more than reimburse the expenses of the treaty. Henry Rice, an easterner who had been engaged in sutling at Fort Snelling and Fort Atkinson (in northeastern Iowa), probably typified the popular feeling when he wrote to Sibley shortly before the treaty was made: "I hope to make the St. Peters my future home... [It] is destined to become the center of a great state." He added: "There will be great opportunities for speculation and we ought to be prepared to act. I mean to be in on the ground and invest at every opportunity." Surely Rice was not the only man to see those opportunities. Mr. Brown, no doubt, was on pins and needles.[26]

On July 31 the chiefs and headmen of the Sisseton, Wahpeton and Wahpekute placed their marks on the treaty. In doing so they relinquished title to all their lands bordering the Minnesota (or St. Peters) River from its mouth to its source and all its tributaries north to the boundary with the Chippewa, some 35,000,000 acres, more than 54,600 square miles, stretching from Iowa to the Crow Wing River, from the Mississippi to the coteau. One-half million acres bordering the Minnesota on the north were reserved for the Sioux; the south bank was destined to become home to the other displaced tribes yet in Wisconsin and Iowa. Doty had been commissioned to purchase land suitable for the proposed Indian territory near the mouth of the Blue Earth River – "as extensive a tract of land as you can obtain," directed Bell, suggesting five million acres would be adequate. Instead, Doty bought all the land occupied by the Sioux in Minnesota, thirty-five million acres, saying it was the only way to convince them they must settle down to agriculture; if they had any land

---

26. *Madison Express* Sep. 8, 1841; John Bell to I. T. Morehouse, Sep. 9 1841, Record Books III: 19, OIA; Sibley New Hope Daybook Jun. 30, 1841, and Henry M. Rice to Sibley, July 1841, Sibley papers. The news of the treaty was not generally known until Doty arrived back in Madison the last week of August, 1841. Some interested parties, including Joshua Pilcher, Henry Dodge and his son Augustus, delegate from Iowa Territory, were taken quite by surprise.

remaining, he reasoned, they would continued to roam it as hunters. The purchase price was just over $1.3 million.

Most of the purchase money was to be invested in annuities, but considerable amounts were earmarked for schools, houses, farm implements, doctors, blacksmiths and other necessities of civilized life. Two new forts were to be built on the upper Minnesota River, the river improved for navigation and a road built to the forts and the seven new settlements that would be established between Traverse des Sioux and Lake Traverse. The unique details of the treaty were Bell's, formulated by him through years of service on the House committee on Indian affairs. The basic idea was to create a buffer zone between settlers and Sioux to protect the Indians from the degradation that inevitably followed from that juxtaposition. Bell had hoped to abolish the credit system, but Doty had been forced to accept a modified version, since the Indians had more confidence in their traders than in the government. Still, the treaty encouraged the Sioux to become farmers by providing that the reserved lands be allotted 100 acres to each family. Those who settled down would be furnished livestock, seed and implements plus government farmers to teach them agriculture, as well as teachers for the mechanic and domestic arts. In a radical departure from previous U.S. Indian policy, the treaty provided that those Indians who cultivated their land for two years would become owners of the land and would acquire along with the real estate, if they desired, the rights of U.S. citizenship. The final article provided for the payment of their debts to the traders, the claims not to exceed $150,000.[27]

Before he left the St. Peters area, Doty convened the Mdewakanton at Mendota assisted by their agent. On August 11 the Mdewakanton chiefs, excepting Wabasha and Wakute, signed a treaty ceding their remaining lands west of the Mississippi for $206,000 and agreed to move to a reservation near the Blue Earth River. Agent Bruce recommended that the two holdouts be persuaded to remove to the upper Zumbro River if they would not sell. A third cession was made by the halfbreeds of their lands on Lake Pepin for $20,000 plus compensation for their improvements thereon. All in all it was a very neat package, and a bargain for the United States at less than $2 million. Doty was back in Madison by the end of August. Albert Parris took the July 31 treaty on to Washington, where it arrived in time to be introduced to the Senate on September 3, just before the end of the special session. Unfortunately the dissension in President Tyler's cabinet had just then reached its peak. On September 11, Bell, along with the other cabinet members except Secretary of State Daniel

27. Doty to Bell, Aug. 4, 1841, enclosing "Treaty with the Sisiahto, Wofpato and Wofpakoota" concluded July 31, 1841, OIA LR St. Peters superintendency. (Doty had his own method of phonetic spelling of Indian words, which is also reflected in the name of his Madison "organ," the *Wiskonsan Enquirer*.) For more see Smith *Doty* 259–260; Thomas Hughes "Treaty of Traverse des Sioux... with notes of the former Treaty there in 1841 under Gov. James D. Doty of Wisconsin," *Minnesota Historical Collections* X (part 1): 101-102, 119; Folwell *Minnesota* I: 457–459.

Webster, resigned in protest of Tyler's politics. The Senate, other things on their minds, tabled the treaty on the last night of the session.**28**

To all appearances, Joseph R. Brown took no part in the treaty proceedings. It is inconceivable, given his interests and friendships, that he did not have some input. To keep his credibility as a representative to the legislature he would not want to appear overtly in the negotiations; his role appeared later when he used that office to spearhead territorial support for the treaty. While most of the other Western Outfit traders were being recommended by Doty for positions as subagents, government traders and farmers and Sibley was contemplating the governorship of the second Indian State, Brown appeared to get no preferment from the treaty. But Brown's main interest was the opening of the reserve, and this treaty, pushing the Indians far upriver and removing the reason for Fort Snelling's strategic importance, would probably do it – newspapers quickly reported that that fort would become a supply depot with much-reduced garrison.**29** There would be, as Rice had put it, opportunities: two forts and seven settlements to build and supply with goods in the Indian country, countless settlers to accommodate as they moved into the ceded lands. There was just one little thing Brown wanted from Doty, and right after he got to work mustering legislative support for the treaty the following winter he got it: a recommendation from Doty that Joseph R. Brown be considered for Sioux Indian agent. This recommendation drew some censure. On the heels of Doty's letter to John Bell came an anonymous warning to the Indian office delineating Brown's moral character as unfit for that office: "He has for the last few years lived in open debauchery with Sioux squaws, is bankrupt in his affairs, was by fraud and deception elected to the legislature of Wiskonsan; he is an unprincipled loco foco."**30**

Well, let's leave that topic for the moment. Besides promoting his interests with Doty, Brown had plenty to keep him busy that summer. The county commissioners met dutifully every one or two months, but rarely did more than one commissioner count himself present: the only constant at these meetings was the clerk, Mr. Brown. Because of his many other activities, Brown, the contractor, had reneged on building the courthouse. The June board meeting gave him a year's extension to complete the work,

---

28. Doty to Bell, Aug. 14, 1841, enclosing "Treaty with the Minda Waukanto on the 11th Inst." OIA LR St. Peters superintendency; Folwell *Minnesota* I: 458. Doty apparently did not mention that two prominent chiefs had not signed; Sibley was charged with convincing them, had authorization to pay them $600 for their signatures (Doty to Sibley, Aug. 22, 1841, Sibley papers). A draft of the halfbreed cession in Doty's hand dated July 31, 1841 is in the Sibley papers.

29. *Madison Express* Nov. 3, 1841, from *National Intelligencer*.

30. Doty to Bell, Aug. 9, 1841, OIA LR St. Peters superintendency; OIA Register of Applications and Recommendations for Appointment, Mar. 18, 1842, in territorial papers of Iowa, microfilm in MHS. The traders were rewarded generously: J-B. Faribault, Joseph Laframboise and Joseph Renville Senior were to be subagents "on location" in the villages; Alexander, David and Oliver Faribault, Philander Prescott, Alexander Graham, Antoine Findley, Joseph Renville Junior, Hazen Mooers and Norman Kittson were to be government traders; Louis Provençalle was down for superintendent of agriculture and Henry Sibley for governor. The letter quoted, signed "One that knows," was received by the Indian Office Mar. 24, 1842 (OIA LR Prairie du Chien) and was probably written by Alfred Brunson who by then had good reason to dislike Brown and who was also angling for a job as Indian agent.

"say until the first day of July next." But by November, despite vast quantities of nails and sash lights being purchased, the construction was still uncompleted. Brown, the clerk, was instructed to advertise for proposals for building a jail, courthouse and eight offices at Dacotah, the work to begin the following May. It is not evident there were any takers.

One great asset to the beleaguered county machine that summer was young Samuel Fletcher Brown. Fletcher had just turned twenty-one, and his half brother found he could use both his help and the fees he could command as a county officer. Fletcher was placed on the grand jury panel for district court, appointed deputy sheriff and made an election judge for a new precinct established at Dacotah. Amazingly, seven people voted at Dacotah in the county elections on September 27 and, along with the twenty other voters at Kawbakunk (St. Croix Falls) and Chanwakan, elected Fletcher one of three assessors, while returning JRB as treasurer, register of deeds and surveyor and coming out soundly for reelection of Henry Dodge as delegate. Fletcher was probably of some use to Joseph Brown in the matter of serving summons too. The justice was kept busy bringing judgments against about a dozen old American Fur Company employees who were in possession of some of its property for Sibley's clerk, William Forbes (it wouldn't be surprising if Brown himself had suggested this dragnet). But for all these activities, Brown seems to have collected very little cash: in November he picked up county orders for $2 for Fletcher as election judge, and for himself $12 as county clerk, $10 for "extra services" and $31 for poll books and carrying election returns to the Prairie. During the summer he recruited David Hone, a timber cruiser for the Marine mills, to help run his Grey Cloud operation. Hone got a tavern license for Chanwakan in November, and made himself useful in Brown's other enterprises as well.31

Brown went down to Madison in November of 1841 armed with several petitions designed to muster support for the treaty and shake loose the reserve. But before he could do anything about introducing them, he had the contested election to resolve. On December 8 Commissioner Brown reported that between October 9 and November 17 he had interviewed all the disputed voters in the St. Croix precincts except four who could not be located – he had waited this long, he said, expecting daily the arrival of the contestants – and found that of the 38 votes for Brunson (and incidentally for himself) 20 were cast by non-citizens and 3 were doubtful. If the 20 votes were thrown out, Lachapelle would have a majority of two and be entitled to the seat. Brunson asked Brown if he had not been told there were 14 votes from Pokegama "of the right sort," which had arrived too late to be counted? The commissioner replied that there was no evidence an election had ever been held at Pokegama as no poll books had been turned in. Brunson was furious. Had he needed them,

31. "Proceedings of St. Croix County Board," 2, 3, 6, 11; Brown Docket Jul. 1, 1841; Sibley Account Book 1839–1843 shows Hone making purchases on Brown's account, selling fresh butter and wheat. Doty and Dodge had changed places in 1840; when Doty was appointed governor, Henry Dodge ran for and was elected territorial delegate.

Brunson knew, Mr. Brown would have found the votes from the unorganized precinct perfectly legal. Changing tactics, Brunson tried to discredit the commissioner, contending that Brown had not given the contestants thirty days notice of the time and place the depositions were to be taken and consequently neither he nor Lachapelle was in attendance. Joseph Brisbois' affidavits had to be sent for to prove Brown had done so, although the committee on elections felt he had not done so according to the spirit and meaning of the resolution. The argument went on for several days. Brown was willing to admit the whole election had been illegal, as only one election clerk had been in attendance, thus throwing out all 38 votes, but in the end one fact was distilled out; there were at least 20 illegal votes for Brunson and that was enough to unseat him. "Lachapelle's proof is strong as holy writ," chortled the Democratic *Wiskonsan Enquirer*; "An election rode over by the car of loco-focoism," was the Whig *Madison Express'* bitter comment. On motion of Mr. Brown, Lachapelle was seated January 18.**32**

The interesting aspect of this election dispute is that it shows how far the education of Joseph R. Brown as an election manager had advanced. Obviously he could count votes. He had used the ballots given by the French Canadians and other "foreigners," most of whom had worked for him at one time or another and of whose nationality he was well aware, and held in reserve the undoubtedly legal votes of the missionaries and loggers, American citizens all, given at Pokegama. It was clear from their testimony that the greater part of the "illegal" voters did not know for whom they were voting: "I voted a ticket given me by Mr. Clewet," swore John Campbell; "I cannot read, but I voted the same ticket as the rest voted," averred Pierre Parrant; "I voted for two, but only recollect the name of Mr. Brown," said Jean-Baptiste Terrepain, a statement that was repeated with minor variations by the greater share of the deponents. (Interestingly, Parrant swore he was a naturalized citizen; it had happened like this: "I went before Judge Doty [five years ago] and told him I wished to be naturalized – the Judge inquired how long I had been in the United States – I answered about sixteen years. He told me I was already a citizen. I told the Judge I would like to be certain and would pay for it and inquired what it would cost. The Judge answered, that if I would absolutely be naturalized, it would cost five dollars. I gave him five dollars, and he took down my name and I left the court.") In the reported debates we can catch a glimpse of Brown managing the floor discussions,

---

32. Report of the Commissioner... 31–39; *House Journal*; *Wiskonsan Enquirer* Dec. 11, 18 and 25, 1841; *Madison Express* Jan. 24, 1842. It may be of interest to know who was in the county at this early date. The poll books show the voters at Marine Mills were Samuel Burkleo, Hiram Swesey, William B. Dibble, Steven Scott, Orange Walker, David Hone and Hiram Berkey; at Red Rock (all proved to be "aliens") were John Foy, William Evans, Pierre Jervais, Jacques Lefevre, Louis Lasarte, Joseph Labissonierre, François Gamelle, John Camble (Campbell), Henry Belland, Joseph Bourcier, Vital Guerrin, Joseph Monjeau, François Trudelle and James R. Clewet; at Chanwakan legal voters Joseph R. Brown, Joseph Haskell, Hazen Mooers, Joseph M. Hall, James S. Norris, Orson H. Caswell, James McCormick and aliens Peter Parrant, J.-B. Terrepain, J.-B. Deniger, Pierre Felix, Bartholemew Baldwin, Charles Lousiasse, J.-B. Le Rock (Baptiste Rocque), Marcier Courterier, Pierre Rouilliard and Jean Yeartin.

or using his influence to manipulate a vote. At one point the business of the House was delayed after lunch, there being no quorum until Mr.

Figure 25 Madison was a typical frontier town in the 1840s. This view shows King Street and the first capitol. The Madison House on the left was built in 1838. This drawing was made by Johann Wengler, an Austrian traveler in America 1850-51. Wis. Hist. Soc.

Brown could be found, as well as Messieurs Burt, Gray, Mills and Whiton, all of whom had been voting with Brunson to reject Brown's evidence. It could have been a coincidence they were all out together, and not at all a matter of Brown trying to influence the afternoon's vote. And one other thing should not be lost sight of: at the end of the session J. R. Brown was owed by the territory of Wisconsin, in addition to his pay and mileage, $350 for "reasonable expenses" in taking the depositions plus $5 for transporting books from the Prairie to the St. Croix.[33]

While Joseph R. Brown was in his element in Madison, the Reverend Brunson was understandably soured by his experiences there. Brunson had tried hard, during his brief stay in Madison, to bring a sense of financial and moral responsibility to the legislators and to check their extravagances. Naturally, he was not well loved. In his autobiography he commented:

> "The place was then small and the vice and wickedness of the territory seemed to be concentrated at this one spot. While the legislature was in session gambling, dancing and profanity ran rampant. Besides this there was a great gathering of "sharpers" trying to skin "Uncle Sam," and if they failed this to skin somebody else... [Patronage offices] provided places for political friends who had favored and perhaps secured the elections of the squandering majority."[34]

---

33. Report of the Commissioneer... 6–23; Treasurer's Report Feb. 18, 1842, *House Journal* 467–485.

34. J. Christian Bay, editor *Going West: The Pioneer Work of Alfred Brunson* 43 (Cedar Rapids, Iowa 1951). Brunson returned to Prairie du Chien, secured an appointment as Indian agent for the Wisconsin Chippewa and in another capacity made himself objectionable to the army. Major William Davenport, commanding Fort Crawford, commented "He [Brunson] holds here the appointment of Supreme court commissioner, an appointment which is believed unknown to the law organizing the government of the Territory of Wisconsin. In this capacity he has recently discharged nineteen enlisted

It was true Madison was a rough-and-ready town in 1841. Practically the first hovels knocked together in 1838 had been saloons and gambling houses: men drank "Rock River" and "Peckatonica," played faro, rolled dice at the "Tiger" and patronized Uncle Jacob George's "Worser" (refused a tavern license, George said he would keep something worser, and so indeed he did). Some forty or fifty houses were, as one visitor said, "rained about here and there sparingly at the corners of the projected streets and thoroughfares." Hogs, "of the true snake-eating, half rat, half alligator variety," infested the doors and found shelter in the unoccupied basement of the capitol and oxen browsed about the streets. Nowhere could our visitor find wagon, cart, mule, or jackass to take him further. The capitol, a rosy sandstone structure standing alone in a large square overgrown with brush, "its tin dome glittering in the sun," was still unsightly and full of chips, shavings and mortar, but by the end of the legislative session changes had been wrought, the worst holes patched, stoves installed, carpets laid and the legislators furnished with desks and cushioned chairs."35

It was after Christmas before the matter of the disputed election was far enough settled to permit of any other business being considered by the House. Brown took advantage of the interval between December 27 and January 10 to return to Dacotah, where he celebrated a rather belated Christmas with his family and the Carlis in Tamarack House. Paul and Lydia were in truth babes in the woods when it came to providing for themselves in the cold of a northern winter. Joe found them rather suffering for want of supplies. They had no livestock, no cow for milk for Lydia's babies, no chickens, no garden vegetables, not even potatoes. There was fresh bear meat and venison if they could get it, but until Sylvester Stateler, former blacksmith at the St. Croix mills, helped them repair an old gun they were unable to hunt. And there was catfish from the St. Croix when they could get nothing else, but they lacked salt to give it savor. The pork sent up in barrels was of what Lydia called "the condemned variety," as was the flour, which had to be smashed apart with a hatchet before biscuits could be made. The clay that chinked the logs of which Tamarack House was built began to drop out in chunks as the house creaked and groaned in the subzero cold. The green floorboards shrank, leaving cracks big enough to run a hand through. The cold was bone-chilling and the open hearth fire inefficient. Coffee would freeze in their cups while they ate. Lydia said she froze her feet three times that winter – "our privations were severe."

But when Joe Brown blew in from Madison, picked up Susan and his children from their home on Grey Cloud, bundled them into buffalo robes for the twenty-mile trip to Dacotah and delivered them all up at Tamarack

soldiers at this post as foreigners, and holds himself bound by his practice to discharge any others who will give him a bribe of ten dollars" (Wm. Davenport to Secretary of War, Oct. 19, 1842 OSW LR).

35. Knapp, "Early Reminiscences of Madison"; Morleigh A Merry Briton 16, 20; Daniel S. Durrie A History of Madison... 136–140 (Madison 1874).

House, their spirits lifted and they made a merry, if overdue Christmas. Laughter rang in the log house as Lydia Ann and Susan produced tiny dolls and "zoological impossibilities" of flour-clay for gifts to delight the children – there were six of them now, Lydia's little John had just turned one, Maria was five and Joseph seven, while Susan still had baby Ellen in arms, Angus was a sturdy three and Lydia Ann, named after her aunt as Joseph Renshaw Carli had been named after his uncle, was six. All the inhabitants of Dacotah, which consisted mainly of several lodges of Sioux who were wintering there and perhaps Joe's younger brothers and a passing traveler or two, were invited to the Christmas feast. Lydia got up a dinner for the Indian women and children of pemmican, salt pork, black dried apples, bread, coffee and sugar, which their guests proceeded to dispatch with gusto, even though unaccustomed to eating with forks and drinking from cups. "It is hardly necessary to remark," Lydia chuckled in remembrance, "that we were shy on napkins." Meanwhile Brown brought out a jug of whiskey to entertain the men, and so the day passed in great merriment.[36]

Brown was back in Madison by January 10, making this a whirlwind trip; he had paused only long enough to deliver his family back to Chanwakan and attend a county board meeting at which a slate of jurors was drawn up for the next June's court (never say die). After some preliminary skirmishing the legislative body seated Theophilus Lachapelle and was free to consider other business. Brown had some. He opened with a memorial to Congress for an appropriation for the survey of a road from Fort Howard on Green Bay to Fort Snelling by way of the Plover Portage on the Wisconsin and Dacotah on the St. Croix (Brown's Ferry was momentarily considered as the western destination, then crossed out); this was followed by a resolution for the survey of the public lands within the territory north of the Wisconsin River. These measures were presented as being necessary inducements to attract settlers to the region – the road alone would cut 200 miles off the 500-mile trip from Green Bay to the St. Peters via the Fox-Wisconsin waterway. Both measures passed without much opposition although it was clear that the benefit to Brown might be equal to or greater than the benefit to the territory.[37]

The direction of the government road was assured by the simple expedient of adding to another road bill a provision for a territorial road "from the Menominee Mills in Crawford County (on the Red Cedar River at present Menomonie) to Dacotah in St. Croix County," thus saving the government surveyors much trouble in locating their road's western end. Improvement of this route would also make it easier for the loggers on the Chippewa and Red Cedar rivers to look west for their supplies and legal transactions, and perhaps would encourage their eventual inclusion in St. Croix county. This measure, too, was approved. In furtherance of this last

36. Easton *St. Croix Valley* 15; Carli to Williams, Sep. 20, 1871; A. B. Easton (presumed author) "Mrs. Lydia Ann Carli," manuscript in Brown papers.

37. "Proceedings of St. Croix County Board," Jan. 3, 1842; Papers of the third Wisconsin territorial legislature: petitions, resolutions.

scheme, Brown attempted to amend a bill organizing several townships in Crawford County, originally sponsored by Brunson, to attach "all that part of Crawford County as lies west of the Chippewa River" temporarily to St. Croix county for all county purposes – elections, assessments, taxes. This he might have managed but for the lateness in the session. On February 3 the bill was ordered to lie on the table and never revived.

As a last hurrah during his last month as a member of the third Wisconsin territorial legislature, Brown introduced and was able to get passed his long-sought ferry bill. This may have been handed him as compensation for his disappointments (more of this in a moment) or by way of recompense for his adroit removal of Mr. Brunson, Whig and Doty supporter, from that predominantly Democratic body. Although Brown had changed the licensee to Dr. Christopher Carli, members of the legislature were well aware it was Brown's request. Some members had been reluctant to tangle with the army over the issue and doubted they had the power to interfere on government property, but Brown convinced them that the Ordinance of 1787, which declared navigable streams should be forever open and free of passage, allowed them the power. Moreover, he thought that if the bill passed and was approved by Congress (which all territorial laws must be) it would have the force of an Act of Congress. By whatever means, Brown finally had a legislative charter to keep a ferry at Sintomonee for ten years. Using this as a wedge, he then applied to the secretary of war through Delegate Henry Dodge with a petition signed by some fifty citizens to have the reserve removed or, if that were not possible, to have the sanction of the secretary for the ferry. Dodge, in forwarding this petition to the new secretary of war, John C. Spencer, commented that "Brown can be relied on," adding to his endorsement, "Mr. Carli is unwilling to bear the expense of boats without your authority." Response from the war department was swift: Mr. Brown had addressed the commanding officer on this subject before and had always been turned down – it was deemed that his object was not one of accommodating the public with the ferry, but a wholly private one, and with this opinion Spencer concurred.[38] The authority of the army over the reserve stood firm.

But Brown had come to this legislature with another purpose more urgent than the contested election, territorial roads or ferry permits. He was charged with getting the legislature to endorse the Sioux treaties, not an easy feat in view of the antagonism toward Governor Doty in both houses. Legislative approval wasn't just a nicety here, it was a necessity. The treaties stood almost no chance in Congress if there was no support for them from the people of Iowa and Wisconsin. Both territories' delegates were personally opposed to them, but Henry Dodge could be counted on to carry the ball if presented with a memorial from his

---

38. *House Journal*; *Wiskonsan Enquirer* Jan. 15, 22, 1842; *Madison Express* Feb. 19, 1842; Brown to Dodge, May 14, 1842, Dodge to Spencer, Jun. 6. 1842, and Spencer to Dodge, Jun. 9, 1842, all in Fort Snelling record collection, microfilm in MHS, originals in OSW LS & LR and OQG consolidated correspondence.

legislature. To this end Brown had wrangled a position as chairman of the select committee on removal of the Indians, formed in response to the governor's opening message, which had requested that the legislature produce a plan. He had reported from this committee before Christmas the strongly-worded statement that "nothing is more likely to retard our settlements or interrupt the peace and tranquillity of our citizens than retaining within our limits Indian tribes... not amenable to our laws," recommended that measures be taken to remove the Indians from their present homes and hunting grounds in Wisconsin to a place west of the Mississippi outside the jurisdiction of any state or territory and submitted that the place that best met these needs was the land recently ceded by the Sioux. He presented a resolution asking for the removal of the Indians still in Wisconsin to the lands recently negotiated for by Governor Doty and also for the speedy ratification of the treaties, so there would be no more delay in their removal. There was hot debate on the propriety of this resolution. When the motion was made for the House to rise on Christmas eve, Brown opposed it on the grounds it would cause delay to their final passage of the resolution, which he thought the public interest demanded. It was especially important to Brown that the measure be put to a vote before Lachapelle was seated, for he knew his fellow Democrat was very much opposed to the Fur Company interest and would do all in his power to defeat the resolution. However, the House refused to consider the measure at that time and the resolution was tabled just before they broke for Christmas.**39**

Brown attacked the problem with renewed vigor when the House sat again in January. The resolution was restated to avoid mention of the treaty and now simply asked that the Indians be removed to lands "which would be provided" west of the Mississippi. During debate Brown tried several times to amend the resolution to support the treaty, at first obliquely, by adding the words "within the country purchased in July from the Sioux of the St. Peters," and then overtly by reinserting the clause soliciting Senate ratification of the treaty "as it will afford the government the means of favorably locating the Indians yet in the territory with a view to their future permanency and ultimate civilization" – to which one member attempted to add "and the benefit of the American Fur Company." Mr. Brown debated that point. The Fur Company, he said, would have small claim on the upper Sioux; independent traders and the old Columbia Fur Company would have the greatest demands against the Indians under this treaty. Might not Brown himself get something out of the $150,000? queried a member. Brown professed the upper Indians did not owe him a cent and if he received any benefit from the treaty, it would be in fair trading. Still, some members – Lachapelle, as Brown had feared, among them – said for the record they considered it a "stupendous system of fraud" to the benefit of those who got it up, and that it was so considered by not only the former Iowa agent, Joshua Pilcher, but by the

---

39. "Removal of the Indians 1841," House documents 1841, series 171.

chairman of the committee on Indian affairs, Missouri Senator Thomas Hart Benton. Brown spoke at some length. The object of Mr. Pilcher and the whole opposition to the treaty could easily be understood, he thought: it was money, and money alone that influenced them. "A large disbursement of public money must of necessity attend the removal of these Indians, and if the opposition have their way this money will be disbursed in Missouri." He could assure the House that the northwestern Indians could not be removed peaceably to a country south of the Missouri; any such attempt would be sure to lead to a war. He could not agree with the member who felt this was a matter they should not interfere with. It was pointed out to Brown that he was not himself a disinterested party. Of course, countered Brown, he would not profess to be disinterested – he was interested in all that would benefit the people of Wisconsin; he was interested in preserving the peace of the territory.**40**

After considerable debate the resolution passed the House without Brown's amendments on January 30. In the Council, Crawford County member Charles Learned tried and failed to append Brown's amendment. The resolution ended up simply asking that the Indians should be located in a district unspecified "to which the white settlements shall not extend." The best Brown could do toward mustering a show of support for the treaties was to secure a petition of the members of the legislature (he had about two-thirds of their signatures) requesting that the Senate confirm the Dakota treaties. Wrote a discouraged Doty to Sibley shortly thereafter, "Brown was unable to carry his resolution – he was assisted in another form and you have the result. The resolution and the petition together present the subject I think in the best way. They have been forwarded to the President of the Senate."**41**

Brown's rather crude assessment of the treaty opponents' monetary motives may have had some basis in fact, but he must have meant to mislead the honorable members about the lack of interest of the American Fur Company. Ramsay Crooks desperately needed that $150,000 to keep the company afloat. The year before Crooks had had to sell the Western Outfit and other assets. Many Mississippi traders, including Henry Sibley and Hercules Dousman, owed him large sums. That fall Sibley and Dousman went to St. Louis to make a deal with old Joe Rolette and Pierre Chouteau Junior for a new partnership. Sibley traveled to Washington City in January, where with Dousman and Robert Stuart he spent the winter lobbying for the ratification. Crooks remained in New York rather than risk stirring up greater opposition by his presence in Washington, exhorting Sibley by post that "the first great object desirable to secure is the ratification of Gov. Doty's late treaty with the Sioux upon which depends very much the result of the Western Outfit 1841." A second object was payment for the $13,000 in vouchers Sibley held, should the

<hr />

40. *House Journal* Dec. 21, 1841, Jan. 27, 29 and 30, 1842; *Wiskonsan Enquirer* Dec. 30, 1841, Jan. 29, Feb. 5, 1942; *Madison Express* Feb. 5, 1842.

41. Doty to Sibley, Feb. 28, 1842, in Sibley papers; the petition, dated at Madison February 16, 1842, is enclosed in Doty to Secretary of War, Feb. 19, 1842, in OIA LR, Wisconsin superintendency.

treaty fall through. The unpopular Doty, like Crooks, lay low. His attempts the previous fall to conclude an agreement with the Sac, Fox and Winnebago to remove to the new northern Indian-state-to-be had failed signally. When the supplementary Sioux halfbreed agreement appeared in Washington that fall, along with Doty's definition of "halfbreed" to include those with one-quarter Sioux blood, there was widespread condemnation of the Wisconsin governor.[42]

Not the least formidable opponent was Missouri Senator Thomas Hart Benton who, along with Bell's old Tennessee political rival John Sevier, was a member of the Senate committee to which the treaties had been referred. They were, as Sibley said, avowedly hostile. Benton believed that Henry Dodge and Joshua Pilcher should have been the agents of removal of the Indians. In a memorandum to President John Tyler he condemned the articles of the treaty as inappropriate to the law of the land, providing as it did for a system of government. And the vast sums involved set a dangerous precedent. After the cabinet's resignation, John Bell had devoted himself to lobbying for the treaty, causing at least one newspaper to condemn it as "a Whig measure designed purely and simply to advance the political fortunes of Mr. Bell." By March it was pretty obvious that Benton's view would not moderate even though Pierre Chouteau had thrown his not inconsiderable influence into support for the treaty and the new secretary of war, John Spencer, had come out openly for it.[43]

Hope was kept alive as April and May passed and the Senate had still not put the treaty to a vote. In June there was a report at the Prairie that it had been ratified; in July Robert Stuart wrote to Doty that he was assured it would be ratified in a few days; in August word was that it had been laid over until the winter session.[44] Back at the St. Peters Joseph R. Brown was going ahead with cheerful optimism on his plans for the reserve. His enthusiasm wasn't always contagious. In April a laconic Alexander McLeod wrote to Martin McLeod:

> "There is some rumours of a part of the reserve to be withdrawn, that is, the east side of the Mississippi. In that case your claim you promised to share half with me. Brown, or rather Squire Brown, was here a few days ago. And he swears that it will be withdrawn and that he is coming up to take possession of a claim that he has and to keep a ferry opposite Mr. Kittson's. Won't we be in town then, oh yes, and grog shops."[45]

---

42. Sibley articles of agreement with Chouteau, Feb. 25, 1842, Crooks to Sibley, Mar. 7, 1842, Sibley papers; see also Sibley's reports to Crooks, Feb. 2, 9, 11, Mar. 11, 15, 26, 1842 in American Fur Company papers.

43. *Washington Globe* Jan. 14, 1842; Holcombe *Minnesota* II: 288–289; Smith *Doty* 260–262.

44. Dousman to Sibley, Jun. 20, Jul. 5, 1842; Crooks to Sibley, Aug. 1, 1842, all in Sibley papers.

45. Alexander R. McLeod to Martin McLeod, Apr. 25, 1842, McLeod papers. The two McLeods were not related. Alexander was an AMF trader, at this time Frank Steele's clerk. Norman Wolfred Kittson had apprenticed under Hazen Mooers and Joe Rolette, been sutler's clerk for Stambaugh, been then an independent trader at Baker's old post near Massie's landing. He joined Sibley in a trading partnership for the 1842–1843 season (for biographical sketches see Williams *St. Paul* 135–136; Holcombe *Minnesota* II: 101–103).

But Stuart, Dousman, Sibley, Brown and McLeod were all to be disappointed. On August 29 the Senate rejected the main treaty by an overwhelming vote of 26 to 2; two days later the supplementary Mdewakanton Treaty was reported out and laid on the table. Results were immediate and sensational. Within a week the American Fur Company had suspended payments: crowed one of its competitors, "The Great American Fur Company... has exploded." Dousman put words to the general feeling within the company in a letter to Sibley in September: "Here is death to the great Panacea which was to cure all the lame Ducks and give the wherewith to so many to be joyful... It is no use to cry we have to swallow it as bitter a Pill as it may be – we shall have to work harder & spend less."**46**

Defeat of the treaty had no less striking effect on Joseph R. Brown. In April his hopes had been high. In August they were dashed. Typically, he wasted no time on regrets. In September he moved his family and much of his trade equipment to a wintering house on the Sheyenne, temporarily laying aside his plans for the county and the reserve.

---

46. Lavender *Fist in the Wilderness* 419; Dousman to Sibley, Sep. 23, 1842, Sibley papers. All was not as bad as it appeared in 1842; Ramsay Crooks eventually paid off every cent of his $300,000 debt. Although the American Fur Company ceased to exist, its successor, Pierre Chouteau Junior and Company, carried on with the same traders on the upper Mississippi and was generally, although incorrectly, known by the old name.

Map 12 Posts and routes on the Coteau des Prairies and in the Red River valley in the 1840s. The site of McLeod's post is now Hartford Beach State Park. The site of Brown's Sica Hollow post near Sica Hollow State Park has been partially excavated.

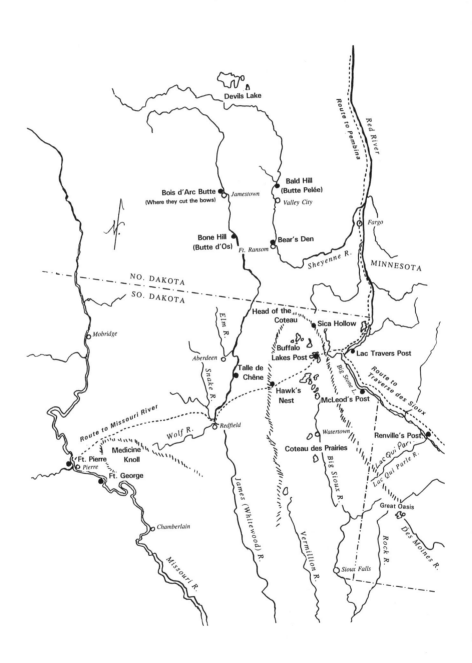

CHAPTER IX

"BROWN EXPECTS TO BE MOST SUCCESSFUL IN CAJOLING THE INDIANS." Martin McLeod 1845

What now seems to have been an abrupt decision actually was very much in character for Joseph R. Brown. Those who have found it inexplicable that a man of Brown's abilities would give up a promising political career, a county organization under his control, the prospect of becoming an important and respected country squire to return to a life "half Bedouin" and have laid it to a restless disposition or vagabond habits have got hold of the wrong end of the stick.1 Joe Brown was a man who knew when to cut his losses. He hadn't gone into politics to become a politician, but to open up the St. Peters cession to settlement and consolidate his claim on the reserve. Roads, ferries, courts, squatters' rights, treaties had all been aimed at this objective, but the failure of the Doty treaty had frustrated his hopes, at least for the foreseeable future. It might be years before the land was surveyed and sold. Meanwhile his debts were mounting – he owed Sibley over $1,000 at this juncture, had given Kenneth Mackenzie a $1,000 note in 1840 – and had no real money-making prospects in St. Croix County.2 In the fall of 1842, Joe Brown was going where the money was.

It was also in character that he had prepared for this eventuality. In June, even while hopes were high, he had descended the river to St. Louis to contract for trade goods and whiskey for the coming season. Chouteau was still in Washington flogging his dead horse, but there were in town several other men who were exultant about the money to be made in trade

---

1. Joseph R. Brown did not conform to the paradigm of the public figure. Even William W. Folwell, who admired Brown as "a man of energy and genius, of admirable personal qualities" was at a loss to explain why he failed to have a great career, suggesting it might have been his restless character, his love for the roving life, even his part Indian family (Folwell *Minnesota* III: 350). Almost every historian has been influenced by the character assessment of Brown produced for his obituary by Joseph A. Wheelock, a prominent St. Paul editor who did not know J. R. Brown intimately, but knew him well enough to realize he had failed to meet the standards of a respectable Victorian businessman: "If his mental powers had been disciplined to the routine of some profession or regular occupation, if he had not been dragged down by the slipshod half-vagabond associations and habits of his frontier life, from the high career for which he was formed, he would have been one of the foremost men of his day" (*St. Paul Press*, Nov. 12, 1870). Joe would have laughed: let the "little big men" think what they liked so long as he got what he wanted.

2. Sibley Ledger, Notebook 1842–1849, Sibley papers.

with the plains Indians. They knew that with Crooks' and Chouteau's interests diverted by the treaty the time was now, if ever, to attack the American Fur Company's hold on the Missouri River trade. No less than six new companies formed oppositions that summer. Among them was the Union Fur Company – sometimes called Fox, Livingston and Company – who were planning to headquarter at the bend of the Missouri, just twenty miles downstream from the AMF's Fort Pierre. Their intention was to buy robes and skins of the Yanktonai and Cuthead who wintered on the James, Vermillion and Big Sioux rivers. Those Indians should have been in the grasp of the American Fur Company, but William Dickson and Jacob Halsey, two of the Fur Company's strongest arms, were no more – Halsey died that summer in St. Louis, Dickson had been found dead near his post on the Vermillion, an apparent suicide.[3] Several of Sibley's traders – Laframboise, the Frénières, Renville – who had been successful trading on the James from bases near the coteau had grown old and preferred their comfortable cabins to the rigors of the derouin. Yes, there was a window of opportunity there.

The Fur Company was aware of the peril. Into the gap they threw Andrew Drips, once their agent, now with Chouteau's influence and connivance President Tyler's appointee as special agent for the Sioux of the upper Missouri, to be headquartered at Fort Pierre. Stakes in this game were high. Over 90,000 buffalo robes and hides came out of that country yearly. They sold in St. Louis for better than $3.50 each, by far the most profitable item of the western trade. Brown would have heard – it was common knowledge in St. Louis that summer – that the buffalo had returned to the eastern parts of the plains. The Indians couldn't help but take a big harvest at the expense of the Red River hunters and the Hudson's Bay Company. Taken together with the mushrooming domestic market for buffalo robes, it looked as if it would be easy to make a killing trading hides.[4] It looked especially appealing to someone who didn't jib at using spirits, banned (at least in theory) to Fur Company traders. The agents at Council Bluffs and Fort Pierre were particularly conscientious about stopping the importation of whiskey by way of the Missouri, but there was little they could do about that which seeped in from the Minnesota River. The door was open.

Henry Sibley, having once been burned by the Sisseton, preferred not to extend his operations past Lac qui Parle. His 1842 agreement with Franklin Steele and Norman Kittson proposed posts at Lac qui Parle,

---

3. Brown to Doty, Jul. 14, 1842. For the events of that summer see Chittenden *American Fur Trade* I: 367–370.

4. While beaver, muskrat and raccoon pelts were mainly sold in Europe for hat-making, the demand for buffalo robes was an American phenomenon. Although often used interchangeably, technically "robes" are the dressed hides of winter-killed bison with the thick fur left on, while "hides" are hairless skins of summer-killed cows. "Skins" usually refers to deer, bear or raccoon, and "furs" to pelts of other fur-bearing animals. For the changing nature of the western fur trade see James L. Clayton "Growth and Economic Significance of the American Fur Trade 1790–1890" in *Minnesota History* XL: 211–215 (St. Paul 1966). For the Fur Company's concern over insinuating Drips on the upper river, see Pierre Chouteau Junior to T. H. Crawford, Sep. 23, 1842, and D. D. Mitchell to Crawford, Jun. 8 and Aug. 25, 1842, all in OIA LR. St. Louis superintendency.

Little Rapids and Traverse des Sioux. Brown knew Sibley was cautious, but Kittson was bold. He might decide to push out into the northern plains and could corral a vast trade by the move; it would be well to anticipate him. Brown's business dealings with the lower Sioux – in trade goods and whiskey which they in turn traded westward to the upper bands – were extensive, but were not making him rich. He had, in fact, amassed over $4,000 in unpaid credits with them, credits that would not be redeemed for many years, now that the treaty was quashed.5 They were a good investment to be sure, but what Brown needed now was cash. It was time to make a move.

So it was that the end of September 1842 found Joseph R. Brown once again at Lake Traverse with a small party consisting of Susan and his children, Akipa, Winona, Gabriel and one or two engagés. Already there was a nip in the air. The prairies were straw-colored and in some places blackened by the fires that the strong winds of autumn whipped through the dry grasses. Hundreds of waterfowl passed down the Red River flyway, settling in the marshes and lakes of the coteau before continuing south. The Sisseton were gone. The village of Tatankanajin (Standing Buffalo), where Susan's relatives might have been found, was deserted; they had packed up everything portable and started for their winter camp on the Sheyenne. It was clear the Indians were not far ahead of Brown's party for their tracks were fresh. At one place they came upon an old woman of the band. Too sick and weak to travel, she had been left alone on the prairie with a small amount

Figure 26 Martin McLeod. Minn. Hist. Soc.

of food to sing her death song. Susan found her – perhaps recognized her – and brought her into camp, insisting that she not be left to be killed by wolves. So they made room for the old woman on a pony travois and carried her along until they caught up with the Sisseton. Susan returned the woman to her family, berating them for holding to so barbaric a custom as leaving the infirm to starve or be killed, even if it was their own wish.6

5. Agreement Jun. 30, 1842, forming N. W. Kittson and Company to trade at Cold Water, Little Rapids, Traverse des Sioux and Lac qui Parle, Sibley papers; J. R. Brown claims, 1851 Treaty of Mendota.

6. S. J. Brown to Doane Robinson, Mar. 12, 1924, Robinson papers, South Dakota Historical Society, Pierre. Sam thought his father traded with the Yankton that winter, and JRB may well have put a

The band had established a camp in the sheltered valley of the Sheyenne near the Butte Pelée. The Indians allowed Brown to set up his camp near them. This area is much changed today because a large dam north of Valley City, North Dakota, backs up water to fill the valley with Lake Astabula. Then it was a deep V-shaped valley, filled with trees and berry bushes, an oasis in the prairie. The landmark bald hillock was not really a hill at all but a large clay bank that had been undercut by the river leaving a vertical face devoid of vegetation. As Brown settled his family in with their relatives, François Frénière, comfortably ensconced on the island in Lake Traverse and loathe to move, wrote to Sibley (via a passing priest) that "Braund" had gone to Bald Butte on the River Sheyenne and promised to send his son Xavier Frénière to oppose him there. Brown, meanwhile, decided prospects looked good. He had withdrawn over $1,000 of Gabriel's and Lydia Ann's halfbreed allotment (which he had banked with Sibley) to finance his outfit. With Gabriel and François Dejarlais, he turned about to descend the river for additional trade goods. He had easily procured a license from Amos Bruce; on October 28 he signed an agreement with Sibley who agreed to furnish an additional small assortment of goods, about $500 worth. Brown obligated himself to bring all his furs and peltries to the Traverse or Mendota where Sibley would pay highest market price for them and agreed not to interfere in any way with Sibley's other outfits.[7]

It was late in the season and turning bitterly cold, but Brown's business delayed him several days at the St. Peters. His first necessity, while Sibley, Gabriel and Dejarlais were making up the equipment, was to visit his farm on Grey Cloud Island, which he had left under the supervision of David Hone. There on October 17 he wrote out a conveyance from himself to "Susan Frenier of Dacotah," for the sum of $500 in hand releasing all claim to "Chanwakan Farm," its dwelling house, buildings, fences, land under cultivation together with the stock of cattle, hogs, tools and articles of every description accruing under stipulation with David Hone. This he obviously did to keep clear title to both claims, at Dacotah and Chanwakan. Witnessing the deed were Fletcher and another of Joe's half brothers, John Wesley Brown, who had followed the other members of his family west, and had been living with Paul and Lydia since April.

While John surveyed the possibilities, Fletcher had made up his mind what to do – he wanted to become a fur trader. This may even have been Joe's idea; he had only a few experienced men in his outfit and could use

---

man on the James River where Waanatan was wont to winter. Known to be working for Brown this season were François Dejarlais, Pierre Rouillard and a man identified only as Shepherd.

7. F. Frénière to Sibley, Oct. 11, 1842 (written by Father Augustin Ravoux); Sibley/Brown agreement Oct. 28, 1842, both in Sibley papers; Guardianship for Gabriel Renville and Angus and Lydia Ann Brown filed by Brown Jan. 6, 1840, Crawford County Probate Book B; Payment to "legal guardian" under treaty of 1837, Sep. 4, 1842, OIA LR, St. Peters superintendency; Martin McLeod Diary Oct. 25, 1842, McLeod papers. The area between Lake Traverse and the coteau is described in *Joseph N. Nicollet on the Plains and Prairies*, Edmund C. Bray and Martha Coleman Bray, editors and translators, 181, passim (St. Paul 1976).

another hand, especially one who was proving as useful as his half brother. Accordingly, Fletcher's resignation as collector was handed in to be read at the November board meeting, at which time Paul Carli was made deputy to finish out Brown's terms as county clerk and treasurer. Nathaniel, at fifteen, was too young for the trade, so remained at Chanwakan with his mother and Hone. Brown and Hone talked over the running of the farm. They decided not to cut hay, planning to graze the forty or so cattle on the dry marsh grass and reeds as soon as the swampy lowlands froze solid. This as it turned out, nearly proved a disastrous decision. Deep drifts kept the cattle from getting to their fodder that winter, and only Hone's resourcefulness in cutting twiggy tree branches and dragging them up for the animals to browse on saved the stock. Many others lost cattle that winter.[8]

The results of the September 11 election, which Brown surely heard as soon as he set foot back at the St. Peters, couldn't have surprised him much. He had run for county clerk (now an elective office), register of deeds, treasurer and legislative representative; he had easily won the clerk's and register's races, garnering all but one vote. But the only precinct casting a majority for him in the other two races was St. Croix Falls – from his "home" precincts he gathered just three votes. This may seem incomprehensible until one realizes that Brown had by election day announced his intention to leave the county, and had without doubt informed the voters (except those at the falls) that he would have to decline the offices anyway if he were elected, although he might have continued as clerk, having already earmarked Paul as deputy. The fact that Fletcher also won reelection as assessor and collector also seems to confirm that Brown had not fallen out of favor with the voters – yet. It's true that reapportionment had resulted in only one representative to the House being chosen from Crawford and St. Croix counties combined, and it would seem that Brown could never win against a Prairie du Chien candidate, since the Prairie regularly gave 150 votes, while St. Croix County could muster but 49. However, he need only have struck a deal with the Democratic candidate for the Council to have ballots printed with both names. Indeed, it almost looks as if this move had been anticipated. Lachapelle abandoned the race for representative to Brown and ran instead for the Council. John Manahan, the Whig candidate, won the House seat almost by default.[9]

Brown probably also quickly learned that one of the new county commissioners, Joseph Haskell, was getting up a petition to have the county offices removed to Red Stone (or Red Rock) Prairie. Dacotah, Haskell felt, was an inconvenient location, there being no courthouse in usable condition and no family living there except the Carlis, upon whose hospitality the commission-ers must necessarily have been thrown.

---

8. St. Croix County Deed Book A 5; Proceedings of County Board, Sep. 11 and 26, Oct. 15, Nov. 10, 1842; Case "J. R. Brown's Trading Post".
9. "Proceedings of the St. Croix County Board" Sep. 11, 26, Oct. 15, Nov. 10, 1842.

This didn't bother Brown either. Let them meet where they wished. They couldn't make Red Stone Prairie the county seat since that was located by the organic act on property owned by Brown, and it would take $800 to buy it back – $800 which, if it had ever been in the treasury, had been put to better use by Brown long since. Without a district court and the lucrative position of clerk of court, there was little profit to be made from having the county seat anyway. He could hope this would change. The July previous he had written to the governor seeking to discover if the authority to issue writs could be given him in his capacity as deputy marshal. It could not, but Doty fired off a letter to the secretary of war asking that Judge Irvin, who "had placed all offenders in the county beyond the reach of the laws," be removed and a competent judge appointed. The complaint was forwarded to President Tyler, who had the secretary of state look into the matter. Irvin was asked to answer the charge, and was apparently able to satisfy the state department that the charge was frivolous. But being called on the carpet by the secretary of state did nothing for the judge's humor; he set about preparing a bombshell for the next territorial legislature – an amendment to the St. Croix County organic act that removed the district court to Prairie du Chien.**10** More of this in a moment.

Before Brown returned to the coteau (or possibly even before he had left to reconnoiter prospects on the coteau earlier that fall), he came to an agreement with two former mill company employees who spent the winter as lodgers with Lydia Carli in the Tamarack House. Jacob Fisher and Sylvester Stateler, millwright and blacksmith for the St. Croix Lumbering Company, had parted company with their boss James Purinton and drifted down the lake, looking for opportunities. Supposedly Brown hired them to complete the county buildings that winter, although it's difficult to understand why he should have bothered. Probably he told them he proposed to locate a mill on Pine Creek (and, in fact, a mill was said to have been started there but never finished), asking them to look into the practicality of such a venture. But Fisher was an opportunist. He saw the millsite at Dacotah had a good flow of water, but because the creek's valley was flat and swampy for more than a half-mile back from the lake extensive improvements would be needed to make it practical for a sawmill. Scouting down the lake Fisher came to the present site of Stillwater, outside Brown's claim (which ended at Battle Hollow), ideal for a mill and sidebooms, but lacking waterpower, having only a spring that was likely to be insufficient in summer. Jacob Fisher soon saw that a short canal was all that was needed to divert the waters of Pine Creek through McKusick Lake and down the cliff to supplement the spring. He found some willing capitalists in the St. Croix Lumber Company (many of whose members had had trouble with Purinton and wanted to get clear of him), claimed the land south of Battle Hollow for himself and the rest is

---

10. Papers of the fourth Wisconsin Territorial Legislature: petitions, series 180; Brown to Doty, Jul. 14, 1842; Doty to Secretary or War, Aug. 9, 1842; F. Webster, acting secretary of state to David Irvine (sic), Oct. 31, 1842, Office of Secretary of State Domestic LS, Vol. 32: 448.

history: John McKusick brought up the fixtures for a sawmill and the Stillwater Mill Company began sawing within a year. Lydia Carli believed that her brother Joe took this setback to his townsite hard, that when the commercial development was attracted to Stillwater rather than Dacotah "all the wild dreams and ambitions which [he] had conjured up faded away."[11] However, it's pretty clear that Brown knew by then that Dacotah was not going to be a viable settlement, and that he didn't really care. Dacotah had been a convenience for the voters of the valley, nothing more. Brown's real interest lay on the Mississippi, where he still cherished hopes for the reserve. While he was stymied there, he would direct his efforts elsewhere.

He almost delayed too long. An early winter was upon them. Brown brought his durham boat into the Traverse on November 5 in a cold, driving rain that in a few days turned to sleet, then snow. River navigation closed on the fifteenth. By the eighteenth it was blowing and drifting and the thermometer had plummeted to minus twelve degrees. It was excruciatingly slow going over the prairies with the loaded carts, the men on snowshoes, the oxen breaking their own path through the drifts, no feed to be had without digging. Brown and Dejarlais at last struggled in to Lac qui Parle. There they were obliged to leave the goods to wait for better weather, while they returned to the Sheyenne with what they could carry.[12]

Winter in North Dakota is unpleasant at best. Weak daylight lasts fewer than eight hours, drifting snow covers all landmarks and the bitter cold seeps into the bones. It can be even more unbearable when a man is basically idle and has burning reason to be elsewhere. Brown's chief activity while his men were on derouin would have been teaching Gabriel and Fletcher the tricks of the trade. It took several seasons to turn an inexperienced young man into a trader, and until they had served that apprenticeship Brown could not put them at a wintering post alone, or even with an experienced hand whose life might depend on his partner. Normally, he would have made one or two trips to check on the winterers, bringing back the fall hides that had been dressed by the women over the winter, but given the one to two-foot snow cover and biting cold, that may have been impractical. By mid-January the weather had moderated somewhat, enough anyway to allow Brown to retrieve his possessions from Kittson at Lac qui Parle. By March it was fine. Driven by necessity – and no doubt cabin fever – Brown set off alone to make the 1,200-mile round trip to Madison.

---

11. Carli to Williams, Sep. 20, 1871; Easton *St. Croix Valley* I: 347; *Stillwater Daily Gazette*, Jun. 3, 1903; Holcombe *Minnesota* II: 108. Lydia Carli's vitriolic attack on Jake Fisher ("prowling adventurer," etc.) more than fifty years later may indicate that she, at least, thought Fisher had had an understanding with Brown on which he had welshed. It could have happened the other way around, too: Brown may have promised Fisher and Statelar great things, then decided to leave for the coteau. We'll probably never know.

12. McLeod Diary Nov. 5, passim; Climatological records Fort Snelling, now in records of the weather bureau, NARG 27; Louis Provençalle to Sibley, Dec. 18, 1842, Sibley papers.

Although he was keenly interested in knowing whether Doty's attack on Irvin had had effect and if this legislature would pull itself together to petition Congress for statehood, he was even more interested in getting the money the territory owed him. He had not been paid a cent for his legislative activities, not per diem nor mileage nor the expense reimbursement granted him in the disputed election tangle; neither had anyone else. For the past two years there had been no money in the territory. The banks had gone bust, Doty and his henchmen had collared the appropriation for the capitol building (well, to be fair, no one ever proved Doty had misused public funds, yet no one believed him wholly innocent either) and previous legislatures had squandered the money earmarked for expenses (printing, furniture and even stationery proved to be very costly on this frontier). As a result the treasurer had been forced to issue drafts for the amounts owed so the members could pay their bills. The secretary received some funds in June of 1842, insufficient to cover even half the debt; it could be guessed that more money would be appropriated by Congress, as indeed it was in December. A prudent man, knowing the governor's ability to soak up money like a sponge, would try to be on hand when the scrip was redeemed to be sure he got his $727. So Brown strapped on his snowshoes and started for Madison.13

Figure 27 Norman Wolfred Kittson.
Minn. Hist. Soc.

13. It is not impossible Brown held considerably more than the $727 scrip assigned to him (see Treasurer's Report May 8, 1844, in "Appropriations for the Legislative Assembly of Wisconsin Territory," *U.S. House Document 251*, 28th Congress, 1st session) because there was considerable speculation in the negotiable drafts, especially after it was noised abroad that the issue was worthless. See *Madison Express* Jun. 29, 1842, and Dec. 28, 1843.

Figure 28 Sioux Indians moving camp with pony travois. Watercolor by Seth Eastman about 1850. Courtesy of W. Duncan MacMillan.

Figure 28 Sioux Indians moving camp with pony travois. Watercolor by Seth Eastman about 1850. Courtesy of W. Duncan MacMillan.

The trip was not without dangers, and not all of those were weather-related. Brown was followed by several young men of the village who aimed, he surmised, to do him mischief. Probably much to their chagrin they were outdistanced. Brown was anxious to reach his destination and so pressed on all night instead of stopping to rest as his stalkers evidently thought he would. J. R. Brown, when he got going, was a great walker. "He always preferred footback to horseback, or any other mode of travel," declared his son Samuel, who also pointed out that among the Sioux his father was noted for feats of travel and often outstripped the best Indian hunters. It may have been a nearer thing than this casual story-telling indicates. Speaking of this affair later Brown is supposed to have said: "I outran the rascals and saved my scalp, and, By George, snowshoes came in handy!" Below The Entry the snow was less deep and travel on the river by sleigh was perfectly possible, making the last 200 or so miles much easier going.**14**

---

14. Two letters of S. J. Brown to Doane Robinson (Mar. 7 and May 5, 1921, Robinson papers) tell of Brown's snowshoe feat but misdate it to the winter of 1840–1841, probably because Sam thought it pertained to one of the years his father was a member of the legislature instead of the year after.

Figure 29 Spearing mustrats in winter. Rat skins were the staple of the trade and prime winter pelts the most desirable. Seth Eastman watercolor about 1850. Courtesy of W. Duncan MacMillan.

As it turned out he needn't have hurried. Doty had circumvented the fourth territorial legislature, which was bent on removing him, by refusing to convene it, citing lack of funds as his reason. The members stewed until March 6, 1843, when the governor at last called a special session to order. Judge Irvin was on hand to swear in the new lawmakers. During this session a bill was introduced that freed the judge from the inconvenience of having to hold a court in St. Croix County and from any further accusations of dereliction of duty. Council bill #30, which repealed part of the St. Croix County Organic Act and annexed the county to Crawford for judicial purposes, was seen by members as the only logical answer to Irvin's adamant refusal to set foot at the St. Croix. There was nothing Brown could do except comment on the inexpediency of removing all officers of the court – including sheriff and judge of probate – from the county and placing them some 200 miles away where they were of little use. The citizens of St. Croix County found themselves in the same position they had been in before organization, with no means of settling estates, trying criminal cases or even posting legal notices, except that they were now burdened with the expense of running the rest of the county administration. Brown's fellow citizens complained bitterly over the next three years, many blaming him – it may be with good reason – for the loss of the court through antagonizing Judge Irvin, and grumbling that he had manipulated the county board and misused county funds.[15]

In Madison Brown may well have been relieved to find the statehood push had fizzled. It had been a popular concept with the legislators, many of whom hoped thus to rid themselves of the curse of government by appointee, with specific reference to Doty. Brown's last session as one of them had mandated a general referendum on the question of statehood for Wisconsin, but it had been rejected by the voters in September and the idea was dropped. If a memorial to Congress had been adopted by the fourth legislature, it would likely have suggested that the state be admitted with the same boundaries as the territory. That would have been of little use to Brown. On the other hand, had the Doty treaty been ratified, there would have been a great deal of ceded land west of the Mississippi that would have required territorial government. Brown's expectation had been that the land north of the incipient state of Iowa and possibly north of the Chippewa River would have formed that new territory, with the St. Peters area right in the middle. The preceding July that had seemed a sure thing – Doty had even referred to "the interest of northern Iowa or the 'Minnesota territory' that summer – but now that expectation appeared futile.[16] Brown could expect to mark time for a year, at least.

Did he even get his money? Probably, although the appropriation had once again come up short, so some of the scrip could not be redeemed until the following summer. All in all, it was rather a disappointing reward for an extraordinary effort that must have occupied him more than a month traveling. He arrived back on the Sheyenne sometime in April to find himself the father of a baby girl, born April 5. A twin, another girl, had died at birth or shortly thereafter; Brown recorded no name for her. The surviving baby, named Harriet Cordelia Brown (convincing proof that the relative he had found in Baltimore was his aunt Harriet Renshaw), would remain with Susan and her other children in the Sisseton's summer village at Lake Traverse while Brown took the furs down.[17] The Indians' hunts had been very, very good. Brown had over 350 dressed robes and a fine selection of valuable furs – beaver, otter, fisher, bear, wolf, fox, mink. What he didn't have was horses. The severe winter and more "mischief" by the young men he had humiliated had left him short of draft animals. In May Joseph Laframboise wrote from Little Rock that he had no news from Brown, but had heard that he could not get out. It was not until early June that JRB was able to return to Mendota, but he had with him quite a haul. Brown sold well over $1,000 worth of peltries and prime robes to

15. *House Journal* 1842 164; Papers of the Territory of Wisconsin, Documents of the Council, series 160.

16. Doty to Sibley, Jul. 20, 1842, Sibley papers.

17. Brown Bible. Brown recorded only the name Harriet Cordelia with her birth and death dates in the Bible and did not give the names of her parents, but the child was obviously Susan's. The probate file of Abigail Crawford shows that twin girls were born to Susan between Ellen and Samuel, and all family members agree that Susan bore twelve children, eight girls and four boys. See S. J. Brown to Warren Upham, Jun. 1, 1923; Historical information file, MHS; and probate of Abigail Crawford, file #3732, BIA records, Sisseton. For more on Brown's family see Appendix A.

Sibley, paying his expenses and enabling him to clear part of his previous debt to the Western Outfit. In comparison, François Frénière had brought in about $1,500 worth of furs, Renville $1,200, Provençalle and Laframboise each about $1,000. Further research by someone with an accountant's eye revealed that Sibley's books were in error: in Brown's account there was a double charge for repairing a plough for Hone, no credit was shown for $200 worth of furs delivered in 1840 and for hams and pork sold Sibley that year and the interest on the balance had been incorrectly figured. These adjustments reduced his old debt to Sibley to just $260 and left him with a $100 credit on the current books. Brown had done very well indeed.[18]

Sibley may have felt that Brown had prospered at his and Kittson's expense. There had been complaints about Brown's methods and a certain amount of trouble with the Sioux. Kittson got down first that spring and made an agreement with Sibley that effectively circumvented Mr. Brown. The other partner, Franklin Steele (now Sibley's brother-in-law), pulled out, agreeing to stay out of the Indian trade while being guaranteed by Sibley all the profits of the fort's sutling trade – this to squelch complaints from Pierre Chouteau Junior that Steele was supplying goods and whiskey to opposition traders on the upper Mississippi. By the agreement Kittson was given all the Western Outfit's territory above Lac qui Parle, retaining his very favorable 10 percent advance for three years. His houses were to be on the western side of Big Stone Lake, on the Sheyenne River and on the James at Talle de Chêne, midway between Elm and Snake Rivers. (This last site being the wintering grounds of the Yankton from Lake Traverse was by custom assigned to the St. Peters division, although the lower James belonged to the Missouri outfits.) Since Kittson was taking all the risks, Sibley was unwilling to supply Brown in opposition. Brown could, if he liked, take an outfit from Kittson. Faced with the impasse, Brown took goods on Kittson's terms and awaited his opportunities. He would operate Kittson's Sheyenne post; the trader at Big Stone Lake would be Martin McLeod; François Frénière would go to the Talle de Chêne.

Brown made some arrangement for other goods as well, probably visiting the Prairie in early June to secure them. At any rate the *Otter* arrived at the St. Peters July 8 with goods that cost $34 freight, say seventeen or eighteen barrels or the equivalent. These goods were perhaps sent on ahead with Akipa and Gabriel while Joseph and Fletcher Brown were charged with assisting Kittson make up the equipments for the posts. By the twenty-fourth of July they were ready to depart.[19]

18. Laframboise to Sibley, May 30, 1843, supplement to Sibley papers; Sibley Daybook, Jun. 28, 1843, and Ledger 1842–1843, Sibley papers.

19. Agreement, Kittson and Sibley, May 22, 1843; lists of materials in Brown's hand, undated but falling between July 13 and 17, 1843, in Sibley Memo Book; Sibley Daybook Jul. 8, 1843, all in Sibley papers.

They encountered no problems getting the durham boats up to the Traverse, but once there they found that Frénière had left no carts to forward his additional goods. Frustrated, Kittson wrote to Sibley that Frénière would just have to make two trips himself to get it all, for neither Brown, who had lost a horse, nor Renville would take any of his goods. They were further balked at Big Stone Lake by news that the Indians would not allow Brown to winter at the Bear's Lodge (near Fort Ransom)

Figure 30 Red River cart with driver. Although this picture was taken in St. Paul in the 1850s, the vehicle and Red River halfbreed it shows are typical of the 1840s as well. Similar carts had been used by traders to move goods from the Minnesota River to their posts from at least 1823. Minn. Hist. Soc.

on the Sheyenne as he had planned. Moreover they found nothing would convince the Lake Traverse Wahpeton to hunt the more valuable furs in the big woods while there were buffalo in plenty on the prairies. It was a disappointment to Kittson, even though robes formed the bulk of the Fur Company's western trade, because he knew from Dousman that "rat fever" was up in St. Louis; there would be premium prices paid and plenty of buyers for fine furs in the spring if the Indians could be persuaded to hunt them. If Brown had been able to locate on the Sheyenne it would have been of less concern, for there the hunters would all be after buffalo and would do well, returning more robes in the spring. After scouting the area, Brown decided that a location on the coteau would be most advantageous. It would put him between McLeod and the James River, and if Frénière did not show up, as seemed likely in September, there would be no Fur Company trader at the Talle de Chêne. Kittson had made plans to go with Joe Rolette Junior to Pembina to assess the potential of supplying the Red River hunters from depots on the St. Peters. Brown's original plan may have been to locate on the old Indian trail from the Red River to the Missouri where it passes near the Buffalo Lakes, but if so, he quickly abandoned the idea, as the site lacked good wood and a reliable water supply. A more convenient location was in Sica (Bad) Hollow on the eastern flank of the coteau near the headwaters of the Little Minnesota River and so it was there he built his unfortified wintering house. "I believe he will do well," commented Kittson to Sibley as he prepared to leave for Pembina.[20]

And so he did. He also took the first opportunity that presented itself to vent his dissatisfaction with the arrangement into which he had been forced. The excellent hunts the Cutheads were having sent him down at least once to Mendota for more goods, provisions and a horse to replace the lost one. In May, when he was sure Kittson was back from Pembina, Brown sent him a letter in which he complained that François Frénière (who had indeed turned up, but probably not in time to make the usual credits) and his son had traded many of Brown's robes. By this treachery, Brown indicated, he had sustained a loss of at least $600. Indignantly, Kittson wrote to Sibley, "[Brown] is fully determined not to deliver his returns to the Company until reparation is made to the full amount – this is no more than could be expected from such a source." Kittson was the more irascible because the Frénières and Renville had but few robes and furs among them and prospects for the entire outfit were not bright. "How far the Frénières have traded with his Indians is impossible for me to tell," pursued Kittson, "however, he cannot make us responsible for any collision which may have happened between them." According to Brown's own statement he had about 500 robes on hand plus a large quantity of meat and tallow and about $200 in unpaid credits due half from the plains Indians and half from the Wahpeton of the coteau. Kittson was dumbfounded! "How he can make his loss so heavy, I can't imagine," wrote Kittson with barely disguised temper. "[As] he still has nearly half his goods left, there certainly must be some error in his statement." What, he asked Sibley, should he do if Brown persisted?[21]

It isn't exactly clear how this contretemps was resolved, but it appears from Sibley's books that Brown was paid a 40¢ differential over the price paid Kittson for robes, with the provision that an additional $50 would be forthcoming if the robes fetched more than $3 in St. Louis, which they did. Brown may have held out some of his returns; the total turned in to Sibley was 430 robes, mostly number one painted, commanding the premium price, plus a few furs for a total take of $1,200, not counting what he received for the meat and tallow. As Kittson had taken a loss on the outfit as a whole (and still owned $2,800 inventory), Brown manifestly came out very well even though he was left holding considerable unpaid

---

20. Kittson to Sibley, Aug. 2, Sep. 18, 1843; Dousman to Sibley, May 22, 1843, Apr. 12, 1844, Sibley papers. Sica or Bad Hollow was so called because of a supposed spirit that gave the place a bad reputation among the Sioux. Brown may have deliberately chosen "wakan" locations (such as Olivers Grove, Chanwakan) to prevent the Indians settling too close. The Wahpeton winter village was probably in Long Hollow, six miles south, where Samuel Brown was born in 1845. Both sites are identified in H. S. Morris *Historical Stories, Legends and Traditions of Northeastern South Dakota* 76, 108 (Sisseton 1939). Brown's post atop the coteau overlooking Sica Hollow State Park was partially excavated under the South Dakota historical preservation plan in 1989 and evidence of a log building was found; no palisade was apparent. See Todd Kapler *1988 Brown's Post (39RO38) Excavation; An Archaeological Investigation of an Historic Fur Trading Post* (Vermillion, SD, 1989). The post stood for several years after Brown left the area and was known to the Indians as Siharmi-totiwota – Crooked Foot's Abandoned Home (S. J. Brown to J. B. Irvine, Feb. 28, 1921, Robinson papers, Pierre).

21. Kittson to Sibley, May 7, 1844, Sibley papers.

credits.**22** Presumably the whole altercation with the Frénières was got up simply to better Brown's position at year end. If so, it had worked.

Business had been good, but Brown had other problems. His baby daughter Harriet may already have been very ill when Brown decided to move his family back to Dacotah for the summer. Possibly she was injured in the birth that killed her twin. If that was the case, it might be her father concluded the fourteen-month-old child would have a better chance if treated by Dr. Carli. Susan and her children accompanied the cart train that brought out Brown's peltries that May. By July, when Brown was compelled to return to the coteau, the infant was too ill to move. There was no alternative but to leave her and Susan as well with Lydia. Susan did return to the coteau, probably with another party headed for the upper Minnesota that fall, but without her baby: by August 5 little Harriet was dead. She was buried in the small cemetery "in the wild" near Dacotah where only a few halfbreed children and two unknown travelers had been laid to rest. As if in recompense for her loss, Susan discovered that fall that she was again pregnant. Her son Samuel John was born in the Sisseton village in Long Hollow in March of 1845.**23**

Joe had taken the time while he was at the St. Peters that summer to make a deal with Henry Sibley for the old Gaspar Bruce claim on St. Marys Point, at the mouth of Bolles Creek, apparently so Lydia and Paul could open a farm. The price for this 160 acres of land lying between the lake and the north side of Bolles Creek within sight of the little halfbreed settlement at Afton was 100 bushels of oats and 25 barrels of potatoes, deliverable at Chanwakan (any deficit in oats to be payable in turnips at 75¢ a barrel or potatoes at $1 a barrel at Sibley's option). Before he left for the coteau Brown hired Jake Fisher and Joseph Hall to build a fine two-story frame house on the point, which they had ready for the Carlis to move into by November. The townsite at Dacotah was virtually deserted, although people were pouring into its immediate neighborhood, thanks to the new sawmill now up and running a mile and a half down the lake. John McKusick had built a big frame boarding house there for the mill hands and already the place boasted a public house, a store and several families. That summer or the next Brown rented the Tamarack House to Robert Kennedy, who operated it as a hotel for several years before removing to St. Paul. The pretentious courthouse fell to ruin. Obviously by 1844 Brown had no further interest in Dacotah as a townsite.**24**

An aside here on some of Brown's other real estate arrangements. The summer of 1843 David Hone and family had left Brown's Chanwakan farm in a hurry, having had some trouble with the Indians – a raid,

---

22. J. R. Brown account was closed out Jun. 24, 1844, Sibley Ledger, Sibley papers.

23. Brown Bible; "Lydia Carli" manuscript; S. J. Brown to J. B. Irvine, Feb. 28, 1921.

24. Purchase agreement Jul. 11, 1844 in Sibley Memo Book, Sibley papers. Brown never ran the farm; it was operated by Paul Carli until his death in 1846, although older settlers referred to it as Brown's Farm. He sold the western part in 1846 to Lemuel Bolles, who built the first flour mill in the valley on the creek in that year. It's possible Brown made another purchase in the area; early settlers thought he also owned the land north of the creek as late as 1849. Case "Trading Post;" Folsom *Fifty Years* 32–33, 37–38, 359, 640).

perhaps, similar to that experienced by Mr. Mencke at another of Brown's establishments back in 1839? Hone removed his little family to the settlement called Lake St. Croix, later Point Douglas, where he built a hotel and happily remained. Fortunately, Brown had a new manager for his farm near to hand. John Wesley Brown took charge of the farm that summer, living there alone with his mother until 1846 when he brought his bride, Mary Mooers, daughter of neighbor Hazen Mooers, to the farm. Brown also had taken an interest with Jim Clewet in "the old Johnson claim" and cabin in what became St. Paul's lowertown area, bought when that party (first name unknown or unremembered) decamped in 1839. This circumstance allowed Brown to boast that he had been "part owner of the first building erected within the limits of St. Paul." In the summer of 1843 Clewet wanted to move to another claim, which is why he and Brown jumped at the chance to sell the 50-acre parcel to Norman Kittson for $300. They probably heartily congratulated themselves at having unloaded the marshy claim so easily, doubling their investment to boot. It was, however, Kittson's investment that really paid off: that land was platted and added to the city of St. Paul as Kittson's addition a few years later, making Norman's fortune. Also in 1842 Pierre Parrant's property on Kittsons' Point (Baytown) had been sold at a sheriff's sale; Brown bought "all claims and improvements" for $27.50. In 1843 he deeded it to his half brother Fletcher. It should be remembered that Brown held only Dacotah in his own name. Chanwakan Farm had been deeded to Susan in 1842; he kept the claim at Prescott, which was in Gabriel Renville's name until 1844 (having contracted with Philip Aldrich to hold it), then apparently sold it. How many other deals he may have had a hand in can only be guessed at now.**25**

At the time it must have still seemed more logical to Brown to return to the coteau than to speculate in (to him) unpromising townsites. Therefore he made two contracts that summer; one with Sibley to sell him all the tallow and meat he could get, and one with Steele to finance his outfit. He started back to the coteau the second week in July, a day or two behind Kittson's boats. All were seriously hampered by water so high the polers could find no bottom and had to resort to pulling the boats along by grasping the willows overhanging the bank. On the sixteenth, Brown overtook Kittson at the Traverse, cheerfully letting him know that Sibley had offered him a good price for tareau and tallow and he was going to get it. "He arrived here this morning with his boat and leaves immediately," Kittson scribbled in a quick note to William Forbes, Sibley's clerk. "He seems to be in a hell of a hurry – he expects to get all the tallow in the country." Kittson, dead tired after a grueling trip up over mucky tracks on a skittish horse, knew that he had to race Brown to the coteau if he expected to prevent loss to his own outfit. Leaving behind the heavier

---

25. Case "Trading Post;" *Henderson Democrat* Apr. 17, 1856; *St. Paul Daily Pioneer* May 31, 1868; *Minnesota Democrat* Apr. 1, 1854; Williams *St. Paul* 71 and interview with James R. Clewet, April 1875, in Williams papers; St. Croix County Deed Book A. Brown paid $200 for one lot in Kittson's Addition in 1851 (Account Book, Brown papers).

items, he loaded the carts lightly so as to make the best time. Brown was now a day ahead. Part of his cargo had been kegs of whiskey.

Kittson managed to steal a march on Brown by sending Antoine Findley on ahead to apprise McLeod at Big Stone Lake of Brown's intentions. McLeod quickly got off three cartloads of goods to trade tallow with the Yankton on the day before Brown's arrival. But Brown still had the advantage because he had the whiskey. The Cutheads would trade all the meat and tallow they had for whiskey, which they, in turn, could trade to the bands further west for horses.**26** Brown had another good reason for traveling fast. He was going not just to the Cuthead camp on the James River, but all the way to the Missouri to strike a deal with the traders at Fort Pierre or Fort George, although McLeod didn't tumble to this until the ensuing winter. Then he realized that there was "an understanding between Brown and some of the Missouri traders, concocted when he was there last summer, to oppose and injure this post as much as possible this season." He further understood, as he informed Sibley, that Brown intended to bring an outfit from the Missouri opposition the following year. "Mr. Brown," threatened McLeod, "may find out, however, that in his anxiety to do too much he has overshot his aim; had he confined himself to the legitimate articles of trade and opposition all would have been fair and I, for one, would not have said a word to the contrary."**27**

That trip to the Missouri added to the Brown legend. As he passed his house in Sica Hollow about the first of August, Brown told Tatankanajin's village that he was going to Fort Pierre and would return in ten days. When he did not appear in the allotted time, there was great consternation in camp because the Cutheads that he had gone to find were not noted for their pleasant dispositions and there were many others who might want Siharmi's (Crooked Foot's) scalp in the James River flats through which he had to pass. The Sisseton thought he must have been waylaid and killed, and so set up their dismal mourning wails. Akipa, Tiwakan and other friends consulted a medicine man to whom Susan gave a pony and some trade goods to help his vision. After a night's vigil the shaman said that he had dreamt of a white man dressed in gray clothes with a pack upon his back ascending the western slope of the coteau near the Hawk's Nest (a hill overlooking the James flats west of Webster), and that this man would arrive at the setting sun. Sure enough, just at sunset, Brown came striding down the hillside into his trading post dressed in gray clothes no one had before seen.**28** This story was told and retold to show the remarkable powers of the Sioux medicine men, although it might as

26. Kittson to Sibley, Jul. 16, 1844 and to William H. Forbes, Jul. 16, 1844; McLeod to Sibley, Jul. 30, 1844, all in Sibley papers. Brown had approximately a $2,000 inventory that season that he must have obtained from Steele (whose books are not extant) or other suppliers. He was over $2,000 in debt to Steele the following year. Steele had promised only to stay out of the trade himself, not to refuse credit to independents.

27. McLeod to Sibley, Feb. 21, 1845, Sibley papers.

28. S. J. Brown to Robinson, Mar. 7, 1921. Just who Brown cut the deal with would be interesting to know. Honoré Picotte, Chouteau's factor at Pierre, complained of interference that spring, so Brown must have found one of the opposition opportunists who was willing to finance him (and treat him to a new suit).

well have served to illustrate the swiftness of their messengers. But it is also a good example of Brown's walking prowess; it is 210 miles in a straight line from Sica Hollow to Pierre and the time elapsed was less than two weeks.

That summer the Indians were prosperous. It had been the best season for growing crops and drying meat in years and there was plenty available for trade. The nearby tribes, even the Wahpeton of the coteau, wrote McLeod, were on good behavior. However, the Sisseton had lost eight men in a skirmish with the métis, halfbreeds of Red River, and were in fighting mood, at least the young men were. This incident had created a problem for Kittson, since the friends of those killed would not hear of his sending any goods to the halfbreeds, and indeed had sent out war parties toward the Red River trail to intercept anyone traveling north. It would be an act of kindness, Kittson mentioned to Sibley with considerable understatement, to inform those people from the Red River then at the St. Peters of the difficulties that would lie in the way of their return.**29**

The belligerence of the Sisseton had an unfortunate, if predictable, result. In August a party of drovers taking cattle from northern Missouri to the garrison at Fort Snelling so far lost themselves as to be in the vicinity of Otter Tail Lake in western Minnesota (they had, it seems, crossed the Minnesota upstream of the Traverse des Sioux and mistaking it for the Turkey River of Iowa, had proceeded north-northwest). The Sisseton war party, claiming to have taken them for Red River métis, shot one man on the spot and brutally treated the remaining three while pillaging their supplies and killing some of the cattle. Only one man, Notley Bennet by name, survived the ordeal. He stumbled into the camp of the Sisseton chief Ishtaba (Sleepy Eyes) near Swan Lake two weeks later in a pitiable, half-starved condition. Both Kittson and the Reverend Stephen Riggs, missionary at Lac qui Parle, pleaded with the Indian agent and the commanding officer at Fort Snelling to take some action to punish the villains responsible for the deaths. The agent, Amos Bruce, sent men to round up the cattle not killed by the Indians and to bring in the unfortunate Mr. Bennet; meanwhile he reported to the war department that in his opinion a party of dragoons would be needed to restore order. "The halfbreeds," he said, "come to hunt in large bands, well armed and in too much force to fear the Indians; and as to the threatened interference of our Government, they laugh at the idea." According to Brown's report to Bruce later that winter, the halfbreeds scorned the Sisseton as well and would not bother to appease them by sending goods to cover the dead, even though they admitted that the eight men had been killed in mistake for Indians of the Missouri. So sure were they of their power they told the

29. McLeod to Sibley, Jul 30, 1844; Kittson to Sibley, Aug. 22, 1844, both in Sibley papers. The Métis, offspring of centuries of contact between white traders and Cree Indians, formed a unique society centered on the Red River on both sides of the border. Buffalo hunters and free traders, they controlled the northern plains, often clashing with the Sioux for the immense trade in hides and meat. Living as neither white nor Indian, the Red River halfbreeds even had their own language, a mixture of French and Cree. (See Thomas Flanagan "Louis Riel and the Dispersion of the American Métis" in *Minnesota History* XLIX 49/5: 180-181 (Spring 1985).

Sisseton chiefs they would pass Lake Traverse the following spring and would then offer them their hands, and as they would be in force they would disregard the consequences of a refusal.30 The Sisseton were much offended. Without intervention, there would undoubtedly be a war.

Colonel Wilson's expedition against the Sisseton was designed to be a show of military might. At Traverse des Sioux his detachment met Captain E. V. Sumner's company of dragoons from Fort Atkinson, Iowa, and the party proceeded together up the Minnesota. They ran across Joseph R. Brown at Beaver Creek (near Redwood Falls), who at their request delayed his trip down to Mendota to help them. Putting his carts at the expedition's disposal, Brown and the Indians who were with him returned to the Sisseton camp near the head of the James River to try to induce the chiefs to bring down those guilty of the attack upon the drovers. Ever confident, Brown had told Colonel Wilson he would meet him with the murderers at his trading house on the coteau within eight days. It was not to be quite that simple.

The Indians were a good deal excited by this turn of events. Afraid that they would not be able to persuade the murderers to turn themselves in, the several camps were in total confusion, some wanting to go meet the troops parading their American flag, some preparing to flee to the prairies. On the coteau Brown found a small party of the Sisseton band running from the soldiers and was able to convince them to return and meet the detachment. But it was only with some difficulty and hazard that he succeeded in inducing the principal men of the band to accompany him to his post with three men they said were implicated in the attack. Two others, Itehinyanza (Sullen Face) and Heyugaga (Forked Horn), had fled beyond the James. An influential relative was dispatched to locate the offenders and, if possible, to convince them to come to Brown's post and give themselves up.

Wilson's troops made camp on the east side of Lake Traverse and waited for Brown. On October 11, twelve days after Brown had set out on his errand, they convened with the Sisseton at Brown's Sica Hollow post. Brown distributed gifts of powder, lead and tobacco to the head men who then delivered over the three prisoners. After some delay the messenger returned without Sullen Face and Forked Horn, but the Sisseton promised to bring them in in the spring, if not sooner. Two others, one Sisseton and The Plume, a relative of Shakopee's who was wanted for the murder of a Chippewa at the St. Peters the previous July, were given up by the band from the island in Lake Traverse. Brown accompanied the detachment back to Fort Snelling – in the capacity of guide, he said in his memo to Bruce, although no guide had been asked for.31

30. Kittson to Sibley, Mar. 22, 1844, Sibley papers; Steven R. Riggs to Commanding Officer Fort Snelling, Aug. 26, 1844, enclosed in Bruce to John Chambers, Aug. 30, 1844 and Brown to Bruce, Feb. 13, 1845, enclosed in Bruce to T. H. Crawford, Feb. 17, 1845, both in OIA LR. St. Peters agency; Bruce report Sep. 1, 1844, in *U. S. Senate Document 60*, 28th Congress, 2nd session.

31. Brown to Bruce, Feb. 13, 1845; Brown to Bruce, Sep. 1, 1846, in "Joseph R. Brown," *U. S. House Report 317*, 30th Congress, 1st session; Lieutenant Selden report, Dec. 28, 1844, in records of

On October 18, at 2 A.M. of a dark and windy night, all five prisoners escaped from Wilson's encampment near Beaver Creek. Martin McLeod couldn't believe it. He, too, was traveling down with the soldiers and scribbled a note to Sibley from the Traverse that the affair was "too ridiculous for comment," confessing that he was unable to understand how naked and unarmed Indians could escape from an armed guard of six men. "It tends to bring the troops, particularly the infantry, into contempt," was his opinion. Brown chose not to mention the incident in any of his reports, probably because it tended to make him look bad as well. The dejected detachment returned to Fort Snelling empty-handed.[32]

To avoid the cost of another military expedition, Colonel Wilson and Major Bruce requested Brown to use his influence among the Sisseton to persuade Sullen Face and Forked Horn to turn themselves in. It was a mission needing great diplomacy, to be sure, because Sullen Face belonged to one of the most important families of the Sisseton and it was certain the chiefs would not dare to deliver him over if he did not want to go. Brown's earlier success with the chiefs had impressed the officers and had established him as the expert on the western bands of Sioux. "Mr. Brown is probably quite as well informed on the subject as any person in this country, and is no more interested than the other traders with the Sioux," reported Captain Electus Backus as he forwarded Brown's account of the troubles to the adjutant general.[33]

Brown's opinion was that much of the blame for the disturbances should be laid at the door of the Red River halfbreeds. Not only did they come out every summer with immense hunting parties trailing 800 to 1,400 carts to carry the meat and cutting off the buffalo from the Sioux, which gave the Indians much trouble simply providing for their needs, but they also visited the Sioux in their winter camps with liquor to buy horses. This, Brown felt, was injurious both to the Indians and to the traders who were "to a man anxious to prevent the introduction of that poison among the Upper Sioux." Indeed, Brown could have added, they are especially anxious to prevent competition with that article from Canada. He suggested that a military force be permanently stationed on the upper Minnesota as a deterrent to the Sioux. The recent expedition, he reported, had created in them a respect for the U.S. government not previously shown. "They are now convinced troops can be brought to their country at short notice, and that our government is determined to punish offenses against citizens, and while they believe this, they will respect us." As a further objective, since these bands were so far removed from military posts and white settlements, a military force would serve to keep evil counselors from among them, and also to prevent their visits to Mendota where, Brown averred, they got liquor to carry above. He made it clear in

the headquarters of the Western Department, AGO, NARG 98, copy in Fort Snelling record collection, MHS; Fanny Huggins to Cordelia Pond, Oct. 1, 1844, Pond papers, MHS.

32. McLeod to Sibley, Oct. 21, 1844, Sibley papers; Bruce to Chambers, Nov. 2, 1844, OIA LR St. Peters.

33. Electus Backus to H. L. Turner, Feb. 17, 1845, copies in Fort Snelling record collection, MHS.

his report that the halfbreeds must be prevented from carrying out their plan to come south in the spring, for the influence of the headmen and chiefs would not be sufficient to prevent the relatives of the slain from attacking them. The resulting war would endanger the lives of all whites in the country because, Brown explained, "it would be erroneous to suppose that the Sioux would make distinction between halfbreeds living as whites and the pure white man." One principal man of the Sisseton had told Brown that he would kill the first halfbreed he saw and continue to kill until he was himself killed. "By this means he can satisfy the *manes* of his relations and the Americans at the same time," he noted. Brown's remarks were forwarded to the secretary of war.[34]

Figure 31 Hunting buffalo on the North Dakota prairies. Watercolor by Alfred Jacob Miller. From sketches made c. 1837. Courtesy Public Archives of Canada.

Sullen Face returned to the vicinity of Sica Hollow as soon as the troops left; however, it wasn't until Brown returned from his second trip to the St. Peters that winter (after making his report to Bruce) that the Indians appeared to be willing to talk. Hearing that the agent was expecting them to give themselves up, Sullen Face and Forked Horn sent a letter to Major Bruce in which Sullen Face promised: "When it is warm weather, my Father, look in this direction, for I shall come to see you," and Forked Horn added, "I certainly shall shake hands with you." The message could have been delivered by Brown when he made a third trip down in March.[35]

---

34. Brown to Bruce, Feb. 13, 1845.

35. Backus to AGO, Jan. 1 and May 5, 1845 transmitting communiqués of Sullen Face and Forked Horn translated by P. Prescott, copies in Fort Snelling record collection, MHS.

In late spring, at a general council of the Lake Traverse Sisseton bands held at Brown's house, Sullen Face announced that he was turning himself in and would go with Brown to the agency, but he wished to be accompanied by his chiefs and friends. Brown said he then requested they be given gifts of ammunition and tobacco and that Sullen Face himself be newly outfitted, as "he was throwing himself away at my solicitation." In early June an entourage of 80 to 100 Sisseton and Yankton, escorted and provisioned by Brown, appeared in all their grandeur at the agency. Mounted on fine horses, dressed in colorful calico shirts and bright leggings, their vests and moccasins garnished with intricate beadwork, their headdresses resplendent with fur and silver and feathers, they presented an awesome spectacle. Sullen Face and Forked Horn solemnly gave themselves up, and after being examined by the agent were sent by steamboat to Dubuque for trial.36

Impressed by Brown's report, Captain Backus requested a party of dragoons to make a show of force on the upper St. Peters and beyond. Despite General Winfield Scott's argument that interposing troops between the hostiles would be of doubtful practicality, the request was granted. Captain Sumner's mounted troop left Fort Atkinson about the first of June 1845, and joining another company of dragoons led by Captain J. Allen from Fort Des Moines at Traverse des Sioux proceeded to Big Stone Lake. Their orders show that they were to select a site for a temporary post above the Blue Earth River – this even though Lieutenant Selden had reported the fall before that the land above Little Rapids, being one vast prairie with scant oak edging the lakes and streams, was insufficient for military operations on any scale, and that the high-banked rivers would impede maneuvers by troops – and to warn the intruders from Canada off U.S. territory. They found the upper Sioux ill-disposed. When informed the soldiers were there to intimidate the Red River people, the chiefs seemed unwilling to let them interfere in the quarrel and professed ignorance as to who had made the complaint. Brown, who could have cleared this point up, was not yet back from Mendota with the Sisseton party. The Indians did, however, turn over three of the miscreants that had escaped from Colonel Wilson's party the season before. These were sent under better guard to Dubuque.

After a certain amount of harassment by some of the Indians, Sumner and Allen met the Pembina hunters in their camp at Devils Lake in mid-July. The métis professed only the most peaceable intentions. They did not consider themselves intruders in the United States since their ancestors, and many of themselves, had been born and lived on the U.S. side of the border. There were about 180 men in the halfbreed camp, but they did not impress Captain Sumner as formidable opponents; in his report he noted that "a few regular troops have nothing to fear from them" Sumner had also heard indirectly that because they were finding their trade with

36. Kittson to Sibley, Mar, 23, 1845, Sibley papers; Brown to Bruce, Sep. 1, 1846. Martin McLeod supplied this vivid description of the upper Indians as they appeared when visiting his camp in McLeod to Sibley, May 6, 1845, Sibley papers.

Kittson more profitable than with the Hudson's Bay Company at Fort Garry, several of them were planning to move across the line in the fall. Sumner strictly prohibited them from hunting in U.S. territory, and his duty done wheeled the squadron and marched them back to Traverse des Sioux. The halfbreeds, who were more unnerved by the encounter than might have been expected, quickly fired off a petition to the United States government protesting the injunction and reiterating their claim to the territory in question.[37]

Figure 32 "Indians of the Plains, Siseton Dakota," an 1899 watercolor by Frank B. Mayer, shows how splendidly these bands arrayed themselves for ceremonial occasions. Courtesy of Goucher College, Baltimore.

There the story should end, face having been saved all around and possible war averted. The military had flexed its muscle, and the chief perpetrators of the attack on the drovers were in custody. It was expected that the imprisoned Sisseton would be released after a time, having been given a much-needed "touching up." But fate took an ironic turn: a person, who undoubtedly thought it was for the best, aided the five Sioux to escape from the Dubuque jail. Two of them managed to reach their village after enduring weeks of hardship, starvation and suffering, but the others, including Sullen Face, died on the journey home. The news caused an uproar in the Indian camp. Brown wrote to the agent that the death of Sullen Face was attributed to him. "By my advice he had gone below; if he had remained with his band he would not have incurred the hardships that caused his death; his wife would not have been a widow, or his

37. Sumner to AGO, Aug. 23, 1845, AGO LR. This report is supported by T. S. Williamson to S. W. Pond, Aug. 1, 1845, in Pond papers.

children orphans! I was the cause of his death: through my instrumentality alone was he cut off in the flower of his age, and through me alone were his friends now deploring the loss of one of their bravest comrades!" Such reasoning, Brown acknowledged to Major Bruce, however light and trivial it might appear in a populous white settlement, "assumes a different aspect and become strong and convincing when uttered by a band of wild Sussetons at the door of the only white man within fifty miles of them."38

To save his property, and perhaps his life, Brown distributed presents liberally among the bereaved relatives and friends. This settlement proved satisfactory and the hostilities came to an end. Brown later turned in an account for $175 spent by him in subsisting the Indians on the trip to Mendota, dressing the prisoners in new finery and appeasing the relations of Sullen Face, but payment was denied him because it was unauthorized.

Brown approached Bruce. He had always, he declared, done the duty requested of him to the best of his ability. In the whole transaction he had been guided solely by a desire to preserve peace between the Sioux and the government. "I firmly believed," he emphasized to the agent, "that on the voluntary surrender of Sullen Face depended peace or war with the Sussetons," adding interrogatively, "unless the Government, after demanding the offenders, had rested satisfied without their delivery." He had also, he noted, saved the cost of a punitive expedition. Brown was fully supported in his request for payment by the officers of the First Infantry including Colonel Wilson and Captain Seth Eastman, as well as by Agent Bruce. (It should also be noted that his suggestion of an expedition against the halfbreeds had been seconded by Commissioner of Indian Affairs T. Hartley Crawford, and been concurred in by James Buchanan, President Polk's secretary of state.) In endorsing Brown's claim, James Clark, Iowa superintendent of Indian affairs, concluded, "It is in the power of a trader so remotely situated as Mr. Brown to do much good in assisting the agents of government in enforcing the laws of the U.S." Clearly he welcomed Brown's efforts. Brown, for his part, had acted as agent ex officio for the upper Sioux, handing out presents, holding councils as the representative of the agent and writing reports that were passed on as being the views of the agent. His growing influence with the Indians did not pass unnoticed. The suspicion that his influence might once more be required may have helped get him his money in October of 1850, when a treaty with the Sioux was again being contemplated.39

---

38. Brown to Bruce, Sep. 1, 1846. Kittson confirms that the Sisseton were assured that no harm would come to the prisoners. In a letter to Sibley he says: "All the principal men and particularly the Burning Earth have requested our assistance in his (Sullen Face's) behalf, which I have promised. They requested me to say that they depended entirely upon your assistance for his safety. As I suppose there is very little probability of his being condemned, your assistance to him might be of some advantage to us hereafter." (Kittson to Sibley, May 30, 1845, Sibley papers)

39. Bruce to Crawford, Feb. 17, 1845, enclosing Brown to Bruce, Feb. 13, 1845; James Clark to W. Medill, Jun. 30, 1846; James Buchanan to William Marcy, Oct. 31, 1845, all in OIA LR, St. Peters agency; U.S. treasury appropriation #10883, Oct. 5, 1850, paid to Hugh Tyler for J. R. Brown.

Brown had a reasonably good season in spite of the commotion over the halfbreeds and the murder of the drovers, and despite the fact that he made three trips to the St. Peters and back between October of 1844 and April of 1845. Since Brown spent most of his time traveling, it is obvious that he had some capable people in charge in his absence. He had acquired the services of Benjamin Dionne (rendered mysteriously in English as Benjamin D. Young), an experienced winterer from Prairie du Chien who may have been allied with traders from the Missouri the preceding seasons. With Gabriel, Fletcher, Pierre Rouillard and George Provençalle (Dejarlais had quit in a huff the season before) plus several Indians on his payroll, Brown could work the bands wintering on the James and on the Sheyenne as well. He was after number one buffalo robes; rats didn't interest him. McLeod could, in fact, report to Sibley that he himself had gone to the James and brought back all the rats and the few other furs those bands had "to save Mr. Brown the trouble of doing so." Apprised that Brown had a man at the Sheyenne, McLeod sent his man to oppose him at the Bear's Lodge, "as it is in that direction Brown expects to be most successful in cajoling the Indians."**40**

On the James the Missouri traders met the Minnesota traders head-on. Pierre Menard and Henry Angé were there taking robes from the Indians who had been credited by McLeod; even Xavier Frénière, who had been financed by McLeod, sold to the opposition. McLeod had also been double-crossed by Renville, who had neglected to send his sons to the James to collect the thousand or so robes the Five Lodges band had amassed there. According to Kittson, McLeod had no one to send and so the whole of them were lost to the Missouri traders, except for several hundred taken by Joseph R. Brown, who got them by means Kittson considered foul. "This post, and also the Cheyenne, have been very much injured by the introduction of spirituous liquors among the Indians, by and through the assistance of Mr. Brown," Kittson exploded to Sibley at the end of March. He added, "Several of our credits have been traded and some of our Indians have been prevented from hunting by this cause [alcohol]. Mr. B. has also procured many robes through the means of giving [it] and the promise of more. This is a business that certainly should not be allowed and steps should be taken to prevent it." Kittson was indeed sore; "I have no particular desire to be on friendly terms with him at the cost of such unlawful advantage over me in the trade," he steamed.

Kittson had, of course, first approached Brown on the subject, stopping at Sica Hollow on his return from Pembina in March. He got little satisfaction. "[Brown] may give his word that he tries to prevent its introduction, but this is all false," Kittson reported to Sibley. "His father-in-law [Akipa], whom he says introduces the liquor, is an Indian who lives in the same room with him, eats at the same table and is supplied in all his wants by him. It would therefore be the easiest matter in the world to

40. McLeod to Sibley, Jan. 1, Feb. 21 and Mar. 23, 1845 in Sibley papers.

prevent his doing so!" During the course of the conversation Brown had informed Kittson that he had got ten robes from one of McLeod's Indians for a small keg, "at least my father-in-law did" he had said. This scamp, Kittson informed Sibley, had been braced by McLeod and had promised not to give Brown any more robes, "nor do I think he will excepting he can get another keg." McLeod, totaling up his take in May, noted that "a certain individual" did not get all that particular Indian's remaining robes as the other promised keg was not forthcoming.[41]

There can be no doubt that whiskey was showing up more and more as an element in the western trade in the mid-1840s and that a large part of it was introduced by the Indians themselves. Special Agent Andrew Drips reported that during the summer of 1844 a number of Sioux from the St. Peters came to the Missouri with whiskey, trading it for twenty or thirty horses from the Yankton. "And I am credibly informed that they are coming in great numbers this winter with that article to trade robes," he continued. The following spring Captain Backus was constrained to report to western department headquarters that one of his sentries at Fort Snelling had shot and wounded an Indian, a Wahpekute, one of several who had been spotted taking canoes loaded with whiskey up the St. Peters and who had refused to come in when summoned. The injured one, said Backus, made it home with his friends, all of whom had come down from Lake Traverse for the explicit purpose of obtaining a supply of the commodity.[42]

Akipa was not the only Sioux dealing in whiskey. In 1846 McLeod indicated that he was being much injured by Indians from below opposing him. "They trade goods at less than their value and give whiskey besides," he reported to Sibley, naming among others the new chief Little Crow from Kaposia, Taoyateduta. It was no secret where they got it. The Halfbreed Tract on Lake Pepin was headquarters for the whiskey trade. Liquors destined for Sioux and Chippewa alike were landed at Wabasha village. Lieutenant Hall, sent there in the summer of 1845 to arrest Duncan Campbell for selling whiskey to Indians, was informed by Alexis Bailly (now often referred to as "The Emperor") that the residents of the tract considered themselves beyond the pale of civilized law, and yet outside Indian country. "I myself saw ten barrels of whiskey landed at Wabashaw," asserted the Lieutenant. In truth, every boat up carried some spirits. From Lake Pepin it was but a short distance inland to the villages of the Sioux or a short trip up the Chippewa River to those of the Chippewa. The Campbells, Brown's old partner Buisson, the La Pointe

41. Kittson to Sibley, Mar. 30, 1845; McLeod to Sibley, May 6, 1845, both in Sibley papers.

42. Andrew Drips to T. H. Harvey (undated, received Dec. 7, 1844), OIA LR Missouri agency; Backus to AGO, Apr. 23, 1845, copy in Fort Snelling record collection, MHS. Before 1844 the bulk of the spirits imported to the Missouri River had been smuggled past the agent at Council Bluffs or had been carried overland from Fort John on the Platte River and even from Santa Fe; the effort alone speaks to the profits to be made. For the extent of the problem see letters from D. D. Mitchell to Crawford, Jun. 8, 1842, Jan. 2 and Oct. 9, 1843, and others in OIA LR St. Louis superintendency.

brothers all made their living in the trade, reported Lieutenant Hall, who prudently decided against trying to make the arrest.**43**

The lower Sioux, Mdewakanton and Wahpekuta, performed the role of middlemen in the trade, many having done so since the early 1830s. They could purchase the spirits and other goods on the Halfbreed Tract with impunity; once it was in Indian hands there was little the army could do about it. Captain Backus solicited help from the Mdewakanton chiefs who, understandably nervous about the possibility of their annuities being held up, did what they could to root the evil out of their villages. But mostly it didn't stay long in their villages. It was traded to the plains Sioux for skins. They, in turn, traded it farther west for horses. And very quickly it got to the Missouri.

Another source of the firewater was Imnijaska, the Old Cave settlement, now metamorphosing into St. Paul. By 1843 Henry Jackson, James Simpson and William Hartshorn were all operating groceries there. In 1845 the steamboat *Lynx* put off fifty-five barrels of whiskey at St. Pauls for Hartshorn and Jackson, although it wasn't immediately distributed because of their reluctance to pay 50¢ a gallon for it. A traveler from Fort Garry described the place in 1846 as a "wretched little village." Said he "Almost every house is either a shop or a 'Grocery' for the supply of the farmers in the neighboring country and for the Sioux Indians... Drinking whiskey seems to occupy at least half the time of the worthy citizens of St. Pauls, while the balance of their time is employed in cheating each other or imposing upon strangers." Another newcomer that year depicted it as a village of five stores, one tavern and a few dwellings, mostly built of logs, with a few U.S. soldiers and Indians lounging about the stores, "some drunk, some sober." One of the stores was Henry Sibley's; a considerable amount of furs bought from Indians, settlers and small traders up and down the Mississippi and St. Croix valleys found its way through this store, which was looked after by David Faribault. David's father-in-law, a Sioux, distributed quantities of whiskey up the Minnesota.**44**

Sibley and Chouteau, while they might rail publicly about the evils of whiskey and stand firm against its importation into Indian territory, were not entirely blameless in the matter. Sibley had been accused by other departments of the Fur Company of interfering in their trade by supplying independents with goods and whiskey – not directly, it would seem, but through his partners Kittson and Steele. In the fall of 1846 Honoré Picotte at Fort Pierre angrily complained that Sibley's men were opposing him on the James "not only with a good assortment of goods, but with liquor, which they succeed to smuggle from the St. Peters." (This controversy

43. McLeod to Sibley, Jan. 24, 1846, Sibley record collection; Hall to Backus, Apr. 11, 1845, copy in Fort Snelling record collection. For lower Sioux involvement in the whiskey trade see Gary Clayton Anderson *Little Crow: Spokesman for the Sioux* 43 (St. Paul 1986).

44. J. Atkinson to Sibley, Jan. 12, 1846, Laframboise to Sibley, Sep. 16, 1845, Sibley papers; Elaine Allen Mitchell "International Buying Trip: Ft. Garry to St. Louis in 1846," *Minnesota History* XXXVI: 41 (St. Paul 1958); A. L. Larpenteur "Recollections of the City and People of St. Paul," *Minnesota Historical Collections* XIV: 367–372 (St. Paul 1901).

was not all one-sided; McLeod was irked that Picotte's men went to the Talle de Chêne and beyond trading rats with Indians who had credits from the post at Big Stone Lake.)**45**

This was an internal squabble, the result of one Fur Company trader impinging on another's turf, and could be arbitrated. The real competition in the western trade came from north of the border. Traders supplied by the Hudson's Bay Company had plenty of liquor and were using it to lure peltries north. By the 1845–1846 season even Pierre Chouteau had given up on the "no whiskey" rule and in a remarkable letter, written by his clerk Benjamin Clapp to Sibley in January of 1846, proposed to smuggle it himself! The article, some five to six hundred gallons of alcohol would be put up in boxes filled with sawdust and topped with rags "that they might appear as merchandise" and would be transported by team from Sibley's frontiers to a suitable point on the Missouri above Council Bluffs. There it could be cached. The wagons would be sent back immediately "so as never to be seen at any Fur Co. establishment," and the person in charge could then go downriver to meet the company's steamboat and superintend taking the cargo on board. Clapp stressed the reliability required of the individual: "In case of seizure he must at all hazard stand as the owner of the property, as it would on no account do that our name should be dragged in – such exposure would forfeit all our licenses." Sibley refused to have anything to do with it on the grounds it could not be done without detection and referred Clapp to the British colony on the Red River "where there are several private stills" and whence "the article" might be transported overland to the Missouri.**46**

Chouteau, Dousman and Sibley – and Rolette and Bailly before them – were quite sincere when they pledged not to make improper use of liquor in the trade, but when the chips were down they were as bad as any of the independents against whom they were wont to hurl accusations. Business, after all, was business. What alcohol did to the Indians did not seem to enter into their calculations, excepting the objection that it led to quarrels and bloodshed that prevented the hunters from bringing in enough furs to make a profitable year. They castigated Brown because he had seen the opportunity, and, taking advantage of his Indian trading network through Akipa and Gabriel, had got the jump on the Fur Company traders.

Brown's tactics had, after all, worked rather well in the 1844–1845 season. McLeod could crow that he had bested JRB "six to one" where they were opposed, although admitting that Brown had done better toward the Sheyenne. However Brown had gone after the more valuable painted robes and had acquired over 300 of them to sell to Sibley in the spring, along with 60 unpainted robes and a few furs, for a total of over $1,260 (keeping in mind the equivalent in 1990s dollars is about forty to one, so that $1,000 then would be at least $40,000 in today's prices). This was

---

45. Benjamin M. Clapp to Sibley, Aug. 18, 1843; Charles W. Borup to Sibley, Jul. 21, 1843; McLeod to Sibley, Mar. 8, 1846; all in Sibley papers.

46. Clapp to Sibley, Jan. (no date) 1846, Sibley papers; Sibley to Chouteau and Co., Feb. 23, 1846. Chouteau papers.

probably gratifying to Sibley who was beset on every side by fur buyers from St. Louis and Fort Wayne, all paying top dollar and skimming off the best pelts and skins, whereas the Company's policy was to offer a fair price and take the bad along with the good. (Sibley was egged along all spring by Dousman, who panicked every time he saw a competitor take passage for Mendota and wrote often to Sibley to "look sharp after them" – they were pirates, he said, only wanting the best furs.) Brown had a good return but should have done better off the $2,000 worth of goods received from Sibley; it may be he sold some robes on the Missouri as well. In any event he had enough cash to pay off Sibley, Chouteau and Kittson and two notes on his half brother Fletcher, who had evidently been trading on his own account with disappointing results. Brown also had a high percentage of uncollected debts.**47**

Kittson's outfits had been somewhat more successful. Although not making as much as he had hoped for from the halfbreeds of Pembina, Kittson nevertheless had turned a profit, and in May of 1845 sent down the first of the long lines of creaking oxcarts that would become a spring fixture in St. Paul. McLeod reported a good return notwithstanding the "whiskey, 'pewter medals,' and all the 'nine farrow of that sow' that a certain individual brought to his aid." Only the Lac qui Parle Outfit, mismanaged by an ailing Renville and sons Antoine and Joseph Junior ("too thoughtless and too indolent to be of much service," was McLeod's assessment of this pair), lost money and even that was partially saved by the good rat hunt made by their Indians that spring.**48**

Steele must have been happy with results from Brown; he advanced him another $2,200 in goods for the next season, and there is a good chance Brown got a small outfit from the Missouri too, as McLeod feared he would. Dionne had left him, but he had acquired the services of another Missouri trader, James Hayes, an experienced hand who had worked for Picotte at Fort Pierre for several seasons and was well acquainted with the Yankton. Hayes was likely the trader who was opposing Picotte so strongly on the Snake River that season, although Kittson also had a man nearby at the Talle de Chêne. Fletcher and Gabriel were fully fledged as traders and had their own wintering posts, Gabriel at the Bear's Den on the Sheyenne, Fletcher probably on the upper James, although he may have been the trader at Brown's subsidiary post at Big Stone Lake. Young Nathaniel was getting his feet wet as a clerk at Brown's new post at Traverse des Sioux, which had been established as a depot to avoid the long trip to Mendota every time supplies were needed. It was a good post for the eighteen-year-old; his clientele would be the band of lower Wahpeton headed by Mazasha (Red Iron) whose village was at the Traverse. Mazasha, who that spring had succeeded his father Tankamani (Big Walker), was a progressive agriculturist, a firm friend of the whites

---

47. McLeod to Sibley, Apr. 12, 1845; Dousman to Sibley, Apr. 18, 1845, Sibley papers. For more on the value of money then and now see Appendix D.

48. McLeod to Sibley, Apr. 12 and May 6, 1845; Kittson to Sibley, Mar. 30, 1845; Sibley Ledger; all in Sibley papers.

and a close relative of Akipa. Nathaniel was also under the watchful eye of the Reverend Robert Hopkins. The American Board missionary seems to have made friends with the youngest Brown, who had incidentally, along with his brother John, become quite active in the Methodist mission at Red Rock Prairie. For this season Joseph R. had moved his main post and his family from Sica Hollow to the Buffalo Lakes on the coteau. Weighed against the disadvantages of the site was its convenience to the hunters on the lakes of the coteau. And there were rats in plenty on the coteau.[49]

Brown needed those rats. The buffalo had disappeared from the James River and from Devils Lake, although some thought there were herds in between near the Bone Hill (south of Jamestown). Business was so bad on the Snake Brown pulled his man out in January, bringing back the goods he had there. Things were not much better on the Sheyenne where Gabriel was up against the Frénières; no buffalo were to be found and no one got many robes. The spring rat hunt, however, was excellent, partly because there were no buffalo to attract the attention of the hunters. Mr. Brown did very well. He brought in over 15,500 rats for which Sibley paid him 10¢ each, 233 mink at 62¢ (more than double the price paid in 1843), 79 raccoon skins at 75¢ (also doubled), plus other fine furs along with a scant 64 robes, all of which netted him $2,446 and a very handsome profit. It appears he also disposed of some furs to Frank Steele who paid top dollar, either by pre-arrangement or mistake. By May 10 Dousman was quoting just 8¢ for rats and 50¢ for mink and coon. The bottom had dropped out of the market leaving a good many speculators holding big inventories, among them Steele. In St. Louis Steele was able to dispose of his furs only at great sacrifice. Possibly he felt had been outmaneuvered by Brown; at least by the fall of 1846 Sibley believed that from what Steele said Brown was unlikely to get any more goods from him.[50]

Brown may have considered pulling out right then. There were dismal prospects for buffalo the next season, and every prospect that the Indians would clash, with highly unfavorable results, with the Red River métis who, true to their promise, were coming across the border to live and hunt. The almost military operations carried out by these hunters would surely net them all the buffalo there were to be had at the expense of the Sioux, and although this might fatten Kittson's profits, it would not aid Brown one whit. Then, too, it was likely that Brown would have to subsist his

49. McLeod to Sibley, Jan. 26 and Mar. 9, 1846, Sibley papers; Sibley to McLeod, Oct. 6, 1846, McLeod papers; Robert Hopkins to S. W. Pond, Dec. 17, 1845, Pond papers; Bruce report Sep. 1, 1846, OIA LR St. Peters agency; Chouteau papers. Ledgers. For location of Brown's trading post at the southeast corner of Buffalo Lakes, see Brevet's South Dakota Historical Markers 74, 78 (Sioux Falls 1974). For Mazasha see Hughes Indian Chiefs 93–94, 99.

50. Sibley Ledger, Clapp to Sibley, Aug. 31, 1845, Sibley papers; Sibley to McLeod, Sep. 1, 1846, in McLeod papers. Brown's trade books have never surfaced, but it is evident that he increased the size of his outfits each year, maintaining about a $2,000 inventory base and adding up to $2,500 new goods each season. He ran a slight cash loss each year because of uncollected credits, which totaled about $5,600 when he sold out in 1846. He was paid these in full with interest under the 1851 treaty. His net for four years on the coteau can be calculated at about $3,800 ($150,000 in 1990's value) after all expenses and former debts were paid, but was not realized until the treaty payment in 1852.

Indians just to keep them alive, as they had consumed all their stored corn over the winter, along with most of their horses. As the summer progressed the weather became drouthy, making it alarmingly evident that the corn crop would fail once again, leaving the Indians starving and unable to hunt.[51]

Still, there was one great change that gave Brown hopes for a good year: the death of old man Renville in April left much disorganization among his adherents and a gap in the Fur Company line of posts. Over the summer of 1846 Brown put considerable effort into building a new post at Patterson's Rapids, just downstream from Lac qui Parle, with the evident expectation of being able to cajole Renville's Indians into trading with him. Rather than set up an opposition to Brown at that place, Sibley and Kittson decided to move McLeod in to Lac qui Parle, much to the disappointment of Antoine and Joseph Renville, who had expected to run that important post. McLeod expressed no worries about Brown's opposition: "B. may safely be left to my tender mercies," he confidently told Sibley. But he was nervous enough to quiz Sibley about Brown's prospects for being well supplied with goods, since it appeared Brown planned even greater expansion into McLeod's district – "he has already three posts... established, and others talked of."

Kittson had tried to hire Antoine Renville to manage the subsidiary post at Big Stone Lake, but that young man refused, having, as he told him, an arrangement with Joseph R. Brown to run his post at Traverse des Sioux. McLeod, also, was brushed off by the Renvilles. He informed Sibley "the Renvilles have some expectation from Brown. Antoine... says he will ask for $300 which B. will perhaps promise him as at present he deals largely in the article of high wages. Joseph is waiting to see if Brown will be able to come up with his promises." Sibley didn't try to dissuade the Renvilles from signing on with Brown; in fact he encouraged them. "I wish them both to get a taste of B. this year," he told McLeod. On September 1, Brown was preparing to leave Mendota for the Traverse with Antoine, although no goods had yet arrived for him. Sibley reported that fact to Mac to allay his anxieties, adding "prospects are so bad so far as furs are concerned that I doubt if Brown will succeed in getting advances from any other quarter."[52]

That was the first of September. A few days later, on his return from Traverse des Sioux, Brown opened a letter from Wisconsin Delegate Morgan Martin that caused him to make drastic alterations in his plans. For Martin's letter contained the information that Congress had passed the enabling act for the State of Wisconsin after altering the western border. Since the new line, the St. Croix River, would leave much of the counties of St. Croix and La Pointe (which had been erected from the northern part of St. Croix in 1844) outside the state and therefore without government,

---

51. Kittson to Sibley, Aug. 7, 1846, Sibley papers; Brown to Bruce, Sep. 1, 1846.

52. McLeod to Sibley, Aug. 20, 1846 and Kittson to Sibley, Aug. 7, 1846, Sibley papers; Sibley to McLeod, Sep. 1, 1846.

Martin would introduce the bill for the new territory in the upcoming session.

With the same celerity that characterized his entry into the western fur trade four years previously, Brown was out. On September 28 he sold his three posts to Sibley with all their inventory and within ten days was on his way to the coteau to remove his goods and family. The long wait was over.

CHAPTER X

"WITH MUCH ENTHUSIASM AMONG ALL PRESENT
FOR THE WORK BEFORE THEM." HENRY MOSS, 1848

Brown was elated as he sat down to answer Morgan Martin's letter on September 16.

It's easy to see why. As a part of Wisconsin, St. Croix County could have expected to have little or no influence in the state assembly. Mendota, in a similar situation across the Mississippi, would languish in the part of Iowa left outside that state if the constitution approved that August were acceptable to Congress. The practically unpopulated Iowa rump might remain unorganized Indian territory for years, consequently gaining few white inhabitants. But the proposed St. Croix boundary line left territory outside the state of Wisconsin that had been open to settlement for nearly ten years and would require immediate inclusion in a governmental organization so as not to deprive its inhabitants of their courts, local government and representation in Congress – hence, Martin's bill.[1]

A few moments' cogitation on this change in expectations will lead one to several happy conclusions, viz.: with the population confined east of the Mississippi, the territorial capital must be established between that river and the St. Croix, where one of the best if not the best site is Brown's claim on the reserve; the government will have to act quickly to treat with the Mdewakantons and Wahpetons and will at last be forced to buy off the Lake Pepin halfbreeds so as to open the land west of the Mississippi for settlements; the displaced Indians most logically will be removed up the Minnesota River and a new fort or forts and agency built to serve them, making Fort Snelling and the reserve superfluous; the reserve will be abandoned by the military and returned to the public land sales. In other words, all the hopes and expectations of the summer of 1841 will at last be realized.

---

1. As the Morgan Martin papers are filled with solicitations from hopeful office seekers bearing dates from September 17 on, it is evident that shortly after Congress passed the enabling act for Wisconsin on August 6, 1846, it was known or generally surmised that Martin would submit a bill for the new territory in the next session and that he would probably have some influence in filling the posts of secretary and judge. There is no evidence that JRB concerned himself with the territory bill up to this time. Congress admitted Iowa in December of 1846.

Great wealth would accrue to those who got in on the ground, as Henry Rice had anticipated. Money would flow into the new territory – payments for the Indians, halfbreeds and traders; appropriations for government, a capitol, roads and other improvements; and most of all, cash from the expected thousands of newcomers who would require transportation, housing, provisions, lumber and every service and article of commerce imaginable. There would be a rash of appointments. President Polk would, of course, fill most high positions with deserving eastern Democrats, but it was generally understood that the territorial delegate would have disposal of a few choice jobs to westerners, and there would be many local appointments as well as elective offices to aspire to. Brown had shown himself a good Democrat and could confidently look forward to pulling out a plum.

To take full advantage of the situation, Brown needed to reestablish his headquarters in the St. Peters area. It meant disposing of his western trade, but this, too, could be profitable. Sibley would be only too happy to consider an agreement that would remove Brown as an aggravation to the Sioux Outfit. Exceedingly pleased with his prospects, he wrote to Martin from a convenient stopping place at The Entry:

> "I have taken the opportunity of speaking to the settlers on the subject of the proposed line of the State of Wisconsin and generally find them well satisfied that it is no worse. We would all have been better pleased, probably, if the Chippewa, instead of the St. Croix, had been designated. The business portion of the population on the St. Croix apprehend some difficulty, owing to their being on the line and the probability that the western county of the state will for some years be attached to Crawford for Judicial purposes and thus give trouble where suits of law with their neighbors may become necessary, but I believe there are but few, if any, who would not prefer the St. Croix to being included in the state by having the line farther west.
>
> "With a trifling exception it leaves the population of St. Croix County without the state lines and instead of forming the western settlements of the State of Wisconsin, whose representation in the national or local Legislature would be only through the Tax list, we will constitute the eastern settlements of the future Territory (I hope of Dacota) and must in the natural course of things always hold a commanding influence in the government."2

2. Brown to Morgan Martin, Sep. 16, 1846, Morgan Martin papers, Neville Museum, Green Bay, microfilm in WHS Madison. Brown's choice of the name Dacota is consistent with his previous thinking and may have been influenced by a previous attempt to form a territory from northern Iowa for which the name Dacotah had been suggested. This, and the fact that Doty had referred to the area as the Minnesota Territory as early as 1842, should end speculation that Brown suggested the name Minnesota to Martin, even though Martin himself confused the issue by stating he had got the name from J. R. Brown, who had been with him in the Wisconsin legislature (Dwight Follette, editor of the *Green Bay Gazette*, quoted in Holcombe *Minnesota* II: 350). Martin's daughter was likely correct when she suggested, "Brown told my father the Indian name, but not with the idea of naming the Territory" (Deborah B. Martin to Wisconsin Historical Society, Oct. 5, 1906, in Kellogg Public Library, Green Bay). Missouri, Illinois, Wisconsin and Iowa territories were all named for their largest rivers; Nebraska Territory was proposed in 1845 from the Indian name for the Platte River. Propounded Henry Schoolcraft (*Galena Advertiser*, Jun. 26, 1847): "As it appears to be a settle[d] principle to give the new territories the

Possibly Martin had asked Brown to feel out the settlers on the topic. Many of those to whom Brown talked first heard of the territory bill from him, and in later years not a few were convinced that Joseph R. Brown had himself proposed it to Martin.

Brown's letter was carefully designed to give the delegate the ammunition he needed to successfully prosecute the territory bill in the next session of Congress. Optimistically, Brown verified that the future territory contained the requisite 2,000 inhabitants, 1,000 in St. Croix County and about the same in Iowa (a gross overestimation). He reckoned that the county had doubled its population within the preceding eighteen months and would undoubtedly double again within the year. As to the eagerness of the inhabitants for territorial government, he could confirm: "It is the general wish that a Territorial organization of the country west of the states of Iowa and Wisconsin may be affected at as early a day as possible, that we may not be left in the predicament that Dubuque was previous to the Territorial organization which included them."3

Figure 33 Henry M. Rice. Photo by Mathew Brody. Minn. Hist. Soc.

This letter suggests that Brown, along with other inhabitants of the area, was taken by surprise by the choice of the St. Croix River as the state boundary. He could hardly have failed to be aware that Martin's statehood bill, introduced in January of 1846, had specified that the Territory of Wisconsin be admitted as a state "with its ancient boundaries," thus fulfilling the clause of the Northwest Ordinance that specified not more than five states could be formed of the old Northwest Territory. As their correspondence shows, many prominent citizens of St. Croix County expected, early in 1846, to remain in Wisconsin's jurisdiction. In April Henry Jackson asked Martin's help in petitioning for the removal of Sioux Agent Amos Bruce (a man disliked by the small traders because he was effective in keeping them away from the annuity payments). His letter concludes "... I am in hopes the time will arrive when I can return favor for favor, and I am certain not to forget." By that Jackson meant that if his campaign to be elected representative to the Wisconsin legislature was successful, he would be in

name of the principal stream run[n]ing through them, the word Minesota... is quite appropriate." Nonetheless, there was considerable discussion over the name in Congress for no discernible reason except to delay passage of the bill.

3. Brown to Martin, ibid.

a position to support Martin in his bid for Senator, Senators at that time being chosen not by popular vote, but by the state assembly. Another county resident, Joseph Bowron of St. Croix Falls, wrote in May to request that the pine timberlands of the upper St. Croix be soon surveyed and sold to help promote settlement of the territory, "I hope soon to become a state," as it would let people know "Wisconsin is somewhere."[4] He, however, was unaware of what had transpired in Congress that spring.

Bowing to considerable pressure to form smaller states of the western territories, the committee on territories, headed by Stephen Douglas, had in May reported Martin's bill amended to divide the territory at the St. Croix River so as to leave as much of the old Northwest Territory out of Wisconsin as in it to form a sixth state. This fact was made known in the *Wisconsin Democrat* of May 30, so it is hard to believe that the inhabitants of St. Croix County were not informed of the proposed boundary change. However, during floor debate, Martin had very nearly succeeded in having the bill amended to allow the citizens of Wisconsin to choose their own western border, which unquestionably would have been placed coincident with that of the territory, and word of this scheme may have given rise to false expectations in the western counties. In September Brown was obviously aware of a plan, originating in St. Croix Falls, to have the split made at the Chippewa River, but this had not yet been publicly proposed.[5]

The idea of splitting the territory was certainly not new. As early as February 3, 1845, David Keeler, editor of the *Milwaukie Daily Sentinel* stated in an editorial what was clear to many, that a state with a western border of 1,200 miles would be unmanageable and that it would be necessary for part of the territory to seek a new political existence. Keeler had been to St. Anthony Falls and the mouth of the St. Croix in the summer of 1843, had talked to the people there and had become enamored of the idea of a new territory, which he proposed to call Superior, being formed of the northern parts of Wisconsin. He suggested the line be drawn between Prairie La Crosse and the mouth of the Menominee River on Green Bay. He felt, he said, that if a combine were formed to colonize the area, set up a provisional government and send a delegate to the next session of Congress, the territory would be organized within the year. This marvelous idea fell on deaf ears in southern Wisconsin, although there was considerable support for the notion in St. Croix County and, indeed, it may have originated there. Throughout the summer of 1845 there had been considerable debate in the newspapers over the advisability of splitting not only Wisconsin, but also Iowa territory, which had rejected its first constitution that April. Dubuque interests thereupon proposed a

---

4. Henry Jackson to Martin, Apr. 4, 1846; Joseph Bowron to same, May 28, 1846, both in Martin papers.

5. The enabling act in full was also printed in the *Wisconsin Democrat* on Aug. 29, 1846. For debate on the bill see Folwell *Minnesota* I: 234–234, Holcombe *Minnesota* II: 351–353 and the *National Intelligencer* Jun. 9, 11, 1846.

division of that territory at the forty-second parallel, throwing themselves into the northern part, which they suggested should be called Dacotah.[6] It is not improbable that Brown, who was a great reader of newspapers, knew about this, although how much it may have influenced his proposal to Martin of a name for the new territory cannot be known. Brown obviously thought the name most suitable and had promoted its use since 1839.

That spring of 1846 occurred another phenomenon, which added impetus to the movement to divide the territory of Wisconsin: precious metals – copper, silver and gold – had been found along the Keweenaw peninsula and the Wisconsin shore of Lake Superior and were thought to exist (as part of the same ore-bearing formations) in the St. Croix valley as well. Even before government surveyor Jacob Houghton's survey report appeared in the spring of 1846, eastern speculators had flocked to the Lake Superior region, anxious to exploit this wealth. By February forty-eight organized mining companies had located mineral permits in the region; among them was the St. Croix and Lake Superior Mining Company, which had located permits at both places included in its name. Boston owners Rufus Choate, Robert Rantoul Junior and Caleb Cushing were unenthusiastic about doing business within the new state of Wisconsin, which they could presume would be dominated by Milwaukee interests. They preferred to be a part of the new territory. Cushing, formerly representative to Congress and in 1845 ambassador to China, thought he could use his not inconsiderable influence to have the territory divided, although surely he did not advocate division at the St. Croix – that slip may most probably be laid to the fuzzy geographic knowledge of the area possessed by most members of Congress.[7]

Cushing liked the idea of Superior Territory, which may have come to his attention through his mining engineer George Brownell, who spent much of 1845 and 1846 scouting potential mineral and timber sites in the valley and near the south shore of the great lake. Cushing's interests went far beyond the development of mineral wealth in the region: he was also interested in acquiring pine timber lands, developing townsites and exploiting the water power at St. Croix Falls. Since all these activities centered on the falls, the notion soon took form that St. Croix Falls should be the new territory's capital. There were some said Cushing thought he should be its governor as well.[8]

In August of 1846 Cushing set out to view firsthand his investments in the west, accompanied by James Purinton, part-owner of the none-too-

---

6. *Milwaukie Daily Sentinel* Feb. 3, 1845. Keeler's plan proposed a limited government, judges and governor only, that would not have suited Brown. Among the other papers discussing the issue were the *Madison City Express* (Mar. 27 and Jul. 13, 1845), *Niles Register* (May 3, 1845) and the *Wisconsin Democrat* (Apr. 18, 1846).

7. Jacob Houghton *Report on Mineral Regions of Lake Superior* 92, passim (Detroit 1846); Alice E. Smith "Caleb Cushing's Investments in the St. Croix Valley" in *Wisconsin Magazine of History* XXVIII: 8; Robert Rantoul Junior *Personal Recollections* 24–26 (Cambridge, MA 1916).

8. Smith "Cushing's Investments"; William R. Marshall "Reminiscences of Wisconsin 1842–1848" in *Magazine of Western History* VII: 248–249.

prosperous St. Croix Falls Lumbering Company. Purinton had been to St. Louis and some eastern cities, trying to raise capital on the failing concern. He interested Cushing, who returned with him by way of La Pointe and the St. Croix River, and who was impressed enough to buy into the company, reorganizing it October 1 as the St. Croix Falls Company with himself and William S. Hungerford as principal stockholders. Cushing was also induced to visit St. Anthony Falls by Boston broker Benjamin H. Cheever, who had been approached by Franklin Steele about development of that water power and desired a first-hand report. He had advised Cushing to talk to Steele, who was, he said, "full of information in relation to this new country." Cushing made no commitment then, but in 1847 sent Cheever back as his agent to negotiate an agreement with Steele. After several abortive attempts to develop the resources of St. Croix county, things were definitely looking up. Comments one reporter: "Westerners rejoiced at the prospect of a vast outlay of capital in their midst and anticipated 'big things' from the Boston folks."[9]

It would be safe to say that when Brown left in 1842, St. Croix County as a political entity had for all practical purposes ceased to exist. In March of 1843 Judge Irvin had succeeded in having the court dissolved and the county attached to Crawford for judicial purposes. The high rent Brown was charging at Dacotah led Joseph Haskell and others to petition to have the county offices removed to Red Stone Prairie, and this proviso was attached to the judiciary bill. Apathy prevailed. Only eighteen voters turned out in 1843; in 1844 only one poll opened, and that one made no return, according to County Clerk William Holcombe. Holcombe, one of the few who showed any interest in maintaining the county machinery, petitioned the legislature of 1843–1844 for a law to allow some legal functions to be handled by other officers and for reinstatement of the office of judge of probate, which was granted. But efforts to regain other court functions met with a brick wall: Judge Irvin absolutely refused to return to the St. Croix and the lawmakers were unwilling to force the issue.[10]

Needless to say, Mr. Holcombe had no great love for Mr. Brown. Brown had tied the commissioners' hands by owning the county seat; so far as they knew, the lease was still running, and if Brown cared to collect, their debt would be considerable. At one point in 1844 Clerk Holcombe was pressured by some nervous citizenry to make a public statement of the county's indebtedness. In 1845 he petitioned the legislature to retract the original county bill because "owing to a premature organization of the county, the offices were held by irresponsible persons and the funds to

9. Smith, op. cit. 7, 11; Lucile Kane *The Waterfall That Built a City* 16 (St. Paul 1966); Folsom *Fifty Years* 87, 728. Documents in St. Croix County Deed Book A (pages 14, 19, 24 and 33) show Purinton mortgaged the property several times. William B. Hungerford took control of operations in March of 1846 and Purinton set off for the east to try to scare up new backers.

10. "Proceedings of St. Croix County Board" 33; Records of Secretary of State, Wisconsin Territory, series 160, 180 and 211.

arise in pursuance of the act locating the county seat [Brown's $800 contribution] had been deeded away by the then commissioners."

Grown weary of complaints from the north, the legislature of 1845 finally approved a bill to allow the people of St. Croix County to elect a special board of commissioners to locate a new county seat, and to vote for or against a district court. If the vote were in favor, provided 150 votes were cast, the court would be held in June of 1846. Judge Charles Dunn of the first judicial district had agreed to preside.11

Figure 34 William Holcombe, St. Croix Co. clerk and delegate to the first Wisconsin constitutional convention, 1846. Minn. Hist. Soc.

No election was held. A correspondent to the *Madison City Express* signing himself "Crawford" intimated that the people of the St. Croix had been kept from voting – "frightened out of their vote" – by secret machinations of the district court judge or some other clique. This sally was answered by one calling himself "St. Croix" who laid the non-election to public apathy and a populace not ready for county government, saying "if it is thrust upon them before they ask for it, their only reply will be a reference to Brown's Organization." Capital B. Capital O. Neither correspondent was in possession of all the facts. The board of commissioners – still by default of elections Joseph Furber, William R. Brown and Philip Aldrich who had been elected back in 1843 – were the ones who failed to act, probably through fear that Henry Jackson's St. Paul Democrats would gain control of the special commission and establish the seat of justice at St. Paul, as they very assuredly attempted to do the following year.12 The commissioners' delaying tactics paid off in 1846. In January, after much maneuvering, the legislature passed a bill making Stillwater the county seat of St. Croix County. That point settled, the board gave notice of election and in September the county had new officers and a temporary courthouse set up in the upper room of John McKusick's store at the corner of Main and Myrtle streets. It appears that someone with some political savvy made a deal with the powers that be of Prairie du Chien to split the representation in the legislature, the member of the House being chosen from St. Croix candidates and the Council member from Crawford. Since St. Croix County could, by this time, poll more votes than Crawford, such an

11. "Proceedings of St. Croix County Board" 43; Petition Jan. 31, 1845, papers of the Wisconsin Territorial Legislature: petitions, series 180; *Acts of Wisconsin Territorial Legislature*, 1845.

12. *Madison City Express* Nov. 6, 1845 and Jan. 15, 1846.

agreement made sense. Democrat Henry Jackson and Whig Joseph Furber fought out a close race for representative, Furber winning by just four votes. William Holcombe was reelected county clerk and register of deeds and was elected delegate to the Wisconsin constitutional convention by the voters of St. Croix and La Pointe counties.13

So things stood when Joseph R. Brown reappeared in the fall of 1846 to "locate permanently" at his old townsite of Dacotah, which he now called Head of Lake St. Croix. He had made an exceptionally favorable deal with Henry Sibley for his Indian trade, Sibley assuming all his debt to Steele, taking his posts and inventory at book value and guaranteeing Gabriel's and Hayes' salaries would be paid for one year. By October 7 Brown was heading upriver with Kittson to inventory the posts and move the excess goods to Big Stone Lake, where Mac would spend the winter laconically evaluating it: "8 soldiers coats, damaged; 10 temperance medals; 1 tea kettle (no cover); 1 old tent and mosquito bar, used; 1 flag all 'tattered and torn.' " By the twenty-eighth he was in a hurry to go down with Susan and the children, impatient to hear the news from Madison.14

William Holcombe had gone down as delegate to the October 5 convention anxious to have the state's western boundary removed from the St. Croix River, which, despite Brown's sanguine statement to Martin, was highly objectionable to the people of the valley. He advocated instead a division of the territory on a line through the "great barrier of uncultivable land between the Wisconsin and Chippewa Rivers," but it was December 9 before he got the committee to agree to a compromise line fifteen miles east of the St. Croix. It was better than nothing, and it kept hopes for Superior Territory alive. In debate Holcombe had mentioned that he was informed the U.S. government intended to establish the territorial seat of government at the St. Croix River, an unsupported bit of information likely given him by Caleb Cushing. The notion that the capital would be at St. Croix Falls was firmly entrenched on that river; in a letter written nearly a year later, B. H. Cheever still asserted the fact was "beyond question."15 J. R. Brown, we can be sure, kept himself informed on this subject.

It may well have been Brown who suggested to Morgan Martin that the capital of this brave new territory would be better placed at the head of navigation of the Mississippi, "at or near the mouth of the Minnesota or

13. Candidates for the Council were Crawford residents Benjamin F. Manahan and Alfred Brunson (Manahan won easily); only Jackson and Furber were on the ticket for representative to the House. "Proceedings of St. Croix County Board" 57; Election returns Sep. 7, 1845, papers of Wisconsin Territory, series 211.

14. Agreement Sep. 28, 1846; Sibley to McLeod, Oct. 6, McLeod to Sibley, Oct. 28, 1846, Sibley papers; inventory memo Aug. 8, 1847, copy in McLeod papers.

15. William Holcombe "Report on the Expediency of Dividing the Territory of Wisconsin" in Journal of the Convention to Form a Constitution for the State of Wisconsin 242–244 (Madison 1847); Benjamin H. Cheever to Isaac Green, Sep. 25, 1847 in Caleb Cushing papers, Library of Congress, microfilm in MHS. The debates are covered in the Wisconsin Democrat Dec. 12, 1846, ff. On the convention, see Frederick L. Holmes "First Constitutional Convention 1846" in Proceedings of the State Historical Society of Wisconsin 1905 229–251 (Madison 1906).

St. Peters River," as section 14 read when Martin presented the bill December 13. The phraseology, it will be noted, does not confine the site to Mendota as later bills did, but leaves open the possibility of a new capital city located on the reserve. Brown did write to Martin again that fall (the original letter is lost, but its contents are referred to in another dated January 11, 1847), sharing with him his plan for the Indians and the reserve. He knew then that the Winnebago had made a treaty, at that time before the Senate, in which they agreed to move to lands in the west. Brown's plan was to locate them south of the Minnesota River, a plan designed to force a treaty with the Sioux for the cession of land required for their reservation.

By January of 1847 he had learned that the treaty confirmed October 23 had provided for location of the Indians north of the Minnesota in Chippewa country; however, he had also heard that Congress contemplated treating with the lower Sioux for their lands on the Mississippi. He wrote again to Martin outlining a new plan, arising, he says, from "a deep interest in the welfare of our Northwestern Indians."[16] It is true, of course, that many of Brown's ideas for advancing the Indians' welfare also advanced his own, but there is no reason to doubt his sincerity on this point. Like most of the traders, he realized that unlimited contact with white "civilization" not only corrupted the native people morally, but destroyed their usefulness as hunters and food gatherers as well. Humanitarian interests did not conflict with economic interests on this score. Like many other people – Bell and Doty come to mind – Brown temporized about the inevitability of the extinction of the red race, or at least its absorption into white civilization, by contemplating removal of the native population to reserves so remote as to remain out of reach of undesirable influences. That this could not long work must have been clear. Still, it would provide a breathing space while the problem of what to do with the Indian was debated by Congress. Again, it will be noted, adoption of Brown's proposal would result in the general removal of the Indian population to reservations far up the Minnesota, eventually forcing abandonment of the reserve by the military.

Brown's suggestion to Martin was that the Winnebago and the Sioux of the Mississippi be located west of a line running south from the mouth of Crow Wing River to Patterson's Rapids on the Minnesota River, the former nation north of the river and the latter south of it. The Menominee might be placed on the Crow Wing and the Chippewa that were still on the ceded land could move to a location above Crow Wing between the upper Mississippi and the Red River. To be effectual, cautioned Brown, the removal must be complete; that is, the government must treat not only with the Sioux of the Mississippi, but with those on the lower St. Peters as well, for if suffered to remain, they would become carriers of liquor for those of the interior, just as those Indians were presently furnishing liquor to the Sisseton and Yankton. He further proposed a complete separation of

---

16. Brown to Martin, Jan. 19, 1847, Martin papers, Kellogg Public Library, Green Bay.

red and white by establishment of a fifty-mile-wide zone east of the line, extending to about the mouth of the Blue Earth River, which is, he says in an incredibly short-sighted or deliberately obtuse statement, "all to which the white settlements need extend for the next fifty years." Without the buffer zone, according to Brown, whiskey would reach the Indians and prevent any progress in agriculture and civilization. One must grant Brown some expertise in this area.

Brown had, as a matter of fact, taken the trouble to inform himself just what the facilities for tempting the Indians with liquor really were, so as to add weight to his argument. "From Prairie du Chien to Crow Wing River, a distance of five hundred miles where the Mississippi is the line between the Indian and the ceded lands, there is two hundred and seventy one persons whose business is the sale of liquor to Indians," he informed Martin. He calculated their average sales at fourteen barrels each, making 3,794 barrels annually. "There is also on the Black, Chippewa and St. Croix rivers and their tributaries about one hundred more," he added; also "on the St. Croix above the lake there is nineteen whiskey selling establishments for the especial convenience of the Chippeways." He estimated their stock at 180 barrels, guessing it would exceed 300 by spring. Although this census may have been undertaken somewhat in the nature of a market survey for Brown's own activities, it nonetheless supplies a good idea of the immense business done in this commodity. If the average barrel held 32 gallons, this one year's stock amounted to 128,000 gallons with a wholesale value of well over $55,000 in 1847 dollars! Of course, this prodigious amount of liquor was not destined to go down only Indian throats; much of it found its way to the thirsty white population as well.[17]

Brown's interest in what would happen to the Winnebago was echoed in other quarters. Apparently Morgan Martin was supposed to have some influence in making the decision. Hercules Dousman, who, through the Fort Atkinson trading house run by Henry M. Rice, controlled most of the tribe's annuity money, was, he told Martin in February, deeply interested in the result. Rice also had influence over the Winnebago and it was said to be the tribe's wish that Rice select their new homeland for them. Accordingly, it was Henry M. Rice and Isaac A. Ver Plank who came upriver to dicker with the Chippewa for a suitable tract for the Winnebago reservation. It was not to be expected they would consult J. R. Brown. That August they purchased from the Chippewa a trapezoidal tract about thrity miles wide between Crow Wing River and the Sioux-Chippewa boundary line extending from Otter Tail Lake to near Sauk Rapids on the Mississippi. The Winnebago were expected to occupy the land around Long Prairie River, where the agency was to be established. In the fall of 1847 Henry Rice moved his trading operation to the mouth of Crow Wing River.[18]

---

17. Brown to Martin, Jan. 19, 1847. Other accounts of the fur trade bear out Brown's figures.
18. Dousman to Martin, Jan. 19, 1847, Martin papers.

Joseph R. Brown was not idle while waiting for some of these plans to mature. His fertile mind had suggested quite a number of other enterprises to undertake in the interim. He lost little time settling accounts with the new St. Croix County board in January. There must have been an interesting scene when Brown presented his itemized bill covering lease of his property for six years, use of his house for county purposes, special services rendered and other contingencies. The board, then composed of Orange Walker, Socrates Nelson and Harley White, rejected the amount out of hand, allowing only $47.57 for taking the census back in 1842 and $1 for service as election judge. The next day Brown was back, and "after a full and free discussion" (County Clerk Holcombe's words) the following was agreed upon: Brown was allowed the $800 he had paid into the treasury plus $169.95 for use of his house by the officers of 1841 and 1842. He agreed to allow a balance against him as treasurer of $391.53, remitted the $400 paid on the lease back in 1841 and allowed he had made some overcharges amounting to $39 – total due J. R. Brown $140. Obviously the math was designed to get to this point, which was the amount the board members felt they could afford to pay to be shut of Mr. Brown. Magnanimously Brown returned $20 to the county till by taking out a license to maintain a tavern "in the home of Brown and Carli."[19]

It's safe to conclude that this tavern was to be in the Tamarack House, which had been used as a convenient stopping place by valley residents from its inception, being first known as "Carli's", then as Kennedy's Hotel. Robert Kennedy had only recently removed to Stillwater proper. The Carli currently in residence was Christopher Carli, still a single man, who called the place home although his medical practice and timber rafting ventures took him up and down the river for many days at a time. Lydia Carli, too, had moved back to Tamarack House and joined the Browns in keeping the new public house. She had been made a widow in March of 1846 when Paul drowned near Catfish bar, leaving her five youngsters and the farm to care for. It had happened on a blustery spring day; Paul had been hauling wheat from Brown's Grey Cloud Island farm to Stillwater for milling and while passing near the lake had stopped to shoot a duck which fell into the water. He got out a small canoe and retrieved the duck, but waves overturned his canoe and being weighted down with a heavy coat he was unable to swim to shore and so drowned in sight of one of his sons. Lydia Ann must have moved out that summer; Brown sold the western part of the farm that fall. However, at Tamarack House romance bloomed, and in the spring of 1847, after the prescribed year of mourning, Chris Carli and Lydia Ann Carli were married. Officiating at the ceremony was Joseph R. Brown, J.P. for the Stillwater precinct, his commission regained at a special election held February 6. The newlyweds soon left Head of Lake St. Croix for the burgeoning town

19. "Proceedings of St.Croix County Board" 64–67.

of Stillwater, where the doctor built an office and pharmacy, with living quarters attached, on lower Main Street.[20]

The firm of Brown and Carli appears to have been founded in the fall of 1846 when Joseph returned to the St. Croix valley. This was a diverse business venture. Obviously they were the proprietors of the Tamarack House tavern; from Steele's records, we know that Brown and Carli did business in furs and lumber, logs and whiskey; in December of 1846 they purchased a lot in downtown Stillwater fronting on Main Street and backing on the steamboat levee, an ideal place for a store or warehouse (the lake's high water line then came within 120 feet of Main Street; Water Street must literally have been in the water!). The record is blank on Brown and Carli's activities until May of 1847, at which time they owed Franklin Steele about $1,500. This large sum suggests they had been doing substantial business in some commodity with financing from Steele. They ran up additional debts of $1,800 during the winter of 1847–1848 and closed their account out that year with a cash payment of over $2,900, a sum that seems small until one realizes that in 1990s dollars that is more than $100,000. That Steele would finance Brown to such an extent after his previous two years' experience in the fur trade with him further suggests that the commodity was one in which Steele had more confidence – lumber.[21]

Since the first rafts had been sent downriver from the St. Croix Lumbering Company in 1842, lumbering had mushroomed in the valley, amounting in 1847 to about sixty million board feet. Brown had been logging the river since 1832; he had sent rafts down from the pineries unhampered by laws or Indians, and had probably piloted the first ones himself to lower markets. Practically everyone on the St. Croix had some interest in logging and Chris Carli was no exception. During Brown's absence he had taken out a least one raft in partnership with a man named H. H. Rhemy, probably under contract with the Stillwater Lumber Company.[22] The pair probably had as much experience and as good contacts as anyone else in the valley for engaging in timber cutting and rafting on a small scale.

What isn't clear is whether they cut their own logs or purchased them from other small-time loggers. Certainly Brown had the expertise to outfit his own crew and bring the logs out in the spring. It is clear they speculated in timber already cut. In the spring of 1847 they purchased over a million feet of logs from Anson Northrup, a Stillwater businessman and hotel proprietor. Many of these logs were lying in the lake below

20. "Proceedings of St. Croix County Board" 80; Case "Trading Post." The marriage took place March 12, 1847, almost exactly one year after Paul's death on March 15, 1846 (see Lydia's account in Easton *St. Croix Valley* 12). Dr. Carli speculated in Stillwater lots, by 1848 owned four on Main Street and one on Second, where he later built his residence, and had an interest with his brother-in-law on another (St. Croix County Deed Book A 44, 65, 119, 120, 155, 159). JRB's reentry into valley politics as a J.P. shows a certain unsinkability as a political force, even though the special election was probably one of the things the commissioners had had to agree to to buy Brown off.

21. Steele General Ledger 1847–1852, Steele papers; St. Croix County Deed Book A 65.

22. Easton *St. Croix Valley* 19. Carli's first partner, Rhemy, was a carpenter who had come out to work for the Stillwater Lumber Company.

Stillwater, having got loose from the boom on Wood River, and Northrup was eager to sell. He had in March purchased a half interest in the Osceola mill (which had commenced operation in 1845 a few miles north of Marine) and was in a poor cash position; Brown contracted to buy his scattered wealth a few days later. One of the loggers, Daniel McLean, had a lien on the logs for $700; possibly the reason Brown was able to make so advantageous a deal with Northrup was his offer to buy back this obligation with interest as soon as the logs were sold – Steele and Carli would give bond. McLean agreed to wait for his money and also to take charge of the logs, bringing down those that were upriver to Lake St. Croix, assisting in making the rafts and helping run them to St. Louis, for which services Brown and Carli would pay him $39 a month. Everything seemed hunky-dory until the other two parties appeared.

Northrup had conveniently forgotten to mention that he had already mortgaged the logs to West and Van Deventer of St. Louis, and also that he owed a hefty percentage of them to the loggers, among them McLean, who had labored all winter cutting them, in lieu of salary. In May William Holcombe, now attorney for West and Van Deventer, descended upon Northrup along with the nine loggers. At last a better-than-nothing deal was struck: the logging crew would take their logs first, 640,000 board feet by the scale equal to the $2,800 owed them; Brown and Carli would then recover 268,000 board feet, taking their logs from those already in the lake; West and Van Deventer would get a half million feet plus additional security consisting of notes on the Osceola mill, and commence taking their logs at the pineries. Where the two groups met, somewhere on the St. Croix, they would make adjustments, splitting on a pro rata basis.23 It was nearly June when all this was sorted out and Brown could begin making the rafts. Brown and Carli had some additional logs – their sales at St. Louis amounted to at least 350,000 board feet – but it was a far cry from the 1.4 million feet they had intended to purchase. With Franklin Steele willing to finance the venture and Cheever and Company, a St. Louis company owned by brothers Benjamin and William Cheever, eager to buy anything they could deliver, Brown and Carli could have cleaned up – and they still had an opportunity to turn a good profit. But before their diminished supply of logs could be moved, other matters commanded J. R. Brown's attention.

That spring had been, on the whole, one of disappointments. On April 6 the new Wisconsin constitution hammered out by the convention had been put to referendum, as prescribed in the enabling act, and although it squeaked by in St. Croix and four other counties, it was soundly rejected by the majority of the voters. The hot issue in St. Croix County had been the boundary, which would have been set just east of the river, reserving the valley for Minnesota territory; the rest of the voters took issue with other provisions, especially one which would have granted property rights

<hr />

23. Agreements, Mar. 4, 1847 between Anson Northrup, William Kent and William Mahoney; Mar. 7, 1847 between Daniel McLean and Brown & Carli; and May 27, 1847 between West & Van Deventer, Daniel McLean et al. and Brown & Carli, St. Croix County Deed Book A 73, 77, 81.

to married women and another which forbade bank charters (the ruinous failure of unregulated banks at the turn of the decade had not been forgotten).**24** A new constitutional convention was called for December, but the failure of the first was a setback to those interested in the early establishment of the new territory. However, one bit of very good news did arrive with Joseph Furber from Madison about the first of March: the legislature had at last reinstated the St. Croix County district court.

Furber had pulled off this unlikely coup with the panache of a seasoned politician. When the Council voiced objections that the bill was unnecessary (since the citizens of the county would soon be included in a different government anyway), Furber quietly made a deal not to create any roadblocks to a pet Council measure waiting to be approved by the House in the February rush of last-minute bill-passing. (It's not difficult to imagine Mr. Furber looking up Mr. Brown before he left to take his seat in January; he would have received excellent advice on how to force passage of a bill.) Judge Irvin remained obdurate, but a satisfactory solution had been found by placing St. Croix County in the first judicial district presided over by Judge Charles Dunn. Brown wasted no time in seeking appointment as clerk of court, a post he had no trouble getting this time. In early May the judge confirmed Brown's appointment and set the opening day of court for June 14. Brown's first official act on May 12 was to prepare the jury slate; his second to buy a desk. Perhaps fearing that the judge would not, on second thought, find it convenient to attend after all, Brown prudently held on to his J.P. commission until the court was a fact, not resigning it until June 21.**25**

He need not have worried. Not only the judge, but every potential office holder and eager lawyer in the western part of Wisconsin – and his wife – was on the steamboat that arrived at Stillwater June 14. Ben Eastman, Thomas P. Burnett, Daniel G. Fenton, Alfred Brunson, Wyram Knowlton and Nelson Dewey, among others, made rather a pleasure party of it. A considerable percentage of these travelers entertained notions of getting appointments in the new territory and had frankly come to look over the situation. The resources of Stillwater, which consisted of but one street three blocks long stretching from John McKusick's mill and store to Anson Northrup's Cosmopolitan Hotel (already stuffed with hopefuls), must have been severely strained to accommodate them all, not to mention the contingents from St. Paul, Marine, Red Rock and other points who crowded into the town.**26**

Judge Dunn opened court on Tuesday, a day late, in the only meeting room in town, the room over McKusick's store across the street from the mill that continued to whine and rumble all day long. The court lasted just

24. Alice E. Smith, *The History of Wisconsin* I: 664 (Madison 1973); "Proceedings of St. Croix County Commissioners" 59; Milo M. Quaife, *Struggle over Ratification 1846–1847* (*Wisconsin Historical Collections* XXVIII) 698, passim (Madison 1920).
25. *Council Journal* 1847 118, 198; *Wisconsin Democrat* Jan. 16, 23, Feb. 6, 13, 1847; "Proceedings of St. Croix County Board" 80–83.
26. Moss "Early Days of Minnesota" 73–75; Folsom *Fifty Years* 33, 38, passim.

four days, much of the time being taken up with organization, jury selection and the making of new voters from among the foreign-born (including Chris Carli, Jim Clewet and Vital Guerin) by taking their affidavits of intent to become citizens in open court. By Wednesday they were ready to get down to the main business, the trial of Notin, a Chippewa Indian, for the murder of Henry Rust, a whiskey seller.

Rust had distributed his wares on the Snake River not far from Elam Greeley's Ann River lumber camp. He had been shot during a drunken brawl, a tragedy precipitated by the spirits he had sold the Indians. This episode quite properly scared the loggers, who determined to put an end to the commerce in whiskey. Taking courage in hand they proceeded en masse to the whiskey store to retrieve Rust's body and collar the Indians involved. Before the eyes of the now-sober Chippewa they knocked in the heads of the remaining whiskey barrels and fired the cabin, the spilled spirits greatly aiding the conflagration. After Sheriff William Folsom had secured the accused Indians, the group of vigilantes marched on to other whiskey shops in the vicinity, destroying the article as they found it and scaring off a number of other entrepreneurs. This was considered the moral and just thing to do and no one thought to take action against the loggers. Notin was the only one brought to trial. After one day of deliberation, the jury, who may have considered it poetic justice, found Notin not guilty of murder. At the insistence of the lumbermen a criminal charge was also brought against Rust's employer and supplier, Andrew J. "Jack" Drake (since Rust was now beyond reach) for selling liquor to Indians. Drake was quickly found guilty and fined $40, and the court adjourned until the second Monday in December.27

Unfortunately for the county, this highly gratifying district court was not repeated for several years. December 13 came, with a jury panel selected and four cases on the docket (one of which was Jack Drake suing Elam Greeley for trespass), but no judge appeared, and Clerk Brown was forced to adjourn the session. The same thing happened the following June. St. Croix County saw no regular court until August 1849 when Minnesota had finally become a territory. However the proceedings in June had given new life to St. Croix County. The board authorized a tax assessment in July to pay for county operations, anticipated to be $1,566; roads were authorized to be surveyed and built to open up communications between Stillwater and St. Paul, Point Douglas and St. Croix Falls. In December the commissioners contracted to build a fine courthouse on the bluff at the end of Chestnut Street on a lot donated by John McKusick and a subscription was got up to raise money for it, although this project was stopped by temporarily by a petition from St. Croix Falls asking that the board not give away the county's right to preempt a quarter section. They wanted no action taken "until the bounds

---

27. Folsom *Fifty Years* 46–48; St. Croix County District Court Calendar 1848 and Calendar Journal 1847–1848, in Washington County district court papers, MHS.

of Minnesota Territory are firmly established" – note that the interest was not in where Wisconsin was, but where Minnesota was to be.[28]

A full year had gone by and the territory was still on hold. There were two new additions to Brown's family, twins Amanda Cecilia and Emily Mary Ann, born September 6, 1847 in the log house at the head of the lake. The Democrats had convened in Madison July 24 and appointed Joseph R. Brown a member of the central and corresponding committee from St. Croix County, probably at the behest of the official delegate from St. Croix and Crawford, D. G. Fenton.[29] Brown himself could not attend; like everyone else on the St. Croix that July he was busy getting out his raft. When he finally returned to Stillwater on the *Prairie Bird* November 2, he allowed it had been a long and unprofitable summer.

Early in July an immense fleet of log rafts, covering some ten acres, had moved slowly through lakes St. Croix and Pepin towed by the steamer *War Eagle*. Brown's two relatively small log rafts were among them. One was anchored at the far side of Lake Pepin while the other made the trip to St. Louis without a hitch and was delivered to Cheever and Company in about two weeks, if we may judge by the salary of $18.25 paid one of the crew. (Men running logs were paid $1 a day and $1 a night while on the moving raft, although on dark nights and in tricky parts of the river the pilot played it safe and made fast for the night; windy weather could hold them up for days. Eighteen "watches" was very good time.)[30] Another log raft consigned to Cheever and Company was delivered July 26 and Brown's raft may have accompanied it in order to take advantage of the skills of its pilot, Phineas Lawrence. In early August Brown returned to Wabasha Prairie to bring down his second raft.

This one, 186,000 feet of white pine, proved more troublesome. All summer the river had been falling and by August it was getting dangerous. Even though the second raft was started immediately, it was exceedingly slow going. Another of Cheever's rafts went to pieces going over the rapids at Rock Island that August; it cost considerable time and 40¢ a log to unstick it from the sandbars where it fetched up. Brown must have been equally unlucky. What happened we don't know, but in mid-October he had got it no farther than Montrose at the head of the Des Moines Rapids. Being apprised that the water was too low to run a raft down with any probability of success, he bit the bullet and hired a man named Pike to

---

28. "Proceedings of St. Croix County Board" 80, 86.

29. Brown Bible; *Wisconsin Democrat* Jul. 24, 1847.

30. Steele Ledger; Folsom *Fifty Years* 49. A bit of background on rafting may be wanted. Rafts of logs or lumber were made up of "cribs," 16-foot squares, coupled together for flexibility. Lumber cribs were strongly framed, boards and lath built up in courses to 24 inches deep; log cribs were simply logs floating side by side, butt to butt, held together by 16-foot poles laid across them and pegged to each log. The cribs were chained together in "strings" with a sweep oar at each end to guide the raft. Small river rafts consisted of three strings ten to twelve cribs long; Mississippi rafts of six strings by twenty-two cribs were built at Stillwater for the journey downriver. Except for steamboat tows through Lake Pepin where there was no perceptible current and considerable sideswing, the rafts were floated with the current and sometimes rigged with sails. The only means of stopping a raft was to take lines to shore to snub it, which was usually done each night. At major rapids, rafts were broken up and additional crew taken on to man the sweeps. Good accounts are in Agnes M. Larson *History of the White Pine Industry in Minnesota* (Minneapolis 1949) and Walter Blair *Raft Pilot's Log* 27–30 (Cleveland 1930).

insure its safety over the winter. Pike would complete the run to St. Louis in the spring as soon as navigation opened for $200, payable only on delivery of the entire raft uninjured in the eddy at St. Louis, he reported to Cheever and Company's agent Isaac Green. He said, however, that he had had to ante up $50 advance to Pike and so had given him a draft on Cheever and Company, which he hoped would be honored. All parties must agree that it was better to be tied up in safety than to share the fate of other rafters on the river that fall – Lawrence lost his last rafts, was reported at Montrose drunk shortly after Brown returned to Stillwater, another's logs were frozen in near Burlington. At least Brown's logs got safely to St. Louis in the spring, although at considerable expense. The costs incurred in that last run practically guaranteed Brown and Carli was not going to break even that year. The venture, if not their first, was certainly their last. When they received payment from Cheever and Company the following August, Brown and Carli closed out their account with Steele and dissolved the partnership.[31]

Christopher Carli may have been unwilling to take further risks, but Joseph R. Brown still believed there was money to be made in lumbering. On his return home in November he learned that Steele still planned to log that winter, despite losing the logs cut that fall by an exploratory party at Dutchman's Grove on the Rum River to the season's first big ice and snow storm, which had taken out a temporary boom at the mouth of the Rum and sent the logs down over the falls. Brown immediately made a deal with Steele to put two crews on the upper Mississippi that winter.

On the strength of his provisional agreement with Cushing and several other Boston businessmen, Steele had begun building at the falls during the summer of 1847. A mess hall, blacksmith and carpentry shop, bunkhouse and stables were already up, built with lumber hauled from the St. Croix, some 2,200 feet of which had been supplied by Brown and Carli. His millwright, Ard Godfrey, was proceeding to frame the mill and finish constructing a dam, started the preceding season by Jake Fisher, with local hardwood (since the pine had been lost), and there was every prospect they would be sawing by summer. Steele's timber cruiser, Daniel Stanchfield, who had had such bad luck with logs on the Rum, nonetheless brought back a glowing report of unlimited amounts of pine on the Mississippi and Rum rivers – "enough to last for fifty years" – growing practically at the water's edge and easily harvested. Since the nearer Rum would have to be cleared of driftwood snags before logging there would be feasible, Steele thought it better to locate the winter camps on the Mississippi, on the land recently ceded by the Chippewa. True, the young Gull Lake chief Hole-in-the-Day was still in possession pending treaty ratification, but Henry Rice (who had become as influential with the Chippewa as he had been with the Winnebago) thought an advantageous deal could be made with him for the timber near Crow Wing River. On

---

31. Brown to Isaac Green, Oct. 23 and Nov. 4, 1847; W. L. Cheever to same, Aug. 30, 1847; B. H. Cheever to same, Jul. 6, Sep. 21 and 25, memo Jul. 26, 1847; John Atchinson to same, Nov. 11, 1847; Green to B. H. Cheever, Aug. 31, 1847; all in Caleb Cushing papers.

December 18 Steele's loggers were at Rice's store at the mouth of the Crow Wing, and at this place, after a week of scouting the possible sites, Stanchfield signed an agreement with Hole-in-the-Day. He had selected a stand of timber four miles below Crow Wing and promised to pay the band 50¢ a tree in the spring. Brown came up about the same time and installed his crews somewhere north of the Crow Wing, contracting separately with Hole-in-the-Day for similar terms. In short order, axes were ringing.32

It is easy to see why, as one historian says, eastern men often made money in the pineries where western men could not. Although it was their first season and they were hampered by lack of snow, not to mention having to take time to build their shelter – sort of a long log bunkhouse-cum-dining hall dug partly into the ground that would be home to the twelve or so men on each crew – Stanchfield's cutting parties managed to bank 1.5 million feet of timber by March first and had cut a mile and a half of long logs for the boom. Their contract specified that they should not be bothered in any way by Hole-in-the-Day's people and the few that approached were summarily shooed away. Brown, we may be sure, ran a different operation. His men, experienced French Canadians and halfbreeds from the St. Croix pineries, were used to and welcomed the Indians. They probably lived in winter lodges similar to those built by the Chippewa. Indian women likely served as cooks and sold them game, wild rice and cranberries, welcome supplements to the daily fare supplied by Steele of salt pork, cornmeal, beans and biscuit washed down with sugar-laced coffee. Brown's men were not as efficient as the easterners. Although he had two crews working, and being his own contractor had a lively interest in keeping them hard at it, his apparent cut was just 600 trees (to judge from the $300 he paid Hole-in-the-Day that spring), which scaled 488,000 feet at St. Anthony. Still, at $4 per thousand delivered at the boom it should have been a profitable year for Brown.33

However, nature once again intervened. Since there had been little snow, there was not enough spring meltwater to run the logs. Brown abandoned his drive in late April. Stanchfield's men started their drive, but at Watab Rapids they got into trouble and a Frenchman was drowned. Then, according to Caleb Dorr, who had superintended a cutting crew and had charge of the drive, the whole crew got scared and stampeded. Dorr made two trips up that spring for the logs and succeeded in floating down the boomsticks, oversize logs desperately needed for construction of the

32. Daniel Stanchfield "History of Lumbering on the Upper Mississippi and Its Tributaries..." in *Minnesota Historical Collections* IX: 329–336 (St. Paul 1901); Rodney C. Loehr "Caleb D. Dorr and the Early Minnesota Lumber Industry," *Minnesota History* XXIV: 127–129 (St. Paul 1943); *St. Anthony Express* Jan. 31, 1952; H. M. Rice to Sibley, Dec. 18, 1847, Sibley papers.

33. Steele Ledger; Stanchfield "History of Lumbering" 337–338; Stephen B. Hanks "Reminiscences" 59, manuscript in Bill papers, MHS. The rigors of winter in the lumber camps can hardly be better expressed than by looking at a list of the supplies JRB took up in early January 1848: 2 castor oil, 1# "sal petre," 2 British oil, 1 peppermint, 1 balsam, 1 laudanum, 1 bushel apples, 1 pepper sauce (this latter evidently for Brown himself; he was partial to pepper sauce), 12 pair moccasins. We can see how he kept busy: 1 quire paper, 1 bottle ink, 1 penholder and pens, 1 blank book, 7 2/3 # tallow candles, 3 packs cards.

permanent boom above the falls. It was July before the other logs were retrieved from near Watab Rapids where they had been left and the first drive came down to St. Anthony. Brown's logs, higher up, evidently were not dislodged until late in the summer, and some were still there the next spring. but at least there was enough timber for Steele's mill to begin sawing in September of 1848.**34**

Despite the setbacks of the spring drive, the potential was there. Brown quickly saw how things could be improved to boost his return. It was obvious that the murderous expenses involved in dragging all the provisions – including remarkable quantities of feed for the oxen – all the way to Crow Wing was eating up profits. His haulage charges alone that season for the better than nine tons of supplies taken up on the ice topped $400, a noticeable percentage of the $2,000 grossed on the logs. There were three steps he could take to alleviate these burdensome costs: shorten the route, get into the transportation business himself and provide some of the produce required at its point of use. It didn't take long for him to figure out how to do all three to some extent.

A way to accomplish the first two steps occurred to him as he returned with the carters just after Christmas. Everything taken to the upper country started its overland trip from St. Pauls landing where the steamboats docked, although the head of navigation was actually at Fort Snelling (and sometimes steamboats could even get through to just below the falls of St. Anthony). Several miles could be cut off the land route if the goods could be landed at his old claim on the reserve or just below it. There he would be able to warehouse supplies needed by his and Steele's operations and arrange for their delivery upriver. He might also be able to turn a profit acting as middleman for goods needed in the Indian trade and by the new agencies and fort which would soon be established on the upper river for the protection of the Winnebago and Chippewa. Besides, it was becoming imperative that he get some legal claim on the reserve before others beat him to it. Steele, for example, already had the approval of the commanding officer for a ferry just below Brown's old site and was awaiting sanction of the war department for permission to build a store and warehouse opposite the fort. Steele, as well as Brown, had seen the area's potential for a townsite. As sutler, Steele already had a recognized claim at the old Baker post on the west side. Now he was attempting to muscle in on Brown's "fancy spot" on the east side as well.

Before the new year Brown penned a letter to the new Wisconsin territorial delegate John H. Tweedy, asking him to present his application for permission to erect a warehouse on the Fort Snelling reserve to the secretary of war. The theme was familiar: "The extension of the military reserve of Ft. Snelling over so large a tract... east of the Mississippi has long been a source of serious annoyance to business operations of the country – now more than ever, due to the increase of business above the

34. Caleb D. Dorr to Folwell, interview Sep. 9, 1917, Folwell Notebooks 32; "Caleb Door Tells of Early Days," *Minneapolis Journal* Jul. 8, 1917; Loehr "Caleb Dorr" 130–131.

Falls of St. Anthony." He wished to build at Fountain Cave, three miles below Fort Snelling, a warehouse and other necessary buildings for storing supplies for the upper Mississippi and promised: "I will enter into bonds not to traffick in liquor and will store government property required for the Indians free." He told Tweedy that this site was the most convenient landing below the fort; however, if he could get him permission to build one mile above the fort (the site of his old ferry and grocery) that would be preferred, for it would shorten the distance by road another mile and a half.[35]

Tweedy dutifully forwarded the request. It was rejected on the grounds that allowing one person the privilege of building on the reserve would make it "the cause of constant difficulty between the military and the citizens." This reasoning apparently did not apply to Steele's request; his ferry was deemed a necessity by the quartermaster general and since the ferryman (Samuel J. Findley) needed a house to live in and a store as additional means of support, the request for buildings was also granted. This ferry, incidentally, was by 1854 producing an annual income of $1,500 for Steele, retrospectively proving that Brown had been right about the possibilities all along.[36]

Brown made one further attempt to gain control of the site: he composed a memorial to Congress asking that preemption rights be secured to John Rex, J. R. Brown, Antoine and Samuel Findley and Martin McLeod for their claims on the reserve. A copy, in McLeod's papers, is undated, but since it contains survey descriptions must have been written after mid-1847. This probably served as the model for a memorial introduced by Jackson in the 1848 Wisconsin legislature asking that the reserve be raised and preemption rights granted the original settlers. It passed, but did little good. Jackson too was waiting to pounce on the reserve. In April of 1848, after passage of his memorial, he purchased Vital Guerin's preemption rights to a claim fronting a half mile of the Mississippi including the cave, very close to the site for which Brown had petitioned the preceding winter. Henry Rice looked first at the reserve near Mendota as an advantageous location for his warehouses meant to supply the new fort and agency, but ran up against Sibley and his brother-in-law Steele who also had plans to make the St. Peters "a great town" and so moved his operation to the Dayton's Bluff area below St. Paul, where he hoped to found a rival town that would become the territorial capital. But the best townsite in the territory was understood to be the one across from the fort; it was called the "best townsite in the west" by Hercules Dousman. Nine years later Seth Eastman, who had been commanding officer at Fort Snelling in the 1830s, expressed surprise it was still undeveloped, commenting: "I have always supposed a town would be built there; I suppose that if the reservation had been sold seven

35. Brown to John H. Tweedy, Dec. 21, 1847, in "Sale of Ft. Snelling Reservation," Serial 1372, *U. S. House Executive Document* #9, 17–18 (40 Congress, 3 session).

36. *U.S. House Ex. Doc. #9*, 2, 20, 59.

or eight years ago, before St. Paul was established, the town would have been there."**37**

By May of 1848 Brown had made arrangements to solve the third part of his supply problem in a very characteristic way, by persuading some Chippewa to open farms near the Rabbit River rapids, not far from his logging camps. Among the merchandise he sent up the first week of May were presents of calico, grey list and scarlet cloth, trade beads, combs and other trinkets, and probably seed stock. If the Indians could successfully grow corn, potatoes and other vegetables and cut marsh hay for feed, there would be that much less tonnage to haul north so laboriously the next fall. He also interested some of the Indian men in becoming loggers, or so he told William Welsh many years later. We may take with a large grain of salt his statement that "I got several farms started and used Indians to work in the Logging Camps... simply to satisfy myself whether Indian men could be induced to labor, instead of depending upon the chase." This experiment naturally created a certain pro-Brown faction among the Chippewa, much as it had among the Sioux of Lake Traverse, and contributed greatly to problems Brown encountered the following year. However, for creative thinking without the advantages of hindsight, it is hard to fault it.**38**

Before Brown returned to the pineries in December the political climate had changed dramatically. Wisconsin had been admitted. Henry Sibley, who had not previously taken enough interest in politics to run for election as J.P. and who had been viewed by many in the St. Croix country with suspicion as the agent of the all-powerful Fur Company, had emerged its shining hope. As duly elected delegate of the resuscitated Territory of Wisconsin, he was en route to Washington to assist at the birth of the Territory of Minnesota. Brown himself, after playing Warwick to Sibley's York, had neatly positioned himself to control the machinery of territorial politics – or so he thought.

How this came about is a tangled tale. Perhaps the way events arranged themselves that summer was purely copacetic. However, it seems where JRB is involved, few things occur by chance. There is no evidence to point plainly to Brown as the prime mover in the events of that summer, but just as geologists infer vanished mountains from their debris, so we can by looking at the effect deduce the cause. In this case the effect was that Henry Hastings Sibley was practically assured election as Minnesota's first delegate to Congress. In three months Sibley went from a private businessman, relatively unknown and vaguely disliked in some communities for his fur company connections, to Minnesota's most popular political figure and something of a hero. It took his rival, Henry M. Rice, two years to catch up. Sibley didn't accomplish this entirely on his own.

37. Memorial to Congress (undated), McLeod papers; St. Croix County Deed Book A 139–140; Rice to Alexander Ramsey, Dec. 2, 1849, Ramsey papers; "Fort Snelling Investigation 1858," Serial 965, *U. S. House Document #351*, *93*, 226, 292, 374–375 (35 Congress, 1 session).

38. Steele Ledger; Welsh *Taopi* 68–69.

The apparent agency of these events was a scheme originating in Madison, an offshoot of Wisconsin's tortuous jockeying for statehood. When the second constitutional convention met in Madison in December of 1847, the new delegate to the convention from St. Croix and La Pointe counties was George Brownell, mining and land agent for Cushing's St. Croix Falls operations. Brownell planned once again to push for the territorial split and felt certain he would be able to get at least the line of the last convention, fifteen miles east of the St. Croix. As he told Isaac Green: "A first position will be taken south of the Chippewa River only to be abandoned in time to save a total rout. The future fortune of St. Croix County is involved in the success of this measure." That the future territorial capital would be at St. Croix Falls seemed to him to be beyond question.[39]

A week later the situation had taken a nasty turn. Brownell had discovered that with few exceptions the members of the committee on boundaries felt they were pledged to include the falls of St. Croix within the new state, and some were opting, at the instigation of the delegate from Prairie du Chien, Daniel G. Fenton, to claim a boundary at the Rum River, thus grabbing for Wisconsin not only the mineral-laden south shore of Lake Superior and the St. Croix Valley, but the extensive Snake River pineries and half the water power at St. Anthonys Falls as well.[40] That news finally jarred Henry Sibley into entering the political arena.

Ever since the first surge of activity for creation of the territory in 1846 Sibley had been contemplating the dim prospects for the fur trade and was steadily coming to the conclusion that his future lay in politics. Throughout 1847 D. G. Fenton, though a most egregious blockhead, fed Sibley's vanity by encouraging him to run for delegate ("You will be elected; Holcombe won't run against you"). Fenton's letters seem to imply he has a direct pipeline to Washington. When he wrote to Sibley in April, Fenton confidently asserted that everything was set for Ben Eastman of Platteville to become judge and he himself secretary of the new territory, "and that arrangement I can assure you will stand good." He prophesied the bill would pass next session and that Sibley could become governor "for the asking."[41]

Sibley, who had no party connections save a personal friendship with the Democratic presidential hopeful Lewis Cass, must have realized this was no more than wishful thinking. He did, however, broach the subject of his running for the delegacy to John McKusick of Stillwater. McKusick's reply was mildly encouraging: he thought Sibley could expect considerable support from the St. Croix. He himself felt Sibley's fur trade connections were a recommendation, rather than otherwise, because he

39. George Brownell to Green, Dec. 16, 1847, Cushing papers.
40. Brownell to Hamlet H. Perkins, Dec. 24, 1847, Cushing papers.
41. Fenton to Sibley, Mar. 3, 17, Apr. 13, 1847, Sibley papers. It is hard to see why would anyone believe: (1) that Martin, or some Wisconsin Democratic committee, could nominate the governor, or (2) that if he could, he would pick someone who had never done anything for Wisconsin Democrats and whose nomination, as an agent of the Fur Company, to a position that included the duties of superintendent of Indian affairs would be sure to cause a stink.

believed it would give him "heavy influence" in Washington. St. Croix lumbermen could appreciate another solid businessman. But, thought McKusick, since there was likely to be no election for some time, Sibley's campaign seemed a bit premature. Sibley was still toying with the idea in September of 1847 when he told Charles Trowbridge, an old friend, "it needs no prophet to foresee that affairs in this country are now in a transit state and... the fur trade must soon be brought to a close. Perhaps I may turn politican or office seeker."**42** It is not impossible that Joseph R. Brown, having decided that Sibley would be exceedingly useful in Washington, helped persuade him to take the plunge.

In any case, Sibley's mind was quickly made up when he received the latter from Fenton about the proposed Rum River line. Despite Fenton's assurance that "you will have a Territory on your own side and the capital at the mouth of the St. Peters River," Sibley considered the move outrageous, as did many others in the St. Croix area to whom he spread the news. Angry citizens organized a public meeting of protest in St. Pauls on January 24, and with Sibley as one of the leaders produced a memorial to Congress opposing the action of the convention as unjust and oppressive – those were the milder terms. Sibley took charge of posting the document with its 345 signatures to Delegate John Tweedy at Washington and followed up with a trip to the Capital in February to personally lobby against the line.

Hercules Dousman, trying to smooth Sibley's ruffled feathers, professed not to know why Sibley felt "so savage." He reminded Henry that they all were anxiously anticipating a treaty with the Sioux – the sooner, the better chance of getting something, he felt – and he thought this would be more likely to happen if the St. Croix settlements were not included in the new territory. He admitted Prairie du Chien interests had promoted the line because without the St. Croix voters "we will be swallowed up by the eastern counties and have no influence in the state," adding the clincher, "you are now sure to have the seat of government of the new territory fixed on your side of the river."**43**

It is not hard to see that whatever his professions to Sibley, Dousman's (and Rice's) real interest was in preventing territorial organization west of the Mississippi for several years, thus keeping that country unsettled Indian territory over which he hoped to exercise considerable influence. If Sibley did not see this, Brown did, and would have lost no time in pointing it out. Only a fool would believe that Congress would set up the ponderous and expensive machinery of territorial government for the few

42. John McKusick to Sibley, Apr. 22, 1847; Sibley to Charles Trowbridge, Sep. 6, 1847, copy; both in Sibley papers.

43. Fenton to Sibley, Dec. 24, 1848; Dousman to same, Jan. 28, 1848; Tweedy to same, Mar. 3, 1848, all in Sibley papers. On the memorial see Holcombe *Minnesota* II: 347. Dousman tried to counteract the citizens' memorial, telling Tweedy, "The principal movers in the petition...do not live in Wisconsin and never have," a reference to his old business associates Sibley and Steele. He suggested to Tweedy that the waterpower at St. Anthony should be saved to Wisconsin, especially since "there is a Boston Company at work there; they have laid out a large city and of course, it must be the capital of the Northwest" (Dousman to Tweedy, Feb. 15, 1848, Tweedy papers, microfilm at MHS).

souls who would be left west of Wisconsin should the Rum River line prevail. Perhaps some of the members of the committee on boundaries had been lulled into thinking otherwise, for the committee chairman, Byron Kilbourne, had made known his desire to be made governor of the new territory and Fenton thought his chances of becoming secretary were "number one." Fenton also had delusions of becoming Indian agent at the St. Peters when Bruce should be replaced. They allowed their eager hopes to overcome common sense. The convention chairman, Morgan Martin, meanwhile had encouraged the Wisconsin-firsters, if only to assure himself of their support in his bid to be the state's first Senator. Cooler heads, such as Tweedy and Brown, knew Congress would never permit the Rum River line to be adopted – northern interests alone would see that more that one state was produced from the old Northwest territory – but Brown may not have taken pains to reassure Sibley of this. Let him get into fighting mettle.**44**

If these political shenanigans made Sibley savage, they made Brownell positively livid. He produced a minority report to the convention laying out reasons why the northwest boundary recommended should not be adopted, then refused to sign the constitution produced, even though the convention, anxious to do nothing that would jeopardize chances of statehood this time, had accepted the boundary specified in the organic act, that is the St. Croix River. They did, however, add that the Rum River line was the preference of the convention if Congress should consent. In this form the new constitution was accepted by an overwhelming majority of the voters March 3, and Congress, ignoring the stated preference of the convention, admitted Wisconsin May 20, 1848, with the St. Croix River as the western boundary.**45**

Congress, however, failed to act on Stephen Douglas' bill, basically the same as Martin's bill of the previous session, to create "Minasota" territory and adjourned in August without making any provision for the governance of the former territory of Wisconsin left over beyond the St. Croix River. This situation, as we know, had been foreseen by Joseph R. Brown in 1846. Others on the St. Croix were well aware of the possibility they would be left without government early in 1848. In February, and again in March, William Holcombe wrote to ask John Tweedy's opinion of what their legal and judicial status would be if this were the case. In April he proposed a practical solution: "The question has been seriously considered here whether we do not still remain under the Territorial Govt. of Wisconsin after the State of Wisconsin shall be admitted into the Union with a boundary not including us on the west side of the St. Croix."**46**

---

44. Fenton to Martin, Sep. 21, 1846, Byron Kilbourne to same, Oct. 24, 1846, Martin papers; Fenton to Sibley, Mar. 3, Apr. 14, Jun. 28, 1847, Sibley papers.

45. The convention is thoroughly discussed in Holcombe *Minnesota* II: 343–348 and in Milo M. Quaife *Attainment of Statehood* (*Wisconsin Historical Collections* XXIX), especially 127, 262, 415 (Madison 1928). A copy of Brownell's minority report *Boundaries of Wisconsin*, (Madison 1848) is in MHS.

46. Holcombe to Tweedy, Dec. 31, 1847, Mar. 4, Apr. 28, 1848, in Green Bay–Prairie du Chien papers, Madison.

In Madison John Catlin, erstwhile territorial secretary, came to the same conclusion. At the end of June, when it became obvious the new

Figure 35 John Catlin & wife Clarissa. Catlin was secretary and ex-officio governor of the rump of Wisconsin Territory in 1848. Wis. Hist. Soc.

territory would not be organized, Catlin asked Henry Dodge, the new Wisconsin state senator, to get an opinion from the state department as to whether Wisconsin territory did not, in fact, exist. Catlin had failed to get either a state office or federal appointment and wished to continue drawing his salary as a territorial officer. To Morgan Martin he confessed: "It is of some importance to me to know whether I am in office or not." He told Martin the subject had been discussed in Madison at length; the opinion generally prevailing among the lawyers was that the territory was still in being, that the division of a territory and organization of a state out of a part of it did not necessarily abolish the territorial government. What did Martin think?

Mails being what they were, Catlin had to wait until the first of August for Dodge's answer to his query. Enclosed was the unofficial opinion of Secretary of State James Buchanan that the laws of Wisconsin territory did remain in force in that portion of it now beyond the state and that all local officers were still in office. But Buchanan would not commit himself to say that the general officers, such as governor, secretary and judge, were still authorized to perform their duties. Congress would never make an appropriation, of that he was sure.[47]

Catlin was not put off by this ambiguous advice. He had by then concluded, or been advised, that he need not settle for the secretary's salary; as surviving territorial officer, he was ex officio governor and also superintendent of Indian affairs, offices worth $2,500 per annum. The question was how to draw the salary. Wisconsin territory might be said to exist, but it had no voice in Congress. Former delegate John Tweedy, loser

---

47. John Catlin to Dodge, Jun. 26, 1848, Secretary of State's papers, NARG 59; Catlin to Martin, Jul. 5, 1848, Green Bay–Prairie du Chien papers; Dodge to Catlin, Jul. 20, 1848, Catlin papers, WHS Madison; Buchanan to Dodge, Jul. 18, 1848, Secretary of State's papers, LS, NARG 59. John Catlin was an early resident of Mineral Point with his law partner Moses M. Strong, had served in the second territorial legislature at Burlington (Burgman, ed. *History of Bench and Bar*).

in the race for state governor, remained out east after being replaced by the new state Congressmen, but Catlin felt sure he would not consent to reassume his seat in Congress without some assurance of pay. Catlin thought Tweedy would, however, formally resign, leaving the way open for him, as acting governor, to call a special election to fill the seat. If Congress seated a delegate from the presumed Wisconsin territory, half the battle was won; the delegate could then attempt to procure an appropriation to run the territorial government. There was another possibility, suggested by Judge David Irvin sometime that summer, which might make the expense more palatable to Congress: Minnesota territory, when erected, could be attached to Wisconsin for legislative and judicial purposes, obviating the need for a second set of officers. Of course, an easterner would be appointed governor, but Catlin and Irvin thought they could get judgeships. All Catlin needed to set the wheels in motion was word that Congress had adjourned without taking action on the Minnesota bill.**48**

No sooner were the results of Wisconsin's statehood bid known than political hopefuls began to make tracks for the soon-to-be organized territory of Minnesota. One Madison lawyer-cum-surveyor-cum-editor, David Lambert, turned up in St. Pauls early in July with a letter of introduction to Henry Sibley from Senator Dodge in his pocket and within weeks had become Sibley's "firm friend and confidant." Lambert was a seasoned Wisconsin politico who had made his mark, first as editor of Whig papers in Arkansas and Kentucky, then as the Tylerite editor of the *Wiskonsan Enquirer*, the organ of then-Governor Doty. When that paper expired in 1845, a casualty of the political wars between Governor Doty and Delegate Dodge, Lambert bounced back as messenger in Doty's Wisconsin superintendency of Indian affairs. He managed to maintain the appointment under Governor Dodge, but by 1847 was considered to be "used up" politically in Wisconsin. In the summer of 1848 Lambert was seeking new opportunities and the new territory looked like a good bet. He hung out his shingle in St. Pauls, doing some legal business for Sibley and others. He also had hopes of starting up a newspaper (which might net him the public printing) provided suitable capital could be found. By mid-August he had an arrangement with Andrew Randall, a member of the U.S. geographic survey corps headed by U.S. Geographer David Dale Owens. Randall, becalmed in Stillwater awaiting funds to continue the survey, decided he, too, wanted a piece of the action in the new territory. He told Lambert he had a press and type in Cincinnati and they came to an agreement. While Randall returned east to prepare for the first publication, Lambert began soliciting subscriptions and business advertisements in St. Pauls, Stillwater and St. Croix Falls.**49**

Lambert had been a driving force in the push to resuscitate Wisconsin territory (he later said he had suggested the idea to Catlin). When Lambert

---

48. This part of the scheme is outlined in Dodge to Catlin, Sep. 20, 1848, Catlin papers.
49. Dodge to Sibley, Jun. 8, 1848; David Lambert to Steele, Aug. 23, 1848; Sibley papers.

moved to St. Pauls, Catlin was still seeking advice as to the advisability of resuming the territorial offices in St. Croix County. By late August Lambert had received word that Catlin had decided to come to St. Croix County to take up the duties of governor if the Minnesota territory bill was not acted upon by Congress. Catlin told him he was not willing to take this step, however, unless he received some assurance that the people of the territory would recognize him as acting governor and were indeed eager for territorial organization. There was also the question of whether there was a candidate for replacement of Tweedy as delegate who could be relied upon to get the job done in Washington, and who would be willing to undertake it at his own expense with the possibility of getting paid only if and when an appropriation was made. Henry Sibley may have been suggested; he was known in Madison and Washington, and had not been exactly quiet about his aspirations to enter politics. We can presume Lambert was asked to report on the political climate and sound out Sibley. Catlin more than hinted that if all went well the post of secretary to the acting governor would be David Lambert's.

When Lambert wrote to Catlin on just these topics September 6, he pointed out that he had been "rather active in this whole matter" and reminded Catlin of his suggestion in reference to making him private secretary if he decided to open the executive office in St. Croix County.50 He also mentioned that he would "communicate the subject of your letter" to Sibley – possibly the first time Sibley was to hear of the proposal to open Wisconsin territorial offices in St. Croix County. As Lambert had been absent from St. Pauls since August 25, when he left for Stillwater and the land sales at St. Croix Falls, it is clear that before that date he must have received knowledge of Catlin's plans. By August 25 Lambert was supporting Sibley for delegate with the help of J. R. Brown, so it's a good bet that all three were aware that Catlin proposed to open Wisconsin territorial offices in St. Croix County at that time, if not earlier. What this portends will be clear in a moment.

It is not likely that Joseph R. Brown or Henry Sibley were originally privy to Catlin's plan, or that either did anything to encourage it. On the contrary, their interest was entirely in the early organization of Minnesota territory, which would include the leftover portion of Iowa as well as that of Wisconsin. However, they could hardly help being aware of the talk about reviving Wisconsin territory: Brown himself assumed Wisconsin laws were still in effect when he spent the summer thoughtfully preparing for a possible election in the fall by filing declarations of intent from St. Pauls' British and Canadian inhabitants, automatically qualifying them as voters, in his role as clerk of court, St. Croix County, Wisconsin Territory. It was wise to do this while the fate of the Minnesota bill was yet

---

50. Lambert to Catlin, Sep. 6, 1848, Catlin papers. "It fell to my lot to be among the first to proclaim the doctrine that this country was still entitled to the territorial government of Wisconsin, and to take the lead in extending to the acting Governor of the old Territory an invitation to come among us and issue his proclamation for the election of a Delegate to Congress," said Lambert in the *Minnesota Pioneer* (July 19, 1849).

unknown. Brown collected more than thirty such declarations, which were in the hands of Henry Jackson (who had been qualifying voters for his own run at the legislature the preceding fall) and J.P. Aaron Foster, and filed them July 3. Toward the end of the month and the first week of August Brown rounded up many of Sibley's employees (some technically residents of Iowa, but potential Minnesota voters) and with the help of Aaron Foster filed for many of the other foreign-born residents from Lake St. Croix to St. Anthonys Falls. By October, there were sixty-seven new voters in St. Croix County, among them eight who had voted illegally for Brown in the 1840 election. Many were present or former employees of the American Fur Company, many were evacuees from the reserve, all could be relied on for unswerving loyalty to Brown and Sibley, both of whom had been active in protecting their interests. Sibley himself helped collect these declarations; several are in his handwriting and not a few are in David Lambert's.[51]

Brown made no move to run for delegate or solicit any other office. (Being an astute vote counter, he was aware that he was too well-known as a Democrat to garner votes in the Whiggish St. Croix river and St. Anthonys Falls precincts, and in predominantly Democratic Crow Wing and St. Pauls he would be opposed by Henry Rice and Henry Jackson.) He had the inspiration to prod Henry Sibley into the public eye and remain out of it himself. Elective office held no lure for JRB unless he could use it to his own advantage, and in this case Sibley would act in his behalf. After all, Sibley's interests ran with his; full territorial government (with its attendant contracts, jobs and appropriations); full payment of traders' claims upon removal of the Sioux; a lucrative settlement for the Lake Pepin halfbreeds so those lands could be sold; and last, but not at all least, the "hidden" issue, return of the Fort Snelling reserve to the public domain with the rights of the original settlers protected. (Sibley never for a moment forgot he was on the reserve solely at the discretion of the military officers and could be removed at any time without being paid a dime for his extensive improvements; Franklin Steele wanted similar resolution of the status of his claim at the old Camp Coldwater and may have helped convince his brother-in-law to enter the political arena.) The Rice–Dousman faction had a heavy influence and could be expected to oppose these interests; witness Rice's surreptitious scrabbling that very summer to acquire a power of attorney from the halfbreeds of Lake Pepin that would have given him carte blanche in the disposal of their very desirable lands.[52] And although Brown had supported Sibley in opposing the removal of Amos Bruce as Sioux agent, it no doubt would have suited him down to the ground to be appointed in Bruce's place. Part of Brown's hidden agenda could have been to place Sibley where he could use his influence to urge Brown's appointment; however, by the time Sibley was

---

51. Declarations of Intent, Records of the Clerk of Court, St. Croix County, MHS.

52. "The Sioux lands of the Half Breed Tract on the Mississippi at Lake Pepen can be got cheaply now," Rice wrote to the Indian office in June. "The halfbreeds are anxious to sell.... Speculators will get hold of it" (Rice to Medill, Jun. 4, 1848, OIA LR St. Peters).

in a position to do something about it, a Whig administration had taken over and Democrats could expect no preferments.

As the summer wore on it became increasingly obvious that Congress was not going to take action on the Minnesota bill that session; Sibley could put his plan to be elected delegate on hold for awhile. Concerned St. Paulites held a meeting in the street outside Jackson's store that July to bruit the question of whether they might not then inherit the abandoned territorial government of Wisconsin. Among the participants were Henry Sibley and David Lambert. After some rousing oratory, the spirited assembly determined to assert their right to territorial government and resolved to call for a convention of all the people.[53]

Before that plan could be put in action, some fertile intellect in the Sibley camp realized that here was an unprecedented opportunity. Such a convention not only would demonstrate the readiness of the population for territorial organization, but also could authorize an official representative to act in behalf of the citizens of Minnesota. Obviously its management could not be left to the storekeepers and traders of St. Pauls, who might well move to block participation from those on the Iowa side of the river. It would be better to hold the convention in Stillwater, where it was felt Sibley could expect to obtain support. Accordingly, on August 4 Sibley, Brown and Steele met in Stillwater with some of that city's most prominent businessmen – including Christopher Carli, Henry Moss, William Holcombe, Socrates Nelson, John McKusick and Anson Northrup – to draft a call for a full convention of all the citizens from both sides of the river. The eighteen signers describe themselves as "citizens of Minnesota Territory;" conspicuously absent are the names of David Lambert and other St. Paulites. The date of the convention is set for August 26, two days before public land sales are to begin in St. Croix Falls for tracts in the southern part of the county. The place is to be Stillwater, which will be a convenient stopping place for everyone planning to attend the land sales. The stated purpose is to "take steps to secure early territorial organization of Minnesota." There is no mention of a delegate being chosen.[54]

Anyone who has been following Brown's career thus far will see that this gambit has been used before. Back on the sixteenth of November 1839, the citizens about to be displaced from the reserve had met "pursuant to public notice" to take steps to assert their rights to claims on the reserve and had ended by appointing Brown their representative to the Wisconsin territorial legislature, authorizing him to use his best endeavors to procure needed legislation. It was the endorsement of that citizen's group that gave Brown an entrée to Madison and a very similar effort

---

53. There are several accounts of the St. Paul meeting that do not agree in particulars; some are probably confused with the later meeting on September 6. See Sibley "Reminiscences" 395; Williams *St. Paul* 181; W. B. Hennesey *Past and Present of St. Paul, Minnesota* 58 (Chicago 1906).

54. Documents relating to the convention are collected in "Organization of Minnesota Territory," *Minnesota Historical Collections* I: 33–46.(reprint St. Paul 1872) The originals of several documents are in the Sibley papers.

could propel Henry Sibley to Washington as the official representative of the disfranchised Minnesotans. Some misdirection was needed. William Holcombe, among others, thought the best case could be made for the continuance of Wisconsin territory. Someone took the trouble to convince him otherwise and persuaded him to sign the call. There was, of course, the convincing point that Congress was unlikely to appropriate funds for Wisconsin, or if they did, it might well be for a limited form of government without legislature or representative – a galling situation. Another consideration was that if Henry Jackson or Henry Rice were allowed to control a convention in St. Pauls, short shrift would be given to valley interests. It would be wise for influential St. Croix businessmen to take the lead in promoting the early organization of Minnesota territory and forget the red herring of Wisconsin. St. Croix businessmen got the picture.

At some time before the convention, Brown, Lambert and Sibley learned of Catlin's plan, which doesn't seem to have been formalized much before the end of July and could hardly have been conveyed to St. Pauls (mails taking between fifteen and eighteen days) before mid-month. The obvious response was to keep quiet about it and let the convention take place under the assumption the Wisconsin issue was dead. If Catlin did not put his scheme into action, Sibley was no worse off than before; if he did, the effect of the convention would have been to endorse Sibley as a candidate for delegate from Wisconsin. Providing Sibley with credentials to Washington, from whatever territory, was the primary consideration. Once he was admitted, he could work for the erection of Minnesota. When Catlin's plan became known, there would be no end of candidates; several men from the St. Croix were known to be eager to run, among them William Holcombe. Whigs would put up candidates just to oppose the Democrats. Henry Rice, Sibley's partner in the Chippewa and Winnebago Outfit, was most ambitious and would certainly come out if he thought there would be an election. As it was, Rice considered the Stillwater convention idea a waste of time, and although he was staying with Sibley at Mendota that summer, refused to attend. To Dousman he scoffed: "At the mass meeting held at Stillwater, I am told that there was only 38 persons present, a central and corresponding committee was appointed (God knows what for, I don't) and Mr. Sibley was appointed special agent to go to Washington and get the Territory organized (or baptized) I don't know which, but presume some great good will be the result."[55] He soon understood.

It is clear from the minutes preserved – taken by David Lambert – that Joseph R. Brown was the conductor and very likely the orchestrator of the "mass meeting." The delegates, in number somewhere between Rice's thirty-eight and Moss' estimate of one hundred, came from the upper Mississippi, St. Anthonys Falls, St. Pauls, Red Rock and Cottage Grove

_____

55. Rice to Dousman, Aug. 25, Sep. 1, 1848, Rice Letterbook, MHS.

as well as from the St. Croix valley. They assembled in the courtroom, McKusick's upper room, the morning of August 26, 1848.

Brown had the meeting well under control. He began by organizing a committee to select officers for the convention and another to draft a memorial to Congress for the early organization of the territory and "to report such further proceedings as they may think proper." Brown and Sibley sat on both committees. When the convention recessed for lunch, the memorial committee, consisting of Sibley, Henry Moss, Socrates Nelson, Calvin Leach, Morton S. Wilkinson and Henry Jackson with Brown as chairman, stayed behind to do its work. As Moss remembered it, "Mr. Lambert immediately submitted the draft of a preamble, series of resolutions and a petition to Congress which evidently had been prepared with careful deliberation." This is probably accurate. Lambert, while not a member of the committee, likely served as secretary, and had been given the draft copies, which we may assume had been prepared by Brown.

Figure 36 Stillwater's Minesota House at right and the St. Croix House at left were built before 1848 and probably housed some of the "delegates" to the Stillwater Convention. Photo by E. F. Everett taken in 1865. Washington Co. Hist. Soc.

That all was in readiness is evident; by half past one, the committee was ready to report four resolutions and two memorials – one to Congress and one to the President.[56]

Sibley, says Moss, informed the convention (although he must mean the committee) of his intention to spend the winter in Washington in the interests of the territorial movement, and suggested the adoption of a resolution requesting him to represent the people in their behalf, which he

56. Sixty-one people signed the memorial to President Polk, which was not presented. (Sibley papers); however, that may not represent actual attendance since the memorials were not forwarded to Sibley until the following Monday or later, having been held for signatures (Lambert to Sibley, Aug. 28, 1848, Sibley papers). Minutes of the meeting in Lambert's hand and a certificate of delegacy in Brown's are also in the Sibley papers. Quotations here and below from Moss "Early Days of Minnesota" 76, 79.

felt would give him more credibility in Washington. He also stated that his stay in the east would be at his own expense, and that he should ask contributions from no one. "A series of urgent resolutions was adopted authorizing him to go to Washington as the representative of the people," recalled Moss. The committee had been skillfully led to recommend the appointment of a delegate "with full power to act, whose duty it shall be to visit Washington during the ensuing session of Congress and there to represent the interest of the proposed Territory, and to urge an immediate organization of the same," and also a corresponding committee to keep in touch with him. The resolutions were quickly approved by the full convention, which then proceeded to chose a delegate. On the first ballot Henry Sibley had a majority and was, on motion of Joseph R. Brown, declared unanimously elected by the convention. Brown and P. A. R. Brace then retired to produce the convention's choice for an acceptance speech and, we may imagine, an enthusiastic round of hurrahs. A few more chores – Brown's motion to notify the newspapers of the convention's proceedings, the production of a certificate of accreditation for Sibley as the unanimously elected delegate of the people, the selection of a committee of correspondence to keep in touch with the delegate, the approval of Brown's motion to request the delegate cause the orthography "Minnesota" be used for the name of the territory, the signing of the memorials – and the convention adjourned "with much enthusiasm among all present for the work before them."

William Holcombe's enthusiasms were considerably dampened when just ten days later he received a letter from Catlin outlining his plan to proclaim an election. Being no fool, Holcombe realized that Brown and Sibley had been aware of Catlin's plans before the convention and had railroaded the participants into giving what now looked like an endorsement of Sibley for territorial delegate. As a signer of the petition, Holcombe could hardly withdraw his support to run himself. To Catlin he wrote:

> "Mr. Sibley seems to have been anxious for some time to procure Ter. organization & is willing to undertake his office at his own expense, & to procure his appointment got up the convention without intimating in the notice that a delegate was to be elected or appointed at that convention, but from the result & the movements that produced it, it is very evident the whole plan was concocted before he crossed the Mississippi river, as he brought about 30 Frenchmen who are entirely under his controul, being engaged in the fur trade, by which means got himself appointed – the people of this district having no notice of any such proceedings."

He added that although Sibley was no doubt very competent, the use of such tactics would make him unpopular.[57]

Holcombe chose to misunderstand Sibley's entourage. The thirty Frenchmen were not in evidence at the convention, nor did they sign the

---

57. Holcombe to Catlin, Sep. 5, 1848, Catlin papers.

memorials. Sibley, too, was en route to the land sales, where he had offered to bid in the claims of some of the original French-speaking settlers, and these, of course, accompanied him to ensure no opposition arose. (As they were reported to have been quite fierce at the land sales against anyone who might try to bid up their claims, they may have seemed threatening to Holcombe as well.) It seems fair to infer from Holcombe's remarks that he believed if the convention had known a legal election would soon be held, no delegate would have been appointed. As it was, the endorsement helped to override the erroneous notion held by many, including Holcombe, that a resident of Iowa was not eligible to run for office in Wisconsin and generally gave credibility to Sibley's candidacy.

So eager was Holcombe to effect a reorganization of the government and judicial system in St. Croix County, under which he felt the law could not be enforced, that he quickly espoused Catlin's plan to hasten territorial organization, even if it meant Sibley would be the delegate. On Lambert's advice he called a hurried meeting of Stillwater citizens on September 5 at which he read the opinions he had gathered from Catlin, Buchanan and "many other gentlemen" and asked for support for Catlin's plan. He got it in the form of a resolution that Tweedy be asked to resign and Catlin be asked to take up the duties of governor and proclaim a special election for delegate. Enclosing the proceedings of this meeting in a letter to Catlin, Holcombe was moved to explain the actions of the Stillwater convention, stating that that the time it was not supposed that any commission could be obtained for a delegate, nor was it known that Tweedy would resign. He assured Catlin that the people "will act under the contemplated proclamation."**58**

The following day, September 6, a second meeting was held in St. Pauls by Sibley and Lambert, who read the Catlin letter and Buchanan opinion to the assembly. This meeting, guided by Sibley, produced a similar set of resolutions, with one important addition: one clause stated that "no measures should be taken to procure the passage of an act for the separate government of Wisconsin, but that every means should be used to effect a full and complete organization of the Territory of Minnesota." Thus did Sibley tell Catlin that the Irvin plan to annex Minnesota was not going to fly. Since time was of the essence, and the boat for the Prairie was getting up steam on the levee (there was not even time for a copy to be made), it would have been pointless for Lambert to argue against the inclusion of the clause. Hastily scribbling a note to Catlin to accompany the resolutions, Lambert wrote: "There is no time for a general Territorial

---

58. Holcombe to Catlin, Sep. 5, 1848, enclosing minutes of the September 5 meeting erroneously dated August 5. In this copy the word August has been lined out and September substituted. This misdating has led to a lot of confusion, as the copy used to produce "Organization of Minnesota Territory" was evidently not corrected. In his letter dated Sep. 6, Holcombe writes: "Yours of 22nd ult. with the accompanying opinion of the Hon. Jas. Buchanan per the hand of J. Bowron Esq. was received early yesterday morning—a meeting of the citizens was immediately convened as you will find by the enclosed proceedings." As Buchanan had only written his opinion to Dodge on July 18, Catlin could hardly have been in possession of it July 22; therefore Catlin's letter must have been dated August 22.

convention, but I presume the action of the two most important towns in the Territory will be a sufficient warrant for you and Mr. Tweedy." He made no comment on the "Minnesota" resolution, but did feel the need to inform Catlin of the convention in Stillwater that had already "elected" Sibley to go to Washington on behalf of Minnesota, concluding "I take it for granted that if you issue the proclamation he will be the candidate for delegate to Congress and if so will be elected." In other words, Catlin was stuck with Sibley as the ball carrier and had been effectively out-flanked.[59]

He was also running out of time. Unable to act until he heard that Congress had adjourned, he could not reveal his plan to Holcombe – the chosen correspondent by virtue of his position as county clerk – until late August. About a week after posting his letter of August 22, and without waiting for reply from Holcombe, he wrote to Tweedy to ask for his resignation. The letter, misaddressed, did not reach Tweedy in Connecticut until mid-September; Tweedy's official resignation was tendered September 18. Meanwhile the prospect that Catlin would be paid for his efforts was beginning to look exceptionally dim. Moreover, the commissioner of Indian affairs had commandeered the papers of the Wisconsin superintendency, believing that office to have expired with the erection of the state, although Senator Dodge had given his opinion that an act of Congress was required to abolish the position claimed by Catlin. Still, it must have seemed worth a try. Armed with Tweedy's resignation, and with no time to spare, Catlin set off for Minnesota on October 3, arriving a week later, and immediately issued a proclamation for an election to be held October 30, thus giving the requisite twenty days notice. It was going to be close; navigation generally closed by mid-November, and Catlin had no intention of remaining in his hyperborean territory all winter.[60]

Electioneering had not waited on his arrival, but was in full swing by mid-September, a chief issue being the relocation of the land office. Rumors flew that Sibley was in the pocket of St. Paul boosters who wanted him in Washington to oppose the Stillwater petition for the land office. Brown sent word to Stillwater that if they preferred, Sibley would withdraw, and they could field their own candidate against Henry M. Rice, who had emerged the only other contender. That brought them quickly into line. Rice was considered a sure winner if Sibley withdrew, and was thought to be far less disinterested. It was too well known how he had managed the Winnebago removal to his own advantage, reserving the government jobs, contracts and licenses to those Norman Kittson called his "new creatures." From downriver came word that his supporters thought he had the governorship of the new territory sewed up.

Other candidates would appear if Sibley did not run. A disgruntled William Holcombe toyed with the idea of coming out as "the St. Croix

59. Lambert to Catlin, Sep. 6, 1848, enclosing minutes of September 6 meeting, Catlin papers.
60. Catlin to Tweedy, Aug, 20, Sep. 16, 1848 in Tweedy papers, microfilm in MHS; Dodge to Catlin, Sep. 26, 1848, Tweedy to Catlin, Sep. 18, 1848 in Catlin papers.

candidate," and Mort Wilkinson for a while favored a convention to bring out a popular Whig, perhaps Joshua Taylor of St. Croix Falls. But by September 20, Henry Moss could promise Sibley that measures would be taken to prevent Taylor from accepting such a nomination: "From present appearances, I can assure you that there will be no candidate upon the St. Croix, unless he comes out independent, and in that case his vote will be small and not affect you much." Moss proved right; the men who had chosen Sibley their spokesman in August felt now they owed him their support. As a friend later remarked, "After the proceedings of the convention held at Stillwater, it would have been treating you badly to take up another man and elect him over you."61

Rice, who had a good deal of support in St. Pauls and St. Anthonys Falls, as well as upriver, took his campaign to Stillwater with promises to get them the land office. By mid-October he was seen to be gaining ground. On October 20 Moss reported to Sibley that something was afoot that "smacks much of duplicity and treachery." This, it turned out, was the out-and-out purchase of Anson Northrup's hotel by Rice's man, John Banfil, and, reported Moss, "I am told that Mr. N. is now in favor of Mr. Rice." A few days later Wilkinson defected from the Sibley camp; according to Dr. Carli, Wilkinson and Holcombe were sitting around counting votes. Carli urged Sibley to take a stand on the land office question. He could not take a stand on a party platform since he had run as a neutral, saying the need for organization of the territory transcended party politics; although he was believed to have Whiggish principles he knew he could not win if he declared himself a Whig – "Hence the necessity to remain mum," as a Rice backer put it.62

But Joseph R. Brown could count votes, too, and he knew Stillwater was safe. Out of 80-odd votes, Rice would get no more than 35. What worried him was the possibility of fraud at Crow Wing, where Rice had imported some forty or fifty voters. At Rice's insistence, new precincts were established at Crow Wing and Sauk Rapids. Catlin was also pressured by Rice to relax the voting challenge so as to admit the unnaturalized French population as well as Rice's men, many of whom were British citizens. Sibley objected to the irregularly established precincts; he wanted the election to be strictly "legal" to forestall any challenge. He also objected to allowing the "alien" vote, but there he felt on shaky ground, because he feared the opposition would use against him any refusal to allow these voters. He was naturally perfectly aware that Brown's efforts had already legitimized much of the French vote in St. Pauls and lower St. Croix County, all of whom would support him.

61. Letters to Sibley from Jacob Fisher, Sep. 24; Henry Moss, Sep. 20; Norman Kittson, Aug. 16; C. S. Whitney, Dec. 30, 1848; Sibley papers. Many other letters in the Sibley collection also refer to the election.

62. Letters to Sibley from J. B. Covey, Oct. 9; Moss, two letters dated Oct. 20; Carli, Oct. 21; W. H. Forbes, Oct. 23, 1848; Sibley papers; William D. Phillips to Robert Smith, Nov. 16, 1848, in Phillips file, general records of the department of state, applications and recommendations for public office.

Catlin, who was mainly interested in getting as large a voter turnout as possible, went along with the new precincts and voter qualifications.63

Brown, who had so far foreseen the situation as to have given his place or residence as Crow Wing in August when he signed the petition to the president, must have expected no less. Someone saw to it that Brown was appointed an election judge at Crow Wing. Someone saw also that Catlin's only official act, other than proclaiming the election, was to issue Joseph R. Brown a permit to cut timber in Chippewa country on the upper Mississippi, even though by no stretch of the imagination could Wisconsin territory's superintendent of Indian affairs (if indeed Catlin held that office) have any jurisdiction whatsoever in Iowa territory (provided either political entity existed).64 Nevertheless, a week before the election, Brown was on his way to Crow Wing.

On the eve of the election, a disquieting communiqué arrived at the home of J. W. Furber, which happened to be the place of election for Lake St. Croix precinct. It was from Brown, on his way to Crow Wing, who reported he had heard at Sauk Rapids that Rice's true plan was to confine the new territory to the east side of the Mississippi and the white settlements below Rum River "so that white settlements will not trample on the Indian trade and competition can be kept away." One of Rice's friends, he said, had told him that Rice would advocate locating the land office, as well as the territorial capital and the county seat of a new county that would be organized west of Red Rock, at Rice's claim near the cave (Dayton's Bluff), where he intended to build a new town. Declared Brown:

> "It appears to me this does not fit the professions of his friends down with you, but then, if he said so there he could expect no votes. Here the interests of his supporters are identified with his own, and he can give his views without danger. And this has long been my impression. It was the interest of Dousman & Rice to have the state line at Rum River, to prevent the organization of a new Territory. Is it then reasonable to suppose that if elected, Mr. Rice will go diametrically against his best interests, and through patriotism and love of the people support measures that will materially injure his business prospects? I for one do not believe he will, and the views he expresses here are those he will endeavor to carry out."

As further proof that Rice was not to be trusted, Brown said he understood that Mr. Myrick (Nathan Myrick, of the Sauk Rapids trading firm of Myrick, Sloan and Rice) had tried to buy out a trader there named Poncin, but had been unsuccessful until a few days earlier when, while Rice and Dousman were there, Winnebagoes had robbed the man and threatened his life. Rice had told him the leader of the renegades had killed several families in Iowa "and this was about the time he should have another fit" and so Poncin had sold to Myrick at half the value "and it bears monopoly on the face of it." Arriving, as it did, on the eve of the

---

63. Lambert to Sibley, Oct. 12; Sibley to Lambert, Oct. 12; Henry Jackson to Sibley, Oct. 14; Sibley to Jackson, Oct. 14; Moss to Sibley, Oct. 20, 1848; Sibley papers.

64. Catlin to Buchanan, Nov. 6, 1848; Catlin papers.

polls opening, this last-minute smear campaign would have swung any undecided voters. Rice got no votes in that precinct.**65**

Was that letter merely an insurance policy, or were similar epistles sent to Stillwater, Marine, St. Pauls and St. Anthonys? Others have not been found, but it would have been like Brown to sit up all night writing them. Any effect on the actual outcome of the election would have been minimal; more effective, no doubt, were the usual election-day tactics that prevailed at St. Anthonys Falls, and probably elsewhere, of buying votes and befuddling the voters with free whiskey (one Sibley supporter apologized for the results at St. Anthonys Falls: "We should have done better but they commenced buying votes in the morning"). At Crow Wing, where Sibley lost 12 to 44, someone, probably Brown, threatened to have the entire election thrown out because of the irregular establishment of the precinct and a plethora of imported votes.

Sibley need not have worried. He won handily, losing only two precincts, by a vote of 236 to 122 for Rice and a smattering for Socrates Nelson of Stillwater. Within a week, Sibley was on his way to Washington, and his political career was off and running. By the time he returned the following April, the bill creating the new territory of Minnesota had been passed and Henry Sibley, to whom all credit for that feat was given, deserved or not, was probably the best-known man in the territory. Thanks were due his campaign manager, Joseph R. Brown. After nearly thirty years in the wilderness, Brown found "civilization" growing up around him. He was thoroughly educated in the ways of frontier politics, content to use Sibley and others to further his designs for the new country and perfectly positioned to reap the harvest of his long apprenticeship. With irrepressible good humor and unbounded optimism, Joseph R. Brown looked forward to a lucrative and satisfying future.**66**

---

65. Brown to Joseph W. Furber, Oct. 26, 1848, in Furber papers, MHS.

66. William Dugas to W. H. Forbes, Oct. 31, 1848. As soon as the polls closed a petition was got up by Rice supporters to Catlin pleading that the vote at Crow Wing be counted (John H. McKenny to Catlin, Oct. 30, 1848, Catlin papers). The abstract of votes, also in the Catlin papers, is as follows:

Name of precinct	H. H. Sibley	H. M. Rice	Socrates Nelson
Stillwater	57	26	0
Marine Mills	37	0	0
Rice River (Nelson Lumber Camp)	0	0	19
Lake St. Croix	47	0	0
St. Pauls	59	14	0
St. Anthonys Falls	12	30	0
Sauk Rapids	12	8	0
Crow Wing	12	44	0
Total	236	122	19
Total Votes	377		

APPENDIX A: GENEALOGY

THE ANCESTRY AND FAMILY OF JOSEPH R. BROWN

JOSEPH R. BROWN'S PATERNAL GRANDPARENTS

Joseph's paternal grandfather, Solomon Brown, was born in Scotland in 1729, immigrated to New Jersey c. 1750 and by 1760 had moved to Harford County, Maryland. He bought a farm on the headwaters of Little Gunpowder Falls River just south of Black Horse named 'Poteet's Pleasure' and added to it over the years. Solomon died in Harford County in 1803, is buried at Bethel Presbyterian, Madonna, Maryland. He married twice. His first wife, Huldah Smith, daughter of Ralph and Huldah Smith of Baltimore County, died sometime after 1773; she was of English extraction. Her five children (presumed order of birth deduced from estate distribution) were:

- John, born in Harford in 1761, died in 1855 in Wellsburg, Brooks County, West Virginia. He was a millwright and owned a farm near Bethany, West Virginia. His one daughter Margaret (1791–1827) by his first wife Eliza Ann Grimes (d. 1791), married Alexander Campbell, founder of a sect called the Campbellites or Disciples of Christ. After Eliza's death, John married Anna (Ann), widow of Samuel Glass.
- James, about whom nothing is known except that he went to "the west country," is possibly the James who married Hannah Hitchcock in Harford County in 1780.
- Mary, married to John Chambers, moved with or soon after John to Bethany, where she and her husband were members of the same congregation.
- Thomas, born c. 1768 in Harford, moved to Baltimore City where he set up as a cooper and where, in 1816, he died of the effects of wounds received in War of 1812. He was buried at Bethel Church. He was married, left a wife, Rebecca, and children (unnamed) who may have died young as the family believed he had no issue.
- Solomon, Jr., born c. 1771 in Harford, died in 1813 in Baltimore as a "result of wounds received defending Baltimore," leaving his second wife, Mary, and no offspring. He was a carpenter, is buried at Bethel.

Solomon Brown's second wife was Althea Foster who was 18 years his junior (born 1747). Her family is said to have been Welsh, and has not been traced, but there are several Fosters in the Baltimore/Harford County area. She died in 1815 and is buried at Bethel Church. Her four children were:

- Holliday (or Huldah), born c. 1780, who married Edward M. Guyton, son of Joshua and Elizabeth Guyton, in 1810. She died two years later leaving one daughter, Sarah (1811–1861), who died unmarried. (Guyton remarried, had a large family, was the person called 'Uncle Ed' by the Hendersons. He was said to have at one time owned the farm on which JRB was raised, that is, 'Poteet's Pleasure.')
- Margaret, born 1782. She married Robert T. Henderson in 1806 and they ran the Brown farm until her mother died; Henderson then bought it from the estate. Several of their nine children were good friends of Joe Brown. Margaret died in 1857. She is the aunt who raised Joe Brown and for whom he named the town of Henderson. Brown's cousins were John Brown 1807–1808, Andrew 1809–1873, John B. 1811–1908, David 1814–1897, Eleanor b. 1816, Robert 1819–1831, Thomas 1821–1905, Huldah 1824–1855, Archibald 1829–1831.
- Samuel, Joseph's father and youngest son of Solomon Brown, born c. 1785 in Harford County, died in 1828 in Girard, Erie County, Pennsylvania.
- Martha, born c. 1787, died in 1815 unmarried and is buried at Bethel Church.[1]

JOSEPH R. BROWN'S MATERNAL GRANDPARENTS

Joe Brown's maternal grandfather, Joseph Renshaw Junior, was born in 1746 in St. George's parish near Perryman, Maryland. Sometime before his marriage he purchased or took over the farm originally patented by his uncle John in 1750 in Bush Hundred. He was a loyalist officer in the revolution, signed the oath of loyalty to the crown in 1777, but later accepted a commission in the colonists' militia. He was a son of Joseph Renshaw Senior (c. 1718–1809) and Elizabeth Wells (c. 1718-1831) who were married in St. George's parish in 1742, and grandson of Thomas Renshaw and Jane Cole Renshaw. Thomas Renshaw, who died in 1751, was of English ancestry, appeared in Baltimore County c. 1710 and is a possible descendent of the Joseph Renshaw who came to Jamestown in 1681, died 1715.

Joseph Renshaw Junior married at least twice (dates uncertain and birth dates of children unknown), the first wife being Elizabeth Hughes, daughter of John Hughes and Elizabeth Norris. Their children were:

---

1. Information derived from Henderson papers, MD Historical Society, Baltimore; will and estate of Solomon Brown, Bel Air, Harford County, MD; estate settlement of Solomon Brown Junior, Baltimore County, MD; Bethel Presbyterian Church records, Madonna, MD; federal tax list, Maryland state records, Annapolis, MD; collections of W.T. Phillips Memorial Library, Bethany, WV; Brown papers, MHS; and genealogical information from Brown family members.

- Harriet S., who was still living in 1870. There is no evidence she ever married. She was cut out of her father's 1830 will with the remark, "(she) had so little affection for me that I think twenty-five cents is as much as she deserves." This is probably the aunt Joe found living in Baltimore in 1841.
- Fanny (Francis), who married John Johnson, "a drunken, dissapated" Irish weaver, in 1809. She was also cut out of her father's will.
- Emily, Joseph R. Brown's mother, who married Samuel Brown c. 1804 and died only a year or two later in or near York, Pennsylvania.
- Otho N. (Norris?) was his father's sole heir. He was married and had four children.

Joseph Renshaw Junior's second wife (married c. 1808) was Naomi Calder, a widow with grown children. **2**

JOSEPH R. BROWN'S HALF BROTHERS AND SISTERS

Samuel Brown married twice. His first wife, Emily Renshaw, daughter of Joseph Renshaw Junior, was the mother of Joseph Renshaw Brown. She died c. 1806 in Pennsylvania. The second wife was Mary, born 1788, the daughter of Valentine and Catherine Hart of Martic Township, Lancaster County, Pennsylvania. After Samuel's death in 1828, Mary married a widower, Colonel James Hall, a veteran of the War of 1812. On his death in 1838 she moved to Chicago, then to Minnesota with some of her children. She died in Red Wing in 1866. She and Brown had ten children:

- Solomon, born in 1810 in Conestoga township, Lancaster County, moved to Lower Canada (Ontario) where he married Elizabeth (unknown), lived in Maryland and Pennsylvania before finally moving in 1853 to Minnesota. He was school superintendent at the Yellow Medicine agency in 1860, a photographer in Henderson in the 1870s. He died in 1881 in St. Peter, Minnesota.
- Jeremiah, born in 1812 was a painter and probably a Mexican War vet as he had free land in Texas in 1850s. In Kentucky he married an Irish girl, Mary (born c. 1840), about 1857 moved to Keokuk, Iowa, where he was a sign and house painter.
- Mary was a milliner. According to Lydia Carli she was crippled and never married and probably remained in Erie County.
- John Wesley was born in 1816 near Columbia, Hempfield township, Lancaster County, and came to Minnesota in 1842. He lived some time at Grey Cloud, Eagan and Red Wing, where he

2. Will and estate settlement of Joseph Renshaw Senior and Junior, Harford County records, Bel Air, MD; Grace Parke Renshaw *Renshaw Reflections* (1983); federal tax list, Harford County, MD; records of Spesutie Church, Harford County, MD; Harford county land records, Bel Air; Brown papers; and information from Brown family members.

died in 1903. John was asked to run for the territorial legislature in 1849 but refused. He married Mary Mooers, daughter of Hazen and Margaret Aird Mooers (Marpiyarotawin or Grey Cloud).

- Lydia Ann was born in 1818 near Lancaster City. She moved, she said, with her family at age 7 to Girard (now Fairfield) township, Erie County. Lydia went to Chicago with a wagon train from Springfield in 1834, and there married Paul Carli (born 1804 in Germany). They moved in 1839 to Fox River, Wisconsin, to Dacotah in 1841, to Afton (St. Mary's Point) in 1843. Paul drowned in the St. Croix in 1846 and Lydia married Dr. Christopher Carli, Paul's brother, in an 1847 ceremony performed by Joseph R. Brown, J.P. She died in Stillwater in 1904.
- Samuel Fletcher was born in 1820 in Pennsylvania. He was apprenticed to a tailor, came with his sister's family to Stillwater in 1841, joined Joe in the fur trade in 1842. He set up as tailor in St. Paul in 1849, in partnership with P. K. Johnson. He married Hepzibah Maria Snow in St. Paul c. 1850; they later divorced. His son Joseph Henderson (born 1855) was one of first children born in Henderson. He later married Sarah Otis and moved to Blakely, MN, where he kept a tavern.
- Wilson went as an acolyte to the Methodists (in Erie) and the family never heard of him again.
- Florence is mentioned only in a list given by John Wesley, and probably died in infancy.
- Welsley died in childhood
- Nathaniel Reeder, born in Erie County in 1827, was nine months old at time of his father's death. He came to Minnesota in 1841 with Lydia Ann and his mother, joined Joe in the fur trade in 1846. He was married to Mary Dixon of Sibley County in 1860, may also have been father of mixed blood children Lydia Ann and William Brown. Family letters refer to a daughter of his by a woman named Anita. (In 1915 a Berdie Brown Williams tried to get an allotment, saying she was the daughter of Lydia Ann Brown, a half blood, and granddaughter of Nathaniel Brown and Winopeska). Nathaniel (Than) was an army contractor in Dakota territory in 1880, had then a white family living in the states (no mother listed). He must have remarried as he left a widow who died in 1902. **3**

JOSEPH R. BROWN'S WIVES

Joseph R. Brown married three times. He wed his first wife, Helen Dickson, in Prairie du Chien in 1825 and divorced her in District Court, Wisconsin Territory, in 1834. Their one son, Solomon W. D. Brown, died

---

3. Brown papers, MHS; census records and city directories; John Fletcher Williams papers, MHS: John Case papers, MHS, and article in *Hastings Gazette* Dec. 4, 1920; various cemetery records.

at the Choctaw Academy. Brown married Margaret McCoy, a part-Chippewa and daughter of his foreman Francis McCoy, in June 1836 at Mendota and obtained a divorce from her in 1840 from the Wisconsin Legislature, which was finalized in District Court in 1842. He began living with Susan Frénière in 1835, but waited until 1850 to marry her before a Justice of the Peace in St. Paul. He had one son by Helen who died in childhood, two daughters by Mary, and twelve children in total by Susan – eight of whom survived childhood.

HELEN DICKSON

Brown's earliest marriage produced important ties, some of which persisted after his divorce. His marriage to Helen Dickson in 1825 allied him to the Sisseton. Helen's mother was Totowin or Ixtatowin (Green Eyed Woman), also known as Elizabeth Winona, a sister (or possibly niece) of Wakinyanduta, (Red Thunder, also known as Capa, the Beaver). Wakinyanduta was of Sisseton lineage descended from Wasuboide (Fans Blaze) and supposed to have fathered Waneta (Charger). Helen's father was Colonel Robert Dickson, a Scot who came to Canada about 1781 and for many years traded from Prairie du Chien and on the upper Minnesota River for various Canadian firms. Dickson and Elizabeth were married in Indian fashion about 1795, and by a priest May 6, 1818. Helen's mother was supposed part white: she was very small and fair-complected. Her father was very tall, over 6 foot and 200 pounds; because of his red-blonde hair the Indians called him in French Faites Jaune (Yellow Crest) and in Dakota Pahaxaxa (Red Head).

Helen Dickson had three siblings (one report says five, but no trace has been found of any others): William (Magaxa or Red Bird) was the eldest (born about 1798) and was a licensed trader on the upper Minnesota River in 1816. He was married three times, first to a Chippewa, then to a Laframboise, finally to a Yankton woman; he died in 1841. Helen was the second child, born in 1808. The third was Thomas (born 1812) who never married, became a trader and interpreter and was killed near Fort Union in 1832. The youngest was Mary (born 1814) who married Henry Angé, a grandson of Wabasha, and had a large family. Helen and Joe were married eight years but apparently lived apart many of them; they had one son, Solomon W. D. Brown (surely the initials stand for William Dickson), born in 1826. Helen had other children. She was living on the Sheyenne with her 'little son' in 1839 (father unnamed); she also had at least two more children from her marriage to Moses Arconge, an AMF engagé.4

---

4. Tohill papers, MHS; records of St. Gabriel's parish, Prairie du Chien, WI; Grace L. Nute, ed., *Documents Relating to Northwest Missions* 1815–1827 (1942); Louis Tohill "Robert Dickson"; Brown vs Brown, Oct. 1833, Michigan territorial circuit court files, WHS Platteville, WI; Choteau papers, St. Louis; census records.

MARGARET MCCOY

Margaret (diminutive Mary) McCoy's father Francis (born c. 1782) was supposed to have come to the St. Croix country from the Red River about 1830. There is some evidence that her mother's maiden name was Margarette Cadotte. Francis McCoy worked for Joe Brown from the early 1830s, was left in charge of the Hastings trading post site during the 1840s, later retired to a small farm in eastern Washington County. Margaret 'Mary' Brown was the oldest child and was born at Red River, as were brothers Francis and Antoine c. 1820 and 1828; Joseph was born near Fort Snelling about 1834. Mary and JRB had two daughters, the eldest, Margaret, born in 1835, married one of Joe's boatmen, Marcelle Vervier dit Courturier and lived on Grey Cloud Island in 1847 when she was only twelve years old. She died in 1887. Mary, born in 1838, married Matthew Jerdine in 1853, is said to have also married Henry Bunnell.[5]

SUSAN FRÉNIÈRE

Susan's mother Madeleine Crawford, called in Dakota Mazardewin or Tinkling Iron, was generally known as Winona (the Dakota name for a first-born daughter) and later by her baptismal name of Abigail. She was born c. 1805, probably in Red Wing's village on the Mississippi, to Mazadehdegawin, a daughter of Tatankamani (Walking Buffalo), chief Red Wing, and British Captain Lewis Crawford, son of William Redford Crawford of Kingston, Ontario. Winona was therefore of the Mdewakanton band. The lineage of the chiefs known as Red Wing is obscure, but her grandfather was probably Red Wing I (c. 1745–1829) later known as Xakea (Xakiya? To Paint Red), and her father Red Wing II who took the name Tatankamani when he became chief. Winona had six children, but only the one child, Susan, with her first husband Narcisse Frénière. She bore Susan on Christmas Day 1819 and parted from Frénière shortly thereafter. A few years later she married Victor Renville (Ohiye or Tamazakanhotanka), who was a brother of the trader Joseph Renville, and by him had two girls – Leader of the Wind who died young and a baby girl who died in infancy – and one son, Gabriel Renville (Tiwakan), born in 1825. Victor died in 1832 and Winona then married Akipa (Meeting) whose full name was Tacandupahotanka (His Big-voiced Pipe), a brother of Mazaxa (Red Iron) and Mazomani (Iron Walker) and had by him two boys, Thomas Renville Crawford and Charles Renville Crawford.[6] These last two boys were therefore grandsons of the

5. Brown papers, ABCFM papers, Case papers, MHS; Case articles in *Hastings Gazette* Jan. 1 1926, and in *Minnesota Historical Collections* XV; census records; article on Courturier in *St. Paul Pioneer Press* May 27, 1894; Dakota County and Ramsey County marriage records, Washington County death records.

6. S. J. Brown to Doane Robinson Mar. 12, 1921 and Jul. 28, 1904 in Robinson papers, South Dakota Historical Society, Pierre, SD; Brown papers, MHS; Victor Renville "A Sketch of the Minnesota Massacre" in *Collections of the North Dakota Historical Society*: Vol V.

Wahpeton chief Tankamani (Big Walker) whose village was in historic times near Traverse des Sioux. Gabriel was, however, related to Little Crow, because Mineyuhe, his father's mother, was a woman of Little Crow's village on the Mississippi and his grandfather Joseph Rainville, an early trader with the Sioux. (Akipa called himself Joseph Akipa Renville and also gave his sons the Renville name, but Samuel J. Brown says he was a full blood Wahpeton, so this was likely a gesture of respect or admiration). The Brown children called Akipa "grandfather." Winona Crawford died in 1897 and is buried at Goodwill, SD.

Winona's father, Lewis Crawford, was a General Society trader and later had the rank of Captain in the British army. He abandoned his trade at Prairie du Chien to return to St. Joseph's Island, Canada, where in 1806 he married Jesse, daughter of Dr. David Mitchell and Elizabeth Bertrand, an Ottawa woman. After the War of 1812 he left the U.S. permanently. Winona also had half siblings in Prairie du Chien: before 1805 Crawford had married Pelagie Lapointe, whose father was Pierre Lapointe and whose mother was a daughter of chief Wabasha. This marriage produced a son, Lewis Crawford, and a daughter, Pelagie, who married Antoine Burch dit Lachapelle. Winona moved with her mother to the Big Stone Lake area shortly before the war; there Mazadehdegawin married Makaayoncitamani. Julia Hazatainwin, Winona's half sister and the Brown family's "Aunt Judy," was born to them near the coteau in 1813.[7]

Susan's father, Narcisse Frénière (Cekpa or Twin), had at least two other wives. His children by a woman of the Elm River Yanktonai were Daniel Antoine (Sataka), Anthony (Yonka) and a daughter who married the trader Francis Chardon. At least two other offspring, Thomas and Narcisse, were his sons by another Yanktonai woman. These last two died young, but did have families. Daniel Antoine (called 'Uncle Antoine' by the Brown children) did not marry, but had a least two illegitimate sons, Thomas and Antoine. Although it was rumored that Narcisse had died on the Missouri River in 1838, that Frénière was his son Yonka. It may have suited some folks to have Narcisse be thought dead. Narcisse died in 1858.

Narcisse's twin brother, François, also married into the Sisseton. His sons were Louis (born c. 1812 and died in a scrap in 1839), Xavier (Pejiskaya) and Narcisse (Maza). François also had several daughters: Marguerite (married Baptiste Peloquin) Angelique (married Jean Rousseau), Rosalie (married Pierre Felix) and Josette. A third brother, Louison (the one who accompanied Nicollet), had at least two wives and many offspring. Their father is presumed to be the Charles Jacques Fresniere (Venire) who traded with the Sisseton in the 1780s and was married to a daughter of Tokokotipixni (He Who Fears Nothing), then one

---

7. John Askin papers, Burton Historical Records II, Detroit; BIA records, Goodwill, SD.

of the most powerful Yankton chiefs. It is likely François and Narcisse were born about 1790; Louison may have been younger.[8]

There is some confusion about the relationship of Winona Crawford to Waanatan. Blanche Allanson Merkle (Winona Crawford's great-great-granddaughter) believed that Winona was a "daughter of Waanatan of the Red Thunder dynasty." However, her uncle Samuel J. Brown said the relationship was that Waanatan's wife was a sister or cousin of Winona's mother, Mazadehdegawin. At other times he said a sister or cousin of Mazdehdegawin married a relative of Wamdiupiduta (Scarlet Plume, the Sisseton chief) and it was her daughter who married Waanatan. One of Sammie's versions is likely to be right. Gabriel Renville was said to be a nephew of Wamdiupiduta. Waanatan (Little Charger) was born about 1830, a son of Waneta (Charger), the powerful chief of the Pabaksa (Cuthead Yanktonai) who died in 1840, and grandson of Wakinyanduta I (Red Thunder, killed by the Chippewa in 1821). His mother was a Sisseton related to Tatankanajin (Standing Buffalo).[9]

With Joseph R. Brown's marriage to Susan Frénière he became a relative of all of the above people, as well as of many other cousins and siblings of whom we have little or no information. These relationships were extremely important to a trader; as he was expected to take care of his wife's family, so they were obligated to back and protect him. Susan Brown died in 1904 and is buried at Goodwill.

THE CHILDREN OF JOSEPH R. BROWN

From a Brown family Bible that belonged to Mrs. Allanson that she made available to W. W. Folwell. He notes that the original is JRB's hand.

- Solomon W. D. Brown, son of Joseph R. Brown and Helen Brown, born Dec. 26, 1826, at St. Peters, died Feb. 1841 at Choctaw Academy.
- Margaret Brown, daughter of Joseph R. and Margaret Brown, born Nov. 14, 1835 at St. Peters. (Was married to Marcell Courterier – this last added by WWF)
- Lydia Ann Brown, daughter of J. R. Brown and Susan Frenier. Born at Lake Travers Nov. 21, 1836. (Died Nov. 188(?) – last statement is WWF)
- Angus Mitchell Anderson Brown, son of J. R. Brown and Susan Frenier. Born at Grey Cloud Island the 14th day of August, 1838. (Died Sept. 1886 – added in pencil by WWF)
- Mary Brown, daughter of Margaret Brown and Joseph R. Brown. Born at St. Peters May 14, 1838.

---

8. *Michigan Pioneer and Historical Collections* XI and XXIII.

9. Blanche Allanson *Indian Moons* (1927); Robinson papers, SDHS, Pierre, SD; Hughes *Indian Chiefs of Southern Minnesota*.

- Ellen Brown, daughter of J. R. Brown and Susan Frenier. Born at Chanwaukan, Jan. 2, 1841.
- Harriet Cordelia Brown, born on Cheyenne River April 5, 1843, died at Dakota (St. Croix) August 5, 1844. (Mother not named – WWF)
- Samuel Jno. Brown, son of Joseph R. Brown and Susan Frenier. Born on Coteau des Prairies, head of St. Peters, Mar. 7, 1845. (Died Aug. 29, 1925 – WWF).
- Amanda and Emily Brown, twin daughters of Joseph R. Brown and Susan Frenier, born at Dakota (head of Lake St. Croix) Sep. 6, 1847.
- Marie Augusta Brown, daughter of J. R. Brown and Susan F. Brown, born in St. Paul (Minnesota Ter'y) June 23, 1850.

This Bible record leads to the inescapable conclusion that it was written by Brown himself, probably at the time of presentation of the Bible, which may have been at his and Susan's wedding in 1850. There is no reason to doubt any of the birth dates.

Susan Frénière Brown gave birth to twelve children, eight girls and four boys. A list of Susan's heirs prepared about 1917 for the settlement of her mother's estate agrees with this, and indicates that twin girls were born between Ellen and Samuel, both of whom died in infancy. This gap coincides with the birth of Harriet Cordelia in 1843, noted by JRB in the Brown family bible. An oddity is that for all the other children listed both parents' names are given, but not for Harriet. This might lead to the conclusion that Joe did not care to name the infant's mother, but it is most likely that as this child was dead, he did not feel the information was needed. It is also true that he did not note the birth of the other girl baby, whether Harriet's twin or not. Samuel Brown agreed that his mother had eight girl children, but says the two who did not live were single births, one between Angus and Ellen and one between Ellen and himself. Although certainly possible, as there are 27 months between Angus and Ellen, it is less likely. Samuel and the other children living in 1897 were born years after these babies died and therefore did not have direct knowledge of what happened – possibly Gabriel Renville supplied the BIA with the correct dates.

Samuel J. Brown (he changed his name from John to Jerome) produced this list of his siblings for Warren Upham in 1923:

- Lydia Ann, born 1836, died 1885.
- Angus Mitchell Anderson, born Aug. 24, 1837 at Medicine Wood.
- Ellen, born Jan. 2, 1841 at Medicine Wood.
- Samuel Jerome, born Mar. 7, 1845 (note: the Indians say it should be one year earlier).
- Amanda Cecelia, twin, born at Dakotah Sep. 6, 1847.
- Emily Mary Ann, twin, born at Dakotah Sep. 6, 1847.

- Augusta, born in St. Paul July 24, 1850.
- Joseph Renshaw, born on St. Paul's west side about 1853.
- Sibley Henderson, born in Henderson in 1855.
- Susan Frenier, born at Yellow Medicine, 1857 or 1858.

In addition, BIA records yield this information:

- Sibley H. Brown died in 1863, age 7.
- Susan F. Brown died in 1863, age 4.**10**

---

10. Information compiled from: Brown Bible; S. J. Brown to Warren Upham, Jun 1, 1923, historical information files, MHS; probate of Abigail Crawford, file #3732, BIA records, Sisseton, SD.

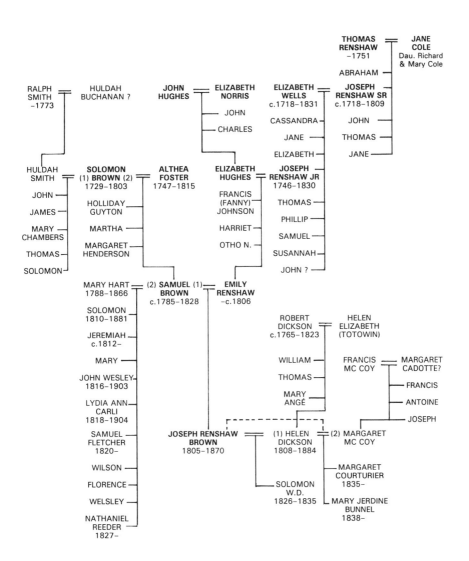

SUSAN FRÉNIÈRE BROWN'S FAMILY TREE
& The Children of Her Marriage

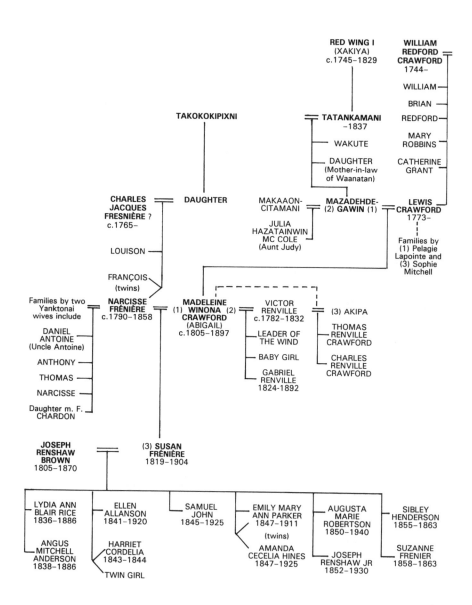

APPENDIX B:

THE WEST OF 1820

Although at the end of the American Revolution the Northwest Territory was ceded to the United States by Great Britain, British influence over its aboriginal inhabitants remained unbroken. The Louisiana Purchase added the land as far west as the Rocky Mountains to United States territory; however, the boundary between Canada and the United States was not well defined and, in any case, could not be defended. Exploration of this vast possession had scarcely begun – Lewis and Clark had ascended the Missouri to its headwaters and Zebulon Pike had explored the Mississippi as far north as Cass Lake by 1806 and obtained the land on which Fort Snelling would be built – when the festering war with the British broke out again, preventing further attention being given to what John Quincy Adams called America's "howling wilderness." During the War of 1812 many of the Indians had been enlisted as British allies. They had been promised by their traders that their hunting lands would be protected if they backed the British, and their loyalties were very strong, especially since few Americans had penetrated to the upper Mississippi and Missouri rivers.

The Treaty of Ghent in December of 1814 crushed British and Indian hopes alike. The British had intended to set aside land for their Indian allies to serve as a buffer zone between the countries and to enable the powerful Canadian fur trading companies to continue their exploitation. The United States intended to acquire and colonize the Indian lands when the population demanded it: to many, the extermination of the Indian's way of life was inevitable, a matter of time, until the tide of western expansion should roll over them. "Foreigners," by which were meant British traders, were excluded from participation in the lucrative fur and hide trade to protect American economic interests, such as the American Fur Company; however, in 1820 the Hudson's Bay Company was openly operating posts at the Grand Forks of the Red River, Red Lake and Lake Traverse (225 miles south of the present boundary) and were considered a source of constant menace. Having disappointed their Indian allies (and in many areas having overharvested the animals, leading to depleted profits) British traders resorted to ever more lavish gifts, including liquor, to placate the hunters and exhort them to greater efforts.

As much as was possible, the United States government took advantage of the disaffection of some Indians with their former allies to win them over to the American side with presents and promises and treaties of friendship. They even, somewhat belatedly, paid the Sioux for the cession made to Pike in 1805. One result of American and eastern Canadian expansion was the displacement of many Indian nations to the west with the further predictable result that bloody fights over greatly depleted hunting grounds became more and more frequent. All these factors served to crystallize United States policy.

U.S. military strategy after the war was aimed at controlling the trade routes through the Great Lakes and the Mississippi by means of strategically placed forts, which could protect American traders and drive out those being supplied from British Canada, counteract the British influence over the tribes of the upper Mississippi, and keep peace between warring tribes. For the time being, no settlers were allowed, but ultimately the forts would serve to encourage expansion while providing future settlements with protection from attacks by Indians (or by the British, with whom another war was thought to be likely). Indian agencies and factories were to be established at these forts to oversee the conversion of the indigenous people into "civilized" agriculturists. President Monroe's message to Congress in 1818 makes the mission perfectly clear: "to civilize [the Indians], even to prevent their extinction, it seems indispensable that their independence as communities should cease, and that the control of the United States over them should be complete and undisputed. The hunter state will then be more easily abandoned and recourse will be had to the acquisition and culture of land..."

To implement these policies, a line of frontier forts had been established at Mackinac Island (Michigan), Green Bay and Prairie du Chien (Wisconsin), and Warsaw and Rock Island (Illinois) to supplement the older Fort Dearborn at Chicago, Fort Shelby at Detroit and Fort Gratiot on Lake Huron. From these bases in 1819, two armies were sent out, one up the Missouri to establish frontier posts at the mouth of the Yellowstone and at the Mandan villages, the other up the Mississippi to the mouth of the St. Peters, the site selected by Pike in 1805. In the summer of 1820 when Joe Brown arrived on the scene, General Atkinson and the first prong had not be able to advance further than the Council Bluffs on the Missouri, establishing there Camp Missouri (later Fort Atkinson), but Colonel Leavenworth had, after much delay, reached the mouth of the St. Peters and was making plans to build a permanent fortification to serve as Regimental Headquarters.

Lewis Cass, Michigan Territorial Governor and Superintendent of Indian Affairs, negotiated with the Saulteurs (Ojibwe) that summer to acquire a site for a fourth post at Sault Ste. Marie, then proceeded through Chippewa country to the Mississippi, making the American presence felt and attempting to promote peace between Chippewa and Sioux. Cass and other government officials tended to attribute the attacks made by Sioux, Fox, Sac and Winnebago on Americans during 1819-1820 to the influence of British agents among them, but a far more pressing cause of their restiveness was the presence of the American military itself. The army had come in force to Indian country – something that had never happened in all the years of the French and British regimes – and were apparently engaged in chasing out the very traders the bands depended on for sustenance. It is not surprising some Indians struck out in frustration as the hopelessness of their position was understood. From 1820 onward Indian "troubles" on the frontier to escalated.[1]

---

1. For further information see Wesley *Guarding the Frontier*, Folwell *Minnesota* I ; Prucha *Broadaxe and Bayonet*.

APPENDIX C:

THE FUR TRADE DESCRIBED

Although most people tend to think of the American fur trade in terms of the colorful mountain men and the cutthroat beaver trade, the reality was much more mundane. The trade in peltries, skins and hides was an immensely complex, well-organized and unusually conservative business – the first big business in the Minnesota area, and the first "modern" business in that it had multiple layers of management, subsidiary firms, thousands of employees working on contract, volume turnover (in one single day J. J. Astor sold nearly half a million muskrat skins!) and an established warehousing and transportation network. Its tendrils spanned the North American continent, stretching from the Rockies, via Missouri and Mississippi rivers to New Orleans, Montreal, New York and London, whence came the calicos and woolens and guns and glass beads favored by the native peoples and where the furs were auctioned. The great trading firms of New York and Toronto had agents at St. Louis and Mackinac who every fall would oversee the delivery of merchandise from the east and its packaging into ninety-pound bales called *pièces* that were assortments of dry goods, clothing, blankets, household equipment, hunting needs, trinkets and personal adornments (enabling the trader to open one bale to find everything he might need – sort of a portable store). The *pièces* were shipped to depots each supplying a *department* or trading area at locations such as Prairie du Chien, Rock Island, St. Joseph, Mendota and Fort Pierre. At these locations company clerks would contract for provisions, meticulously invoice all trade goods, hire voyageurs, outfit their licensed winterers at posts (often called forts) scattered throughout the fur-producing region and also furnish goods to independent traders (taking a percentage of their profit and/or loss). The following spring they would receive, grade, inventory and ship the harvest of furs. A ledger was kept for each year's trading venture, which was called an outfit – as for example, Bailly's Cannon River Outfit or Sibley's Sioux Outfit, which consisted of several locations on the Minnesota River.

The factors, originally called by the old French term *bourgeois*, and their clerks were generally British or American, although quite a few of those trading on their own account were French Canadians. Their employees – boatmen, winterers, blacksmiths and interpreters – were French Canadians, many of them halfbreeds who had lived with the Indians, learning perfectly their ways and culture, and were often indispensable to dealing competitively with the bands to which they belonged. Sturdy and indefatigable, these laborers indentured themselves to winter each year for small wages, new clothes, tobacco and promised provisions, including whiskey. Every trader going into Indian territory had to be licensed by the Indian agent and his goods and men accounted for.

The Indians came to the trading locations each fall to receive "credits" – usually traps, guns and ammunition necessary for hunting and clothing and cooking equipment to see their families through the winter – that were expected to be paid for in so many furs or skins (naturally, anyone advancing credit to the hunters would set his prices high enough to cover expenses and to allow for losses, which at some locations ran as high as 50 percent). Such special items as beads and silk handkerchiefs, bells and combs and, of course, whiskey were often given to seal the contract. In the spring the hunter returned with his harvest of furs, hides and buffalo robes, which were packed into compact bales (80 to 100 pounds was the most convenient size for transportation by canoe and for portaging). Sometimes the trader sent men *en derouin* to winter with the band; this was done particularly to protect his investment, stave off competitors and keep the hunters and skin-dressers up to the mark. (This is where the whiskey came in: rival traders would try to seduce each other's hunters with strong spirits – desired by the Indians not only for the euphoria it could produce but also as an article to trade for horses with tribes further west – getting them to hand over furs promised to and already paid for by another.) A running account was kept for each hunter and engagé; all advances and purchases, breakages or losses of equipment were charged against him, and credit given for wages, peltries and meat brought in and goods returned. Obviously, it would be more than a year before anyone saw any profit: goods shipped in the spring from the east would arrive at the trading locations in the fall and furs gathered over the winter would be sent down the rivers the following spring, hopefully to be shipped back east before they had a chance to deteriorate in hot weather. Equally obviously, everyone's profit depended upon setting a markup high enough to cover ruined goods and misjudgments of character.

At each level, the trader or clerk operated much as a banker would today. Goods from the east were invoiced at cost plus 5 to 13 percent markup, depending on where they had originated. Transportation costs were added in as the bales and kegs moved by steamboat, keelboat, canoe and cart to distribution points. Interest was scrupulously applied to all advances (Bailly's books show interest charged on such items as "use of an ax for three months"). A profitable outfit (or hunter) did not often see cash money, except for a token amount given (and usually immediately spent in a drunken frolic) when the credits were redeemed. Most engagés preferred to leave any credit in account with their employer, merely asking for an advance when something was wanted. In point of fact, almost everyone was continually in debt to his supplier, a situation that might have been subtly encouraged, as the accumulating interest provided an additional source of profit – not unlike the modern credit card society.

Gradually, as fur returns fell due to overharvesting, conflicts among the Indians that prevented them from hunting, more intense competition and mounting bad debts, the trading companies came to depend more and more upon the government to bail them out by buying the lands from the Indians for goods and annuities. Instead of paying the Indians directly for the land purchased, the sale price was invested in annuities, the interest on which was supposed to be paid to the band each year. In addition, the government contracted to supply them with provisions, merchandise, farming tools, horses and cattle, blacksmiths and farmers, schools and other means of survival. The powerful traders' lobby tried – often successfully – to have inserted in each treaty provision for repayment of the band's debts in a lump sum. They also began to vie for lucrative contracts to supply the Indians with provisions. Although only certain traders were supposed to trade with Indians that had been removed to reservations, in fact it was almost impossible to prevent others from selling whiskey and advancing credits. Anyone could trade on ceded lands, from which it was often next to impossible to remove the aboriginal inhabitants, and there was no bar to Indians carrying their purchases from the public lands onto Indian lands. The Indians could no longer hunt, so the return changed from furs to cash when the annuities were paid. When the white settlers began to move in, the fur companies changed with the times, running little stores that not only provided a dependable source of manufactured goods to the immigrants but also a source of cash as these small farmers took over trapping of furs.

Today it is difficult to appreciate the influence of the fur trade in early American history. Although it was never of vast importance to the American economy as a whole, on the frontier it was almost the only business. The items carried into Indian country consisted of every conceivable manufactured article, pins and wire to awls, files and knives, from guns and traps to kettles and fire steels, from blankets and woolen cloths to shirts, hats and frock coats, from thimbles and mirrors to horseshoes and hawk bells. Gunpowder and lead pigs (for making bullets) were vital, and a blacksmith was usually employed to make iron objects such as nails and cart wheels on the spot as well as to repair traps and guns. The sale price of an item might be 400 percent of its original invoice, an increase in part justified by the horrendous expenses incurred in getting it to the customer and returning the furs and skins to the eastern seaboard – transportation, packing, warehousing, wages and provisions for the outfits, administrative costs – and the many sources of loss – shipwreck, spoilage, pilferage, wanton destruction, death or dereliction of creditors. Years passed between the buying of a blanket or gun in London and the paying of the debt with furs trapped on the western coteau. Yet the price paid for furs could generate enormous profits for some outfits, even though most traders remained poor and in debt. Beaver was always the luxury fur of the trade; in the late eighteenth century the demand for beaver from the felters of Europe fueled expansion of the trade. Other fine furs, such as otter, mink and fox, commanded premium prices. But at the time of this story the mainstay of the trade was the lowly muskrat. Hunters also took wolf, deer, bear and raccoon, which were popular for hats and coats. In the 1840s demand shifted to buffalo hides, which made excellent carriage robes. Beside peltries, the western posts shipped back east cargoes of swans' feathers, buffalo tongue, pemmican, tallow, cranberries, maple sugar and dried corn, as well as fine items of Indian manufacture.

The fur trade was always of great concern to the U.S. government, for it was evident that its agents interfered with the government's stated policy of civilizing the aborigines, and it was widely, if wrongly, believed that the many foreigners involved in the trade might, with their Indian allies, constitute a threat to peace on the frontier – the French and Indian wars and the War of 1812 had thoroughly proved the hold traders had over their Indian bands. Also it proved very nearly impossible for the government agents to protect their charges from abuse by the traders, many of whom freely used whiskey, cheated, threatened and, if necessary, starved their clients.

APPENDIX D:

This narrative mentions money several times. Almost nothing (save the slavery issue) caused more ferocious political uproars and public controversy in this period than the question of what money should be. Obviously the inwardness of these disputes is not reflected in this brief discussion. Here is a short orientation to money in Joe Brown's times.

What did money mean to the individual in the early nineteenth century? Paper money today is standardised: a dollar bill is a dollar bill. Most people can describe what a dollar looks like and have a pretty exact idea of what it can buy today. Joe Brown's money was a less definite concept. There was no dollar bill, no national paper currency. As for hard money, American gold coins were seldom seen in America; most gold coinage was exported. The chief coins in use were silver twenty-five and fifty cent pieces and copper pennies. On the frontier, American silver and brass were also scarce – "not enough money in town to change five dollars" reported one western newspaper over the winter of 1829. Spanish bits and English shillings still circulated. Alexis Bailly, a lightning calculator, used pounds and shillings, bits, and dollars concurrently on his invoices.

Paper banknotes – mostly promises to pay the face value in silver on demand – were issued by many persons or organizations. Some of this paper money was better – literally – than gold; some had only the value of the paper, say as a spill for lighting a candle. The issuer might be a state bank (a state agency) or a bank chartered by a state legislature or an insurance company. Every issuer used a different design. The purchasing power of a particular dollar tended to decline with its distance from the issuer. The approximate current value of notes in general circulation was listed in the newspapers next to the quotes on whiskey and mackerel in barrels. News of the latest counterfeits and advertisements for up-to-date counterfeit detectors appeared on the same page. Another class of paper was that issued by fictional banks, though some of the duly chartered banks also seemed a little unreal.

As long as most holders of paper did not demand silver, the system worked. As a practical matter, a sensible man would prefer paper or bank drafts to a sack of silver which would identify him as a target for every highwayman and bandit. When Kenneth Mackenzie collected traders' payments at the St. Peters under the 1837 treaties, he received $4,000 cash: the silver coins filled a small keg. To get them to St. Louis on a steamboat filled with sharpers, he had the keg put in a skiff and towed behind the boat, keeping watch with pistols, but a storm loosened the boat and the money was lost – or stolen.

Occasionally, events combined to shake the whole system, and no banks anywhere could be found to pay silver. (Some banks – the "wildcat" banks, located where the wildcats roamed – were widely believed to compensate for their lack of silver by making it unlikely that a noteholder would find their home office.) The result was "general ruin." States defaulted on their bonds. Unemployment was general. As there was not enough silver and gold to do much business, very little business was done. This happened in 1817 when Joe Brown's father was thrown into prison for bankruptcy and again after 1837.

Many organizations and individuals acted like banks without issuing bank notes. The usual advantage of a chartered bank was its ability to issue notes and its limited liability for the incorporators. In most jurisdictions, anyone could be a private banker, accepting deposits and extending credit at their own risk. Mercantile and trading companies often performed the functions of banks. Louis Provençalle, long a Fur Company trader at Traverse des Sioux, died with a large sum to his credit on the company books. His payments had been deposited to his account and his purchases deducted from it. The company paid interest and, in effect, cashed Louis' checks written on the account. Louis probably saw very little hard money throughout his long career, so in this area there was a cashless economy.

An individual might create a bank on the spot, by "writing a draft" on a third party, that is, A would write a note saying that C will pay money to B on A's account. If B took the note in payment, he would expect to be paid by C, who would add this sum to A's debit account. In the trade area where all the parties were known, the draft might pass as currency through several hands before being finally presented to C.

Even if there were no banks, no hard money and no paper money, business was still done. The editor of the *Miner's Journal* took "hay, corn, potatoes, turnips, beets, pickled cucumber (if pickled in salt), sour crout, onions, &c, &c...." Joe Brown bought a land claim from Sibley for oats, or if the oat crop failed, turnips and potatoes.

How much money did people get? A fur company boatman got about $160 for a season's work. Laborers in the lead mines got from $20 to $25 a month. Men on lumber rafts earned $1 a day. François Labisseure, Brown's interpreter at the Flint Hills, got $300 a year. An experienced trader, Joshua Palen, got $900. John Catlin was paid $2,000 as Secretary of Wisconsin Territory. Samuel Swartwout, President Jackson's appointee as Collector of Customs for the Port of New York, was reputed to have stolen more than one million dollars in addition to his normal commissions.

What did things cost? Whiskey in Galena over the winter of 1829 sold for 35 to 60 cents a gallon in the barrel. Army pork there was scarce at $12 the barrel. A Northwest gun in St. Louis in 1831 could be had for $10 to $12. A good horse was valued at $50. Pine boards sold at Galena in 1836 for $60 a thousand feet. Henry M. Rice bought the American House, a four-story hotel with a ninety-five foot frontage, for $3,600 in 1849.

A working man could board in Washington City for $3 a week, but in Madison, where rooms were in high demand, the cost was $5 a week. Scarce, heavy and fragile commodities, such as paper and ink and patent medicines, were very dear in Minnesota. A frock coat and crepe tie cost Joe Brown $31 in 1831. In general, prices and salaries noted in this story can be multipled by a factor of forty to get the equivalent in 1990s inflated dollars. When a trader was given a $3,000 outfit on credit he was being entrusted with almost a quarter of a million dollars in today's money.[1]

---

1 Information compiled from *Miners Journal*, Galena,Il; *Missouri Republican*, St Louis; Chouteau papers; Records of the Washington County District Court, Minnesota Territory. The Chouteau ledgers and Sibley's books (both available on microfilm) have prices and salaries. Useful for banks and currency is Bray Hammond's *Banks and Politics in America, from the Revolution to the Civil War*, (Princeton 1957). Thomas Senior Berry *Western Prices Before 1861* (Cambridge 1943) is good on changes in price levels.

NOTES ON

THE BIBLIOGRAPHY & ACKNOWLEDGMENTS

When first we started this project, we were perplexed that a biography of Joseph R. Brown, a man so well known and acknowledged to be so important in the early days of Minnesota history, had not been written. We soon found out why. The trail he left behind is very dim, and has been, over the years, confused with elements of mythology that are hard to see beyond.

The truth is that Joseph R. Brown left almost no reminiscences or memoirs, and no personal papers that bear on his early life, save a volume of cases he kept as a justice of the peace for Wisconsin territory in 1839 through 1841 and few letters and notes now available in the collection of Brown papers at the Minnesota Historical Society. Brown was a prolific writer, and it is certain that we would have been blessed with a vast collection of his papers, were it not that the Dakota Conflict, so called, of 1862 put an end to his house, his office, his papers and most of his personal belongings by fire.

The bulk of the information about Brown has been gleaned from digging through other collections: the papers of Lawrence Taliaferro, George Davenport, Henry Sibley, Alexander Ramsey, Caleb Cushing, Alexis Bailly, Martin McLeod, John Stevens and John Catlin, among others. These letter collections were supplemented by the American Fur Company ledgers and account books preserved in the public archives of Canada, in the Chouteau Collection at the Missouri Historical Society in St. Louis and in the Burton Historical Collection in Detroit. In addition, there are the U.S. government records including those of the Western Department of the Army, the various Indian agencies and superintendencies and the Secretary of War, stored in the National Archives, and the district court, territorial and state papers of Wisconsin, Iowa and Minnesota, available in the respective state archives. Microfilm covering much of this was, thank heavens, available in the Minnesota Historical Society in St. Paul, and in the Wisconsin Historical Society research centers in Madison, Platteville and River Falls. The trail took us from St. Louis to Canada, from Washington DC and Annapolis to the Dakotas, and many, many points in between.

While oral history can at times mislead the unwary, first person accounts and other materials collected by William Watts Folwell, Lyman Draper, Reuben Gold Thwaites, William H.C. Folsom, Augustus Easton, John R. Case, John Fletcher Williams and other historians have been invaluable aids in reconstructing the period. In addition, we have drawn heavily on newspaper accounts, remembering that they are often admittedly partisan. We have preferred not to rely on secondary sources, going to the original documentation when possible. This policy has proved enlightening: for example, George W. Featherstonhaugh's published account of his trip to western Minnesota is at considerable variance with his unedited diary of the trip in such details as conversations added, personal interpretations overlaying his original observations and significant omissions of facts probably deemed not interesting enough for publication, but interesting to the historian. An idea of what happens to the memory of actual participants in events can be gained by comparing John Fletcher Williams' account of several judicial proceedings in early St. Paul – accounts gained from eyewitnesses forty years after the fact – with Brown's justice of the peace docket, which surfaced years after Williams wrote. Many printed accounts, such as those published by E. D. Neill and taken directly from Lawrence Taliaferro's diary, contain misread words from which misinterpretations have been drawn for 140 years. Even typescripts of various documents in historical society archives have proved treacherous in the matter of omitted or miscopied words: our best advice is, Read it in the original. This is not to denigrate the many fine works available on Minnesota history. On the contrary, we have drawn heavily from the published histories of J. Fletcher Williams, William Watts Folwell and Return I. Holcombe, all of whom did meticulous research and had, indeed, sources no longer available to us.

We have been fortunate to know several descendants of Joseph R. Brown who have given us support and access to family documents, especially the late Carmon Brown, Susan Hinrichs, Joe Martin and Lois Lien, whose extensive genealogical research has been of enormous help. We are also indebted to Alan Woolworth of the Minnesota Historical Society whose research into the life of JRB gave direction to our efforts, and to the many others who preceded us in attempting to reconstruct the life of a very complex man from the limited material readily available, including Everett Sterling, William Watts Folwell and Samuel J. Brown. Thanks also to Minnesota historians William E. Lass, James Taylor Dunn and Judy Yaeger Jones, for reading the manuscript and giving invaluable counsel. We appreciate their comments even if we were unable to carry out all their suggestions.

BIBLIOGRAPHY

UNPUBLISHED SOURCES

Manuscript Collections

American Board of Commissioners for Foreign Missions (ABCFM)
 papers. Microfilm in Minnesota Historical Society (MHS), St. Paul.
American Fur Company papers. Burton Historical Collections, Detroit
 and New York Historical Society Archives, microfilm in MHS St. Paul
Bailly, Alexis. Papers, account books. MHS St. Paul
Boutwell, William T. Papers. MHS St. Paul
Brown, John, family records. Collections of W. T. Phillips Memorial
 Library, Bethany, WV
Brown, Joseph R. and Samuel J. Papers, MHS St. Paul
Case, John R. Papers. MHS St. Paul
Catlin, John. Papers, Wisconsin Historical Society (WHS), Madison
Chouteau, Pierre Junior and Company. Papers, letterbooks. Missouri
 Historical Society, St. Louis
Cushing, Caleb. Papers, MHS St. Paul
Davenport, George. Papers. Special Collections, Augustana College,
 Rock Island
Engle, James. Papers. MHS St. Paul
Folwell, William Watts. Papers, notebooks of interviews. MHS St. Paul
Furber, Joseph. Papers. MHS St. Paul
Green Bay-Prairie du Chien Papers. Bound volume, WHS Madison
Henderson family records. Maryland Historical Society, Baltimore
Jones, George W. Papers. Iowa State Historical Society, Des Moines
Mackenzie, Kenneth. Papers. Missouri Hist. Soc., St. Louis
Martin, Morgan. Papers. Neville Museum and Kellogg Public Library,
 Green Bay, and WHS Madison
McLeod, Martin. Papers, diary. MHS St. Paul
Pond, Gideon. Papers. MHS St. Paul
Robinson, Doane. Papers. South Dakota Historical Society, Pierre
Satterlee, Marion. Papers. MHS St. Paul
Selkirk Papers. Archives of Canada, Winnipeg
Sibley, Henry Hastings. Papers, account books. MHS St. Paul
Steele, Franklin. Papers. MHS St. Paul
Stevens, John. Papers. MHS St. Paul

Street, Joseph M. Papers. Microfilm MHS St. Paul
Taliaferro, Lawrence. Papers, diaries. MHS St. Paul
Tohill, Louis. Papers. MHS St. Paul
Tweedy, John. Papers. Microfilm MHS, St. Paul
Williams, John Fletcher. Papers, notebooks. MHS St. Paul
Williamson, Thomas Smith. In ABCFM papers, microfilm MHS St. Paul

Government records

Baltimore County (MD) land records, Hall of Records, Annapolis, MD
Harford County (MD) land records, population schedules, marriages,
    wills, probates, Bel Air, MD
Bureau of Indian Affairs (BIA) records, Sisseton Reservation, Goodwill,
    SD
Crawford County (WI) deed books, probate records, Court House,
    Prairie du Chien
Erie County (PA) land, sheriff, probate records, Court House, Erie, PA
Federal tax lists, Maryland Hall of Records, Annapolis, and Penn. Hist.
    Society, Harrisburg.
Fort Snelling records and map collection. Copies in MHS, St. Paul
Iowa and Crawford County (WI) records, records of district court, WHS
    Regional Research Center, Platteville, WI
Lancaster County (PA) records, deeds, court records, Lancaster
    Historical Society, Lancaster
Papers of the Wisconsin Territorial Legislature, WHS Madison
Papers of Wisconsin Territory, Records of Secretary of State, WHS
    Madison
Records of Adjutant General's Office (AGO): Muster rolls, post returns,
    inpection reports. National Archives Record Group (NARG) 94
Records of Advocate-General's Office, NARG 153
Records of Chief Engineer's Office, NARG 77
Records of General Accounting Office (GAO): records of paymasters,
    second auditor, NARG 217
Records of Office of Indian Affairs (OIA), NARG 75
Records of Office of Quartermaster General (OQG), NARG 92
Records of Office of the Secretary of War (OSW), NARG 107 and 234
Records of Office of the Surgeon General (OSG), NARG 27
Records of Sisseton and Santee reservations, microfilm, MHS St. Paul
St. Croix County (WI) board and treasurer records, Washington County
    (MN) Historic Court House, Stillwater
St. Croix County (WI) records, in Washington Co. (MN) records, Court
    House and Historic Court House, Stillwater
St. Croix County (WI) records of the clerk of court, in Washington
    County records, MHS St. Paul
Territorial papers of Iowa, Iowa Historical Society, Des Moines
United States Customs records, Mackinac
United States Department of State, general records, National Archives

Manuscripts and other unpublished sources

Bourke, John P. Journal of Transactions in the Sioux District 1819-1820, and Upper Red River Journal 1820-1821, Hudson's Bay Company papers, Winnipeg.

Brown, Samuel J. "Chief Gabriel Renville: A Memoire," manuscript in Minnesota biographical collections, MHS

Brisbois, Bernard W. "Autobiography of Bernard W. Brisbois," MHS.

Featherstonhaugh, George. Journal (1835), microfilm copy, MHS.

Mooers, John. "Memoire of Hazen Mooers," MHS.

Robertson, Thomas A. "Reminscences," Sioux Uprising Collection, MHS.

Hanks, Stephen B. "Reminiscences," manuscript in Bill papers, MHS.

St. Croix Valley Old Settler's Biographies (c. 1875), MHS.

Tohill, Louis Arthur "Robert Dickson, British Fur Trader on the Upper Mississippi: A Story of Trade, War, and Diplomacy," Ph.D dissertation University of Minnesota 1926, MHS; mimeograph ed. Edwards Bros., Ann Arbor, MI 1927.

Wolcott, E. Letter to J. R. Carli, April 29, 1892, MHS. Published as "Reminiscences of the St. Croix River" Nancy Goodman, ed., in *Historical Whisperings* 22/4 Jan. 1995.

PUBLISHED PRIMARY SOURCES

Periodicals

Detroit Gazette 1820
Galena Advertiser 1847
Hastings (MN) Gazette 1920, 1926
Henderson (MN) Democrat 1856
Illinois Intelligencer 1825, 1826, 1827 (Vandalia)
Lancaster (PA) Journal 1820
Madison City Express 1845, 1846
Madison Express 1841-1844
Milwaukie Daily Sentinel 1845
Minneapolis Journal 1917
Minnesota Democrat (St. Paul) 1854
Minnesota Farmer and Gardener (St. Paul) 1860
Minnesota Pioneer, 1849, 1850 (St. Paul)
National Intelligencer, 1846 (Washington)
Niles Register 1820, 1845 (Baltimore)
St. Anthony Express 1852
St. Paul Daily Pioneer 1868
St. Paul Dispatch 1870

St. Paul Pioneer 1870
St. Paul Pioneer Press 1894
St. Paul Press 1870
St. Paul Weekly Pioneer and Democrat 1856
Southern Minnesotian
Stillwater Daily Gazette 1903
Stillwater Messenger 1896
Washington Globe 1842
Wisconsin Democrat 1846, 1847 (Madison)
Wiskonsan Enquirer 1839-1844 (Madison)

Books and Articles

Adams, Ann "Early Days at Red River Settlement and Ft. Snelling: Reminiscences of Mrs. Ann Adams 1821-1829" J. F. Williams, ed., *Minnesota Historical Collections* VI (St. Paul 1894)

Ainse, Joseph "Reply of Joseph Ainse," *Michigan Pioneer and Historical Collections* XXIII (1893)

Allanson, Winona Blanche *Indian Moons* (St. Paul 1927)

Birk, Douglas A. *Grey Cloud; An Archeological Approach* (St. Paul 1972)

Blegen, Theodore C. *The Autobiography of Henry Hastings Sibley* (Minneapolis 1932)

Brandt, Frank Edwin "Russell Farnham, Astorian," *Transactions of the Illinois Historical Society 1930* (Springfield 1930)

Brisbois, Bernard W. "Recollections of Prairie du Chien," *Wisconsin Historical Collections* IX (reprint Madison 1909)

Brownell, George *Boundaries of Wisconsin: Minority Report to the Constitutional Convention* (Madison 1848)

Brunson, Ira "Early Times in the Old Northwest," *Wisconsin Historical Society Proceedings 1904* (Madison 1905)

Case, John R. "The First House in Hastings," *The Hastings Gazette* January 1, 1926

Case, John R. "Pioneer Days In And Around Hastings," *The Hastings Gazette* Dec. 4, 1920

Case, John R. "Historical Notes of Grey Cloud Island and Its Vicinity," *Minnesota Historical Collections* XV (St. Paul 1915)

Chittenden, Hiram Martin *The American Fur Trade of the Far West* I (reprint Stanford 1954)

Draper, Lyman, ed. "Personal Narrative of Captain Thomas G. Anderson" in *Minnesota Historical Collections* IX (St. Paul 1901)

Easton, Augustus B. *History of the St. Croix Valley* I (Chicago 1909)

Featherstonhaugh, George W. *Canoe Voyage Up the Minnay Sotor* (reprint St. Paul 1970)

Folsom, William H. C. "History of Lumbering in the St. Croix Valley," *Minnesota Historical Collections* IV (St. Paul 1902)

Folsom, William H. C. *Fifty Years in the Northwest* (St. Paul 1888)

General Regulations of the Army, (Philadelphia 1821)

Gilfillan, Charles D. "The Early Political History of Minnesota," *Minnesota Historical Collections* IX (St. Paul 1901)

Green Bay-Prairie du Chien papers (extracts) *Wisconsin Historical Collections* X (Madison 1888)

Holcombe, William "Report on the Expediency of Dividing the Territory of Wisconsin," *Journal of the Convention to Form a Constitution for the State of Wisconsin* (Madison 1847)

Holmes, Frederick L. "First Constitutional Convention 1846," *Proceedings of the State Historical Society of Wisconsin* 1905 (Madison 1906)

Houghton, Douglas "Journal" in *Schoolcraft's Expedition to Lake Itasca: The Discovery of the Source of the Mississippi*, Philip P. Mason, ed. (1958)

Houghton, Jacob *Report on Mineral Regions of Lake Superior* (Detroit 1846)

Hughes, Thomas *Indian Chiefs of Southern Minnesota* (reprint Minneapolis 1969)

Hughes, Thomas. "Treaty of Traverse des Sioux . . . with Notes of the Former Treaty There in 1841 under Governor James D. Doty of Wisconsin," *Minnesota Historical Collections* X/1 (St. Paul 1905)

Journals of the Third Wisconsin Territorial Legislature: 1839-1847 (Madison 1840-1848)

Kapler, Todd *1988 Brown 's Post (39R038) Excavation: An Archaeological Investigation of an Historic Fur Trading Post* (Vermillion, SD 1989)

Kappler, Charles Joseph *Indian Affairs, Laws and Treaties II* (Washington 1904)

Kearny, Stephen Watts "Journal of Stephen Watts Kearny," Valentine Mott Porter, ed. *Missouri Historical Society Collections* III (St. Louis 1908)

Knapp, J. G. "Early Reminiscences of Madison," *Wisconsin Historical Collections* VI (reprint Madison 1908)

Kohl, Johann Georg "Johann Georg Kohl; A German Traveler in Minnesota Territory," translated and edited by Frederic Trautmann, *Minnesota History* 49/4 (St. Paul 1984)

Larpenteur, Auguste L. "Recollections of the City and People of St. Paul," *Minnesota Historical Collections* XIV (St. Paul 1901)

Larson, Agnes M. *History of the White Pine Industry in Minnesota* (Minneapolis 1949)

Lavender, David *The Fist in the Wilderness* (Albuquerque 1964)

Lockwood, James H. "Early Times in Wisconsin," *Wisconsin Historical Collections* II (reprint Madison 1903)

Loehr, Rodney C. "Caleb D. Dorr and the Early Minnesota Lumber Industry," *Minnesota History* XXIV (St. Paul 1928)

Long, Stephen H. *The Northern Expeditions of Stephen H. Long: The Journals of 1817 and 1823 and Related Documents*, Lucile M. Kane, June D. Holmquist, Carolyn Gilman, eds., (St. Paul 1987)

Long, Stephen H. "Voyage in a Six-Oared Skiff to the Falls of Saint Anthony in 1817," *Minnesota Historical Collections* II (reprint St. Paul 1889)

Lyman, George D. *John Marsh, Pioneer* (New York 1934)

Marshall, William R. "Reminiscences of Wisconsin 1842-1848," *Magazine of Western History* VII (1888)

Meyer, Roy W. *History of the Santee Sioux: United States Indian Policy on Trial* (Lincoln 1967)

Morris, H. S. *Historical Stories, Legends and Traditions of Northeastern South Dakota* (Sisseton 1939)

Moss, Henry L. "Last Days of Wisconsin Territory and Early Days of Minnesota Territory," *Minnesota Historical Collections* VIII (St. Paul)

Neill, Edward D. "Occurrences In and Around Fort Snelling from 1819 to 1840," *Minnesota Historical Collections* II (reprint St. Paul 1889)

Newson, Thomas M. *Pen Pictures of St. Paul, Minnesota and Biographical Sketches of Old Settlers* (St. Paul 1886)

Nute, Grace Lee ed. *Documents Relating to Northwest Missions. 1815-1827* (St. Paul 1942)

Nute, Grace Lee "The Diary of Martin McLeod," *Minnesota History Bulletin* IV (St. Paul 1922)

Nute, Grace Lee "Posts in the Minnesota Fur Trading Area," *Minnesota History* XV (St. Paul 1915)

"Organization of Minnesota Territory," *Minnesota Historical Collections* I (reprint St. Paul 1872)

Pond, Gideon "Indian Warfare in Minnesota," *Minnesota Historical Collections* III, (St. Paul 1880)

Pond, Samuel W. "The Dakota or Sioux in Minnesota as They Were in 1834," *Minnesota Historical Collections* XII (St. Paul 1908)

Powell, William "William Powell's Recollections," *Wisconsin Historical Society Proceedings 1912*, Lyman C. Draper, ed., (Madison 1913)

Parker, Donald Dean, ed. *The Recollections of Philander Prescott, Frontiersman of the Old Northwest, 1819-1862* (Lincoln 1966)

"Proceedings of the Court of Inquiry Against Joseph Ainse," *Michigan Pioneer and Historical Collections* XV (1890)

Prucha, Francis Paul "Army Sutlers and the American Fur Company" in *Minnesota History* XL (St. Paul 1966)

Prucha, Francis Paul *Broadaxe and Bayonet: The Role of the United States Army in the Development of the Northwest, 1815-1860* (Madison 1953)

Quaife, Milo M. *Attainment of Statehood (Wisconsin Historical Collections* XXIX) (Madison 1928)

Quaife, Milo M. *Struggle over Ratification 1846-1847 (Wisconsin Historical Collections* XXVIII) (Madison 1920)

Renshaw, Grace Parke *Renshaw Reflections* (Baltimore 1983)

Renville, Victor "A Sketch of the Minnesota Massacre," *Collections of the State Historical Society of North Dakota* V (1893)

Schoolcraft, Henry Rowe *Narrative Journal of Travels Through the Northwestern United States*, Mentor L. Williams, ed. (East Lansing 1953)

Schoolcraft, Henry Rowe "Exploratory Trip Through the St. Croix and Burntwood Rivers," *Schoolcraft's Expedition to Lake Itasca: The Discovery of the Source of the Mississippi*, Philip P. Mason, ed. (1958)

Sibley, Henry Hastings "Remininscences of the Early Days of Minnesota," *Minnesota Historical Collections* III (St. Paul 1880)

Sibley, Henry Hastings "Memoir of Jean Baptiste Faribault," *Minnesota Historical Collections* III (St. Paul 1880)

Smith, Alice E. *James Duane Doty: Frontier Promoter* (Madison 1954)

Smith, Alice E. "Caleb Cushing's Investments in the St. Croix Valley," *Wisconsin Magazine of History* XXVIII

Snelling, William Joseph (supposed author) "Early Days at Prairie du Chien and the Winnebago Outbreak of 1827," *Wisconsin Historical Collections* V (reprint Madison 1907)

Snelling, William Joseph *Tales of the Northwest, or Sketches of Indian Life and Character by a Resident Beyond the Frontier . . .* (reprint Minneapolis 1936)

Stanchfield, Daniel "History of Lumbering on the Upper Mississippi and Its Tributaries . . ." *Minnesota Historical Collections* IX (St. Paul 1901)

Stevens, John H. *The Early History of Hennepin County*, pamphlet published by *Northwest Democrat* (Minneapolis 1856)

Strong, Moses M. *Territorial Legislature in Wisconsin* (Madison 1870)

Strong, Moses M. *History of the Territory of Wisconsin from 1836 to 1848* (Madison 1885)

Taliaferro, Lawrence "Autobiography of Major Lawrence Taliaferro," *Minnesota Historical Collections* VI (St. Paul 1894)

Territorial Papers of the United States XXVII, John Porter Bloom, ed. (Washington 1969)

Trowbridge, Charles C. "Charles C. Trowbridge's Journal" Ralph Brown, ed., *Minnesota History* 23/4, December 1942

United States House Document 144, "Reservation at Fort Snelling," 26 Congress, 1 session

United States House Document 251, "Appropriations for the Legislative Assembly of Wisconsin Territory," 28 Congress, 1 session

United States House Document 351, "Fort Snelling Investigation 1858," 35 Congress, 1 session (serial 965)

United States House Ex. Document 9, "Sale of Fort Snelling," 40 Congress, 3 session (serial 1372)

United States House Report 317, "Joseph R. Brown," 30 Congress, 1 session

United States Senate Document 60, 28 Congress, 2 session

United States Senate Document 61, "Commission Report: Ramsey Investigation," 33 Congress, 1 session

Van Cleve, Charlotte Ouisconsin *Three Score Years and Ten: Life Long Memories of Fort Snelling, Minnesota and Other Parts of the West* (Minneapolis 1888)

Welsh, William, compiler *Journal of the Rev. S. D. Hinman Missionary to the Santee Sioux Indians and Taopi by Bishop Whipple* (Philadelphia 1869)

Wesley, Edgar Bruce *Guarding the Frontier: A Study of Frontier Defense from 1815 to 1825* (reprint Westport, CT 1970)

Wilkie, Franc B. *Davenport: Past and Present* (Davenport 1888)

Williams, John Fletcher, "Memoir of Joseph R. Brown" in *Minnesota Historical Collections* III (St. Paul 1880)

Williams, John Fletcher *The History of the City of St. Paul and of the County of Ramsey, Minnesota* (St. Paul 1876)

Winchell, Newton H. *The Geology of Minnesota II* (St. Paul 1888)

Wisconsin Territorial Papers: Crawford County (Madison 1841)

Wisconsin Territorial Papers: St. Croix County I, "Proceedings of St. Croix County Board" (Madison 1841)

Wisconsin Territory, House of Representatives *Elections Committee Report 1841-1842* (Madison 1842)

Wisconsin Territory *Acts of the Third Wisconsin Territorial Legislature: 1842-1843* (Madison 1843)

Secondary Sources and Background Material

Alexander, W. E., ed. *History of Chickasaw and Howard Counties, Iowa* (Decorah 1883)

Anderson, Gary Clayton *Little Crow: Spokesman for the Sioux* (St. Paul 1986)

Baird, Elizabeth Therese "Early Days on Mackinac Island," *Wisconsin Historical Collections* XIV (reprint Madison 1910)

Balistier, Joseph N. *Annals of Chicago 1840*, Number 7 in Robert Fergus' Historical Series (reprint Chicago 1874)

Barrett, J. O. *A History of Traverse County: Browns Valley and Its Environs to 1881*, (n.d.)

Bay, J. Christian, editor *Going West: The Pioneer Work of Alfred Brunson* (Cedar Rapids 1951)

Berry, Thomas Senior *Western Prices Before 1861* (Cambridge 1943)

Blair, Walter *Raft Pilot's Log* (Cleveland 1930)

Bray, Edmund C. and Martha Coleman Bray, editors and translators *Joseph N. Nicollet on the Plains and Prairies* (St. Paul 1976)

Brevet's South Dakota Historical Markers (Sioux Falls 1974)

Burgman, John R. ed., *History of the Bench and Bar of Wisconsin II* (Chicago 1898)

Carter, William G. *History of York County* (Pennsylvania 1834)

Clayton, James L. "Growth and Economic Significance of the American Fur Trade 1790-1890" in *Minnesota History* XL (St. Paul 1966)

Commons, John R. *History of Labor in the United States* I (New York 1921)

Durrie, Daniel S. *A History of Madison, the Capital of Wisconsin, including the Four Lakes Country; to July, 1874, with an appendix of notes on Dane County and its towns* (Madison 1874)

Downer, Harry E. *History of Davenport and Scott County* I (Chicago 1910)

Ellis, Franklin *History of Lancaster County* (1888)

Faris, J. T. *Old Roads Out of Philadelphia* (1917)

Flanagan, Thomas "Louis Riel and the Dispersion of the American Métis," *Minnesota History* XLIX 49/5 (Spring 1985)

Folwell, William Watts *A History of Minnesota* I (revised edition, St. Paul 1956)

Folwell, William Watts *A History of Minnesota* III (revised edition, St. Paul 1969)

Fonda, John H. "Early Wisconsin," *Wisconsin Historical Collections* V (reprint Madison 1907)

Futhey, John S. *History of Chester County Pennsylvania* (1881)

Gregg, Samuel *History of Methodism* (1873)

Hammond, Bray *Banks and Politics in America, from the Revolution to the Civil War* (Princeton 1957)

Hansen, Marcus *Old Fort Snelling 1819-1858* (Iowa City 1918)

Hauberg, John H. "The Black Hawk War 1831-32," *Transactions of the Illinois Historical Society* XXXIX (Springfield 1932)

Heathcote, C. W. *History of Chester County Pennsylvania* (1932)

Hennesey, W. B. *Past and Present of St. Paul, Minnesota* (Chicago 1906)

Holcombe, Return I. *Minnesota in Three Centuries* II (Minnesota 1908)

Jones, Evan *The Minnesota: Forgotten River* (New York 1962)

Kane, Lucile *The Waterfall That Built a City* (St. Paul 1966)

Lass, William E. *Minnesota's Boundary with Canada; Its Evolution Since 1783* (St. Paul 1980)

Lewis, Sinclair *The God-Seeker: a novel* (New York 1949)

McKenney, Thomas "The Winnebago War," *Wisconsin Historical Collections* V (reprint Madison 1907)

McLeod, Martin "Narrative of Martin McLeod," *Army and Navy Chronicle* Jul. 27, 1837 (Washington)

Mitchell, Elaine Allen "International Buying Trip: Ft. Garry to St. Louis in 1846," *Minnesota History* XXXVI (St. Paul 1958)

Morleigh (pseud.) "A Merry Briton in Pioneer Wisconsin" (Madison 1950, reprint from *Life in the West. . .* [London 1842])

Papenfuss, Edward C., Gregory A. Stiverson, Susan A. Collins, Lois Green Carr, eds., *Maryland: New Guide to the Old Line State* (Baltimore 1976)

Parker, Amos A. *Trip to the West and Texas* (Boston 1836)

Parkinson, Daniel M. "Pioneer Life in Wisconsin," *Wisconsin Historical Collections* II (reprint Madison 1903)

Petersen, William J. *Steamboating on the Upper Mississippi: The Water Way to Iowa* (Iowa City 1937)

Preston, Walter W. *History of Harford County* (Baltimore 1901)

Rantoul, Robert, Junior *Personal Recollections* (Cambridge 1916)

Smeltzer, W. G. *Methodism in Western Pennsylvania 1784-1968* (1969)

Smith, Alice E. *The History of Wisconsin* (Madison 1973)

Snelling, William Joseph "Running the Gauntlet," *Minnesota Historical Collections* I (reprint St. Paul 1872)

Spencer, J. W. "Narrative of J. W. Spencer," *The Early Days of Rock Island and Davenport* Milo Milton Quaife, ed. (Chicago 1942)

Thwaites, Reuben Gold "A Wisconsin Fur Trader's Journal 1804-5," *Wisconsin Historical Collections* XIX (Madison 1910)

Van der Zee, Jacob "Fur Trade in the Eastern Iowa Country from 1800 to 1833," *Iowa Journal of History and Politics* XII (Iowa City 1914)

Way, Royal Branson *The Rock River Valley: Its History, Traditions, Legends and Charms* I (Chicago 1920)

INDEX

Bold citations indicate an appearance in a footnote

Brown, Emily Mary Ann (Parker) (daughter), 262, 293

Brown, Harriet Cordelia (daughter), 225, 293; death of, 229

Brown, Helen Dickson, 57, 59, 111, 288, 289

Brown, J. R., 104, 170, 178, 189, 192; 'Jo the Juggler', 9; 2nd marriage re an inheritance from Brown's uncle Thomas (Henderson?), 135; 30 days at Madison accomplish all, 177; accounts of him at his post c. 1829 by visitors, 90; acting sec. at Democratic meeting, Madison, 1/1841, 192; acting Sgt. Major, 72; actions against Olivers Grove establishment, 118; ankle crooked re injury, 25; appointed St. Croix Co. inspector, 189; appointment as St. Croix Co. Clerk, 260; approved as St. Croix Co. clerk, treasurer, 188; April, 1835 finds him setting up at Hidden Falls, 121; as hard trader, methods condoned, 148; as hospital attendant, 56; as intellectual lion, 10; as Justice of Peace, hears criminal case, 181; at his death, Minnesota's oldest white settler, 9; attacked collecting debts from Red Wing's band, 116; back at Ft. Snelling/St. Peters spring, 1830, 95; back at Lake Traverse 9/1842, 217; becomes treasurer, surveyor and register of deeds, 187; born 1/5/1805, York Co., PA, 15; branch house on Sheyenne run by Provençalle, 146; Brown & Carli dissolve firm, 263; Brown's county bill, 174; Brown's Ferry (near Mendota),

156; Brown's Grey Cloud Island farm, 257; Brown's road bill, 193; Brown's running mate, 189; claim at Dacotah becomes county seat, 187; commissioned as justice of the peace, 160; Company K's fifer, 54; considerations on Indian improvement, 89; cost to County Board to be shut of him, 257; counterpetition to est. St. Croix Co., 175; Democratic politics, 188; descendants of, 310; divorce from Helen, 111; divorce from Margaret, stipulations 4/29/1841, 178; divorce requires him to bring suit at Mineral Point for desertion & adultery, Oct. 1833, 112; doesn't want to transfer to Upper Mississippi Outfit, 83; dollar value of an Indian wife, children=$3,000 c. 1838, >$100,000 c. 1990, 145; education in Indian ways, 40; effect of 1841 treaty defeat on, 213; elected representative to 3rd Wis. Territorial Legislature, 188; endorsement of Sioux treaties in legislature, 209; engages Snake River Indians in agricultural pursuits, 107; enlisted in army, 309; epitaphs for, 9; epitaphs for, by Sinclair Lewis, 11; ferry bill, 173; ferry bill passed, 209; ferry license denied, 158; first documented efforts at lumbering 1833-34, 114; first trip into the frontier, 32; fugitive, 25; Grey Cloud Island farm, 218; half brothers & sisters, 287; has legislative charter for ferry at Sintomonee for 10 yrs, 209; his discussion of early army career, 39; his life as an Indian trader, 85; in the middle of the Winnebago War, 72; income from furs 1845 season $2,446, 244; income, other sources 1826, 61; Indian farming project and, 88; is not William Brown, American Fur Co trader at Lands End, 100; issued questionable timber cutting permit, 282; joins a Sunday school class, 44; joins the army, 1920, 27; joins with Farnham & Davenport to run Rock River post in 1828, 82; June 17th, 1835 signs with Sibley to work for American Fur Co.'s Western Outfit, 122; Justice of Peace, 180; knack for languages, 62; legend added to, 231; license at mouth of Chippewa, 97; life seems one chequered waste of unfulfilled dreams??, 9; lives with Susan Frénière, 131; lobbying skills, petition drafting, 171; March, 1843 travels, on snowshoes, from North Dakota post to Madison to collect $727 back pay, 223; marries Helen Dickson, 59; marries Margaret McCoy, 135; Minnesota's premier lumberman, 114; mistress(s), reputation with ladies, 128; mother Emily Renshaw, 287; named to territorial Democratic central committee, 7/24/1847, 262; need to reestablish in St. Peters River (Minnesota) area, 248; Olivers Grove establishment, c. 1832, 114; ousts Renvilles, gets control at Lake Traverse, 134; papers lost in 1862 Dakota Conflict, 309; post at the mouth of the St. Croix, 109; printer's apprentice, 23; promoted to 3rd Sgt., 61; promoted to Corporal, 56; recommended by James Duane Doty to be Sioux Indian agent, 203; reenlistment, 57; refuses order for eviction from Hidden Falls, 121; relationship (lack of) with Joseph Renville, 123; release from Army signed, 6/8/1828, 83; returns from furlough 1826, reporting to Ft. Armstrong, 69; reverses Renville's appeasement policy, 148; seeks removal of Indians from Wisconsin, 210; sells out of fur trade to Sibley, 9/28/1846, 246; sends son Solomon to Choctaw Academy, 113; settles accounts with St. Croix County board, 257; shot by Isannapea over chicken, 147; six month furlough 5/1/1826 to 11/1/1826, 68; sold Davenport claim 'for a box of cigars', 95; St. Croix delegate to territorial temperance society, 192; the fur trade and, 81; trade license issued to by Capt. Wm. Jouett, 109; trading as an independent, 109; trading house searched for whiskey, 118; trading lumber c. 1848 financed by Franklin Steele, 258; Two Rocks location, 141; vice president of Democratic convention, 192; walks 210 miles in under two weeks, 232; wife of Col. John McNeil influences in early army years, 45; wives, 288; works for American Fur Co., 89

Brown, J. R. & Carli purchase logs, 258

Brown, Jeremiah (half brother), 287

Hidden Falls, 121

hivernants, 131

Holcombe, William, 192, 252, 254, 259, 270, 275, 276, 278, 281; reelected St. Croix Co. clerk, reg. of deeds, chosen delegate to Wis. Constitutional convention, 254

Hole-in-the-Day. *see* Pugonakeeshig

Hole-in-the-Day (younger), Gull Lake chief, 263

Hone, David, 189, 204, 218; hurriedly leaves Brown's Chanwakan farm, 229

Hopkins, Reverend Robert: American Board Missionary, 244

hospital books: in a deranged state, 61

hostilities of Fox & Sioux 1828 stop hunting, 81

Hotel Brown: Tamarack House, 198

hotels, 171

House Bill #4: ferry bill, 173

houses of ill repute, 54

Howard, Hiram E., 108; agent of Cephas Mills & Co., 103

Hudson's Bay Company, 51, 137, 194, 216, 297; whiskey (liquor) and the Indians, 242

Huggins, Alexander G., 147

Hughes, Andrew S., 90

Hungerford, William S., 252

hyperborean territory, 280

Iaubaus (Little Buck) of the Follesavoine, 115

Illinois lead mines, 51

immigration, the great western had commenced, 155

income: Brown's enhanced by Justice of Peace fees, 160

Indian ambush, 56

Indian art, 50

Indian bands: traders hold over, 304

Indian credits, 139

Indian Education Fund: government of, 113

Indian free state in California, 138

Indian Intercourse Act 6/30/1834: prohibits liquor trade with Indians, 118

Indian land title extinction demanded, 92

Indian Liberation Army: James Dickson's, 138

Indian Office, 194

Indian quarrels, 67

Indian scares, 31

Indian territory, 171

Indian title: extinguishment opens their former land to settlers, 152

Indian trade, 50, 65, 265

Indian trade goods, 200

Indian wars, 304; involve Yankton, Mandan, Sisseton in 1836, 136

Indians: Brown has serious trouble at Lake Traverse, 147

inflation adjustment: $2,900 c. 1848 equal $100,000+ in 1990 dollars, 258

interruption of trade suit, 66

Iowa: incipient state of, 225

Iowa City, 160

Iowa River, 70

Iowa Territory, 160, 173; created west of Mississippi in 1838, 160

iron objects, 303

Irvin, Judge David, 196, 199, 220, 224, 225, 252, 260, 272; arrives at Ft. Snelling, comedy begins, 197; refuses to hold court in St. Croix Co., 224

Ishtaba (Sleepy Eyes), Sisseton chief, 232

Itehinyanza *see* Sullen Face, 233

Jackson, Henry, 241, 249, 253, 254, 274, 276, 277

Marston, Maj. Morrell, 44
Martin, Morgan, 245, 256, 270; president of Dem convention Feb. 1841, 192
Massie, Louis, 65, 121
Massie's Landing, 157
Mazadehdegawin, 130, 292
Mazasha (Red Iron), 243
McCormack, John, 183
McCoy, Francis, 196, 290; father of J. R. Brown's second wife Margaret, 289
McCoy, Margaret, 127; J. R. Brown's mistress on the St. Croix, 111; second wife of J. R. Brown, 290
McCoy, Margarette (Cadotte), 290
McKenney, Thomas, 66
McKusick Lake, 220
McKusick, John, 221, 253, 260, 275; built boarding house for mill hands, 229; donates land for courthouse, 261
McKusick's store: lodges temporary St. Croix Co. courthouse in upper room, 253
McLean, Daniel, 259
McLeod, Alexander, 212
McLeod, Martin, 138, 139, 170, 212, 234, 266, 309
McNair's coulee, 75
McPhail, Lt. Daniel, 164, 182
Mdewakanton, 8, 35, 73, 98, 116, 130, 136, 144, 145, 163, 172, 202, 241, 247, 290
Mdewakantons: ½ & ¼ blood relations of, payments to, 145
medical training, 130
Medicine Bottle, 109, 144, 149, 152; moved his band off Grey Cloud Island per treaty to Pine Bend bottoms, 149
Menard, Pierre, 239
Mencke, Henry C., 157, 161, 164, 173

Mendota, 73, 96, 301
Menominee Indians, 55
Menominee Mills (Menomonie, Wis.), 208
merchandise: whiskey, 104
Mesquakie, 8, 31; see also Sac and Fox Indians, 8
metals, precious: 48 organized mining companies locate permits by Feb. 1846, 251; found in northern Wisconsin - copper, silver and gold, 251; St. Croix & Lake Superior Mining Company (owners Choate, Rantoul, and Cushing of Boston, 251
Méthode, Claude: murdered with his family 1826 at their sugar camp near Ft. Crawford, 67
Methodist missions: at Kaposia, Crow Wing, 188
métis, 232, 236, 244; see Red River halfbreeds, 232
Michigan Territory: of 1818, includes Wisconsin, Minnesota east of Mississippi, 158; of 1834 includes section between Missouri River and Canada, 160
military reserve see Fort Snelling military reserve, 171
milk: i.e. whisky, 41
mill people, 176
Miller, Dr. B. O., 192
Milwaukie Daily Sentinel, 250
Minasota territory bill, 270
Mineral Point, 112
mink: 50¢, 244
minkskin bullet pouch, 96
Minnehaha Creek, 48, 99
Minnesota: east of Mississippi under jurisdiction of Crawford Co. Wis, 160; territory's capitol must lie between Mississippi and the St. Croix -in or near Brown's holdings, 247

334

raccoon grease: Indians compare
white settlers to, 82

Rainville, Joseph, 291

Ramsey, Alexander, 309

Randall, Andrew, 272

Rantoul, Robert Junior, 251

ratification of treaty, 210

Reaume, Ralph, 115, 121

Red Bird, 74

Red Cedar River of Iowa, 51

Red Cedar River of Wisconsin, 174

Red Hail, 162

Red Lake, 297

Red River, 49, 121, 232

Red River flyway, 217

Red River halfbreeds (métis), 136,
232, 234, 244

Red Rock, 178, 187, 219, 260, 277,
282

Red Rock Prairie: Methodist
mission at, 244

Red Rover: steamboat, 88

Red Stone Prairie, 252; also known
as Newport, 199; see Red Rock,
219

Red Wing, 130

Red Wing band hunting lands, 98

Red Wing II: see Tatankamani,
290

Red Wing -lineage of chiefs known
as, 290

Red Wing's band, 97

Red Wing's village, 93

Renshaw, Emily, 15, 16, 17, 287

Renshaw, Joseph Senior, 17

Renshaw, Joseph, Jr., 16, 287; b.
1746, 286

Renville, Antoine, 243, 245

Renville, Gabriel, 290, 292; ward
of Brown, 157

Renville, Joseph Jr., 125, 243

Renville, Joseph Senior, 130; lived
in Minnesota like medieval
baron, 123; operates Yankton
Outfit for American Fur Co. for

50% of profit (or loss), 124;
polygamy and, 127; relationship
(lack of) with J. R. Brown, 123

Renville, Victor (Ohiye), 127, 290

Rhemy, H. H.: rafting partner of
Dr. Chris Carli, 258

Rice, Henry M., 201, 248, 256,
263, 266, 274, 276; managed
Winnebago removal to own
advantage, 280; moves trading
operation to mouth of Crow
Wing River, 256

rice, wild see wild rice, 33

Riggs, Reverend Stephen, 200, 232

River aux Embarass (Zumbro
River), 97

Roberts, Louis, 152

Robertson, Andrew, 149, 189

Robinette, Joseph, 131; Brown's
blacksmith, 141

Robinson, Dennis, 49

Rock Island, 70, 301

Rock River, 56, 77; bands, 72;
Indians' seasonal movements,
70; post, 82

Rock River post, 85

Rocky Mountains, 297

Rocque, Augustin, post, 97

Rolette, Joseph, 34, 103, 114;
'King' Rolette too big for even
the American Fur Co. to
swallow, 51; American Fur Co.
traders unhappy with, 104; dies
1845, 119; operates gristmill,
supplied beef to Army, 55;
privilege of paying for his own
competition, 97; quarrel with
Col. Snelling, 65; started
sixteen kegs of high wines north
by keelboat, 110; sues Ft.
Snelling C.O. William Jouett,
111; Upper Mississippi outfit,
77

Rolette, Joseph, Jr., 227

Rolette's Road, 105

Rondo, Joseph, 65

Rouillard, Pierre, 218, 239

Rum River, 39, 54, 263, 268, 282; first pine timber cut on, 39; proposed Wisconsin boundary, 270

Rum River line, 270

Rumtown, 162; variously known as The Entry / Mendota / Brown's Ferry, 156

Russell, Jeremiah, 186, 189

Ruyapa (Eagle Head), 73

Sac Indians, 68

Sac war party, 56

Sac's largest village, 70

salt pork, 186, 264

Sandy Lake, 106

Sandy Lake Chippewa, 40

Santee Sioux, 93

satinet, 96

Sauk Rapids, 256, 281, 282

Saukenuk, 70, 88

Sault Ste. Marie, 33, 59, 298

Saulteurs (Ojibwe), 298

Savannah River portage, 40

Scarlet Plume (Wamdiupiduta), 292

Schelinski, Drum Major John, 37

Schoolcraft, Henry, 109; Indian agent at La Pointe, 105; revokes Brown's license, 110

Scott, Gen. Winfield, 54, 67

Secretary of War, 167, 172

Selkirk's (Lord) colony on the Red River, 49

settlers: problem to fur trade, 81

Sevier, John, 212

Shackelford, Barlow, 174

Shakopee: Six's village, 73

Sheyenne River, 109, 126, 127, 218

shinplasters: notes on defaulting banks, 43

Shokokon village, 88

Sibley, Henry H., 113, 124, 140, 160, 173, 182, 211, 229, 241, 272, 273, 275, 276, 278; as Chief Agent, American Fur Co. at the St. Peters, 120; campaign manager J. R. Brown, 283; Sioux Outfit, 301; Wisconsin territory delegate to Congress, 267

Sica (Bad) Hollow, 227, 231, 233, 235, 239, 244

Simpson, James, 241

Simpson, Sir George, 51

Sintomonee: (Known All Over the World), also known as Brown's Ferry, Rumtown, 156; Brown's whiskey store, 157

Sioux: 50 lodges of destroyed, 133

Sioux customs, 42

Sioux Indians, 241

Sioux medicine men: powers of re J. R. Brown, 231

Sioux of Mississippi, 116

Sioux scalp, 186

Sioux territory, 105

Sioux treaty of 1837, 145

Sioux/Sac/Fox wars, 88

Sioux-Chippewa boundary line, 256

Sisseton: attack and kill cattle drovers, 232; camp near head of James River, 233; expedition against by Captain E. V. Sumner's company of dragoons, 233; quarrelsome nature of, 126

Sisseton bands, 172

Sisseton village, 229

Sisseton's summer village, 225

Six's village (Shakopee), 99

Skunk River, 70

smallpox: among the Yankton, 146

smear campaign: Brown conducts last minute against Henry Rice, 283

Smith, Lt. E. K., 165

Snake River, 103, 106, 261

Snelling, Colonel Josiah, 37, 39

Snelling, William Joseph, 46, 47, 65

soldiers: whiskey is their God and Mutiny their watchword -Col. Snelling on new recruits, 44

Spirit Light *see* Medicine Bottle, 109

St. Anthony, 153, 283

St. Anthony Falls, 165, 176

St. Croix Chippewa, 140

St. Croix Co., 176, 187, 191; as part of Wisconsin, would have no influence, 247; board, 188; boundary line, 247; Brown's counterpetition to create, 175; Court irregular until 1849 when Minnesota becomes a territory, 261; created (bill written in J. R. Brown's handwriting), 177; delegate slate to Democratic convention 2/11/1841, 192; district court placed in 1st judicial district, 260; district court reinstated, 260; Judge Irvin refuses to set foot at, 224; moves to establish 1839, 174; organic act, 189; amendment to removes district court to Prairie du Chien, 220; Organic Act repealed in part & annexed to Crawford Co. for judicial purposes, 224; population base of new, 177; Stillwater made seat of, 1846, 253; territorial roads proposed in by Brown, 191

St. Croix Lumbering Company, 176, 189, 220, 258

St. Croix River, 51, 100, 140, 173, 176; Brown's log cutting on, 1837, 114; mouth of (Prescott, Wisconsin), 167

St. Croix valley, 106

St. Cyr, Benjamin, 140

St. Joseph, 301

St. Joseph's Island, Canada, 291

St. Louis, 50, 82

St. Marys Point, 153

St. Paul, 153, 170, 181, 273, 274, 275, 277, 279, 281, 283; a wide-open frontier town, 241; city of, 230

St. Pauls: *see* St. Paul, 282

St. Pauls landing, 265

St. Peters, 45, 74, 106, 120, 122, 298

St. Peters River, 24, 29, 30, 50, 51, 122, 157, 165; Indians of upper, 50; Minnesota River, 167

St. Vrain, Charles D., 77, 83

Stambaugh, Samuel C., 142

Stanchfield, Daniel, 263; Steele's timber cruiser, 263

Stanchfield's cuttings: 1 ½ million feet, 264

Stateler, Sylvester, 207; blacksmith, 220

steam mills: lumber, 114

Steele, Franklin, 226, 252, 258, 259; lumberman from Pennsylvania, 141

Stevens, John H., 99

Stewart, Thomas, 56

Stillwater convention, 11, 276, 279

Stillwater Mill Company, 221

Stone & Bostwick of St. Louis, 52

stone jail, 189

Stone, David, 50

Street, Joseph M., 104; Prairie du Chien agent, 85, 97

Strong, Moses M. U.S. atty, 190

Stuart, Robert, 106, 120, 211, 212

sturgeon, 115; 1,825# of sold by J. R. Brown to Bailly, 114

sugar, 186; maple, 304

sugar-laced coffee, 264

Sullen Face, 234, 235

Sunrise River: forks of, 176

new post at, *c.* 1845, 243;
Columbia Fur Co. post at, 53
travois, 217
treaty: 1804, 1816, 82; 1837
Chippewa ceded 60 million
acres to U.S., 143; 1837
importance of, 144; 1837 Sioux
ceded territory to U.S., in turn
U.S. pays off Sioux's creditors,
144; 1837-ratified 1838 -Sioux
and Chippewa, 160; 1841
halfbreeds on Lake Pepin get
$20,000 plus improvements,
202; 1841 provisions of, 202;
1841, 8/11 Sioux cede
remaining lands west of
Mississippi for $206,000,
removal to Blue Earth
reservation (unratified), 202;
Mdewakanton, 213;
negotiations, 193; of Ghent,
297; official view of, creates
perpetual Indian state, 201;
pressure for grows in 1836, 142;
provisions modified by traders,
303; Taliaferro on 1837 trader
payments 'plain fraud traded on
the helpless Indians', 143;
United States Treaties of 1804,
1816, 82; who benefits, who's
paid off, 200
turnips, 107
Tuttle, Calvin A., 187, 189;
account of re J. R. Brown's
timber cutting, 141
Tweedy, John H., 269, 270, 271;
Wisconsin territorial delegate,
265
Two Rocks, 106
Tyler, President John, 195, 212
U.S. military strategy: control of
water routes, 298
Union Fur Company, 216

United States territory: additions
to, 297; birth in confers
citizenship, 52
upper dalles (Taylors Falls), 106
Upper Mississippi Outfit, 77, 148
Upper Missouri Outfit: transfer of
Brown to, 95
Upper Sioux: *see* Sisseton,
Wahpeton, Yankton, Yanktonai,
234
Van Buren, President Martin, 165
Ver Plank, Isaac A., 256
Vermillion River, 216
Vervier, Marcelle dit Courturier,
290
Vineyard, James R.: as WI
territorial legislator, shot
legislator Chas. P. Arndt in
chamber, 105
Vineyard, Miles, 104, 139; **sheriff**
of Grant Co., WI, 105
Vose, Major Josiah, 72;
commander of Ft. Armstrong,
68; complaints about
Davenport's operations, 71
voting challenge relaxed to admit
unnaturalized French, 281
Waanatan (Little Charger), 126,
136, 292
Wabasha, 97, 98; Chief, 74
Wabasha band hunting lands, 98
Wabasha Prairie, 93, 118, 262
Wabasha village (*see* Winona), 240
Wabokiesshiek (White Cloud), 71
Wahpekute, 8, 42, 172, 240
Wahpeton, 243, 247; warriors, 75
Wakanojanjan, 117. *see* Medicine
Bottle
Wakinyanduta (Red Thunder), 59,
289, 292
Wakinyantanka (Little Crow II),
116, 117; complaints against J.
R. Brown's Olivers Grove, 117
Walker, Orange, 187, 189, 257

Walk-in-the-Water: first steamboat on Lake Erie, 32

Wamdiupiduta (Scarlet Plume), 292

Waneta (Charger), 289

Wanigsootshkau (The Red Bird), 75

war: dance, 186; parties sent toward Red River trail, 232; rumors of, 75

War Eagle: log raft tow steamer, 262

War of 1812, 29, 304

Warren, Lyman, 140; American Fur Company agent NW Wisconsin, 106; leads Pillagers from Leech Lake to press claims, 143

Washington, George, 18

Watab Rapids, 264, 265

water power, 141; at St. Croix Falls, 251

Watkins, Samuel (Company C drummer), 48

Wayzata Bay, 48

Webster, Daniel, 193

Wekau (Sun), 75

Wells, Elizabeth, 286

West and Van Deventer, 259

Western Department of Army, re Brown papers, 309

Western Outfit, 125, 145, 211, 226; $10,000 is approx. normal trade year investment, 200; sold by Crooks to Pierre Chouteau, Jr., 200

Whig election in 1840 ends 40 years of Democratic administrations, 192

Whig threat, 192

whiskey, 110, 118, 160; 'business, after all, is business', 242; 271 dealers on Mississippi sell 3,794 barrels annually to Indians c. 1846, 100 more on other rivers sell additional 1,400 barrels (barrel = 32 gallons), 256; 55 barrrels landed at St. Pauls, 1845, cost 50¢ a gallon, 241; as a necessity, 34; Bailly accused of bringing 10-15 kegs into the country in one summer alone, 118; confiscated turned over to Rolette by Taliaferro, 119; drum, 72; drum, at dinner, 38; drum, in the morning (½ gill per man), 38; how to smuggle, 242; importation, stopping of, 216; purveyors supplied by American Fur Company, 116; rule, 242; Schoolcraft's charge that J. R. Brown was selling, 134; seller Henry Rust, murder of, 261; selling establishments, 19 on St. Croix above the lake do 180-300 barrels per year, 256; shop, 158, 161, 180; shop operater murdered, Indian perpetrator acquitted, 261; shop supplier/owner convicted of selling to Indians, 261; shops destroyed by loggers, 261; shops of, 54; Sioux dealing in, 240; six barrels confiscated, 119; smuggling, 99; St. Paulites spend half their time drinking, other half cheating each other or imposing on strangers, 241; store, construction of Brown's, 20 barrels of whiskey delivered to, 160; trade in *c.* 1843 from Imnijaska (Old Cave), later St. Paul, 241; trade in Halfbreed Tract on Lake Pepin, 240; trade, Henry Sibley in, 241; trading in by Indians in mid-1840s, 240; used to seal contracts, 302

White Bustard (Chief Magasan), 40

White Rock, 182

White, Harley, 257

Whitewood (James) River, 112
wild rice, 264; crop failure, 107
Wilkinson, Morton S., 277, 281
Williamson, Dr. Thomas:
American Board Missionary
at Lac qui Parle, 126; officiates
Brown marriage to McCoy, 135;
treats Brown's gunshot wound,
147; treats Susan Frénière after
she's accidentally shot by her
uncle, Joe Renville, 130
Winnebago, 55, 68, 71; a Siouan
language, 85; bellicosity of
1826, 67; lands vacated 1832,
139; of Rock River, 31;
prisoners, 67; reservation, 256;
treaty, 93; War, 72
Winona, MN: city of, 75
winterer, 239; licensed, 301
Wisconsan Territorial Legislature,
203
Wisconsin: red herring of, 276;
state constitution, 259; state
constitutional convention, 254;
State of; admitted to Union May
20, 1848, 270; state of, enabling
act 1846 alters western border,
245; territory left outside of new
state, 247; western line of, 248

Wisconsin River, 67, 68, 174
Wisconsin Territory, 160, 272;
Doty made governor of, 195;
first legislature, 160; interest in
party politics awakened, 192;
laws of remain in force in future
Minnesota Territory, 271;
legislature, 178; territorial
offices, Catlin proposal to open,
273
Wiskonsan Enquirer, 162, 272
Wolcott, Alexander -agent at the
embryo Chicago, 82
Wolf Creek, 110
Wool, General John E., 161
woolen cloths, 303
worser: Uncle Jacob George's, 207
Wyman, William: Whig editor of
the *Madison Express*, 188
Xunkahaton (The Horned Dog),
147
Yankton: quarrelsome nature of,
126
Yanktonai, 8, 59, 129, 146, 216,
291
Yellow River, 115
zoological impossibilities, 208